Advance prai … ganizations

"Ground-breaker! Game-changer! Brilliant! The most exciting book I've read in years on organization design and leadership models. Sustainability? Employee engagement? Innovation? This elegant, parsimonious way of working realizes those aspirations effortlessly while exceeding traditional bottom-line measures and infusing heart and spirit into work without gimmicks. Like a Zen practice, learning to do less takes discipline, and this book shows how letting go gives back—to you, your organization, your stakeholders, and the world."

—Jenny Wade, Ph.D., Author of *Changes of Mind*

"People have long asked me what a "5th order," or "high stage" organization would look like in the flesh. Frederic Laloux's richly researched book is the closest anyone has come, as yet, to answering this question. This is a stimulating and inspiring read!"

— Robert Kegan, Harvard University's Meehan Professor of Adult Learning, and author of *In Over Our Heads*

"A book like Reinventing Organizations only comes along once in a decade. Sweeping and brilliant in scope, it is the Good To Great for a more enlightened age. What it reveals about the organizational model of the future is exhilarating and deeply hopeful."

—Norman Wolfe, Author of *The Living Organization*

"A comprehensive, highly practical account of the emergent world view in business. Everything you need to know about building a new paradigm organization!"

—Richard Barrett,
Chairman and Founder of the Barrett Values Centre

"Frederic Laloux has done business people and professionals everywhere a signal service. He has discovered a better future for organizations by describing, in useful detail, the unusual best practices of today."

—Bill Torbert, Author of *Action Inquiry*

"Frederic Laloux's 'Teal Organization' is as close a model to what I call a 'conscious organization' as I have seen—an organization and a culture that not only thrives in the unfolding paradigm of collective thought but helps in the unfolding. It could serve as the mid-wife for a new worldview that will allow humankind to consciously evolve to a level where the world works for everyone."

—John Renesch, futurist, founder of FutureShapers, LLC and author of 14 books, including *The Great Growing Up*

"As the rate of change escalates exponentially, the old ways of organizing and educating, which were designed for efficiency and repetition, are dying. Frederic Laloux is one of the few management leaders exploring what comes next. It's deeply different."

—Bill Drayton, Founder, Ashoka: Innovators for the Public

REINVENTING ORGANIZATIONS

A Guide to Creating Organizations Inspired by the Next Stage of Human Consciousness

Frederic Laloux

Foreword to the Indian Edition by

Sarosh J Ghandy

Chairman, Caux Initiatives of Business in India.

Formerly, Managing Director, TELCON and Resident Director, Tata Motors

PRIME

AN IMPRINT OF

KNOWLEDGE PARTNERS

This Special Indian edition is Published by:
Knowledge Partners
403, Prerana, Vasant Leela Phase (XI) CHSL,
Waghbil, Ghodbunder Road, Thane 400615,
Maharashtra, India
Email: madhu@kp-india.com

Quantity Sales: Special discounts are available on quantity purchases of this book. For details contact the Publisher.

First Published in 2014 by Nelson Parker.

ISBN : 978-81-928163-3-3

Printed at Replika Press Pvt. Ltd.

TABLE OF CONTENTS

INDEX OF KEY STRUCTURES AND PRACTICES

FOREWORD

(INDIAN EDITION)

Many of you reading this book might wonder if what you are reading is really true or, that what is stated is possibly true in the US or Europe but would not work in the East, specifically, in our country, India. Let me add to your disillusionment by saying that your supposition is incorrect!!

The "Teal Organisation" that Frederic Laloux describes in this book is what seems improbable and a bit of a fantasy but I myself set up a "Teal-like organisation" in the Company where I worked and it produced results which I could not have foreseen!! The Teal Organisation is really about creating a mature architecture that helps to bring in the humane element to thrive, by using rather than serving the advances in technology! Douglas McGregor in his book "The Human Side of Enterprise" was among the first to talk about 'trust' as being the most important motivator for an employee. Unfortunately, most of us are brought up in an environment of 'fear' and 'mistrust' around which our organisations are modelled. We assume that people need supervision to make them work. This means people cannot work by themselves to produce results. This book suggests the possibility of a much deeper kind of change, more of the heart, brought out many times.

Another interesting perspective suggested by the author is to adopt a more total approach to organisational development. Implementing a deep-change in setting up a new organisation would be fairly straight forward, but implementing it in an older organisation with its established practices, habits, traditions might result in mere incremental changes, and the whole purpose of bringing about basic shifts could be defeated.

An important subject the book deals with is about 'self-management'. It deals with making arrangements and putting in place mechanisms where our intent in empowering the individual finds the right ecosystem for self-expression. For instance, we focused on evolving a variety of such ideas, like overhauling an old scheme on 'Suggestions from Employees' - by trusting and giving the charge to employees and by ensuring that an idea or suggestion, when accepted was implemented quickly so that the employee could be acknowledged and suitably rewarded. We were able to increase the rate of suggestions received from 2500 to 18,000 per year to build a new can-do confidence.Throughout my working life I have always strived to explore opportunities to trust and involve employees to improve quantity and quality. Employees also learn better. Furthermore, in order to increase the involvement of our people in their day to day work, we decided to start what was by then popularly known as "Quality Circles", which we called "Small Groups". This was a way of involving employees in voluntary groups of ten to twelve, responsible not only for the quality of their product, but also for process development, cost control, safety and upkeep of their work places. Employees were trained in basic Statistical Quality Control methods, Brain Storming Techniques, Conflict Resolution and other forms of people-process related work. It was an overall success, benefiting the company to the extent of Rs. 100 million annually, which was a significant value 30 years ago. This resonates so much with the thoughts in this book on developing capacity for self-management!

We then scaled up in terms of building more self-confidence among employees by including larger areas in the supply and value chains, where employees controlled all aspects of their work. Among other benefits it helped to considerably flatten the reporting layers from eight to four; it improved efficiency and retention. Importantly, people were much happier.

Although there were cultural and social challenges typical to the Indian environment, through sheer commitment of the leadership and a motivated team of executives, it was possible to mature to a significant degree of a more holistic ecosystem of possibilities, as explained in the book. I would certainly therefore encourage all business leaders, organisational developers, heads of human resources, faculty and researchers in business management and other institutions in India who are passionate about the subject, to seriously look into the thoughts and actions suggested herein.

Finally, let me acknowledge Kiran Gandhi, who first introduced this book to me - an engineer by qualification but evolved as a senior HR professional and has dedicated his life thereafter to transforming people. Kiran has travelled a good part of this journey with me in the critical years in our search and endeavour to try and build truly humane workplaces! I also appreciate Anant Nadkarni, an Advisor in Value creation, for his support to bring out this special edition.

Sarosh J. Ghandy

Chairman, Caux Initiatives of Business in India.

Formerly, Managing Director, TELCON and Resident Director, Tata Motors.

January 2018, Panchgani, India.

FOREWORD

This is a very important book, deeply significant in many ways, as much for the pioneering research, insights, guidelines, and suggestions that it makes as for the many equally important questions and issues that it raises. It is, without doubt, on the leading-edge of a type of work we are seeing more and more of at this time: namely, that concerned with the extremely profound changes in consciousness, culture, and social systems that we are seeing emerge, in increasing numbers, at this point in human (and, indeed, cosmic) evolution. Frederic Laloux's work focuses specifically on the values, practices, and structures of organizations—large and small—that seem to be driven by this extraordinary transformation in consciousness occurring around the world. He offers a very detailed and practical account—what amounts to a handbook, really—for people who feel that the current management paradigm is deeply limiting and yearn to bring more consciousness to the way we run organizations but wonder if it is possible and how to do it.

The book is highly practical, but don't be mistaken: it is solidly grounded in evolutionary and developmental theory. Books describing the broader transformation of consciousness, not just in organizations but in society, have appeared for at least three decades now, going back to such pioneering works as *The Aquarian Conspiracy, The Turning Point, The Greening of America*, and so on. But there is a major, indeed profound, difference: development studies continue to indicate, with increasing certainty, that what has generally been thought of as a single major transformation in consciousness and culture in the last four or five decades actually contains two major transformations, emerging successively, and known variously as pluralistic and integral, individualistic and autonomous, relativistic and systemic, HumanBond and Flexflow, green and teal, and order 4.5 and order 5.0, among many others. And, as developmentalists are increasingly discovering, these two transformations are simply the latest two in a long line of consciousness transformations that, slightly modifying the terms of Jean Gebser, for example, are called Archaic, Magic (Tribal), Mythic

(Traditional), Rational (Modern), Pluralistic (Postmodern), and Integral (Post-postmodern).

Each of these stages of development occurred to humanity as a whole, and repeats itself in essentially basic ways in individuals today, with everybody starting at stage one and proceeding essentially up to the average level of development in his or her culture (with some individuals lower, some higher). Each of these general stages has a different set of values, needs, motivations, morals, worldviews, ego structures, societal types, cultural networks, and other fundamental characteristics. The two basic transformations that I referred to above are the last two in the series: the Pluralistic stage, emerging in the 1960s and marking the beginning of Postmodernism, and more recently (and still much more rarely) the Integral stage, newly emerging, and marking the beginning of the phase—whatever it may turn out to be—that is moving beyond Postmodernism and its basic tenets.

The profound difference I was alluding to is this: most earlier books heralding a transformation of society speak from a Postmodern perspective, and have a rather simplistic view of human evolution. Laloux's book speaks from an Integral perspective and is grounded in a sophisticated understanding of evolutionary and developmental theory and what in Integral theory is called AQAL (all quadrants, all levels).

Postmodernism, as the name suggests, is that general phase of human development that came after, and in many cases strongly criticized, the previous general phase of Modernism, which began in the West with the Renaissance and then fully blossomed with the Enlightenment—the "Age of Reason and Revolution." What Enlightenment's modernity brought to the scene was a move beyond the previous mythic-literal, religious, traditional era of development—where the Bible was the one source of literal, uncontested truth; humanity had one, and only one, savior; and "no one comes to salvation save by through the Mother Church," whose dogmas delivered truth on all subjects, artistic to normative to scientific to religious. With the Enlightenment, representative democracy replaced monarchy; freedom replaced slavery (in a 100-year period, roughly 1770-1870, every rational-industrial society on the planet outlawed slavery, the first time this had ever happened to any societal type in human history); the experimental modern sciences replaced the revelatory mythic religions (as sources of serious truth); and what Weber called "the differentiation of the value spheres" (the differentiation of art, morals, and science, so that each could pursue its own logic and its own truths outside of their fusion in the dogma of the Church; where the Churchmen refused to even look through Galileo's telescope, researchers by the hundreds and eventually thousands began to do so, with an explosion in all of what are now referred to as the "modern sciences"—geology, physics, chemistry, biology, psychology, sociology).

So successful were the modern sciences that the other major domains of human existence and knowledge—from artistic to moral—began to be invaded and colonized by scientism (the belief that science, and science alone, can deliver any valuable truth). The "dignity of modernity" (the differentiation of the value spheres) soon collapsed into the "disaster of modernity" (the dissociation of the value spheres), resulting in what Weber also famously called "the disenchanted universe."

Such was the state of affairs for some 300 years—a mixture of great advance and stunning discoveries in the scientific arena, accompanied with a reductionism and scientific materialism that rendered all other fields and areas as defunct, outmoded, childish, archaic. "Social Darwinism"—the notion of the survival of the fittest applied to all aspects of human existence as well—began to insidiously invade all the humanities, ethics, and politics of humans, including the two major new economic systems, capitalism and socialism. Scientific materialism—the idea that all phenomena in the universe (including consciousness, culture, and creativity) could be reduced to material atoms and their interactions, which could be known only by the scientific method—and the generally liberal politics that accompanied such beliefs, set the stage for the next three centuries.

Until the 1960s, when not only the reign of scientific materialism was challenged (as being itself largely a cultural construction, not some deified access to universal truths), but also all of the remaining indignities of the Mythic-religious era (some of which were addressed by Modernism, and some of which were exacerbated by it)—indignities such as, overall, the oppression of women and other minorities, the toxic despoliation of nature and the environment, the lack of evenly applied civil rights, the general reign of materialism itself—all were aggressively attacked, and attempted to be remedied, by Postmodernism. What developmentalists have discovered about this new emergence is that it was driven, in large measure, by the emergence of a new and more developed stage of human unfolding (variously referred to as pluralistic, individualistic, relativistic, postmodern). This is not to say that everything Postmodernism pronounced was therefore true, only that it was based on a mode of thinking that was more complex, more sophisticated, more inclusive, and included more perspectives than the typical formal rational structure of the Modern era (and the Modern stage in today's individual development).

This new, more inclusive stage of development drove the first wave of books maintaining that "there's-a-great-new-paradigm-and-major-consciousness-transformation" now underway. These books, which began to emerge in the 1970s and 1980s, and a few of which I already named, usually had a very conspicuous diagram with two columns—one was the "Old Paradigm," which was "analytic-divisive,"

"Newtonian-Cartesian," "abstract-intellectual," "fragmented," "masculine," and which was the cause of literally all of humanities' problems, from nuclear war to tooth decay, and then another column, the "New Paradigm," which was "organic," "holistic," "systemic," "inclusive," and "feminine," and which was the source of a radical salvation and paradisiacal freedom from virtually all of humanity's ills. What's more, these two choices—old paradigm and new paradigm—were the only basic choices humanity had. Its earlier stages (e.g., tribal) were simply earlier versions of the new paradigm, which was repressed and destroyed by the aggressive Modern version of the old paradigm.

In large measure, these books were simply boomer writers documenting the transformation that they had just been a part of—namely, where, to the remains of the Magic, Mythic, and Rational paradigms still in existence to varying degrees, was added the possibility of the newly emergent Post-Rational or Postmodern paradigm, to which the boomers were the first major generation to have access (today in Western cultures, the Pluralistic/Postmodern stage makes up around 20 percent of the population, with 30 to 40 percent still Modern/Rational, 40 to 50 percent Mythic, and 10 percent Magic).

All of these early books had several things in common. By dividing humanity's choices into just two major ones—old and new paradigms—they blamed all of humanity's ills on nothing but Modernity and the Enlightenment paradigm, severely distorting the actual situation, which is that a majority of the really nasty cultural problems faced by humanity are the result of the Mythic-literal structure—from ethnocentric "chosen peoples," to female oppression, to slavery, to most warfare, to environmental destruction. In some cases, Modern technology was added to those Mythic motivations, thus making them more deadly (e.g., Auschwitz—which was not the product of Modern *worldcentric* morals, which treat all people fairly, regardless of race, color, sex, or creed, but Mythic *ethnocentrism,* which believes in out-groups of infidels and in-groups of "chosen peoples," and in which infidels, lacking souls, can be murdered or killed, and jihad in one form or another—from missionary converting to outright crusades—is the order of the day). In many cases, Modernity was in the process of ending these Mythic ethnocentric insults (such as slavery, and using a specific Modern attitude of *tolerance,* a previously quite rare value), but Postmodernity blamed Modernity (and rational Enlightenment values) for all of it, thus, in many cases, making matters considerably worse.

But in other ways, Postmodernity, with its own higher perspectives, brought not only advances in the sciences, but gave equal emphasis to virtually all other disciplines as well (sometimes going overboard, and claiming that no truth at all was possible, only various interpretations, so of course all disciplines should be included). And in its drives for civil rights and environmentalism and gay/lesbian rights and rights for the disabled, the higher moral fabric at least possible with a higher stage of development came clearly to the foreground. It was these advances that all the "new paradigm" books were celebrating. Who can blame them for getting carried away, and assuming the whole world was headed into this Pluralistic phase, this "new paradigm," instead of seeing that that phase was simply the fourth or fifth major transformation in human history and would simply take its place alongside the others, not completely replace them? It still shared many characteristics with its predecessors—all of which, together, Maslow would say were driven by "deficiency needs" and Clare Graves' followers would call "first tier."

But developmentalists of the time began noticing something initially perplexing, and then outright astonishing: among those that developed to the Postmodern/Pluralistic stage, a small percentage (two or three percent) began to show characteristics that were literally unprecedented in human history. Graves called the emergence of this even newer level "a monumental leap in meaning," and Maslow referred to it as the emergence of "Being values." Where all the previous stages (Magic, Mythic, Rational, and Pluralistic) had operated out of a sense of lack, scarcity, and deficiency, this new level—which various researchers began calling "integrated," "integral," "autonomous," "second tier," "inclusive," "systemic"—acted out of a sense of radical abundance, as if it were overflowing with goodness, truth, and beauty. It was as if somebody put a billion dollars in its psychological account, and all it wanted to do was share it, so full it was.

And there was something else about it, too. Where all the first-tier stages felt that their truth and values were the only real truth and values in existence—all the others were mistaken, wrong, infantile, or just goofy—this new Integral stage somehow intuited that all of the previous value structures were true and important in their own ways, that all of them had something to offer, that all of them were "true but partial." And thus, as much as the Postmodern/Pluralistic stage wanted to see itself as being "all-inclusive," it still essentially abhorred Rational and Mythic values; but the Integral stage actually did include them, or embrace them, or make room for them in its overall worldview. It was the emergence, for the first time in history, of a truly inclusive and non-marginalizing level of human consciousness. And this, indeed, would change everything.

Slowly, but with increasing speed, a whole second generation of "new paradigm" books began to emerge. These included such early pioneers as James Mark Baldwin and Jean Gebser, but then, more recently, books by philosophers, psychologists, and theologians such as Jürgen Habermas, Abe Maslow, Bede Griffiths, Wayne Teasdale, Allan Combs, and my own work, to barely scratch the surface. Unlike the first wave of new paradigm books, this second wave had a much more sophisticated psychological component, including at least four or five stages of development, sometimes nine or 10 (but certainly more than two, the "old" and "new paradigm," as the earlier wave had it); and—in addition to those developmental levels, a series of developmental lines, or multiple intelligences that moved through those levels (such as cognitive intelligence, emotional intelligence, moral intelligence, kinesthetic intelligence, spiritual intelligence, and so on). They also found room for an integration of science and spirituality—not reducing one to the other (nor seeing all spirituality as explainable by quantum mechanics or brain neuroplasticity; nor seeing all science as reducible to a mystical ground; but both science and spirituality being irreducible domains of major importance). And they all saw the first wave of "new paradigm" books as describing essentially the Postmodern/Pluralistic stage, and not a genuine Integral/Systemic stage.

Frederic Laloux's book belongs clearly to this second wave of books. But that is not its major claim to significance. We have been seeing, for the last decade or two, books increasingly focusing on business and some sort of "new paradigm" (mostly still first-wave books, but increasingly some second-wave books as well). But more than any other book that I am aware of, Laloux's work covers all four quadrants (to be explained later), at least five levels of consciousness and culture, several multiple lines or intelligences, and various types of organizational structures, moving from Magic to Mythic to Rational to Pluralistic to Integral—and, of course, focusing on the last and most recent emergent, that of the Integral stage, and a sophisticated and fairly detailed description of the business organizations that seem built around Integral-level characteristics, including individual worldviews, cultural values, individual and collective behavior, and social structures, processes, and practices. This makes it a truly pioneering work.

A brief explanation of "quadrants, levels, and lines" is perhaps in order. As Laloux indicates, these technical aspects are taken from my own Integral Theory, which, as the result of a cross-cultural search through hundreds of premodern, modern, and postmodern cultures and the various maps of human consciousness and culture that they have offered, has come up with what might be thought of as a "Comprehensive Map" of human makeup, which was arrived at by putting all of the known maps together on the table, and then using each one to fill in any gaps in the others, resulting in a comprehensive map that is genuinely inclusive of the basic dimensions, levels, and lines that are the major potentials of all humans. There are five basic dimensions in this Framework—quadrants, levels of development, lines of development, states of consciousness, and types.

Quadrants refer to four major perspectives through which any phenomenon can be looked at: the interior and the exterior in the individual and the collective. These can introductorily be indicated by the pronouns often used to describe them: the interior of the individual is an "I" space (and includes all the subjective thoughts, feelings, emotions, ideas, visions, and experiences that you might have as you introspect); the interior of a collective is a "we" space (or the inter-subjective shared values, semantics, norms, ethics, and understandings that any group has—its "cultures" and "sub-cultures"); the exterior of an individual is an "it" space (and includes all the "objective" or "scientific" facts and data about your individual organism—one limbic system, two lungs, two kidneys, one heart, this much dopamine, this much serotonin, this much glucose, and so on—and includes not only "objective" ingredients but behaviors); and the exterior of a collective, which is an "its" space (and includes all the interobjective systems, processes, syntax, rules, external relationships, techno-economic modes, ecological systems, social practices, and so on).

Not only all human beings, but all their activities, disciplines, and organizations can be looked at through this four-quadrant lens, and the results are always illuminating. According to Integral Theory, any comprehensive account of anything requires a look at all of these perspectives—the first-person ("I"), second-person ("you" and "we"), and third-person ("it" and "its") perspectives. Most human disciplines acknowledge only one or two of these quadrants and either ignore or deny any real existence to the others. Thus, in consciousness studies, for example, the field is fairly evenly divided between those who believe consciousness is solely the product of Upper-Right or objective "it" processes (namely, the human brain and its activities); while the other half of the field believes consciousness itself (the Upper-Left or subjective "I" space) is primary, and all objects (such as the brain) arise in that consciousness field. Integral Theory maintains that both of those views are right; that is, both of those quadrants (and the other two quadrants) all arise together, simultaneously, and mutually influence each other as correlative aspects of the Whole. Trying to reduce all of the quadrants to one quadrant is "quadrant absolutism," a wretched form of reductionism that obscures much more than it clarifies; while seeing all of the quadrants mutually arise and "tetra-evolve" sheds enormous light on perpetually puzzling problems (from the body/mind problem to the relation of science and spirituality to the mechanism of evolution itself).

Laloux carefully includes all four quadrants and a detailed description of each as it appears in different organizational types, focusing, again, on the pioneering or Integral stage. As he puts it, "The four-quadrant model shows how deeply mindsets [Upper-Left or "I"], culture [Lower-Left or "we"], behaviors [Upper-Right or "it"], and systems [Lower-Right or "its"] are intertwined. A change in any one dimension will ripple through all the others." He goes on to point out that Mythic and Modern theories of organization focus on "hard" exterior facts (the two Right-hand quadrants), and the Postmodern introduced the interiors of mindsets and culture (the two Left-hand quadrants)—while often going overboard, as Postmodernism in general did, and claimed that only culture was important. Only Integral organizations deliberately and consciously include all four quadrants (as Laloux's book itself is one of the very few to include all four quadrants in its research). Many Integral writers, while fully aware of all the quadrants, focus on the Left-hand quadrants of levels of consciousness and worldviews, and leave out the Right-hand quadrants of behaviors, processes, and practices necessary to help the emergence of Integral Left-hand dimensions. Laloux points out, for example, that Integral organizational culture (Lower-Left "we") is enacted particularly by Integral role-modeling from those in the organization with moral authority (from the Upper quadrant), and, from the Lower-Right or "its" quadrant, supportive structures, processes, and practices.

As for levels and lines, Laloux states that "In their exploration, [many researchers] found consistently that humanity evolves in stages. Our knowledge about the stages of human development is now extremely robust. Two thinkers in particular—Ken Wilber and Jenny Wade—have done remarkable work comparing and contrasting all the major stage models, and have discovered strong convergence. ... The way I portray the stages borrows mostly from Wade's and Wilber's meta-analysis, touching briefly upon different facets of every stage—the worldview, the needs, the cognitive development, the moral development."

Laloux rightly invites us to be extremely careful what we mean by "a stage." As Howard Gardner made popular, and virtually every developmentalist agrees, there is not just one line of development with its stages or levels, but multiple lines or multiple intelligences, and each of those lines are quite different, with different characteristics and different stage structures. But what's so interesting is that although the various lines are quite different, they all develop through the same basic levels of consciousness. For the moment, let's simply number the levels; or, as Integral Theory often does, you can give them a color name (for example, red, orange, or green). But let's say that there are, in this example, seven major developmental levels through which move, say, a dozen different developmental lines (cognitive, emotional, moral, values, needs, and spirituality, among others). Each line—say cognitive, moral, emotional—evolves through each of the levels, so we can talk about red cognition, red morals, red values (red being level 3). But somebody at orange (level 5) cognition can also be at a red (level 3) conventional moral development. So talking about levels without lines is dangerous.

All of the multiple intelligences in humans develop through *actualization* hierarchies. Cognition, for example, moves from sensorimotor intelligence, to images, then symbols, then concepts, then schema, then rules, then meta-rules, then systemic networks. This is a point worth emphasizing, because Laloux's book shows that organizations operating at the Integral or teal stage no longer work with dominator hierarchies, the boss-subordinate relationships that are pervasive in organizations today. But the absence of dominator hierarchy is not the same thing as the absence of any hierarchy. Even if we look at Graves' work, for example, one of the major defining characteristics of Integral or teal is the return of nested hierarchies, after their almost complete removal at green Postmodern pluralism. (The Postmodernists utterly fail to distinguish between dominator hierarchies, which are indeed nasty, and actualization hierarchies, which are the primary form of natural growth, development, and evolution in the world—atoms to molecules to cells to organisms, for example. Postmodernists toss out all hierarchies as being sheer evil. This is a characteristic of the egalitarian Pluralistic stage and is one of its shadow sides.)

But with the emergence of the teal altitude, hierarchies are all over the place—they're literally everywhere. As Elliott Jacques' works have empirically demonstrated, the way most organizations are structured, those at the lower levels of this hierarchy usually work on the floor or assembly line; those at the intermediate levels mostly work middle management; and those at the upper levels work upper management (including CEO, CFO, COO). What these newer organizations do is move all of those levels—the entire hierarchy itself—into teams of usually 10 to 15 people. Any person, in any team, can make literally any decision for the company—and, in fact, virtually all the major decisions in the organizations are made by team members—including sales, marketing, hiring and recruitment, research and development, salary decisions, dismissals, HR functions, equipment purchases, community relations, and so on. This makes each team, and each person in the team, much more Integral—they can operate on any level in the hierarchy they are capable of, as long as they consult with those who will be affected by the decision (although they don't have to follow the advice), where previously they had been constrained by their place in the pyramid. One of the great findings of Laloux's work is that actualization hierarchies can flourish when dominator hierarchies are removed. A company of 500 individuals thus has, not one but 500 CEO, any one of whom might have a breakthrough idea and be able to implement it, a true self-management move that is one of the major reasons for the astonishing success of so many of these organizations. What happens to middle and much of upper management? Mostly, it doesn't exist. Those hierarchies have been relocated.

This work is, as I said, one of the most important books in the entire second wave of "new paradigm" books. As Laloux is the first to admit, we don't know if all the characteristics, processes, and practices that he describes will end up actually describing the structure and form that teal organizations will take. But this research deserves to be taken seriously by every Integral, indeed every conventional, student of organizations and organizational development. In terms of AQAL (all-quadrant, all-level) sophistication, there is simply nothing like it out there. My congratulations to Frederic Laloux on a spectacular treatise. May it help many readers gather inspiration to create businesses, schools, hospitals, or nonprofits inspired by this emerging new wave of consciousness that is starting to transform the world.

Ken Wilber

Denver, Colorado
Fall 2013

INTRODUCTION

THE EMERGENCE OF A NEW ORGANIZATIONAL MODEL

You never change things by fighting the existing reality. To change something, build a new model that makes the existing model obsolete.

Richard Buckminster Fuller

Aristotle, the great Greek philosopher and scientist, proclaimed in a treatise written in 350 BC that women have fewer teeth than men.[1] Today we know this is nonsense. But for almost 2,000 years, it was accepted wisdom in the Western World. Then one day, someone had the most revolutionary of ideas: *let's count!*

The scientific method—formulating a hypothesis and then testing it—is so deeply ingrained in our thinking that we find it hard to conceive that intelligent people would blindly trust authority and not put assumptions to the test. We could be forgiven for thinking that, perhaps, people simply weren't that smart back then! But before we judge them too harshly, let's ask ourselves: could future generations be similarly amused about us? Could we, too, be prisoners of a simplistic way of understanding the world?

There is reason to believe we might be. As an example, let me ask you a simple question: How many brains does a human being have? I imagine your answer is "one" (or, if you suspected a trick question, it might be "two," the often-referred-to right and left brains). Our current knowledge is that we have three: there is of course the massive brain in our head; then there is a small brain in our heart, and another in our gut.

The last two are comparatively much smaller[2], but they are fully autonomous nervous systems nevertheless.

Here is where it gets interesting: The brain in the heart and the one in the gut were discovered only recently, even though from a technological point of view, they could have been identified long ago. All it takes to see them is a corpse, a knife, and a basic microscope. Actually, the brain in the gut *was* discovered long ago, in the 1860s, by a German doctor named Auerbach. His discovery was further refined by two English colleagues, Bayliss and Starling. And then, something extraordinary happened. Medical circles somehow forgot about the brain in the gut. For a century, they completely lost sight of it! It was rediscovered only in the late 1990s by Michael Gershon, an American neuroscientist, along with others.

How could medical circles forget the existence of a brain? I believe it has to do with the belief system of our times: in a hierarchical worldview, there can be only one brain in command, just as there must be a single boss at the head of every organization. Although popular parlance has long used the terminology of "knowing in our hearts" and "knowing in our gut," having three autonomous brains working side by side can't be possible if we believe the world needs clear hierarchies to function. It might be no coincidence that we discovered (or rediscovered) the other two brains at the same time as the Internet became a dominant force in our lives. The age of the Internet has precipitated a new worldview—one that can contemplate the possibility of distributed intelligence instead of top-down hierarchy. With that worldview, we can accommodate the idea that we have more than one brain and that they can work together in shared intelligence.

We can't quite understand how people in the Middle Ages believed Aristotle's claim that women had fewer teeth than men. And yet, it seems we can be prisoners of our thoughts just as much as they were. Modern scientists neglected to look carefully through the microscope because "there can only be one brain," rather like Galileo's contemporaries refused to look through the telescope because it was unthinkable that our God-formed planet would be anything other than the center of the universe.

The limits of our current organizational models

My interest is in organizations and collaboration, not medicine or astronomy. But the conceptual question is the same: could it be that our current worldview limits the way we think about organizations? Could we invent a more powerful, more soulful, more meaningful way to work together, if only we change our belief system?

In many ways, this is a strange and almost ungrateful question to ask. For thousands and thousands of years, people have lived on the brink of famine and in fear of plagues, always at the mercy of a drought or a simple flu. Then suddenly, almost out of nowhere, modernity has brought us unprecedented wealth and life expectancy in the last two centuries. And all this extraordinary progress has come not from individuals acting alone, but from people collaborating in organizations:

- The large and small businesses in our free-market economies have created unprecedented wealth in the Western world, and they are currently lifting millions of people out of poverty in India, China, Africa, and elsewhere. We have built up incredibly intricate supply chains, which increasingly link every human being in relationships that arguably do more for peace between nations than any political arrangement ever has.
- A dense network of organizations—research centers, pharmaceutical companies, hospitals, medical schools, health insurance companies—have meshed into a highly sophisticated medical system that would have been unthinkable just a century ago. Over the last century, this network contributed to adding nearly 20 years of life expectancy for the average person in the United States. Infant mortality has been reduced by 90 percent and maternal mortality by 99 percent. Age-old scourges like polio, leprosy, smallpox, and tuberculosis are mostly part of history books, even in the poorest countries in the world.
- In the field of education, a network of schools—kindergartens, elementary and high schools, colleges, and graduate schools—have brought education that was once the privilege of the very few to millions of children and youth. Never before in human history have there been free public education systems available to every child. The high degrees of literacy that we now take for granted are unprecedented in history.
- All around the world, the nonprofit sector has grown spectacularly for several decades, creating jobs at a faster pace than for-profit companies. An ever-increasing number of people donate time, energy, and money in pursuit of purposes that matter to them and to the world.

Modern organizations have brought about sensational progress for humanity in less than two centuries—the blink of an eye in the overall timeline of our species. None of the recent advances in human history would have been possible without organizations as vehicles for human collaboration.

And yet, many people sense that the current way we run organizations has been stretched to its limits. We are increasingly disillusioned by organizational life. For people who toil away at the bottom of the pyramids, surveys consistently report that work is more often than not dread and drudgery, not passion or purpose. That the *Dilbert* cartoons could become cultural icons says much about the extent to which organizations can make work miserable and pointless. And it's not only at the bottom of the pyramid. There is a dirty secret I have discovered in the fifteen years I have spent consulting and coaching organizational leaders: life at the top of the pyramids isn't much more fulfilling. Behind the façade and the bravado, the lives of powerful corporate leaders are ones of quiet suffering too. Their frantic activity is often a poor cover up for a deep inner sense of emptiness. The power games, the politics, and the infighting end up taking their toll on everybody. At both the top and bottom, organizations are more often than not playfields for unfulfilling pursuits of our egos, inhospitable to the deeper yearnings of our souls.

This book isn't a rant about large corporations gone mad with greed. People who work in government agencies or nonprofits are rarely more exuberant about their workplaces. Even professions of calling aren't immune to organizational disillusionment. Teachers, doctors, and nurses are leaving their field of vocation in droves. Our schools, unfortunately, are for the most part soulless machines where students and teachers simply go through the motions. We have turned hospitals into cold, bureaucratic institutions that dispossess doctors and nurses of their capacity to care from the heart.

> *Instinctively, we know that management is out of date. We know its rituals and routines look slightly ridiculous in the dawning light of the 21st century. That's why the antics in a Dilbert cartoon or an episode of The Office are at once familiar and cringe-making.*
>
> Gary Hamel

The questions that triggered the research for this book

The way we try to deal with organizations' current problems often seems to make things worse, not better. Most organizations have gone through many rounds of change programs, mergers, centralizations and decentralizations, new IT systems, new mission statements, new scorecards, or new incentive systems. It feels like we have stretched the current way we run organizations to its limits, and these traditional recipes often seem part of the problem, not the solution.

We yearn for more, for radically better ways to be in organizations. But is that genuinely possible, or mere wishful thinking? If it turns out that it *is* possible to create organizations that draw out more of our human potential, then what do such organizations look like? How do we bring them to life? These are the questions at the heart of this book.

To me, these are not merely academic but very practical questions. An increasing number of us yearn to create soulful organizations, if only we knew how. Many of us don't need convincing that new types of companies, schools, and hospitals are called for. What we need is faith that it can be done and answers to some very concrete questions. The hierarchical pyramid feels outdated, but what other structure could replace it? How about decision-making? Everybody should make meaningful decisions, not just a few higher-ups, but isn't that just a recipe for chaos? How about promotions and salary increases? Can we find ways to handle such matters without bringing politics to the table? How can we have meetings that are productive and uplifting, where we speak from our hearts and not from our egos? How can we make purpose central to everything we do, and avoid the cynicism that lofty-sounding mission statements often inspire? What we need is not merely some grand vision of a new type of organization. We need concrete answers to dozens of practical questions like these.

Taking this practical perspective does not preclude us from also considering much larger societal and environmental implications. Our way of conducting business has outgrown our planet. Our organizations contribute on a massive scale to depleting natural resources, destroying ecosystems, changing the climate, exhausting water reserves and precious topsoils. We are playing a game of brinkmanship with the future, betting that more technology will heal the scars modernity has inflicted on the planet. Economically, a model of ever more growth with finite resources is bound to hit the wall; the recent financial crises are possibly only tremors of larger earthquakes to come. It is probably no exaggeration, but sad reality, that the very survival of many species, ecosystems, and perhaps the human race itself hinges on our ability to move to higher forms of consciousness and from there collaborate in new ways to heal our relationship with the world and the damage we've caused.

> *The greatest danger in times of turbulence is not the turbulence—it is to act with yesterday's logic.*
> Peter Drucker

Organizations over the course of evolution (Part 1)

Einstein once famously said that problems couldn't be solved with the same level of consciousness that created them in the first place. Perhaps we need to access a new stage of consciousness, a new worldview, to reinvent human organizations. To some people, the notion that society could shift to another worldview, and that from that worldview we could create a radically new type of organization, might pass for wishful thinking. And yet, this is precisely what has happened several times in human history, and there are elements that hint that another change of mindset—and thus another organizational model—may be just around the corner.

A great number of scholars—psychologists, philosophers, and anthropologists, among others—have dissected the journey of human consciousness. They found that in the roughly 100,000-year history of humanity, we have gone through a number of successive stages. At every stage we made a leap in our abilities—cognitively, morally, and psychologically—to deal with the world. There is one important aspect that researchers have so far somewhat overlooked: every time humanity has shifted to a new stage, it has invented a new way to collaborate, a new organizational model. Part 1 of this book recounts this story: how humanity's consciousness evolved, and how at every step of the way we have invented new organizational models. (Those successive models are still around today, so this historical perspective has much to offer toward understanding today's various types of organizations and many of today's debates in the field of management.)

Here is where things become particularly intriguing: developmental psychology has much to say about the next stage of human consciousness, the one we are just starting to transition into. This next stage involves taming our ego and searching for more authentic, more wholesome ways of being. If the past is any guide to the future, then as we grow into the next stage of consciousness, we will also develop a corresponding organizational model.

Empirical research—what pioneers can teach us (Part 2)

The second part of the book describes in practical detail how organizations operate at this next stage. It so happens that the future is not just around the corner—it is already blending into the present. For two years, I have researched pioneer organizations that have already, to a significant degree, started operating on a new organizational model consistent with the next stage of human development. The questions I was trying to answer as I started researching these pioneer organizations were these:

> *What do organizations molded around the next stage of consciousness look and feel like? Is it already possible to describe their structures, practices, processes, and cultures (in other words, to conceptualize the organizational model) in useful detail, to help other people set up similar organizations?*

I didn't know what to expect when I set out to identify pioneer organizations. This field is only emerging; would I find any good examples? Would I stumble only on tiny organizations, with too little history to get to any meaningful insights? I felt that rather strict selection criteria were needed in any case—otherwise there might not be much value in the claims the study would make. To be included in this research, organizations could stem from any geographical area or sector (business, nonprofit, education, health, government), but needed to employ *a minimum of 100 people,*[3] and to have been operating for *a minimum of five years along* structures, practices, processes, and cultures that to a substantial degree were *consistent with the characteristics of the next developmental stage.*

My concerns proved unfounded. The twelve organizations I researched (see chapter 2.1 for an overview) overshoot these criteria by a long shot. Many have been operating on these breakthrough principles for a long time, sometimes 30 or 40 years, and not just with a handful, but with a few hundred and sometimes several thousand employees.

Another surprise: I was expecting to find case examples mostly in service professions—health care or education—where work is often a calling, and the organization's noble purpose helps people transcend their more selfish motivations. I was happy to be proven wrong. Among the pioneers are for-profit as well as nonprofit organizations. There are retailers, manufacturing companies, an energy company, and a food producer, as well as a school and a group of hospitals.

I was also surprised to discover that these organizations didn't know about each other. I had expected, if I found any such pioneers, that they would know about like-minded peers with whom they would exchange insights and experiences. Instead, they were generally delighted to hear that they weren't the only ones out there questioning today's management practices. I came to jokingly think about these organizations as friendly aliens from some old TV series, living right among us for quite a while now, endowed with superpowers but isolated and unrecognized. Perhaps the times are catching up with them; perhaps we are now finally ready to see them for what they are: not merely as friendly but awkward outliers, but as pioneers of our collective future.

Researching these case studies involved two sets of questions (listed in Appendix 1). The first set relates to 45 practices and processes that are commonly discussed in organizational research. They connect to:

- key overarching organizational processes such as strategy, marketing, sales, operations, budgeting, and controlling;
- the main human resources processes, including recruitment, training, evaluation, compensation; and
- critical practices of everyday life like meetings, information flow, and office spaces.

For each of these 45 areas, the research tried to identify in what ways the practices of the pioneers differ—or don't—from conventional management methods. The approach was deliberately broad and open-ended: given the emerging nature of the topic, the research looked at the entire spectrum of structures, practices, and cultures typically considered in organizational research, without preconceived notions. It relied upon publicly available material, internal documents, interviews, and onsite visits.

Spoiler alert

Each of the pioneer organizations is astonishing in its own right and would warrant an entire book to tell its story. But of course, as part of the research, I was curious if there was more to it than a collection of case studies: are there patterns and commonalities that point to a coherent new model? Can the pioneers provide not just inspiration, but a template for those aspiring to create more soulful types of organizations?

The answer, clearly, is positive. These pioneer organizations didn't know about each other and experimented on their own; they work in radically different sectors and locations; some have hundreds, others tens of thousands, of employees. Despite all this, they have—after much trial and error—come up with strikingly similar structures and practices. I find it difficult not to get excited about this. It means that a coherent organizational model seems to be emerging, one we can describe in quite some detail. This is not a theoretical model, not a utopian idea, but a very concrete way to run organizations from a higher stage of consciousness. If we accept that there is a direction to human evolution, then we hold here something rather extraordinary: the blueprint of the future of organizations, the blueprint to the future of work itself.

Organizations researched for this book are like aliens from some old TV series—living right among us, unrecognized despite their superpowers.

I write this with full awareness that we are in the early days of this emerging phenomenon. I don't mean to suggest that this book offers a definitive, fixed description of this upcoming organizational model. As more companies start to innovate in this field, as more researchers look at them from different angles, and as society as a whole evolves, more richness and texture will certainly be added to the picture. But I am confident that, even now, we hold a blueprint for how we can organize entities in ways that make work vastly more productive, fulfilling, and purposeful. Organizational leaders who want to create new types of organizations don't have to start from a blank sheet of paper; they can draw inspiration from the very concrete descriptions in Part 2 of this book outlining the principles, structures, practices, and cultures that support a new way to come together in organizations.

Necessary conditions (Part 3)

The research for this book has also yielded interesting insights concerning the journey to bring such new organizations to life (based on a second set of research questions—see Appendix 1). What are the necessary conditions to making this new model work? If you are planning to start up an organization and want to, from the beginning, eschew the old model and start on a new foundation, what can you learn from pioneers who have done this before? Or, if you lead an existing organization, large or small, and consider transitioning to this new paradigm, what would be good ways to get started and to engage colleagues in that journey? These are some of the questions addressed in Part 3 of the book.

If we are to overcome the daunting problems of our times, we will need new types of organizations—more purposeful businesses, more soulful schools, more productive nonprofits. Anybody breaking out of the mold and venturing into the new is likely to meet resistance, to be called an idealist or a fool. Anthropologist Margaret Meade once said, "Never underestimate the power of a few committed people to change the world. Indeed, it is the only thing that ever has." If you are one of them, if you feel called to create a radically more soulful, purposeful, and productive workplace, then I hope that this book will provide you with some extra confidence that it can be done. May it serve as a practical handbook along your journey. I have no doubt that the world is ready and waiting for you.

— Part 1 —

Historical and Developmental Perspective

CHAPTER 1.1

CHANGING PARADIGMS: PAST AND PRESENT ORGANIZATIONAL MODELS

Seeing is not believing; believing is seeing!
You see things, not as they are, but as you are.
Eric Butterworth

Can we create organizations free of the pathologies that show up all too often in the workplace? Free of politics, bureaucracy, and infighting; free of stress and burnout; free of resignation, resentment, and apathy; free of the posturing at the top and the drudgery at the bottom? Is it possible to reinvent organizations, to devise a new model that makes work productive, fulfilling, and meaningful? Can we create soulful workplaces—schools, hospitals, businesses, and nonprofits—where our talents can blossom and our callings can be honored?

If you are the founder or leader of an organization and you long to create a different workplace, much rides on your answer to that question! Many people around you will dismiss this idea as wishful thinking and try to talk you out of even trying. "People are people," they will say. "We have egos, we play politics, we like to blame, criticize, and spread rumors. This will never change." Who can argue with that? But, on the other hand, we have all experienced peak moments of teamwork, where achievements came joyfully and effortlessly. Human ingenuity knows no bounds and radical innovations sometimes appear all of a sudden, out of nowhere. Who would wager we cannot invent much more exciting workplaces?

So which voice should you heed? Is it possible to set a course away from the land of management-as-we-know-it for a new world? Or are you just going to sail off the edge, because there is nothing beyond the world we know?

Part of the answer, I have found somewhat unexpectedly, comes from looking not forward, but into the past. In the course of history, humankind has reinvented how people come together to get work done a number of times—every time creating a vastly superior new organizational model. What's more, this historical perspective also hints at a new organizational model that might be just around the corner, waiting to emerge.

The key to this historical perspective, interestingly, comes not from the field of organizational history, but more broadly from the field of human history and developmental psychology. It turns out that, throughout history, the types of organizations we have invented were tied to the prevailing worldview and consciousness. Every time that we, as a species, have changed the way we think about the world, we have come up with more powerful types of organizations.

A great number of people—historians, anthropologists, philosophers, mystics, psychologists, and neuroscientists—have delved into this most fascinating question: *how has humanity evolved from the earliest forms of human consciousness to the complex consciousness of modern times?* (Some inquired into a related question: *how do we human beings evolve today from the comparatively simple form of consciousness we have at birth to the full extent of adult maturity?)*

People have looked at these questions from every possible angle. Abraham Maslow famously looked at how human *needs* evolve along the human journey, from basic physiological needs to self-actualization. Others looked at development through the lenses of *worldviews* (Gebser, among others), *cognitive capacities* (Piaget), *values* (Graves), *moral development* (Kohlberg, Gilligan), *self-identity* (Loevinger), *spirituality* (Fowler), *leadership* (Cook-Greuter, Kegan, Torbert), and so on.

In their exploration, they found consistently that humanity evolves in stages. We are not like trees that grow continuously. We evolve by sudden transformations, like a caterpillar that becomes a butterfly, or a tadpole a frog. Our knowledge about the stages of human development is now extremely robust. Two thinkers in particular—Ken Wilber and Jenny Wade—have done remarkable work comparing and contrasting all the major stage models and have discovered strong convergence. Every model might look at one side of the mountain (one looks at needs, another at cognition, for instance), but it's the same mountain. They may give somewhat different names to the stages or sometimes subdivide or regroup them differently. But the underlying phenomenon is the same, just like Fahrenheit and Celsius recognize—with different labels—that there is a point at which water freezes and another where it boils. This developmental view has been backed up by solid evidence from large pools of data; academics like Jane Loevinger, Susanne Cook-Greuter, Bill Torbert, and Robert Kegan have tested this stage theory with thousands and thousands of people in several cultures, in organizational and corporate settings, among others.

Every transition to a new stage of consciousness has ushered in a whole new era in human history. At every juncture, everything changed: society (going from family bands to tribes to empires to nation states); the economy (from foraging to horticulture, agriculture, and industrialization); the power structures; the role of religion. One aspect hasn't yet received much attention: with every new stage in human consciousness also came a break-through in our ability to collaborate, bringing about a new organizational model. Organizations as we know them today are simply the expression of our current world-view, our current stage of development. There have been other models before, and all evidence indicates there are more to come.

Philosophers, mystics from many wisdom traditions, psychologists, and neuroscientists have all delved into this most fascinating question: how has human consciousness evolved from the time we lived in caves to who we are today?

So what are the past and current organizational models in human history—and what might the next look like? In this chapter, I will take you on a whirlwind tour of the major stages in the development of human consciousness and of the corresponding organizational models. The way I portray the stages borrows from many researchers, and primarily from Wade's and Wilber's meta-analyses, touching briefly upon different facets of every stage—the worldview, the needs, the cognitive development, the moral development. I refer to every stage, and to the corresponding organizational model, with both a name and a color. Naming the stages is always a struggle; a single adjective will never be able to capture all of the complex reality of a stage of human consciousness. I've chosen adjectives I feel are the most evocative for each stage, in some cases borrowing a label from an existing stage theory, in other cases choosing a label of my own making. Integral Theory often refers to stages not with a name but with a color. Certain people find this color-coding to be highly memorable, and for that reason I'll often refer to a stage throughout this book with the corresponding color (which should not obscure the fact—let's add this to avoid any misunderstanding—that the way I describe the stages of consciousness stems from a personal synthesis of the work of different scholars, which while generally compatible might not always square entirely with the way Integral Theory describes the same stages).

Reactive—Infrared paradigm[1]

This is the earliest developmental stage of humanity, spanning roughly the period from 100,000 to 50,000 BC, when we lived in small bands of family kinships (some of which survive in remote parts of the world today, which accounts for our knowledge of this stage). These bands typically number just a few dozen people. Beyond that number, things start to break down, as people's capacity to handle complexity in relationships is very limited at this stage. The ego is not fully formed; people don't perceive themselves as entirely distinct from others or from the environment (which causes some to romanticize about this period, seeing it as pre-dualism bliss, ignoring the extremely high rate of violence and murder at this stage). Foraging is the basis of subsistence. This model requires no division of labor to speak of (other than women taking responsibility for the bearing and rearing of children), and so there is nothing like an organizational model at that stage yet. In fact, there is no hierarchy within the band—there is no elder, no chief that provides leadership.

There are only a few remaining bands of people operating from this paradigm in the world today. However, child psychologists study what amounts to the same stage in newborn babies, who engage with the world via a comparable form of consciousness, where the concept of self isn't yet fully separate from the mother and the environment.

Magic—Magenta paradigm[2]

Around 15,000 years ago, and perhaps earlier in some places of the world, humanity started to shift to a stage of consciousness some authors have labeled "magical." This stage corresponds to the shift from small family bands to tribes of up to a few hundred people. Psychologically and cognitively, this represents a major step up in the ability to handle complexity. The self at this stage is to a large degree differentiated physically and emotionally from others, but it still sees itself very much the center of the universe. Cause and effect are poorly understood, and so the universe is full of spirits and magic: *clouds move to follow me; bad weather is the spirits' punishment for my bad actions.* To appease this magical world, tribes seek comfort in ritualistic behaviors and by following the elder and the shaman. People live mostly in the present, with some blending in of the past, but little projection toward the future. Cognitively, there is no abstraction yet, no classification, no concept of large numbers. Death is not seen as particularly real, and the fear of one's death is markedly absent (which accounts for continuing high rates of violence and murder). Organizations don't exist at this stage yet. Task differentiation remains extremely limited, although elders have special status and command some degree of authority.

Today, this stage is typically experienced by children of around three to 24 months of age. This is when they acquire sensorimotor differentiation (*when I bite my finger it's not the same as when I bite the blanket*) and emotional differentiation (*I'm not my mother, though in her presence I feel magically safe*). With adequate nurture, most children grow beyond this stage.

Impulsive–Red paradigm[3]

Historically, the shift to the Impulsive-Red paradigm was another major step up for humanity. It brought forth the first chiefdoms and proto-empires, around 10,000 years ago. From it also emerged the first forms of organizational life (which I'll refer to as Red Organizations).

The ego is now fully hatched, and people have a sense of self that is entirely separate from others and from the world. At first, this realization is frightening: for the first time, death is real. *If I'm just a small part, separate from the whole, I might suffer or die.* The world at this stage is seen as a dangerous place where one's needs being met depends on being strong and tough. The currency of the world is power. *If I'm more powerful than you, I can demand that my needs are met; if you are more powerful than me, I'll submit in the hope you will take care of me.* The emotional spectrum is still rather crude, and people often express their needs through tantrums and violence. One is largely unaware of other people's feelings. The orientation is still mostly to the present—*I want it, and I want it now*—but this impulsiveness can extend somewhat into the future with simple strategies using power, manipulation, or submission. Simple causal relationships such as rewards and punishments are understood. Thinking is shaped by polar opposites, which makes for a black and white worldview—for example, strong/weak, my way/your way.

With ego-differentiation, role differentiation becomes possible—in other words, meaningful division of labor. There is now a chief, and there are foot soldiers. Slavery enters the picture on a large scale, now that tasks can be isolated and given to enemies from neighboring tribes that have been defeated and put into bondage. Historically, this has led to the emergence of chiefdoms ruling not only hundreds, but up to thousands or tens of thousands of people. Impulsive-Red functioning can still be found in adults in many tribal societies in the world today and in underprivileged areas amidst developed societies, when circumstances don't provide adequate nurture for children to develop beyond this stage. Every paradigm has its sweet spot, a context in which it is most appropriate. Impulsive-Red is highly suitable for hostile environments: combat zones, civil wars, failed states, prisons, or violent inner-city neighborhoods.

Red Organizations

Organizations molded in Impulsive-Red consciousness first appeared in the form of small conquering armies, when the more powerful chiefdoms grew into proto-empires. They can still be found today in the form of street gangs and mafias. Today's Red Organizations borrow tools and ideas from modernity—think about organized crime's use of weaponry and information technology. But their structures and practices are for the most part still molded in the Impulsive-Red paradigm.

What are the defining characteristics of Red Organizations? Their glue is the continuous exercise of power in interpersonal relationships. Wolf packs provide a good metaphor: rather like the "alpha wolf" uses power when needed to maintain his status within the pack,[4] the chief of a Red Organization must demonstrate overwhelming power and bend others to his will to stay in position. The minute his power is in doubt, someone else will attempt to topple him. To provide some stability, the chief surrounds himself with family members (who tend to be more loyal) and buys their allegiance by sharing the spoils. Each member of his close guard in turn looks after his own people and keeps them in line. Overall, there is no formal hierarchy and there are no job titles. Impulsive-Red Organizations don't scale well for those reasons—they rarely manage to keep in line people who are separated from the chief by more than three or four degrees. While Red Organizations can be extremely powerful (especially in hostile environments where later stages of organizations tend to break down), they are inherently fragile, due to the impulsive nature of people's way of operating (*I want it so I take it*). The chief must regularly resort to public displays of cruelty and punishment, as only fear and submission keep the organization from disintegrating. Mythical stories about his absolute power frequently make the rounds, to keep foot soldiers from vying for a higher prize.

Present-centeredness makes Red Organizations poor at planning and strategizing but highly reactive to new threats and opportunities that they can pursue ruthlessly. They are therefore well adapted to chaotic environments (in civil wars or in failed states) but are ill-suited to achieve complex outcomes in stable environments where planning and strategizing are possible.

Conformist–Amber paradigm[5]

Every paradigm shift opens up unprecedented new capabilities and possibilities. When Conformist-Amber consciousness emerged, humankind leaped from a tribal world subsisting on horticulture to the age of agriculture, states and civilizations, institutions, bureaucracies, and organized religions. According to developmental psychologists, a large share of today's adult population in developed societies operates from this paradigm.

At the Conformist-Amber stage, reality is perceived through Newtonian eyes. Cause and effect are understood,[6] people can grasp linear time (past, present, future) and project into the future. This is the soil from which agriculture could emerge: farming requires the self-discipline and foresight to keep seeds from this year's harvest to provide for next year's food. The caloric surplus generated by agriculture allowed for feeding a class of rulers, administrators, priests, warriors, and craftsmen; this brought about the shift from chiefdom to states and civilizations, starting around 4000 BC in Mesopotamia.

Conformist-Amber consciousness develops a deeper awareness of other people's feelings and perceptions. Piaget, the pioneer child psychologist, has given us a defining experiment of Conformist-Amber cognition. A two-colored ball is placed between a child and an adult, with the green side facing the child and the red side facing the adult. Prior to the Amber stage, a child cannot yet see the world from someone else's perspective, and he will claim that both he and the adult see a green ball. At the age of around six or seven, a child raised in a nurturing environment will learn to see the world through someone else's eyes and will correctly identify that the adult sees the red side of the ball.

Psychologically, the implications are enormous. I can identify with my perspective and my role and see it as different from yours. I can also imagine how others view me. My ego and sense of self-worth are now very much based on other people's opinions. I will strive for approval, acceptance, and belonging in my social circle. People at this stage internalize group norms, and the thinking is dominated by whether one has the right appearance, behaviors, and thoughts to fit in. The dualistic thinking of Red is still present, but the individual "my way or your way" is replaced with a collective "us or them." Red egocentrism has given way to Amber ethnocentrism. Ken Wilber puts it this way:

> *Care and concern are expanded from me to the group—but no further! If you are a member of the group—a member of … my mythology, my ideology—then you are "saved" as well. But if you belong to a different culture, a different group, a different mythology, a different god, then you are damned.*[7]

In Conformist-Amber, the formerly impulsive Red self is now able to exercise self-discipline and self-control, not only in public but also in private. Amber societies have simple morals based on one accepted, right way of doing things. The Conformist-Amber worldview is static: there are immutable laws that make for a just world, where things are either right or wrong. Do what's right and you will be rewarded, in this life or the next. Do or say the wrong things, and you will be punished or even rejected from the group—and possibly suffer in the hereafter. People internalize the rules and morality and feel guilt and shame when they go astray. Authority to define what is right and wrong is now linked to a role, rather than to a powerful personality (as was the case in Red); it's the priest's robe, whoever wears it, that defines authority.

Any major change of perspective, like the change from Red to Amber, is both liberating and frightening. To feel safe in a world of causality, linear time, and awareness of other people's perspectives, the Amber ego seeks for order, stability, and predictability. It seeks to create control through institutions and bureaucracies. It finds refuge in strictly defined roles and identities. Amber societies tend to be highly stratified, with social classes or caste systems and rigid gender differences as defining features. A lottery at birth defines what caste you are born into. From there, everything is mapped out for you—how you are to behave, think, dress, eat, and marry is in accordance with your caste.

With so much in flux in the world today, some find Amber certainties an appealing refuge and call for a return to a fixed set of moral values. To take that perspective is to ignore the massive inequality of traditional societies that set strict social and sexual norms. It can be unpleasant, to say the least, to be a woman, a homosexual, an untouchable, or a free thinker in a Conformist-Amber society.

Amber Organizations

The advent of Amber Organizations brought about two major breakthroughs: organizations can now *plan for the medium and long term,* and they can *create organizational structures that are stable and can scale.* Combine these two breakthroughs, and you get organizations able to achieve unprecedented outcomes, beyond anything Red Organizations could have even contemplated. Historically, Amber Organizations are the ones that have built irrigation systems, pyramids, and the Great Wall of China. Conformist-Amber Organizations ran the ships, the trading posts, and the plantations of the Colonial world. The Catholic Church is built on this paradigm—arguably it has been *the* defining Amber Organization for the Western world. The first large corporations of the Industrial Revolution were run on this template. Amber Organizations are still very present today: most government agencies, public schools, religious institutions, and the military are run based on Conformist-Amber principles and practices.

Amber breakthrough 1: Long-term perspective (stable processes)

Red Organizations are highly opportunistic; they don't generally eye a prize beyond the next scheme in a few days or a few weeks. Amber Organizations can take on long-term projects—constructing cathedrals that might take two centuries to complete or creating networks of colonial trading posts thousands of miles away to facilitate commerce.

This breakthrough is very much linked to the invention of processes. With processes, we can replicate past experience into the future. *Last year's harvest will be our template for this year's; next year's classroom will be run with the same lesson plan as this year's.* With processes, critical knowledge no longer depends on a particular person; it is embedded in the organization and can be transmitted across generations. Any person can be replaced by another that takes over the same role in the process. Even the chief is replaceable, in an orderly succession, and Amber Organizations can therefore survive for centuries.

At the individual level, people operating from a Conformist-Amber paradigm strive for order and predictability; change is viewed with suspicion. The same holds true for Amber Organizations, which are exceptionally well-suited for stable contexts, where the future can be planned based on past experience. They operate on the hidden assumption that there is one right way of doing things and that the world is (or should be) immutable. What has worked in the past will work in the future. When the context is changing, and *the way we do things around here* stops working, Amber Organizations find it hard to accept the need for change. The idea that *there is one right way* makes Amber Organizations ill at ease with competition. Historically, they have striven for dominance and monopoly, and Amber Organizations today still tend to view competition with suspicion.

Amber breakthrough 2: Size and stability (formal hierarchies)

In Red Organizations, power structures are in constant flux as personalities jockey for influence. Conformist-Amber Organizations bring stability to power, with formal titles, fixed hierarchies, and organization charts. The overall structure settles into a rigid pyramid, with a cascade of formal reporting lines from bosses to subordinates. Below the pope there are cardinals; below cardinals, archbishops; below archbishops, bishops; and below bishops, priests. The plant manager commands the department heads, who in turn oversee unit managers, line managers, foremen, and machine operators. The personal allegiance of the foot soldier to the chief is no longer needed; the foot soldier has integrated his place into the hierarchy. Even if the pope is weak, a priest will not scheme to backstab him and take his place. Much larger organizations become possible, spanning not hundreds but thousands of workers, and they can operate across vast distances. Mankind's first global organizations—from the Catholic Church to the East India Company—were built on a Conformist-Amber template.

Planning and execution are strictly separated: the thinking happens at the top, the doing at the bottom. Decisions made at the top get handed down through successive layers of management. The constant threat of violence from above in Red Organizations gives way to more subtle and elaborate control mechanisms. A whole catalog of rules is set up. Some among the staff are put in charge of ensuring compliance and handing out disciplinary measures and punishments for those found wanting. Show up late at work, and part of your wage will be deducted. Show up late again, and you will be suspended for a day. Show up late again, and you could be dismissed.

> *Why is it that every time I ask for a pair of hands, they come with a brain attached?*
>
> Henry Ford

The underlying worldview is that workers are mostly lazy, dishonest, and in need of direction. They must be supervised and told what is expected of them. Participatory management seems foolish from a Conformist-Amber perspective; management must rely on command and control to achieve results. Jobs at the frontlines are narrow and routine-based. Innovation, critical thinking, and self-expression are not asked for (and often discouraged). Information is shared on an as-needed basis. People are effectively interchangeable resources; individual talent is neither discerned nor developed.

From the vantage point of later stages, this might sound severely limiting. But as a step up from Red, it is major progress. Even for people at the bottom of the organization doing routine work, it feels highly liberating. In Red Organizations, people have to fight to protect their turf (if not their survival)—day in and day out—from their boss, their peers, and their underlings. In contrast, Amber Organizations' order and predictability feels like a safe haven. We no longer need to watch out for threats and danger that might come unexpectedly from any direction. We just need to follow the rules.

Red Organizations are wolf packs. In Amber, the metaphor changes: a good organization should be run like an army. Within a rigid hierarchy, there must be a clear chain of command, formal processes, and clear-cut rules that stipulate who can do what. Foot soldiers at the bottom of the pyramid are expected to follow orders scrupulously, no questions asked, to ensure the battalion marches in good order.

The social mask

Size and stability become possible because people in Conformist-Amber are content to stay in their box and not vie for a higher prize. People operating from this stage identify with their roles, with their particular place in the organization. Amber Organizations have invented and generalized the use of titles, ranks, and uniforms to bolster role identification. A bishop's robe signals that inside is no mere priest. A general's uniform can hardly be confused with a lieutenant's or a private's, even from far away. In factories, the owner, the engineer, the accountant, the foreman, and the machine operator tend to dress differently to this day. When we put on our clothes, we also put on a distinct identity, a social mask. We internalize behaviors that are expected of people with our rank and in our line of work. As a worker, it's not only that I wear a different uniform than the engineer. I eat in the workers' mess; he eats in the factory restaurant. And in these places, the subjects of conversation, the jokes, and the type of self-disclosure are vastly different. Social stability comes at the price of wearing a mask, of learning to distance ourselves from our unique nature, from our personal desires, needs, and feelings; instead, we embrace a socially acceptable self.

Historically, this hierarchical stratification in organizations paralleled social stratification: priests were recruited from peasantry; bishops and cardinals, from aristocracy. The organizational ladder would come with big gaps—a man (and certainly a woman) born into the working class would not climb to a management position. Fortunately, that rigid social stratification has disappeared in modern societies. But today's Amber Organizations still tend to replicate hierarchical stratification, albeit in more subtle ways. In government agencies, schools, and the military, positions higher than a certain level often still require a specific diploma or a certain number of years of service. The promotion can bypass the most qualified and go to the person who happens to tick off the right criteria.

Us versus them

Social belonging is paramount in the Conformist-Amber paradigm. You are part of the group, or you are not—it is "us" versus "them." This dividing line can be found throughout Amber Organizations—nurses versus doctors versus administrators, line versus staff, marketing versus finance, frontline versus headquarters, public schools versus charter schools, and so forth. To deflect internal strife within a group, problems and mistakes are routinely blamed on others. Amber Organizations have definitive silos, and groups eye each other with suspicion across silos. The way Amber Organizations try to restore trust is through control—creating procedures that people across silos have to abide by.

If there are barriers inside the organization, there is a moat between the organization and the outside world. Amber Organizations try wherever possible to be self-contained and autonomous—one simply shouldn't need the outside world. Early car factories had their own rubber plantations and steel mills, operated their own bakeries, and provided social housing. Employees also "belong" to the organization: employment is assumed to be lifelong, and much of people's social life revolves around the organization. The possibility of dismissal therefore carries a double threat: employees risk losing both the identity the work gives them as well as the social fabric they are embedded in. Someone who decides to leave the organization is often met with bewilderment, if not accused of betrayal. In milder forms, today's Amber Organizations—which often come in the form of government agencies, religious organizations, public schools, and the military—still have lifetime employment as their implicit or explicit norm, and for many of their employees, social life revolves heavily around their work life. For those who feel unfulfilled in Amber Organizations and decide to leave, it is often a painful process—akin to shedding an old life and having to reinvent a new one.

Achievement–Orange paradigm[8]

In Orange, the world presents a new face. We see it no longer as a fixed universe governed by immutable rules, but as a complex clockwork, whose inner workings and natural laws can be investigated and understood. There is no absolute right and wrong, though plainly, there are some things that work better than others. Effectiveness replaces morals as a yardstick for decision-making: *the better I understand the way the world operates, the more I can achieve; the best decision is the one that begets the highest outcome.* The goal in life is to get ahead, to succeed in socially acceptable ways, to best play out the cards we are dealt.

The cognitive shift involved in this new paradigm is well described by another of Piaget's experiments, here recounted by Ken Wilber:

> *The person is given three glasses of clear liquid and told that they can be mixed in a way that will produce a yellow color. The person is then asked to produce the yellow color. Concrete operational children* [Piaget's words for Amber cognition] *will simply start mixing the liquids together haphazardly. Formal operational adolescents* [i.e., those that master Orange cognition] *will first form a general picture of the fact that you have to try glass A with glass B, then A with C, then B with C and so on. If you ask them about it, they will say something like "Well, I need to try all the various combinations one at a time."*
>
> *It means the person can begin to imagine different possible worlds. "What if" and "as if" can be grasped for the first time. All sorts of idealistic possibilities open up. You can imagine what yet might be! Adolescence is such a wild time, not just because of sexual blossoming, but because possible worlds open up the mind's eye—it's the "age of reason and revolution."* [9]

With this cognitive capacity one can question authority, group norms, and the inherited status quo. In the Western world, Achievement-Orange thinking started to poke holes in the Conformist-Amber world of Christian certainties during the Renaissance, but it was at first confined to a very small minority, primarily scientists and artists. With the Age of Enlightenment and the Industrial Revolution, Orange thinking emerged on a broader scale within educated circles. After the Second World War, a more significant percentage of the population in the Western world shifted to the Achievement-Orange paradigm. Today, Orange is arguably the dominating worldview of most leaders in business and politics.

Orange cognition has opened the floodgates of scientific investigation, innovation, and entrepreneurship. In a timeframe of just two centuries—the blink of an eye in the overall history of our species—it has brought us unprecedented levels of prosperity. It has added a few decades to our life expectancy, doing away with famine and plague in the industrialized world, and is now repeating the magic at a rapid pace in the developing world as well.

Every paradigm, seen from a higher stage, also comes with its shadows. The dark side of the Achievement-Orange paradigm is hard to ignore these days: corporate greed, political short-termism, overleverage, overconsumption, and the reckless exploitation of the planet's resources and ecosystems. But this shouldn't eclipse the enormous liberation this stage has brought us. It has moved us away from the idea that authority has the right answer (instead, it relies on expert advice to give insight into the complex mechanics of the world) and brings a healthy dose of skepticism regarding revealed truth. It has allowed us to engage, for the first time, in the pursuit of truth regardless of religious dogma and political authority, without having to risk our lives. We have become capable of questioning and stepping out of the condition we were born in; we are able of breaking free from the thoughts and behaviors that our gender and our social class would have imposed upon us in earlier times. Where Red's perspective was egocentric and Amber's ethnocentric, Orange brought about the possibility of a worldcentric perspective.

From an Orange perspective, all individuals should be free to pursue their goals in life, and the best in their field should be able to make it to the top. In practice, though, Achievement-Orange does not deconstruct the traditional Conformist-Amber world as fully as its thinking promises. People's need to be seen as socially successful makes them ready to adopt social conventions when they are helpful. Those who have achieved success are generally happy to recreate forms of social stratification—they move to privileged neighborhoods, join exclusive clubs, and put their children in expensive private schools. People operating from this perspective are often skeptical of religious observance; and yet, many who do not have personal faith will retain a religious affiliation if it is socially beneficial. (And as a hedging strategy, too, in case there is some truth to Revelation after all.)

The worldview at this stage is solidly materialistic—only what can be seen and touched is real. Achievement-Orange is suspicious of any form of spirituality and transcendence because of a difficulty in believing something that cannot empirically be proven or observed. Unencumbered by deep soulful questions, our ego reaches the peak of its dominance at this stage as we invest it with all our hopes of achievement and success. In this material world, *more* is generally considered *better*. We live our lives on the assumption that achieving the next goal (getting the next promotion, finding a life partner, moving to a new house, or buying a new car) will make us happy. In Orange, we effectively live in the future, consumed by mental chatter about the things we need to do so as to reach the goals we have set for ourselves. We hardly ever make it back to the present moment, where we can appreciate the gifts and freedom the shift to Orange has brought us.

Orange Organizations

Street gangs and mafias are contemporary examples of Red Organizations. The Catholic Church, the military, and the public school system are archetypes of Amber Organizations. Modern global corporations are the embodiment of Orange Organizations. Choose any of the defining brands of our time—say, Walmart, Nike, or Coca-Cola—and you are likely to have picked an organization whose structures, practices, and cultures are inspired by the Achievement-Orange worldview.

In terms of outcome, Amber Organizations surpassed anything Red Organizations could even contemplate. Achievement-Orange Organizations ratcheted this up another level, achieving results on entirely new orders of magnitude, thanks to three additional breakthroughs: *innovation, accountability,* and *meritocracy.*

Orange breakthrough 1: Innovation

As Piaget's experiment of mixing fluids illustrates, people operating from the Orange paradigm can live in the world of possibilities, of what is not yet but could one day be. They can question the status quo and formulate ways to improve upon it. Unsurprisingly, leaders of Orange Organizations don't tire of saying that change and innovation are not a threat, but an opportunity. Collectively, Orange Organizations have ushered in a period of unprecedented innovation that has fueled the massive wealth creation of the last two centuries. They invented departments that didn't exist (and largely still don't exist) in Amber Organizations: research and development, marketing, and product management. Amber Organizations are entirely *process* driven; Orange Organizations are *process and project* driven.

Orange Organizations retain the pyramid as their basic structure, but they drill holes into rigid functional and hierarchical boundaries with project groups, virtual teams, cross-functional initiatives, expert staff functions, and internal consultants, to speed up communication and foster innovation.

Orange breakthrough 2: Accountability

A subtle but profound change takes place in leadership and management style. Amber *command and control* becomes Orange *predict and control.* To innovate more and faster than others, it becomes a competitive advantage to tap into the intelligence of many brains in the organization. Larger parts of the organization must be given room to maneuver and must be empowered and trusted to think and execute. The answer comes in the form of *management by objectives.* Top management formulates an overall direction and cascades down objectives and milestones to reach the desired outcome. To a certain degree, the leadership doesn't care *how* the objectives will be met, as long as they *are* met. This attitude has prompted the birth of a host of now familiar management processes to define objectives (predict) and follow up (control): strategic planning, mid-term planning, yearly budgeting cycles, key performance indicators, and balanced scorecards, to name a few. In the Achievement-Orange

> *When I give a minister an order, I leave it to him to find the means to carry it out.*
> Napoleon Bonaparte

worldview, people are driven by material success. Unsurprisingly, Orange Organizations have invented a host of incentive processes to motivate employees to reach the targets that have been set, including performance appraisals, bonus schemes, quality awards, and stock options. To put it simply, where Amber relied only on sticks, Orange came up with carrots.

The breakthrough in terms of freedom is real. Managers and employees are given room to exercise their creativity and talent and the latitude to figure out how they want to reach their objectives, which can make work considerably more interesting. And when the incentive schemes are set up well (when individual and organizational goals are aligned), the often-adversarial relationship between workers and leaders can be smoothed out by the pursuit of mutually beneficial objectives.

Experience shows that unfortunately, Orange Organizations don't always deliver on the promise of management by objective. The fears of the ego often undermine good intentions. Take the notion that decisions need to be pushed down to foster innovation and motivation: this makes perfect sense for leaders operating from Achievement-Orange. But in practice, leaders' fear to give up control trumps their ability to trust, and they keep making decisions high up that would be better left in the hands of people lower in the hierarchy.

Or take the budget process that sets everyone's objectives, a critical piece in the puzzle to give people room to maneuver. It makes perfect sense in principle. But anyone who has gone through such a process knows how quickly it starts breaking down. When top management asks departments to make their budgets, people play a game called sandbagging—they push for the lowest possible expectation to make sure they will achieve the targets and collect their bonuses. When the numbers don't add up, top management arbitrarily imposes higher targets (which they make sure exceed what they promised to shareholders, to ensure they will make their bonuses too), which people lower down have no choice but to accept. Instead of frank discussions about what's feasible and what's not, people exchange spreadsheets with fictive forecasts driven by fear of not making the numbers. In the process, budgets fail to deliver on one of their key objectives: making people feel accountable and motivated for their outcomes.

Orange breakthrough 3: Meritocracy

Orange Organizations have adopted the revolutionary premise of meritocracy. In principle, anybody can move up the ladder, and nobody is predestined to stay in his position. The mailroom boy can become the CEO—even if that boy happens to be a girl or has a minority background. This dramatically widens the talent pool, as nobody is excluded from the outset. The pervasive thinking is that each person's talent should be developed and that everybody should be put in the box of the organization chart where they can best contribute to the whole. The shift from stratified Amber to meritocratic Orange has given birth to modern human resources and its arsenal of processes and practices, which include performance appraisals, incentive systems, resource planning, talent management, leadership training, and succession planning.

It is hard to overstate the historical significance of the idea of meritocracy. It is a breakthrough in social fairness. It gives people the option to choose, at least in principle, the occupation that best suits their particular talents and aspirations. In the process, people often leave aside the aspiration to lifelong employment that was so critical in the previous stage. People take the responsibility of managing their careers and expect to change positions every few years, either inside the organization, or outside if needed.

Meritocracy also largely does away with the symbols of hierarchical stratification. The mandatory uniforms that used to indicate one's rank are dropped in favor of more indistinct business attire. As people change position often during a career, the Conformist-Amber fusion of identity with one's rank and position in the pyramid is weakened. Instead, people tend to wear a professional mask. One must always look the part: be busy but composed, competent, and in control of the situation. Rationality is valued above all else; emotions, doubts, and dreams are best kept behind a mask, so that we do not make ourselves vulnerable. Our identity is no longer fused with our rank and title; instead it is fused with our need to be seen as competent and successful, ready for the next promotion.

> *It is my philosophy that in order to be successful, one must project an image of success at all times.*
>
> Buddy Kane, the "King of Real Estate" in the movie *American Beauty*

In most workplaces, while the precise uniform may be out of fashion, the signs of status are not. Senior managers have spacious corner offices, enjoy reserved parking spaces, fly first class, and receive generous stock options—while their subordinates fly coach and toil away in cubicles. Perks are not incompatible with meritocracy: leaders have the biggest impact on the organization's success, so they must be given the means to succeed. Besides, they deserve it. If you are smart and work hard enough, these benefits could be yours too.

Organizations as machines

Achievement-Orange thinks of organizations as machines, a heritage from reductionist science and the industrial age. The engineering jargon we use to talk about organizations reveals how deeply (albeit often unconsciously) we hold this metaphor in the world today. We talk about *units* and *layers, inputs* and *outputs, efficiency* and *effectiveness, pulling the lever* and *moving the needle, accelerating* and *hitting the brakes, scoping problems* and *scaling solutions, information flows* and *bottlenecks, re-engineering* and *downsizing*. Leaders and consultants *design* organizations. Humans are *resources* that must be carefully *aligned* on the chart, rather like cogs in a machine. Changes must be planned and mapped out in *blueprints,* then carefully *implemented* according to plan. If some of the machinery functions below the expected rhythm, it's probably time for a "soft" *intervention*—the occasional team-building—like injecting oil to grease the wheels.

The machine metaphor, as impersonal as it sounds, also reveals the dynamic nature of organizations in Orange (as compared to Amber, where we think of organizations as rigid, unchanging sets of rules and hierarchies). There is room for energy, creativity, and innovation. At the same time, the metaphor of the machine indicates that these organizations, however much they brim with activity, can still feel lifeless and soulless.

Every paradigm has its leadership style that suits its worldview. Impulsive-Red calls for predatory leaders; Conformist-Amber for paternalistic authoritarianism. In keeping with the machine metaphor, Achievement-Orange leadership tends to look at management through an engineering perspective. Leadership at this stage is typically goal-oriented, focused on solving tangible problems, putting tasks over relationships. It values dispassionate rationality and is wary of emotions; questions of meaning and purpose feel out of place.

The shadows of Orange

As with any new paradigm, the more light it shines, the more shadow it can cast. One of Orange's shadows is "innovation gone mad." With most of our basic needs taken care of, businesses increasingly try to *create needs,* feeding the illusion that more stuff we don't really need—more possessions, the latest fashion, a more youthful body—will make us happy and whole. We increasingly come to see that much of this economy based on fabricated needs is unsustainable from a financial and ecological perspective. We have reached a stage where we often pursue growth for growth's sake, a condition that in medical terminology would simply be called cancer.

Another shadow appears when success is measured solely in terms of money and recognition. When growth and the bottom line are all that count, when the only successful life is the one that reaches the top, we are bound to experience a sense of emptiness in our lives. The midlife crisis is an emblematic disease of life in Orange Organizations: for 20 years, we played the game of success and ran the rat race. And now we realize we won't make it to the top, or that the top isn't all it's made up to be. In principle, work in Orange Organizations can be a vehicle for self-expression and fulfillment. But when year after year things boil down to targets and numbers, milestones and deadlines, and yet another change program and cross-functional initiative, some people can't help but wonder about the meaning of it all and yearn for something more.

> *Ever more people today have the means to live, but no meaning to live for.*
> Viktor Frankl

In light of the corporate scandals of the last decade, some would add that the most obvious shadow of the modern organization is individual and collective greed. A small circle of CEOs grant themselves ever higher salaries; they lobby government for favorable rules; corrupt regulators; play off governments to pay little or no taxes; and merge in a frenzy to dominate their industries and abuse their power over suppliers, customers, and employees.

Pluralistic–Green paradigm[10]

The Achievement-Orange paradigm replaces Amber's absolute truth of right and wrong with another standard: *what works and what doesn't*. The Pluralistic-Green worldview holds that this idea is still too simplistic. There is more to life than success or failure. Pluralistic-Green is keenly aware of Orange's shadow over people and society: the materialistic obsession, the social inequality, the loss of community.

Pluralistic-Green is highly sensitive to people's feelings. It insists that all perspectives deserve equal respect. It seeks fairness, equality, harmony, community, cooperation, and consensus. The self operating from this perspective strives to belong, to foster close and harmonious bonds with everyone. Orange promised a worldcentric stance; Green wants to cash in on the promise. Not only should individuals be able to break free from the prison of conventional roles, but the entire edifice of castes, social classes, patriarchy, institutional religion, and other structures needs to tumble down. In industrialized countries, in the late 18th and 19th centuries, a small circle of people operating from Pluralistic-Green started championing the abolition of slavery, women's liberation, separation of church and state, freedom of religion, and democracy. Ken Wilber puts it this way:

> *With the shift to reason and worldcentric morality, we see the rise of the modern liberation movements: liberation of slaves, of women, of the untouchables. Not what is right for me or my tribe, or my mythology, or my religion, but what is fair and right and just for all humans, regardless of race, sex, caste or creed.*
>
> *And thus, in a mere hundred-year period, stretching roughly from 1788 to 1888, slavery was outlawed and eliminated from every rational-industrial society on earth. In both the preconventional/egocentric* [Red] *and conventional/ethnocentric* [Amber] *moral stance, slavery is perfectly acceptable, because equal dignity and worth are not extended to all humans, but merely to those of your tribe or your race or your chosen god. But from a postconventional stance, slavery is simply wrong, it is simply intolerable. …*
>
> *For almost identical reasons, we would see the rise of feminism and the women's movement on a culture-wide scale, generally dated … from*

Wollstonecraft in 1792, exactly the general beginning period of numerous liberation movements. …

[Democracy], too, was radically novel, on any sort of large scale. The early Greeks had none of this universalism. Let us remember that in the Greek "democracies," one out of three people were slaves, and women and children virtually so; the agrarian base cannot support emancipation of slaves.[11]

In the late 18th and 19th centuries, only a small elite operated from this Pluralistic-Green paradigm, but it profoundly shaped Western thinking. In the 20th century, this paradigm steadily grew in numbers, and some people embraced it wildly in the countercultural 1960s and 1970s. While Orange is predominant today in business and politics, Green is very present in postmodern academic thinking, in nonprofits, and among social workers and community activists.

For people operating from this perspective, relationships are valued above outcomes. For instance, where Achievement-Orange seeks to make decisions top-down, based on objective facts, expert input, and simulations, Pluralistic-Green strives for bottom-up processes, gathering input from all and trying to bring opposing points of view to eventual consensus. Orange glorifies decisive leadership, while Green insists that leaders should be in service of those they lead. Its stance is noble—it is generous, empathetic, and attentive to others. It insists that in light of the continuing inequality, poverty, and discrimination in our world, there must be more to life than a self-centered pursuit of career and success.

Yet this stage has its obvious contradictions. It insists that all perspectives be treated equally and finds itself stuck when others abuse its tolerance to putting forward intolerant ideas. Green's brotherly outreach is only rarely returned in kind by Red egocentricity, Amber certainty, and Orange contempt for what it sees as Green idealism. Green's relationship to rules is ambiguous and conflicted: rules always end up being arbitrary and unfair, but doing away with rules altogether proves unpractical and opens the door for abuse. Green is powerful as a paradigm for breaking down old structures, but often less effective at formulating practical alternatives.

Green Organizations

The Pluralistic-Green perspective is uneasy with power and hierarchy. Ideally, it would want to do away with both altogether. Some have tried to take this radical step—to discard the Amber and Orange models and start from a blank slate. *If power inequality always results in those at the top ruling over those at the bottom, then let's abolish hierarchy and give everybody the exact same power. Let's have all workers own the company in equal shares and make all decisions by consensus, with nobody holding a leadership position (or, if needed, work with rotating leadership).* Some radical experimenters have tried to create a new future along these lines; for instance, in the cooperative movement in the late 19th and early 20th centuries (in response to the glaring inequality brought about by the Industrial Revolution) or in the communes in the 1960s (inspired by the counterculture of the times). In hindsight, we know that these extreme forms of egalitarian organization have not been successful on a meaningful scale for any meaningful amount of time.[12] Bringing about consensus among large groups of people is inherently difficult. It almost invariably ends up in grueling talk sessions and eventual stalemate. In response, power games break out behind the scenes to try to get things moving again. Power can't simply be wished away. Like the Hydra, if you cut off its head, another will pop up somewhere else.

Extreme egalitarianism has proven a dead-end track. Yet Green has, like the previous stages, come up with its own breakthrough organizational model, adding three breakthroughs to the previous Orange model. Some of the most celebrated and successful companies of the last decades—companies like Southwest Airlines, Ben & Jerry's, and The Container Store, to name only few, are run on Green practices and culture.

Green breakthrough 1: Empowerment

Green Organizations retain the meritocratic hierarchical structure of Orange, but push a majority of decisions down to frontline workers who can make far-reaching decisions without management approval. People in the trenches are directly in touch with the myriad of smaller, day-to-day problems; they are therefore trusted to come up with better solutions than experts could devise from far away. Ground teams at Southwest Airlines, for instance, are famous for being empowered to seek creative solutions to passenger problems, whereas their colleagues at most other airlines aren't allowed to depart from the rulebook.

Making decentralization and empowerment work on a large scale is no easy feat. Top and middle managers are effectively asked to share power and give up some control. To make it work, companies have found that they needed to very clearly spell out the kind of Green leadership that they expect from people in senior and middle management. Green leaders should not merely be dispassionate problem solvers (like in Orange); they should be *servant leaders,* listening to their subordinates, empowering them, motivating them, developing them. Much time and effort is invested in helping people become servant leaders:

- Candidates for management positions are rigorously screened on their mindset and behavior: *Are they ready to share power? Will they lead with humility?*
- Green Organizations often invest a disproportionate share of their training budget in courses for newly promoted managers, to teach them the mindset and skills of servant leaders.

- Managers are evaluated based on 360-degree feedback, to make bosses accountable to their subordinates.
- In some innovative companies, managers are not appointed from above, but from below: subordinates choose their boss, after interviewing prospective candidates.[13] The practice naturally induces managers to act as servant leaders.

Green breakthrough 2: Values-driven culture and inspirational purpose

A strong, shared culture is the glue that keeps empowered organizations from falling apart. Frontline employees are trusted to make the right decisions, guided by a number of shared values, rather than by a thick book of rules and policies.

Some people have become disillusioned with and scoff at the notion of shared values. This is because Orange Organizations increasingly feel obliged to follow the fad: they define a set of values, post them on office walls and the company web site, and then ignore them whenever that is more convenient for the bottom line. But in Green Organizations, where leadership genuinely plays by shared values, you en-counter incredibly vibrant cultures in which employees feel appreciated and empowered to contribute. Results are often spectacular. Research seems to show that values-driven organizations can outperform their peers by wide margins.[14]

> *Culture eats strategy for breakfast.*
> Peter Drucker

In many cases, Green Organizations put an inspirational purpose at the heart of what they do. Southwest Airlines doesn't consider itself merely in the transportation business; it insists that in reality it is in the business of "freedom," helping customers to go to places they couldn't go if it weren't for Southwest Airlines' low fares. Ben & Jerry's is not just about ice cream, it's about the earth and the environment too.

In Orange Organizations, strategy and execution are king. In Green Organizations, the company culture is paramount. CEOs of Green Organizations claim that promoting the culture and shared values is their primary task. The focus on culture elevates human resources (HR) to a central role. The HR director is often an influential member of the executive team and a counselor to the CEO. He heads a large staff that orchestrates substantial investments into employee-centric processes like training, culture initiatives, 360-degree feedback, succession planning and staff morale surveys.

Green breakthrough 3: Multiple stakeholder perspective

Orange holds that for-profit companies should operate with a shareholder perspective. Management's primary (some people claim its sole) obligation is to maximize profits for investors. Adam Smith's "invisible hand" is often invoked to explain how this benefits all stakeholders in the long run. Green Organizations insist that there should be no such hierarchy among stakeholders. Businesses have a responsibility not only to investors, but also to management, employees, customers, suppliers, local communities, society at large, and the environment. The role of leadership is to make the right trade-offs so that all stakeholders can thrive.

Every large organization today has to publish a corporate social responsibility report. Green Organizations consider their social responsibility an integral part of how they do business, contrary to their Orange counterparts who often deem such reports a distracting obligation. Social responsibility is often at the core of their mission, and it provides the motivation that spurs them on to innovate and become better corporate citizens. Green Organizations work with their suppliers in developing countries to improve local working conditions and prevent child labor; they try to reduce their carbon footprint and their use of water; they strive to recycle their products and reduce packaging. Leaders in Green Organizations maintain that the "stakeholder perspective" might come with higher costs in the short term, but it will deliver better returns in the long run for all parties, including shareholders.

Family as the guiding metaphor

Where Achievement-Orange views organizations as machines, the dominant metaphor of organizations in Pluralistic-Green is the family. Listen to leaders of Green Organizations and you can't fail to notice how frequently the metaphor pops up in one form or another: employees are *part of the same family* and *in it together*, ready to *help each other out* and *be there for one another*. At Southwest Airlines, one of the eight injunctions to display "a servant's heart" in the Southwest Way is for employees to "Embrace the SWA family." DaVita, a leading operator of dialysis centers that has implemented Green organizational principles and practices with great consistency,[15] uses another community metaphor. Notwithstanding its large size, the company talks about itself as the *Village* and calls its 41,000 employees *citizens*. The corporate headquarters is known as *Casa DaVita*, while Kent Thiry, the chairman and CEO (who is credited with having turned the company around from virtual bankruptcy in 1999 to its current success by virtue of the Green culture he brought about) is referred to as the *Mayor* of the Village.

From Red to Green: co-existence of organizational models

Organizations as we know them are a very recent phenomenon. For the majority of the history of our species, we were busy hunting and gathering, which we can safely assume didn't involve email overload and tedious budgeting meetings. In the overall scope of things, it wasn't long ago that we switched to the age of agriculture, and even then organizations rarely spanned beyond family structures. It was only with the Industrial Revolution that organizations began to employ a large share of *human resources.* Management as a field of academic interest really only blossomed in the last 50 years.

When we plot the successive stages of human and organizational consciousness on a timeline, the result is striking. Evolution seems to be accelerating, and accelerating ever faster. If the trend is to continue, we might well experience the emergence of one or two new stages beyond Green within our lifetimes.

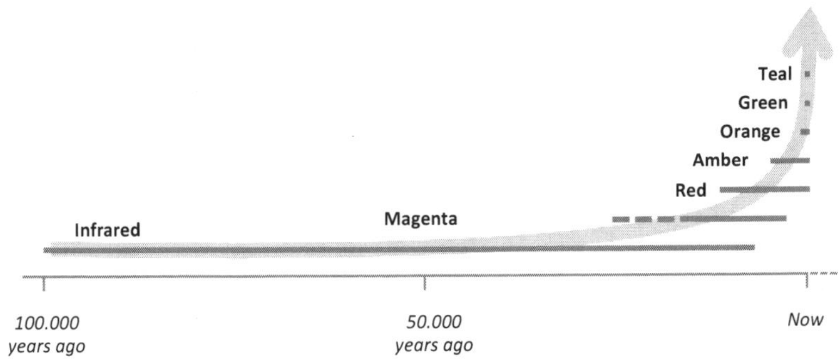

The illustration reveals another interesting phenomenon: Never before in human history have we had people operating from so many different paradigms all living alongside each other. The same is true for organizations: in the same city, if we care to look, we can find Red, Amber, Orange, and Green Organizations working side by side.

In a broad generalization, it is safe to say that, in developed societies, Impulsive-Red Organizations persist only at the fringes of legal activity. Conformist-Amber is still heavily present in government agencies, the military, religious organizations, and public school systems. Achievement-Orange is clearly the dominant paradigm of business corporations, from Wall Street to Main Street. Pluralistic-Green organizational practices are making increasing inroads, not only in the world of nonprofits, but in the business sector as well. The table below summarizes these four organizational models, their breakthroughs, and dominant metaphors. It shows the current state of affairs out of which, perhaps, a new model is about to emerge.

	Current examples	Key breakthroughs	Guiding metaphor
RED organizations Constant exercise of power by chief to keep troops in line. Fear is the glue of the organization. Highly reactive, short-term focus. Thrives in chaotic environments.	• Mafia • Street gangs • Tribal militias	• **Division of labor** • **Command authority**	• **Wolf pack**
AMBER organizations Highly formal roles within a hierarchical pyramid. Top-down command and control (what and how). Stability valued above all through rigorous processes. Future is repetition of the past.	• Catholic Church • Military • Most government agencies • Public school systems	• **Formal roles** *(stable and scalable hierarchies)* • **Processes** *(long-term perspectives)*	• **Army**
ORANGE organizations Goal is to beat competition; achieve profit and growth. Innovation is the key to staying ahead. Management by objectives (command and control on what; freedom on the how).	• Multinational companies • Charter schools	• **Innovation** • **Accountability** • **Meritocracy**	• **Machine**
GREEN organizations Within the classic pyramid structure, focus on culture and empowerment to achieve extraordinary employee motivation.	• Culture driven organizations (e.g., Southwest Airlines, Ben & Jerry's, ...)	• **Empowerment** • **Values-driven culture** • **Stakeholder model**	• **Family**
TEAL organizations ?	?	?	?

CHAPTER 1.2

ABOUT STAGES OF DEVELOPMENT

There is nothing inherently "better" about being at a higher level of development, just as an adolescent is not "better" than a toddler. However, the fact remains that an adolescent is able to do more, because he or she can think in more sophisticated ways than a toddler. Any level of development is okay; the question is whether that level of development is a good fit for the task at hand.

Nick Petrie

A pause might be in order at this moment in our exploration, before we discuss Evolutionary-Teal, the next stage in human consciousness. Some clarifications may be helpful toward better understanding the process of human evolution and avoiding misunderstandings. Sometimes, when people are first exposed to the notion of successive stages in human evolution, they are so fascinated with the insight that they tend to apply it haphazardly, oversimplifying reality to fit the model. Other people have the opposite reaction; they feel uncomfortable with a model that could be used to label people and put them into different boxes.

Let's first get one potential misunderstanding out of the way: the notion, which makes some people uneasy, that successive stages in development would imply that some people are somehow better than others. It's a valid concern. As a human race, we have done much harm to each other by means of colonialism, slavery, racism, and sexism, in the name of one group being "better" than other groups.

Human consciousness evolves in successive stages; there is no wishing away the massive amount of evidence that backs this reality. The problem is not with the reality of the stages; it is with how we view the staircase. We get into trouble when we believe that later stages are "better" than earlier stages; a more helpful interpretation is that they are "more complex" ways of dealing with the world. For instance, a person operating from Pluralistic-Green can integrate people's conflicting perspectives in a way that a person operating from Impulsive-Red most likely cannot. At the same time, every level has its own lights and shadows, its healthy and unhealthy expressions. Orange modernity, for instance, has harmed the planet in a way previous stages never could.

Another way to avoid attaching judgment to stages is to recognize that each stage is well adapted to certain contexts. If we were caught in a civil war with thugs attacking our house, Impulsive-Red would be the most appropriate paradigm to think and act from so as to defend ourselves. On the other hand, in peaceful times in post-industrial societies, Red is not as functional as some of the later stages.

The complexity of human evolution

The discussion of stages and colors is only an abstraction of reality, just like a geographical map is only a simplified depiction of a territory; it gives us distinctions that facilitate understanding of a complex underlying reality, but it cannot claim to offer a full portrayal of reality. In the previous chapter, I took you on a whirlwind tour of human evolution, and by describing the stages one after the other, I may have given the impression that people (or even whole societies) operate neatly from just one paradigm. Research shows—bless it!—that we human beings are wonderfully complex and cannot be reduced to a single stage:

- Every paradigm *includes and transcends* the previous. So if we have learned to operate from, say, Achievement-Orange, we still have the ability, when appropriate, to also react from Conformist-Amber or Impulsive-Red. Even the opposite is true to some extent: were we to be surrounded by people operating from a later stage, for example, Pluralistic-Green, we could temporarily display Green behaviors, even though we wouldn't yet have integrated this stage.
- There are many dimensions of human development—cognitive, moral, psychological, social, spiritual, and so on—and we don't necessarily grow at the same pace in all of them. For example, we might have internalized Orange cognition and be running an innovative business, but on the spiritual side, we espouse an Amber Christian fundamentalist belief.

For these reasons, I cringe when I hear people say that *someone is* Green, or Orange, or Amber. At best, we can say (and I have made every effort to stick to this vocabulary) that in a specific moment a person "operates from" one type of paradigm. Don Beck, a student of developmental psychologist Clare Graves, uses an insightful analogy: If evolution were music, stages of development would be musical notes, vibrating at certain frequencies. Human beings would be like strings, capable of playing many different notes. The range of notes they can play depends on the range of tensions they have learned to accommodate.

Let's also have in mind that people operating from the same stage (that is, playing the same note) can see the world very differently from each other, despite the fact that they share certain cognitive, moral, or psychological traits. A right-wing Christian fundamentalist and a left-wing trade union leader might operate from the same Conformist-Amber world of certainties, yet come to opposite conclusions on almost every issue. At a cocktail party, a flashy Wall Street trader, an introverted scientist, and a trendy graphic designer might not find much to talk about, even though all three likely view the world through an Achievement-Orange lens. We can develop *vertically* by integrating a perspective from a later stage, but there is just as much room to develop *horizontally* within a stage—say, from an intolerant and narrow-minded to a generous and open-minded expression of Amber.

Shifting stages

What triggers a person to open up to a later, more complex stage of consciousness? According to the research, the trigger for vertical growth always comes in the form of a major life challenge that cannot be resolved from the current worldview. When we face such a challenge, we can take one of two approaches: we can grow into a more complex perspective that offers a solution to our problem, or we can try to ignore the problem, sometimes clinging more strongly to our existing world-view (or even shifting back to the reassuring simplicity of an earlier worldview).

> *Every challenge you encounter in life is a fork in the road. You have the choice to choose which way to go—backward, forward, breakdown or breakthrough.*
>
> Ifeanyi Enoch Onuoha

Take the shift from Conformist-Amber to Achievement-Orange. When a person feels allegiance to several groups (say, family, friends, work, and church) and the norms of two or more of these groups enter into conflict, the conformist worldview is out of its depth. Something can't be right and wrong at the same time. In response, one can simply choose to restore a single set of beliefs by staying with one group and rejecting the other, or one can start to question the validity of absolute rules.

Cognitively, psychologically, and morally, moving on to a new stage is a massive feat. It requires courage to let go of old certainties and experiment with a new worldview. For a while, everything can seem uncertain and confused. It might be lonely, too, as sometimes in the process we can lose close relationships with friends and family who can no longer relate to us. Growing into a new form of consciousness is always a highly personal, unique, and somewhat mysterious process. It cannot be forced onto somebody. No one can be made to evolve in consciousness, even with the best of intentions—a hard truth for coaches and consultants, who wish they could help organizational leaders adopt a more complex worldview by the power of conviction. What can be done is to create environments that are conducive to growing into later stages. When someone is surrounded by peers who already see the world from a more complex perspective, in a context safe enough to explore inner conflicts, chances are higher that the person will make the leap[1].

Stage development applied to organizations

To avoid oversimplifying, we need to be careful with organizations, too, in how we apply developmental theory. Sometimes I get asked, "What color is this or that organization?" I'm always careful to explain first what I mean when talking about organizations operating from a certain stage like Amber, Orange, or Green: I'm referring to systems and culture, not people. If we look at an organization's structure, its practices, and its cultural elements, we can generally discern what worldview they stem from. Let's take the topic of compensation to illustrate this:

- If the boss can freely, on a whim, decide to increase or reduce pay, that would be consistent with the Impulsive-Red paradigm.
- If salaries are fixed and determined by the person's level in the hierarchy (or the person's diploma), that sounds like Conformist-Amber.
- A system that stresses individual incentives if people reach predetermined targets probably stems from an Achievement-Orange worldview.
- A focus on team bonuses would be in line with a Pluralistic-Green perspective.

When we look through this filter not only at compensation, but at all the structure, practices, and culture of an organization, we find that they are not scattered randomly among the stages and colors, but cluster around a center of gravity, a stage that defines most practices of the organization. It is this center of gravity that I refer to when I talk about, for instance, an Orange Organization. To be very clear, when I talk about an "Orange Organization," I don't mean to imply that *all* the daily interactions in that workplace are consistent with the Achievement-Orange paradigm, or that all the people in it have reached and operate primarily from an Orange perspective. That is never the case. At any moment in time, different people will operate from different stages in their daily interactions. The term "Orange Organization" means that the majority of the organization's structure, practices, and processes are shaped by the Achievement-Orange paradigm.

> *When you adopt a tool, you also adopt the management philosophy embedded in that tool.*
>
> Clay Shirky

In large organizations, certain units or certain locations can have a different center of gravity than the rest of the organization. A typical example: the headquarters of a large multinational might operate mostly along Orange lines, while some of the factories are steeped in Amber. We should therefore always be careful not to oversimplify and to be clear what the labels refer to (and what they do not).

The pull of leadership—downward and upward

What determines which stage an organization operates from? It is the stage through which its leadership tends to look at the world. Consciously or unconsciously, leaders put in place organizational structures, practices, and cultures that make sense to them, that correspond to their way of dealing with the world.

This means that an organization cannot evolve beyond its leadership's stage of development. The practice of defining a set of shared values and a mission statement provides a good illustration. Because this practice is in good currency, leaders in Orange Organizations increasingly feel obliged to have a task force come up with some values and a mission statement. But looking to values and mission statements to inform decisions only makes sense as of the Pluralistic-Green paradigm. In Orange, the yardstick for decisions is success: *Let's go with what will deliver top- or bottom-line results*. In Orange Organizations, leadership might pay lip service to the values; but when the rubber hits the road and leaders have to choose between profits and values, they will predictably go for the former. They cannot uphold a practice and a culture (in this case, a values-driven culture) that stems from a later stage of development.[2]

The pull of leaders toward their stage of consciousness goes in two directions: they can pull "back" practices from later stages (rendering them ineffective as in the previous example), but they can also exert a strong pull "forward." The structure, practices, and culture they put in place can help employees adopt behaviors of more complex paradigms that they as individuals have not yet fully integrated. Suppose I am a middle manager looking at the world mostly from a Conformist-Amber perspective. My natural style with my subordinates would be to interact in very hierarchical ways, telling them exactly what they need to do and how they need to do it. Now let's say I work in a Green Organization, where my leaders urge me to empower employees that work for me. All around me I see other managers giving their subordinates lots of leeway. Twice a year, I receive 360-degree feedback, including from my direct reports, telling me how well I'm doing on empowerment (which can affect my bonus); every six months, I'm asked to sit down with my team and discuss how well we are doing in living

> *When you change the way you look at things, the things you look at change.*
> Wayne Dyer

company values (which include empowerment). Within such a strong context of Pluralistic-Green culture and practices, I'm likely to espouse some Green management skills and behaviors. The context has pulled me up, leading me to operate in more complex ways than I would if left to my own devices. And just perhaps, over time, when I'm ready for it, the context will help me grow and genuinely integrate into that paradigm.

That is the true genius of organizations: they can lift groups of people to punch above their weight, to achieve outcomes they could not have achieved on their own. This insight is a hopeful one in a time when we need the consciousness of Green and Teal Organizations to start healing the world of the wounds of modernity.

CHAPTER 1.3

EVOLUTIONARY-TEAL

The most exciting breakthroughs of the twenty-first century will not occur because of technology, but because of an expanding concept of what it means to be human.

John Naisbitt

The next stage in human evolution corresponds to Maslow's "self-actualizing" level; it has been variously labeled authentic, integral, or Teal.[1] This stage is the last one identified by Maslow's hierarchy of needs (though he later hinted at another stage of "self-transcendence"), but other researchers and thinkers have established with a fair amount of confidence that evolution doesn't stop there (Appendix 2 gives a short description of subsequent stages). Maslow and other authors agree, in any case, that the shift from Green to Teal is a particularly momentous one in the human journey—so much so that Graves and others in his wake have used the term "first-tier" consciousness for all stages up to Green and the term "second-tier" for the stages starting with Teal. All "first-tier" stages consider that their worldview is the only valid one, and that all other people are dangerously mistaken.[2] People transitioning to Teal can accept, for the first time, that there is an evolution in consciousness, that there is a momentum in evolution towards ever more complex and refined ways of dealing with the world (hence the adjective "evolutionary" that I will use for this stage).

> *[In Teal] the ego becomes more of a variable, less of an absolute.*
>
> William Torbert

Taming the fears of the ego

Each shift occurs when we are able to reach a higher vantage point from which we see the world in broader perspective. Like a fish that can see water for the first time when it jumps above the surface, gaining a new perspective requires that we disidentify from something we were previously engulfed in. The shift to Conformist-Amber, for instance, happens when Impulsive-Red internalizes rules that allow it to disidentify from impulsively satisfying its needs; the shift to Achievement-Orange happens when Amber disidentifies from group norms. The shift to Evolutionary-Teal happens when we learn to disidentify from our own ego. By looking at our ego from a distance, we can suddenly see how its fears, ambitions, and desires often run our life. We can learn to minimize our need to control, to look good, to fit in. We are no longer fused with our ego, and we don't let its fears reflexively control our lives. In the process, we make room to listen to the wisdom of other, deeper parts of ourselves.

What replaces fear? A capacity to *trust the abundance of life*. All wisdom traditions posit the profound truth that there are two fundamental ways to live life: from fear and scarcity or from trust and abundance. In Evolutionary-Teal, we cross the chasm and learn to decrease our need to control people and events. We come to believe that even if something unexpected happens or if we make mistakes, things will turn out all right, and when they don't, life will have given us an opportunity to learn and grow.

> *Fear is the cheapest room in the house. I would like to see you living in better conditions.*
> Hafez

Inner rightness as compass

When we are fused with our ego, we are driven to make decisions informed by external factors—what others will think or what outcomes can be achieved. In the Impulsive-Red perspective, a good decision is the one that *gets me what I want*. In Conformist-Amber, we hold decisions up to the light of *conformity to social norms*. Decisions beyond what one's family, religion, or social class considers legitimate cause guilt and shame. In Achievement-Orange, *effectiveness* and *success* are the yardsticks by which decisions are made. In Pluralistic-Green, matters are judged by the criteria of *belonging* and *harmony*.

In Evolutionary-Teal, we shift from *external* to *internal* yardsticks in our decision-making. We are now concerned with the question of *inner rightness*: *does this decision seem right? Am I being true to myself? Is this in line with who I sense I'm called to become? Am I being of service to the world?* With fewer ego-fears, we are able to make decisions that might seem risky, where we haven't weighed all possible outcomes, but that resonate with deep inner convictions. We develop a sensitivity for situations that don't quite feel right, situations that demand that we speak up and take action, even in the face of opposition or with seemingly low odds of success, out of a sense of integrity and authenticity.

Recognition, success, wealth, and belonging are viewed as pleasurable experiences, but also as tempting traps for the ego. In contrast with previous stages, the order is reversed: we do not pursue recognition, success, wealth, and belonging to live a good life. We pursue a life well-lived, and the consequence might just be recognition, success, wealth, and love.

Life as a journey of unfolding

In previous stages, the pursuit of love, recognition, and success shapes our lives slowly but surely to the point that we end up, in the words of poet May Sarton, "wearing other people's faces." In Teal, our journey toward inner rightness prompts some soul searching of who we are and what our purpose in life might be. The ultimate goal in life is not to be successful or loved, but to become the truest expression of ourselves, to live into authentic selfhood, to honor our birthright gifts and callings, and be of service to humanity and our world. In Teal, life is seen as a journey of personal and collective unfolding toward our true nature.

> *Now I become myself. It's taken*
> *Time, many years and places;*
> *I have been dissolved and shaken,*
> *Worn other people's faces …*
>
> May Sarton

This is like a Copernican revolution in an age that tells us that we can become anything we want, if we only put our mind to it. If we "go Teal," then instead of setting goals for our life, dictating what direction it should take, we learn to let go and listen to the life that wants to be lived through us. Parker Palmer, the author, educator, and activist, writes beautifully about this perspective on life and vocation in his book *Let Your Life Speak*:

> *Behind the understanding of vocation is a truth that the ego does not want to hear because it threatens the ego's turf: everyone has a life that is different from the "I" of daily consciousness, a life that is trying to live through the "I" who is its vessel. …*
>
> *It takes time and hard experience to sense the difference between the two—to sense that running beneath the surface of the experience I call my life, there is a deeper and truer life waiting to be acknowledged.*[3]

Many people transitioning to this stage take up practices like meditation, centering, martial arts, yoga, or simply walking in nature to find a quiet place that allows the inner voice of the soul to speak its truth and guidance. Individuals who live from this perspective and connect to a deeper sense of purpose can become quite fearless in pursuit of their calling. With their ego under control, they don't fear failure as much as not trying. Clare Graves' favorite phrase to describe someone operating from Teal was "a person who has ambition, but is not ambitious."

Growing into their true nature and working toward their calling is their driving force, so much so that to others who don't come from the same perspective, persons operating from Teal can sometimes come across as impatient with people who impede their personal growth, or with situations that don't feel aligned with the purpose they perceive for their life.

Building on strengths

When we set goals for our life that are disconnected from our deeper selfhood, when we wear other people's faces, we don't stand in the strength of our selfhood. Inevitably we will find ourselves lacking and invest much energy in trying to overcome our weaknesses, or in blaming ourselves or others for not being who we think we ought to be.

When we see our life as a journey of unfolding toward our true nature, we can look more gently and realistically at our limitations and be at peace with what we see. Life is not asking us to become anything that isn't already seeded in us. We also tend to focus less on what is wrong or missing in people and situations around us and move our attention instead to what is there, to the beauty and the potential. We trade in judgment for compassion and appreciation. Psychologists talk about a shift from a *deficit* to a *strength-based* paradigm. Slowly, this shift is making profound inroads in different fields, from management to education, from psychology to health care—starting with the premise that, as human beings, we are not problems waiting to be solved, but potential waiting to unfold.

Dealing gracefully with adversity

When life is seen as a journey of discovery, then we learn to deal more gracefully with the setbacks, the mistakes, and the roadblocks in our life. We can start to grasp the spiritual insight that there are no mistakes, simply experiences that point us to a deeper truth about ourselves and the world. In previous stages, life's roadblocks (an illness, a bad boss, a difficult marriage) are seen as unfair rolls of the dice. We meet them with anger, shame, or blame, and these feelings disconnect us from others and ourselves. In Teal, obstacles are seen as life's way to teach us about ourselves and about the world. We are ready to let go of anger, shame, and blame, which are useful shields for the ego but poor teachers for the soul. We embrace the possibility that we played a part in creating the problem, and inquire what we can learn so as to grow from it. In earlier paradigms, we often convince ourselves that everything is all right until a problem has snowballed and hits us like an avalanche, forcing change into our life. Now, we tend to make frequent small adjustments, as we learn and grow from problems we encounter along the way. In previous stages, change on a personal level feels threatening; as of Evolutionary-Teal, there is often an enjoyable tension in the journey of personal growth.

> *With appropriate humility, we accept our inability to control the world. … We accept that losing is part of life. We do not fear adversity or suffering. Out of them comes new learning, new growth, new hope, and new life.*
>
> Dennis Bakke

Wisdom beyond rationality

In Orange, rationality is king and rules unquestioned in the pursuit of the decision that will yield the best outcome. Any source of insight other than facts and logical reasoning is "irrational" and must be discarded. Ironically, however, Orange's attachment to outcomes often clouds the ability to see reality clearly. Amid the stacks of information that are meant to inform complex decisions, we can fail to see information that is incongruous with our worldview or with the future our ego has projected and is attached to; often the writing was all over the wall, and yet people dismissed the clues (or didn't dare to speak up). Teal, less attached to outcomes, can more easily accept the sometimes unpleasant truths of reality; therefore, rational thinking within Teal can be more accurately informed by data.

Beyond facts and figures, cognition at this stage taps a broader range of sources to support decision-making. The Orange modern-scientific perspective is wary of emotions that could cloud our ability to reason rationally, whereas Green sometimes goes to the other extreme, rejecting analytical "left brain" approaches for "right brain" feeling as a basis for decision-making. Teal is happy to tap into all the domains of knowing. There are insights to be gained from analytical approaches. There is also wisdom to be found in emotions if we learn to inquire into their significance: *Why am I angry, fearful, ambitious, or excited? What does this reveal about me or about the situation that is unfolding?*

> *The intuitive mind is a sacred gift and the rational mind is a faithful servant. We have created a society that honors the servant and has forgotten the gift.*
>
> Albert Einstein

Wisdom can be found in intuition, too. Intuition honors the complex, ambiguous, paradoxical, non-linear nature of reality; we unconsciously connect patterns in a way that our rational mind cannot. Intuition is a muscle that can be trained, just like logical thinking: when we learn to pay attention to our intuitions, to honor them, to question them for the truth and guidance they might contain, more intuitive answers will surface.

Many people believe that there are answers to be found in yet deeper sources. Wisdom traditions and transpersonal psychology trust that if we don't simply ask a question, but *live* a question, the universe in its abundance may give us clues to the answer in unexpected events and synchronicity or in words and images that arise in dreams and meditations. Non-ordinary states of consciousness—meditative states, contemplative states, visionary experiences, flow, peak experiences—are available at any stage of consciousness, but from Teal onward, people often take on regular practices to deepen their experience in these states and access the full spectrum of human experience.[4]

Another cognitive breakthrough is the ability to reason in paradox, transcending the simple *either-or* with more complex *both-and* thinking.

Breathing in and breathing out provides an easy illustration of the difference. In either-or thinking, we see them as opposites. In both-and thinking, we view them as two elements that need each other: the more we can breathe in, the more we can breathe out. The paradox is easy to grasp for breathing in and out; it is less obvious for some of the great paradoxes of life that we only start to truly understand when we reach Teal: freedom and responsibility, solitude and community, tending to the self and tending to others.

Put this all together—a fearless rationality and the wisdom that can be found in emotions, intuition, events, and paradoxes—and Evolutionary-Teal turns the page from the rational-reductionist world-view of Orange and the post-modern worldview of Green to a holistic approach to knowing.

Striving for wholeness

Disidentifying from the ego is one more step of liberation on the human journey. But with disidentification comes separation, and people operating at this stage often develop a keen sense of how far we have let separation fragment our lives and how much it has cost us. We have let our busy egos trump the quiet voice of our soul; in our culture we often celebrate the mind and neglect the body; we often value the masculine above the feminine; we have lost community and our innate connection with nature.

With this stage comes a deep yearning for wholeness—bringing together the ego and the deeper parts of the self; integrating mind, body, and soul; cultivating both the feminine and masculine parts within; being whole in relation to others; and repairing our broken relationship with life and nature. Often the shift to Teal comes with an opening to a transcendent spiritual realm and a profound sense that at some level, we are all connected and part of one big whole. After many successive steps of disidentification, as we learn to be fully independent and true to ourselves, it dawns on us that, paradoxically, we are profoundly part of everything.

This longing for wholeness is at odds with the separation that most existing workplaces foster, albeit unconsciously—overemphasizing the ego and the rational while negating the spiritual and emotional; separating people based on the departments they work in, their rank, background, or level of performance; separating the professional from the personal; separating the organization from its competitors and the ecosystem it is embedded in. Vocabulary we use is often revealing: in organizations, we often speak about "work-life balance"—a notion that shows how little life is left in work when we have separated ourselves from so much that truly matters. For people transitioning to Teal, these separations in the workplace often become so painful that they choose to leave organizational life for some form of self-employment, a more accommodating context to find wholeness with themselves and with others.

Wholeness in relation to others

In Evolutionary-Teal, we can transcend the opposites of *judgment* and *tolerance*. In earlier stages, when we disagree with other people, we often meet them in judgment, believing that we must be right and they must be wrong. Our task then is to convince, teach, fix, or dismiss them. Or we can, in the name of tolerance, the Green ideal, gloss over our differences and affirm that all truths are equally valid. In Teal, we can transcend this polarity and integrate with the higher truth of *non-judgment*—we can examine our belief and find it to be superior in truth *and* yet embrace the other as a human being of fundamentally equal value.

In the absence of judgment, relationships take on a new quality. Our listening is no longer limited to gathering information so as to better convince, fix, or dismiss. We can create a shared space safe from judgment, where our deep listening helps others to find their voice and their truth, just as they help us find ours. In Orange, we broke free from the oppressive, normative communities of Amber. Now we have a chance to recreate community on new grounding, where we listen each other into selfhood and wholeness.

Wholeness with life and nature

Paradoxically, again, the more we learn to be true to our unique self, the more it dawns on us that we are just one expression of something larger, an interconnected web of life and consciousness. That realization can be elating but also painful—we now comprehend how deeply our relationship with life and nature has been broken. We strive to repair that relationship, not from a place of moral obligation, but from an inner awareness, knowing that we are not *separate from* but *one with* nature. We see the foolishness and arrogance of mankind's stance of putting itself above the rest of life and try to find a more truthful and humble place in the midst of it. Often, rekindling our relationship with life and nature causes us to pursue a simpler life, less cluttered by possessions we thought we needed until we understood that we are rich not through the things we own, but through the relationships that nourish our soul.

What this could mean for Teal Organizations

In the first chapter of this book we discussed how every new organizational model in the past has achieved outcomes of a magnitude that previous models could not consider. A number of researchers—Clare Graves, William Torbert, Susanne Cook-Greuter, and Keith Eigel, to name a few—have empirically established another interesting phenomenon: within a given organization (say, an Orange Organization), the higher people have traveled on the developmental ladder, the more effective they are. Torbert, for instance, established that the CEO's developmental stage determined to a significant degree the success of large-scale corporate transformation programs (and within that, leaders operating from Evolutionary-Teal were by far the most successful).[5] Clare Graves came to a similar conclusion with a different approach. He put together groups of people based on the paradigm they most often operated from and gave them complex tasks to perform.

> *I took a group of people who thought the same way, and I put them in situations … where they were required to solve problems with multiple answers. … and lo and behold, when the results started to come in I found this most peculiar phenomenon: the [Teals] find unbelievably more solutions than all the others put together. They found more solutions than the [Red] plus the [Amber] plus the [Orange] plus the [Green]. I found that the quality of their solutions to problems were* amazingly *better. … I found that the average time it took the [Teal] group to arrive at a solution was* amazingly *shorter than it took any of the other groups.*[6]

It appears that the law of evolution holds true for Evolutionary-Teal as much as it did for previous paradigms: the more complex our worldview and cognition, the more effectively we can deal with problems we face.

This is a hopeful message for organizations, especially when not only individuals within it, but the organization itself, operates from Teal principles and practices. Based on what we know about how individuals operate from Teal, we can make some conjectures about what might define Teal Organizations. Taming the ego could have deep repercussions on how we structure and run organizations. Many of the corporate ills today can be traced to behaviors driven by fearful egos: politics, bureaucratic rules and processes, endless meetings, analysis paralysis, information hoarding and secrecy, wishful thinking, ignoring problems away, lack of authenticity, silos and infighting, decision-making concentrated at the top of organizations, and so forth. In Teal Organizations, less driven by ego, we can hope to put some of these corporate ills behind us. More generally, the relationship to power could be transformed in quite fundamental ways. When trust replaces fear, will a hierarchical pyramid still provide the best structure? Will we need all the rules and policies, detailed budgets, targets, and roadmaps that give leaders today a sense of control? Perhaps there are much simpler ways to run organizations when the fears of the ego are out of the way.

> *Companies either operate from the fears of the ego or the love of the soul.*
> Richard Barrett

As people in Teal are busy exploring the calling in their lives, they are likely to affiliate only with organizations that have a clear and noble purpose of their own. We can expect that purpose, more than profitability, growth, or market share, will be the guiding principle for organizational decision-making. It's also fair to assume that Teal Organizations will strive for wholeness and community, and will be places that support people's longing to be fully themselves at work, and yet be deeply involved in nourishing relationships.

The above are conjectures, based on what we know about individuals seeing the world through a Teal lens. Thankfully, today we can move past conjectures. Part 2 of this book tells the stories of organizations that are already operating from this paradigm. It examines the structures, practices, and cultures of a dozen extraordinary pioneers and provides a detailed description of what the Teal organizational model can look like in practice. There is a template ready to be copied, emulated, and improved upon by people called to help more soulful, fulfilling organizations come about.

— Part 2 —

The Structures, Practices, and Cultures of Teal Organizations

CHAPTER 2.1

THREE BREAKTHROUGHS AND A METAPHOR

Nothing is as powerful as
an idea whose time has come.
Victor Hugo

Up to this point in history, humanity has experienced four ways to collaborate in organizational settings, based on four very different worldviews: Impulsive-Red, Conformist-Amber, Achievement-Orange, and Pluralistic-Green. Each of these organizational models has brought about major breakthroughs, and allowed us to tackle more complex problems and achieve results of unprecedented scale. (Page 36 summarizes the breakthroughs and the dominant metaphors of the different models).

As more people engage with the world from an Evolutionary-Teal perspective, it's fair to assume that more Teal Organizations will start to arise. What breakthroughs will they bring about? What metaphors will capture their essence? Here, in summary, are some answers that emerged from the research into pioneer Teal Organizations.

A new metaphor: organizations as living systems

Achievement-Orange speaks of organizations as machines; Pluralistic-Green uses the metaphor of families. Several of the founders of the Teal Organizations researched for this book explicitly talk about the need for a new metaphor. Clearly, looking at organizations as machines feels soulless and constraining; these founders don't want to play the all-important CEO who pulls levers at the top to propel the people below into motion like cogs in a machine. From an Evolutionary-Teal perspective, the metaphor of family can feel awkward too. Families, as we all know, don't always bring out the better aspects of our nature; more often than we would want, they are mildly or wildly dysfunctional. And concretely, if I'm your boss and you are reporting to me, does the metaphor imply that I'm a father and you are a child? Green insists on caring, serving leadership, but from a Teal perspective, I don't want to be a father to anybody in the organization, not even a caring, serving father.

The founders of Teal Organizations use a different metaphor for the workplaces they aspire to create. With surprising frequency, they talk about their organization as a *living organism* or *living system*. Life, in all its evolutionary wisdom, manages ecosystems of unfathomable beauty, ever evolving toward more wholeness, complexity, and consciousness. Change in nature happens everywhere, all the time, in a self-organizing urge that comes from every cell and every organism, with no need for central command and control to give orders or pull the levers.

The metaphor opens up new horizons. Imagine what organizations would be like if we stopped designing them like soulless, clunky machines. What could organizations achieve, and what would work feel like, if we treated them like living beings, if we let them be fueled by the evolutionary power of life itself?

Three breakthroughs of Evolutionary-Teal Organizations

The case studies of pioneer Teal Organizations researched for this book reveal three major breakthroughs:

- **Self-management**: Teal Organizations have found the key to operate effectively, even at a large scale, with a system based on peer relationships, without the need for either hierarchy or consensus.
- **Wholeness**: Organizations have always been places that encourage people to show up with a narrow "professional" self and to check other parts of the self at the door. They often require us to show a masculine resolve, to display determination and strength, and to hide doubts and vulnerability. Rationality rules as king, while the emotional, intuitive, and spiritual parts of ourselves often feel unwelcome, out of place. Teal Organizations have developed a consistent set of practices that invite us to reclaim our inner wholeness and bring all of who we are to work.
- **Evolutionary purpose**: Teal Organizations are seen as having a life and a sense of direction of their own. Instead of trying to predict and control the future, members of the organization are invited to listen in and understand what the organization wants to become, what purpose it wants to serve.

Each of these breakthroughs manifests itself through a number of concrete, day-to-day practices that depart—sometimes subtly, sometimes radically—from traditionally accepted management methods. These practices will be described in the next chapters, illustrated with stories and real-life examples from pioneer Teal Organizations. Chapters 2.2 and 2.3 look at self-management, chapters 2.4 and 2.5 detail the practices used in pursuit of *wholeness,* and chapter 2.6 deals with *evolutionary purpose*. Chapter 2.7 discusses organizational culture, the "soft" aspect of the Teal Organizational model.

Readers interested in an overview of the different practices can consult Appendix 4, which outlines Evolutionary-Teal Organizations' practices along the traditional lens of key functional processes (strategy, innovation, marketing, sales), human resources processes (recruitment, performance management, compensation), and key practices of daily life (meetings, decision-making, information flow).

Organizations featured in the research

Like protagonists in a play, the organizations researched for this book will come on the stage at different moments in the next few chapters. Let me introduce each of them here to give you a sense of the type of industries, locations, and sizes involved (and for reference, if while reading you want to be reminded of who is who).

AES
Energy sector—Global—40,000 employees—For profit
AES was founded by Roger Sant and Dennis Bakke in the United States in 1982 and quickly grew into one of the world's largest electricity production and distribution companies, with plants in dozens of countries spread around the globe and 40,000 employees.

BSO/Origin
IT consulting—Global—10,000 employees (1996) –For profit
BSO/Origin was founded in 1973 by Eckart Wintzen in the Netherlands. By 1996, when Wintzen left, after selling it to Philips, it had 10,000 employees in 20 countries.

Buurtzorg
Health care—Netherlands—7,000 employees—Nonprofit
Buurtzorg was founded as a nonprofit in 2006 by Jos de Blok and a team of nurses. It has become the largest neighborhood nursing organization in the Netherlands, providing home care to the elderly and the sick.

ESBZ
School (Grades 7-12)—Germany—1,500 students, staff, and parents—Nonprofit
ESBZ, a publicly financed school in Berlin, was founded in 2007 under the guidance of Margret Rasfeld, the school's director. It has attracted international recognition for its innovative curriculum and organizational model.

FAVI
Metal manufacturing—France—500 employees—For profit
FAVI, a brass foundry, is a family business created in 1957 in the north of France. In 1983, Jean-François Zobrist was appointed CEO and undertook a radical transformation of the organization. It produces, among other things, gearbox forks for the automotive industry.

Heiligenfeld
Mental health hospitals—Germany—600 employees—For profit
Heiligenfeld currently operates a rehabilitation center and four mental health hospitals in central Germany. The company was founded in 1990 by Dr. Joachim Galuska and Fritz Lang, after Galuska had tried unsuccessfully to apply his vision for a holistic approach to mental health problems in traditional mental health hospitals.

Holacracy
Organizational operating model
Holacracy is an organizational operating model, originally developed by Brian Robertson and his team at Ternary Software, a Philadelphia-based start-up. After transferring Ternary to new leadership, Robertson co-founded HolacracyOne, a training, consulting, and research company dedicated to spreading this new organizational model, which has been adopted by large and small for-profit and nonprofit organizations on several continents.

Morning Star
Food processing—United States—400-2,400 employees—For profit
Morning Star was founded in 1970 by Chris Rufer as a single-truck business transporting tomatoes. Today, it holds an overwhelming market share of tomato processing and transport in the United States. If you have enjoyed a pizza or spaghetti sauce in the United States, you are likely to have tasted a Morning Star product.

Patagonia
Apparel—United States—1,350 employees—For profit
Yvon Chouinard, perhaps history's most unlikely businessman, founded what would later be called Patagonia in 1957 to produce climbing pitons. The California-based company has grown into a leading outdoor apparel maker, committed to being a positive influence on the environment.

RHD
Human Services—United States—4,000 employees—Nonprofit
Resources for Human Development (RHD) is a Philadelphia-based nonprofit operating in 14 states, serving people in need through a variety of homes, shelters, and programs in areas such as mental disabilities, addiction recovery, and homelessness. It was founded in 1970 by Robert Fishman.

Sounds True
Media—United States—90 employees and 20 dogs—For profit
Sounds True is in the business of disseminating spiritual wisdom through recordings of spiritual masters, books, online courses, and music. It was founded in 1985 by Tami Simon, who still owns and leads the company today.

Sun Hydraulics
Hydraulics components—Global—900 employees—For profit
Sun Hydraulics, a company that was founded in 1970 by two engineers, designs and manufactures hydraulics cartridge valves and manifolds. Today it is a public company with factories in Florida (where it is headquartered), Kansas, England, Germany, and Korea.

For methodological reasons, only organizations with at least 100 employees were researched in depth. (Admittedly, I gave Sounds True a nudge by adding its 20 dogs into the tally. More about the dogs at Sounds True, and why it is not entirely disingenuous to count them in, at the beginning of chapter 2.4.) When relevant, the next few chapters will occasionally also mention remarkable practices from other organizations such as Ozvision, a Japanese Internet company; the Center for Courage & Renewal, an educational nonprofit supporting Parker Palmer's work with leaders in the field of education, health care, clergy, and business; Realize!, a small Dutch organizational consultancy; Valve, a Seattle based game-software company; and others.

Among the organizations listed above, AES and BSO/Origin have special insights to offer, albeit for unfortunate reasons. They achieved spectacular results during the two decades when they operated with a number of Teal practices and structures; however, under new leadership, they have reverted to more conventional management approaches. Today, not much remains of their pioneer Teal style. Their journeys offer valuable insights about the necessary conditions for Teal practices, a topic discussed in Part 3 of this book.

The way I have linked organizations to stages in human development in Part 1 of this book (see page 40) applies of course to Evolutionary-Teal just as well. When, as a matter of convenience, I talk about a "Teal Organization," I do not mean to imply that *all* people who work there and *all* daily interactions are informed by the Evolutionary-Teal paradigm. As discussed in chapter 1.2, our human nature is (thankfully) far too complex to be reduced to one single label. What I mean to imply, instead, is that many if not most of the structure, practices, and cultural aspects of that organization are consistent with the Evolutionary-Teal stage of consciousness.

A few of the researched organizations are almost pure "Teal." Most are a blend—they have innovated with Evolutionary-Teal practices very consistently in some areas, and work with more traditional Orange-Green practices in other areas. An extreme example is Morning Star, the tomato processing company: it has pushed and refined the breakthrough of self-management to an extraordinary degree, but hasn't much pursued the other two Teal breakthroughs. Calling it a Green-Teal Organization might be more accurate, and the same could be said of some of the other organizations. Fortunately, this doesn't impair the research: while some of the Teal pieces might be missing in some organizations, collectively, in every area, we have more than enough overlapping pieces for the full picture to emerge. Based on their innovations, the Evolutionary-Teal organizational model can be described in enough detail to provide practical guidance for other organizations wanting to operate in similar ways; we can even distinguish between structures and practices that can apply to all types of organizations and those that need to be adapted to the characteristics of specific companies and industries.

CHAPTER 2.2

SELF-MANAGEMENT (STRUCTURES)

> *Why do so many people work so hard so they can escape to Disneyland? Why are video games more popular than work? ... Why do many workers spend years dreaming about and planning for retirement?*
>
> *The reason is simple and dispiriting. We have made the workplace a frustrating and joyless place where people do what they're told and have few ways to participate in decisions or fully use their talents. As a result, they naturally gravitate to pursuits in which they can exercise a measure of control over their lives.*
>
> *In most organizations I have been exposed to around the world, ... we still have the offices "above" the working people ... who, without consulting workers, make decisions that dramatically affect their lives.*
>
> Dennis Bakke

The concentration of power at the top, separating colleagues into the powerful and the powerless, brings with it problems that have plagued organizations for as long as we can remember. Power in organizations is seen as a scarce commodity worth fighting for. This situation invariably brings out the shadowy side of human nature: personal ambition, politics, mistrust, fear, and greed. At the bottom of organizations, it often evokes the twin brothers of powerlessness: resignation and resentment. Labor unions were born from the attempt to confederate power at the bottom to counter power from the top (which in turn tries to break the power of unions).

The widespread lack of motivation we witness in many organizations is a devastating side effect of the unequal distribution of power. For a few lucky people, work is a place of joyful self-expression, a place of camaraderie with colleagues in pursuit of a meaningful purpose. For far too many, it is simply drudgery, a few hours of life "rented out" every day in exchange for a paycheck. The story of the global workforce is a sad tale of wasted talent and energy.

If you think this is too strong a statement, consider the 2012 survey conducted by Tower Watson, a human resources consulting firm. It polled 32,000 workers in the corporate sector in 29 countries to measure employee engagement (as well as the key factors contributing to engagement, such as confidence in senior management and the perceived interest by senior management in employee well-being). The overarching conclusion: just around a third of people are engaged in their work (35 percent). Many more people are "detached" or actively "disengaged" (43 percent). The remaining 22 percent feel "unsupported." This survey is not a negative outlier. The same survey has been administered for years, and in some years results have been worse still. Gary Hamel, a scholar and writer on organizations, aptly calls survey results such as these *the shame of management*.

Pluralistic-Green Organizations seek to deal with the problem of power inequality through empowerment, pushing decisions down the pyramid, and they often achieve much higher employee engagement. But empowerment means that someone at the top must be wise or noble enough to give away some of his power. What if power weren't a zero-sum game? What if we could create organizational structures and practices that didn't need empowerment because, by design, everybody was powerful and no one powerless? This is the first major breakthrough of Teal Organizations: transcending the age-old problem of power inequality through structures and practices where no one holds power over anyone else, and yet, paradoxically, the organization as a whole ends up being considerably more powerful.

This chapter will address in detail the *structures* that make self-managing organizations possible—what becomes of the pyramid, the staff functions, the executive team, the project teams that we know from today's organizations? The following chapter (2.3) will then describe the practices needed to make self-management work: who gets to make what decisions; how information flows; how people are evaluated, promoted, and compensated in these new structures.

A case example: from Orange to Teal

Buurtzorg, a Dutch neighborhood nursing organization, is perhaps the best available case example to illustrate the change from today's dominant organizational model (Achievement-Orange) to the emerging paradigm of Evolutionary-Teal.

First, some background: Since the 19th century, every neighborhood in the Netherlands had a neighborhood nurse who would make home visits to care for the sick and the elderly. Neighborhood nurses are an essential piece of the Dutch health care system, working hand-in-hand with family doctors and the hospital system. In the 1990s, the health insurance system (which over time had taken on footing most of the bill), came up with a logical idea: why not group the self-employed nurses into organizations? After all, there are obvious economies of scale and skill. When one nurse is on vacation, sick, or simply trying to get a good night's sleep, someone else can take over. If one has too much work while another has a lull, the organization can balance the load. And not every nurse knows how to treat every type of pathology, so there are complementarities in terms of skills.

Soon enough, the organizations that grouped the nurses started merging themselves, in pursuit of ever more scale: the number of organizations dropped from 295 to 86 in just five years, from 1990 to 1995. Piece by piece, the Achievement-Orange logic grew deeper roots. Tasks were specialized: some people would take care of intake of new patients and determine how nurses would best serve them; planners were hired to provide nurses with a daily schedule, optimizing the route from patient to patient; call center employees started taking patients' calls; given the growing size of the organizations, regional managers and directors were appointed as bosses to supervise the nurses in the field. To ensure accurate planning and drive up efficiency, time norms were established for each type of intervention: in one company, for instance, intravenous injections would be allotted exactly 10 minutes, bathing 15 minutes, wound dressing 10 minutes, and changing a compression stocking 2.5 minutes. To reduce costs, these different health treatments (now called "products") were tiered according to the expertise they required. The more experienced and expensive nurses perform only the more difficult products, so that cheaper nurses can do all the others. To be able to keep track of efficiencies, a sticker with a bar code is placed on the door of every patient's home and nurses have to scan in the barcode, along with the "product" they have delivered, after every visit. All activities are time-stamped in the central system, and can be monitored and analyzed from afar.

Each of these changes makes perfect sense in the Achievement-Orange pursuit of economies of scale and skill. But the overall outcome has proved distressing to patients and nurses alike. Patients have lost the personal relationship they used to have with their nurse. Every day (or several times a day if their situation calls for it) a new, unknown face enters their home. The patients—often elderly, sometimes confused—must gather the strength to re-tell their medical history to an unknown, hurried nurse who doesn't have any time allotted for listening. The nurse changes the bandage, gives the shot, and then is out the door. The system has lost track of patients as human beings; patients have become subjects to which products are applied. The human connection is lost, and the medical quality is compromised too: there is no continuity in care; the subtle but important cues about how a patient's health is evolving are often overlooked when a different nurse comes along every day.

Nurses find these working conditions degrading. Most of them chose their profession out of vocation to care for those in need—nursing is hardly a profession in which to get rich—and these practices make a mockery of their vocation. One of the nurses now working at Buurtzorg says this about her previous work in a neighborhood nursing organization:

> *The whole day, the electronic registration system that you have to carry with you is making you crazy. Some evenings I had to go and see 19 different patients. Then there is nothing you can do but run inside, put on a bandage or give a shot, and run out. You can never finish your work in a qualitative way. And when you go home, you keep thinking all the time, "I hope the nurse that comes after me doesn't forget to do this or that."*[1]

Another nurse tells a similar story of her experience in one of the neighborhood nursing organizations:

> *The last years I was responsible for 80 patients that I never got to know well. ... The planning was done somewhere else by someone who didn't know the patients. It went wrong so many times that at some point I could no longer explain to patients why nobody would come or why the agreed time wasn't respected. In seven years I had 14 managers and was tired of that too. The organization had become too big and difficult to navigate. Nobody felt responsible for the care of patients. Every day there were complaints and conflicts among colleagues.*[2]

A third nurse tells the following story:

> *The final straw came when my previous organization wanted us to sell stuff to our patients. We had to sell products from the internal pharmacy that the organization had set up. We felt deeply troubled because our expertise and integrity were abused. ... For me and for many colleagues, this was a turning point in our loyalty towards our employer.*[3]

People who work in the headquarters of these organizations don't find work much more meaningful. As these organizations grew, so did the number of levels of management. In good faith, managers at each level are trying to do their job—supervising their direct reports, paying close attention to budget variances, double-checking each request for resources, ensuring that all the bases are covered by all relevant superiors before approving a change in course. In the process, motivation and initiative are choked out.

Buurtzorg, the organization that has caused a revolution in neighborhood nursing, was founded in late 2006 by Jos de Blok. Jos had been a nurse for 10 years and had then climbed the ladder to assume management functions and staff roles in a nursing organization. When he saw that he couldn't effect change from the inside, he decided to start his own organization.[4] An entirely different paradigm would inform the care and the organizational set-up. Buurtzorg, the organization he created, has become extraordinarily successful, growing from 10 to 7,000 nurses in seven years and achieving outstanding levels of care.

Self-managing teams

Within Buurtzorg (which means "neighborhood care" in Dutch), nurses work in teams of 10 to 12, with each team serving around 50 patients in a small, well-defined neighborhood. The team is in charge of all the tasks that were previously fragmented across different departments. They are responsible not only for providing care, but for deciding how many and which patients to serve. They do the intake, the planning, the vacation and holiday scheduling, and the administration. They decide where to rent an office and how to decorate it. They determine how best to integrate with the local community, which doctors and pharmacies to reach out to, and how to best work with local hospitals. They decide when they meet and how they will distribute tasks among themselves, and they make up their individual and team training plans. They decide if they need to expand the team or split it in two if there are more patients than they can keep up with, and they monitor their own performance and decide on corrective action if productivity drops. There is no leader within the team; important decisions are made collectively.

Care is no longer fragmented. Whenever possible, things are planned so that a patient always sees the same one or two nurses. Nurses take time to sit down, drink a cup of coffee, and get to know the patients and their history and preferences. Over the course of days and weeks, deep trust can take root in the relationship. Care is no longer reduced to a shot or a bandage—patients can be seen and honored in their wholeness, with attention paid not only to their physical needs, but also their emotional, relational, and spiritual ones. Take the case of a nurse who senses that a proud older lady has stopped inviting friends to visit because she feels bad about her sickly appearance. The nurse might arrange a home visit from a hairdresser, or she might call the lady's daughter to suggest buying some new clothes.

Buurtzorg places real emphasis on patients' autonomy. The goal is for patients to recover the ability to take care of themselves as much as possible. What can patients learn to do themselves? Can patients structure their support networks? Are there family members, friends, or neighbors who could come by and help on a regular basis? Nurses will often go ring at a neighbor's door to inquire if they would be open to helping support the older lady living next door. Buurtzorg effectively tries to make itself redundant whenever possible. Vocation is restored in its true sense: the patient's well-being trumps the organization's self-interest. The result is that patients are thrilled by how Buurtzorg's nurses serve them. And so are their families, who often express deep gratitude for the important role nurses come to play in the life of the sick or elderly (it is not unusual for nurses to care for terminally ill patients until their last moments).

Outrageous results

The results achieved by Buurtzorg on the medical front are outrageously positive. A 2009 Ernst & Young study found that Buurtzorg requires, on average, close to *40 percent fewer hours* of care per client than other nursing organizations—which is ironic when you consider that nurses in Buurtzorg take time for coffee and talk with the patients, their families, and neighbors, while other nursing organizations have come to time "products" in minutes. Patients stay in care only *half as long,* heal faster, and become more autonomous. A third of emergency hospital admissions are avoided, and when a patient does need to be admitted to the hospital, the average stay is shorter. The savings for the Dutch social security system are considerable—Ernst & Young estimates that close to €2 billion would be saved in the Netherlands every year if all home care organizations achieved Buurtzorg's results. Scaled to the US population, this savings would be equivalent to roughly $49 billion. Not bad for just home care. Imagine if the incomparably bigger hospital organizations were to be run in a similar manner.

> *Humans are born to care. Our institutions magnify or depress the human capacity to care.*
>
> Jane Dutton

These numbers fail to include what might be even more important—how patients feel about the emotional and relational support they receive during their illness or the last years of their life. Trying to put numbers on this would be arbitrary and ultimately meaningless. It would be equally pointless to try to peg a dollar value to the sense of vocation that has been restored to nurses. A common phrase heard within Buurtzorg teams is, "I have my job back." Some numbers do testify to the level of job satisfaction: absenteeism for sickness is 60 percent lower at Buurtzorg and turnover 33 percent lower than in traditional (Orange) nursing organizations. Nurses at traditional organizations are leaving in droves to join Buurtzorg, which has gone from a start-up with 10 nurses in late 2006 to a point in 2013 at which it employs two-thirds of all neighborhood nurses in the Netherlands. Buurtzorg is single-handedly transforming a key component of the health care industry in the Netherlands.

No boss

Buurtzorg teams have no boss. All team members—typically 10 to 12 people—are nurses. They deal with all the usual management tasks that arise in every team context: they set direction and priorities, analyze problems, make plans, evaluate people's performance, and make the occasional tough decisions. Instead of placing these tasks on one single person—the boss—team members distribute these management tasks among themselves. The teams are effectively self-governing and self-organizing.

Anybody who has worked on a team with no boss knows that it can easily turn into a nightmare. Yet that only rarely happens at Buurtzorg. How come? Productive self-management rarely happens spontaneously. Buurtzorg has become very effective at giving teams the specific support (training, coaching, and tools) required for self-management to work in practice. To begin with, all newly formed teams and all new recruits to existing teams take a training course called "Solution-Driven Methods of Interaction,"[5] learning a coherent set of skills and techniques for healthy and efficient group decision-making. Within the training, team members deepen their knowledge in some of the most basic (and ironically often most neglected) building blocks of human collaboration: learning different types of listening and different styles of communication, how to run meetings, how to coach one another, and other practical skills.

> *The question is not how you can make better rules, but how you can support teams in finding the best solution. How can you strengthen the possibilities of the team members so that they need the least amount of direction-setting from above?*
>
> Jos de Blok

Let's take a look, for instance, at a team meeting where important issues need to be resolved. With no boss in the room, no one can call the shots or make the final call. Instead, Buurtzorg teams use a very precise and efficient method for joint problem solving and decision-making. The group first chooses a facilitator for the meeting. The agenda of topics to be discussed is put together on the spot, based on what is present for team members at that moment in time. The facilitator is not to make any statements, suggestions, or decisions; she can only ask questions: "What is your proposal?" or "What is the rationale for your proposal?" All proposals are listed on a flipchart. In a second round, proposals are reviewed, improved, and refined. In a third round, proposals are put to a group decision. The basis for decision-making is *not* consensus. For a solution to be adopted, it is enough that nobody has a principled objection. A person cannot veto a decision because she feels another solution (for example, hers!) would have been preferable. The perfect solution that all would embrace wholeheartedly might not exist, and its pursuit could prove exhausting. As long as there is no principled objection, a solution will be adopted, with the understanding that it can be revisited at any time when new information is available. The meeting process elegantly ensures that every voice is heard, that the collective intelligence informs decision-making, and that no one person can derail the process and hold others hostage trying to impose her personal preferences.

If, despite their training and meeting techniques, teams get stuck, they can ask for external facilitation at any time—either from their regional coach or from the pool of facilitators of the institute they trained with. A team that is stuck can also turn to other teams for suggestions, using Buurtzorg's internal social network platform, as most likely some team somewhere will already have grappled with a similar problem.

Often, nurses joining from other organizations find the switch to self-management quite challenging at first. The job brings up tough questions all the time. For instance, should the team add a second person to the night shift, even though no one likes to work at night? Or take the case of a team that has too much work already, when the family of a patient it has cared for before says to the team, "Our mother is terminally sick; could you please care for her?" Nurses can't offload these difficult decisions to a boss, and when things get tense, stressful, or unpleasant, there is no boss and no structure to blame; the teams know they have all the power and latitude to solve their problems. Learning to live with that amount of freedom and responsibility can take some time, and there are often moments of doubt, frustration, or confusion. It's a journey of personal unfolding, in which true professionals are born. Many nurses report their surprise at how much energy and motivation they discovered in themselves that was never evoked when they worked in a traditionally managed organization.

Let's add an important clarification straightaway, because this can be easily misunderstood: In Buurtzorg's teams, there is no boss-subordinate hierarchy, but the idea is not to make all nurses on a team "equal." Whatever the topic, some nurses will naturally have a larger contribution to make or more say, based on their expertise, interest, or willingness to step in. One nurse might be a particularly good listener and coach to her colleagues. Another might be a living encyclopedia of arcane medical conditions. Another might have a knack for handling conflict within the team or within the feuding family of a patient. Another might be a great planner and organizer. In any field, some nurses will naturally have more to offer than others. Some nurses build up reputations and influence even well beyond their team and are consulted by nurses from across the country on certain topics of expertise. Because there is no hierarchy of bosses over subordinates, space becomes available for other natural and spontaneous hierarchies to spring up—fluid hierarchies of recognition, influence, and skill (sometimes referred to as "actualization hierarchies" in place of traditional "dominator hierarchies").

No middle management

There is no boss within the team. Surely, then, there must be strong leadership coming from higher up in the hierarchy, say, from the regional managers that oversee a number of teams? The answer, as you've probably guessed, is no. There are no regional managers. Instead, there are regional coaches. It's not merely semantics. Unlike typical regional managers, coaches at Buurtzorg have no decision-making power over teams. They are not responsible for team results. They have no targets to reach and no profit-and-loss responsibility. They receive no bonuses if their teams perform well. The vertical power transmission of traditional pyramidal organizations is taken off its hinges: the teams of nurses aren't simply *empowered* by their hierarchy; they are truly *powerful* because there *is no hierarchy* that has decision-making power over them.

In traditional organizations, the position of regional manager is often a breeding ground for young talents on their way up. At Buurtzorg, there is no managerial ladder to climb; coaches are selected for their coaching capacity—they tend to be older, highly experienced nurses with strong interpersonal skills. Those who have held management positions in other nursing organizations have to learn to approach their role from a very different angle, as one coach explains:

> *I had to free myself from previous ways of working, when I was trained to manage and control. I have to let go of that here. The big difference is that, really, I'm not responsible. The responsibility lies with the teams and Jos [de Blok, the founder].*[6]

Coaches have no hierarchical power, but make no mistake, they play a crucial role just the same. Self-management is no walk in the park. Newer teams in particular face a steep learning curve. They are effectively in charge of all the aspects of creating and running a small organization of 12 people (remember, there are no intakers, no planners, no call center operators, no administrators, no managers), and at the same time they are learning to manage interpersonal dynamics within a self-organizing, boss-less team. The regional coach is a precious resource to the teams; upon request she can give advice or share how other teams have solved similar problems. Mostly, though, the coach's role is to ask the insightful questions that help teams find their own solutions. Coaches mirror to teams unhelpful behavior and can at critical moments raise the flag and suggest that a team pause to deal with a serious problem.

There is no job description for the regional coach. Every coach is encouraged to find and grow into her specific way of filling the role, based on her specific character and talents. Nevertheless a few unwritten principles have emerged as part of Buurtzorg's culture:

- It's okay for teams to struggle. From struggle comes learning. And teams that have gone through difficult moments build resilience and a deep sense of community. The coach's role therefore is not to prevent foreseeable problems, but to support teams in solving them (and later help them reflect on how they've grown in the process).
- The coach's role is to let teams make their own choices, even if she believes she knows a better solution.
- The coach supports the team mostly by asking insightful questions and mirroring what she sees. She helps teams frame issues and solutions in light of Buurtzorg's purpose and its holistic approach to care.
- The starting point is always to look for enthusiasm, strengths, and existing capabilities within the team. The coach projects trust that the team has all it takes to solve the problems it faces.

The span of support (what in traditional organizations would be called "span of control") of Buurtzorg's regional coaches is broad; on average, a coach supports 40 to 50 teams. Jos de Blok, Buurtzorg's founder and CEO, explains the intention:

> *Coaches shouldn't have too much time on their hands, or they risk getting too involved with teams, and that would hurt teams' autonomy. Now they take care of only the most important questions. We gave some of the first teams from Buurtzorg quite intensive support and attention, and today we still see that they are more dependent and less autonomous than other teams.*[7]

Buurtzorg teams have incredible latitude to come up with their own solutions. Very little is mandated from the top. There are only a few ground rules that experience has shown are important so as to make self-management work in practice. The list of ground rules includes:

- A team should not grow larger than 12 persons. Beyond that number, it should split.
- Teams should delegate tasks widely among themselves. They should be careful not to concentrate too many tasks with one person, or a form of traditional hierarchy might creep in through the back door.
- Along with team meetings, teams plan regular coaching meetings where they discuss specific issues encountered with patients and learn from each other (using a specific group coaching technique).
- Team members must appraise each other every year, based on competency models they can devise themselves.

- Teams make yearly plans for initiatives they want to take in the areas of client care and quality, training, organization, and other issues.
- The target for billable hours in mature teams is 60 to 65 percent.[8]
- Teams make important decisions based on the specific decision-making technique outlined earlier.

Bare minimum staff functions

In the last decades, we have witnessed, especially in large organizations, a proliferation of staff functions: human resources (HR), strategic planning, legal affairs, finance, internal communications, risk management, internal audit, investor relations, training, public affairs, environmental control, engineering services, quality control, knowledge management.

There is a natural tendency for people in such staff functions, often with the best of intentions, to prove their worth by finding ways to "add value"—devising rules and procedures, building up expertise, finding new problems to solve. Ultimately, they concentrate power and decision-making away from the frontline. People there feel disempowered: they have to follow rules that often make sense only in principle but cannot accommodate the complexity of the concrete situations they face on the ground. Teal Organizations, in contrast, keep staff functions to an absolute bare minimum. They understand that the economies of scale and skill resulting from staff functions are often outweighed by the diseconomies of motivation produced. As a result, there are very, very few people working in staff functions in Teal Organizations. And those that do typically have no decision-making authority. They can provide guidelines but cannot impose a rule or a decision. They truly deserve the name *support functions*, kicking into action only when teams request their support.

> *Bureaucracies are built by and for people who busy themselves proving they are necessary, especially when they suspect they aren't.*
> Ricardo Semler

At Buurtzorg, for example, the 7,000 nurses are supported by only 30 people working from a humble building in a residential part of Almelo, a town in the northern Netherlands—a far cry from the headquarters building you might expect for such a successful company. None of them are involved in the typical headquarters functions of nursing companies (intake, planning, call center). Buurtzorg has incredibly motivated employees (it is regularly elected "best company to work for" in the country) but, like many other Teal Organizations, it has no human resources department. People working at headquarters have a strong ethos of service to the teams of nurses—their duty is to support nurses with the same dedication and responsiveness that the nurses bring to their patients. Calls and emails from nurses are answered on the spot, or within a few hours at most.

How is it possible to manage a 7,000-person-strong organization with such a barebones headquarters? Many of the typical staff tasks are simply devolved back to the teams. Take recruitment for example: when a team feels the need to expand, it does its own recruiting (the regional coach might give advice when asked but is not involved in the decision). Chances are that the team will co-opt somebody who will fit in well. Because the team members make the decision themselves, they are emotionally invested in making the recruit successful.

How about expertise? In every organization, there is a natural tension between the need for expertise and the need to let frontline people make decisions. At Buurtzorg, it doesn't make sense for every one of the roughly 600 Buurtzorg teams to develop expertise in every arcane medical condition they might encounter. The first instinct, in most organizations, would be to create a central pool of experts. The risk, of course, is that over time two castes emerge within the organization: the prestigious, and probably higher paid, group of central experts and the lesser-paid generalists scattered around the country. Buurtzorg has developed a number of effective alternatives to deal with expertise, medical and otherwise:

> *We were used to working in large organizations and to joking about the idiots from HQ that came up with all sorts of things. Now we have to do it ourselves and can't complain about others.*
>
> A nurse at Buurtzorg about the absence of staff functions

- Nurses on the teams are encouraged to build up expertise and become contact points beyond their team. Through Buurtzorg's intranet, nurses can easily identify and access colleagues with relevant expertise in a specific subject matter.
- Occasionally, volunteer task forces of nurses are set up that, in addition to their work with patients, investigate a new topic and build up expertise (for instance, how Buurtzorg should adapt in response to new legislation).
- When needed, an expert can be hired centrally as a freelancer, rather than brought into a staff role.
- If a staff function is hired, that person has no decision-making authority over teams.

A real-life example: one day, in a meeting of Buurtzorg's regional coaches, a suggestion was made to hire a specialist in labor law, a topic many teams occasionally need assistance with. The suggestion made sense. And yet, other avenues were explored; after closer examination, it appeared that most questions were recurring, and so the group decided to create a self-help section of "frequently asked questions on labor law" on Buurtzorg's intranet. This took care of most questions, but a year later, the group realized that some questions still popped up for which the FAQ provided no answers. It was decided to contract a freelance expert for a few days per month who would answer questions from teams on request.

Trying to avoid or limit staff functions is something I encountered not only in Buurtzorg, but in all self-managing organizations in this research. The absence of rules and procedures imposed by headquarters functions creates a huge sense of freedom and responsibility throughout the organization. Why is it then, we might wonder, that most organizations today rely so heavily on staff functions? I believe that there are two main reasons for this:

- Staff functions provide economies of scale, or so goes the usual rationale. Economies of scale can easily be estimated in hard dollar figures, whereas it is virtually impossible to peg a number to the diseconomies of motivation.
- Staff functions give CEOs and leaders a sense of control over employees working out in the field. Rarely do leaders invoke this reason for putting staff functions in place, but it is very real. In the old machine metaphor of organizations, staff functions are like levers that the C-suite leaders use to steer the ship—levers that are conveniently close at hand, just a few doors down the hall at headquarters. Yet it is often an illusion of control: from the perspective of headquarters, rules and procedures always make sense; one must be in the field to experience the counterproductive and dispiriting results they often produce and to realize how often people find creative ways around them or simply ignore them.

Leaders of Teal Organizations therefore must embrace trust twice: they must trust that they can give up a sure thing (economies of scale) for something less certain but probably much more beneficial (unbridled motivation). And, after having already severed the power transmission of middle management, they must give up the illusion that staff functions can provide control over frontline staff.

Blue collars turn Teal

An organization like Buurtzorg might seem the natural place for self-managing practices to emerge. Many nurses wouldn't want to climb a career ladder to become managers, even if there was one. For that reason, when I started the research that led to this book, I wondered if perhaps I would find Teal Organizations only in serving professions—in health care, education, or the nonprofit sector. I was happy to be proven wrong more than once. FAVI, a family-owned French brass foundry, was the first example I stumbled upon of a blue-collar company that operates with Evolutionary-Teal principles of self-management. FAVI was created in the late 1950s and started off creating brass pieces for faucets. Today most of its revenue comes from the gearbox forks it produces for the automotive industry; its other products include components for electrical motors, water meters, and hospital equipment.

Work at FAVI is physically demanding; it's real blue-collar work. The factory is not a squeaky clean automotive assembly where you can see robots perform elegant and silent dances. It's a workshop where operators work hard loading and unloading metal pieces onto noisy workstations. The nature of batch production at FAVI allows for only limited automation. Walking through the factory, you might not notice immediately what is special about it. You could be forgiven for thinking that cranking out gearbox pieces isn't a very sexy or rewarding business. Yet FAVI's results are far from ordinary. All its competitors have moved to China to enjoy cheaper labor costs. And yet FAVI is not only the one producer left standing in Europe; it also commands a 50 percent market share for its gearbox forks. Its product quality is legendary, and its on-time delivery close to mythical: workers are proud of their record of not a single order delivered late in over 25 years. FAVI delivers high profit margins, year in and year out, despite Chinese competition, salaries well above average, and highly cyclical demand patterns. There is virtually no employee turnover; workers who have tasted FAVI's ways of working can't see themselves going back to traditionally run factories.

FAVI used to be operated like a traditional factory, before the family appointed Jean-François Zobrist, a charismatic metallurgist and former paratrooper, as new CEO of the brass foundry in 1983.[9] (He remained CEO until his retirement in 2009, when Dominique Verlant took over that role). Despite its relatively small size (80 people), it was firmly stacked like a pyramid: shop-floor workers reported to a *chef d'équipe* that reported to a *chef d'atelier* that reported to a *chef de service* that reported to the *chef de production* that reported to the CEO. The *chef de production* was part of the management team, together with the heads of sales, engineering, planning, maintenance, HR, and finance, all of whom reported to the CEO. This setup is still typical for a manufacturing organization today, with perhaps one or two layers taken out to flatten the structure and reduce costs. No academic or management consultant would find fault with such a structure.

But with Zobrist at the helm, within two years FAVI was fundamentally reshaped, along lines that bear a striking resemblance to Buurtzorg's way of operating. Today, the factory has more than 500 employees that are organized in 13 teams called "mini-factories" of 15 to 50 people. Most of the teams are dedicated to a specific customer or customer type (the Volkswagen team, the Audi team, the Volvo team, the water meter team, and so forth). There are a few upstream production teams (the foundry team, the mold repair team, maintenance), and support teams (engineering, quality, lab, administration, and sales support). Each team self-organizes; there is no middle management, and there are virtually no rules or procedures other than those that the teams decide upon themselves.

The staff functions have nearly all disappeared. The former HR, planning, scheduling, engineering, production-IT and purchasing departments have all been shut down. Their tasks have been taken over by the operators in the teams, who do their own hiring, purchasing, planning, and scheduling. At FAVI, the sales department has been disbanded too. The sales account manager for Audi is now part of the Audi team, just as the sales account manager for Volvo is part of the Volvo team. There is no head of sales above the group of account managers. In the old structure, white-collar workers in offices with windows overlooking the shop floor planned in detail what the workers needed to do, by when, and how. Now blue-collar workers effectively wear their own white collars and no longer receive instructions from above.

How a client order makes its way through the system perhaps best illustrates how deeply the new model departs from the traditional one. Previously, when an order came in, it would arrive first at the sales department. The planning department would give sales a predicted shipment date and allocate the necessary machine times into the master planning. Then, the day prior to production, scheduling would make the detailed planning of what exactly would need to be produced when on which machine. Based on the scheduling, HR would allocate workers to the machines according to schedule. Workers then simply did what they were told. They had no insight into the order book, whether business was good or bad, and why on that specific day they were allocated to this product or that machine. All they were asked to do was show up at the right place and time and then perform the prescribed tasks for a number of hours. Workers were given no information or say in their work; this state of affairs might or might not have been intentional, but with a fragmented order process, where successive departments refine the planning, it could not be any other way. Workers weren't the only blind ones in the process; the sales account managers did not know what happened on the shop floor any more than workers knew about the order history. They weren't able to understand and tell their customers why certain orders would be delivered on time and others not. Orders, once put in, landed in something of a black box; no one could easily untangle the complex flow that had taken the order through planning, scheduling, HR, and the shop floor.

Now, in the team setup, the process looks very different. Every week, in a short meeting, the account manager of, for example, the Volkswagen team will share with his dozen colleagues the order the German carmaker has placed. Everybody joins in the joy when the order is high or the disappointment when it is low. Planning happens on the spot, in the meeting, and the team jointly agrees on the shipment date. Account managers now have a good understanding of how their agreements with clients affect people and processes in the factory, and when they are put under pressure to reduce prices, they can enlist workers in finding solutions. Can the process be somehow improved, or productivity increased, to shave off another few cents per unit?

The account managers do not report to a head of sales; in practice, they report to their own teams. No one gives them sales targets (you read that right—sales people without sales targets). Their motivation is to serve their clients well and, in the face of Chinese competition, to maintain and when possible increase the number of jobs the factory can provide. Shop floor operators are not faceless workers, but colleagues they know well from their weekly interactions. To account managers, feeding their team with work is a motivation far stronger than any sales target from a head of sales could ever provide. Incidentally, at FAVI, sales orders are always discussed in terms of employment, not in monetary terms; so there is no "we got a $1 million order," but rather "we got an order for 10 people's work."[10]

No executive team, few meetings

The functional structure at FAVI has disappeared, and so there are no more executive team meetings. No one meets at the top! The weekly meetings that used to bring together the heads of sales, production, maintenance, finance, HR, and other departments are now held at the level of every team. At FAVI, each team decides on its meeting schedule—typically they hold three regular meetings: a short tactical discussion at the start of every shift, a weekly meeting with the sales account manager to discuss orders, and a monthly meeting with an open agenda. There are no fixed weekly or monthly meetings across teams that would resemble the previous executive team meeting. When cross-team meetings happen, it's because a specific need has prompted someone to organize it ad hoc. The same holds true for Buurtzorg. Jos de Blok, the CEO, does not meet every week with his regional coaches, for instance. In many ways, such meetings would make a lot of sense: the regional coaches have great insight into what's happening in the field; collectively, they could spot issues and opportunities and determine which actions to take and initiatives to launch. But that would exactly be the problem, in Buurtzorg's perspective—people from up high believing they know what is needed down below. Jos de Blok and the regional coaches have recognized that meeting frequently would most likely spur them to get busy in all sorts of ways. Therefore, they decided to come together just four times a year, with an open agenda to discuss any topics that emerge. This rhythm, they found, is infrequent enough to prevent the risk of their taking the reins from the teams in the way an executive team would.

In a pyramid structure, meetings are needed at every level to gather, package, filter, and transmit information as it flows up and down the chain of command. In self-managing structures, the need for these meetings falls away almost entirely. Meeting overload in traditional organizations is particularly acute the higher you go up the hierarchy. The typical day of a top manager consists of back-to-back meetings. The joke goes that in most organizations, people low in the hierarchy work, while people higher up do meetings. But think of it: in functional pyramidal structures, it could hardly be otherwise. The higher you go, the more lines converge. It is only at the very top that the different departments such as sales, marketing, R&D, production, HR, and finance meet. Decisions are naturally pushed up to the top, as it's the only place where decisions and trade-offs can be informed from the various angles involved. It's almost deterministic: with a pyramidal shape, people at the top of organizations will complain about meeting overload, while people below feel disempowered.

> *Traditional pyramidal structures demand too much of too few and not enough of everyone else.*
>
> Gary Hamel

In the type of structure adopted by Buurtzorg, FAVI, and other self-managing organizations we will meet, the lines converge at the lowest level, within teams. Teams hold short meetings (daily, weekly, or monthly) to align and make decisions; beyond that, there tend to be no regularly scheduled meetings at all. Meetings are planned only ad hoc, when a topic demands attention, with the relevant people around the table. It's an organic way of running an organization, where structure follows emerging needs and not the other way around.

Coordination and knowledge exchange across teams

Of course, coordination is often needed across teams. Traditionally, that's when bosses and staff functions step in. Take load-balancing: because customer orders fluctuate, on any given day some teams might have too much work and others too little. Perhaps a COO role might be needed after all, with an assistant planner to allocate workers across teams. Yet this would be a step back toward reinstating a dominator hierarchy.

FAVI chose a more organic and elegant solution. At regular intervals, a group composed of one designated person from each team comes together for a few minutes; they quickly discuss which teams are over or understaffed; back in their teams, they ask for volunteers to switch teams for a shift or two. The person from the Audi team, for example, might ask who in the team is willing to spend the day with the Volvo team. Things happen organically on a voluntary basis; nobody is being allocated to a team by a higher authority.

Let's look at another example of coordination: the capital expenditure process. Once a year, every team at FAVI establishes the investment budget for the next year—new machines, new tooling, and so on. In most organizations, the finance department challenges these requests and ultimately the executive committee or the CEO arbitrates across departments to channel more money in one direction or another.

This opens up the can of worms of politics. Everyone jockeys for a bigger part of the pie. For middle managers, the size of the budget is often the yardstick by which their status is measured. They try, as best as they can, to influence the decision makers in the executive committee through any formal and informal channels at their disposal.

At FAVI, there are no middle managers that fight for budgets, and Zobrist refused to play the role of the father who would decide how to divide up the candy among his children. Teams know that no haggling will take place, so they don't throw in inflated numbers to start with; they make realistic requests based on realistic needs. In most years, when the budgets of the teams are added up, the resulting number is reasonable, and all plans get the green light, with neither discussion nor scrutiny. Teams are trusted to do the right thing; if one team were to get itself golden-plated machines, other teams would quickly notice, and peer-pressure would self-regulate the problem away. In those years where the combined projects exceed what would be reasonable, the CEO simply asks teams to sit together and to come back to him with a revised plan. Representatives from each team come together and put all the plans on a table. They look at what is most important and what might be deferred in everyone's plans. In one or two meetings, the problem is always sorted out.

When opportunities arise that span the boundaries of several teams, the same mechanism plays out: workers self-nominate to create a temporary project team. Sometimes a person is appointed for a staff role to coordinate across teams, but that person receives no authority to impose decisions on the teams. For example, at FAVI there is Denis, an engineer, whose role is to help teams exchange insights and best practices. He spends his days encouraging machine operators to go and see what other teams have come up with. He can't coerce a team into adopting another team's ideas. He must get them interested and excited. If he fails to do so, if teams stop seeing added value in his work, then his role will naturally disappear and Denis will need to find himself another role to fill. In the true sense of the word, he has a support function. In case you are not familiar with manufacturing environments, let me point out how unusual this is—an engineer who is in service and not in command of less-educated (but highly skilled) blue-collar workers.

> *Every decision made at headquarters takes away responsibility from people elsewhere in the organization and reduces the number of people who feel they are making an effective contribution to the organization.*
> Dennis Bakke

Another support role in the FAVI environment is held by Frank, a former machine operator. He is FAVI's idea scout. Frank joined the factory as an unskilled operator at the age of 18 when he could hardly read and write. Zobrist noticed a fierce curiosity in Frank's eyes. He prodded him to attend local night classes in French literature to feed his curiosity and to build up self-confidence. After a few years of working on the shop floor, Frank felt ready for more. He told Zobrist: "I'm sure we could be more innovative if we were to scout more actively for new machines, materials, and suppliers. I want to do that job." Zobrist gave him an answer in keeping with his usual leadership style: "Go do it. I believe you have what it takes to be successful in that role. But it's not my decision. You need to show the teams that your role is worthwhile to them." Frank made a success of it. He has been traveling the world, looking for new technologies and new suppliers. He works without a budget and without targets, just like everyone else at FAVI. He is trusted to be reasonable in his travel and hotel expenses. Roughly once a month, he comes back to the factory on a Friday morning and holds a conference to share his findings. The topic determines who among the operators or engineers show up. That people choose to attend the meeting and pick up on his ideas is proof that his role is valuable. If at some point colleagues were to stop coming to his Friday morning meetings, his role would naturally cease to exist. In that case, Frank would need to find a new role for himself, possibly rejoining a team as a machine operator.

Just like Denis and Frank, the teams at FAVI that offer staff-like support—maintenance and quality, for instance—have no decision-making power over the shop floor teams. They can only rely on their powers of persuasion. Mostly they act upon request from the shop floor. The general philosophy is one of *reverse delegation*. The expectation is that the frontline teams do everything, except for the things they choose to push upward.

These examples—load balancing, investments, task forces, expert functions—show how Teal Organizations deal with the need for coordination across teams: form follows function. When a problem or an opportunity arises, an ad hoc meeting is convened across teams. When a more permanent form of coordination is needed, a staff function might emerge from the teams in a process of reverse delegation. None of this needs approval from above. The decision to create a role like Frank's, or to put an end to it, is not in the hands of the CEO. Things happen organically. Meetings and roles in self-managing structures emerge spontaneously; they subsist as long as they add value to the ecosystem.

Information technology tools such as internal social networks and knowledge repositories can play a critical role in steering clear of unnecessary structures, especially when companies grow larger and people are spread throughout different locations. At FAVI, where the 500 employees all work in the same factory, a colleague is never far away. Much of the knowledge exchange and coordination happens informally on the shop floor or over lunch. At Buurtzorg, there are 7,000 nurses scattered over the country, and most of them have never met. The company's internal social network helps nurses locate a colleague with a specific expertise; they can then pick up the phone and ask a question. Nurses can also post questions directly on the platform in a continuous Facebook-like stream. Collectively, the 7,000 nurses have an extraordinary breadth of medical and technical knowledge; in almost all cases, the answer to a question is out there somewhere. The trick is to find the right person! The engagement level on the platform is so high (nurses tend to log onto it at least once a day, if not more) that within hours, a new question is seen by thousands of colleagues and will attract one or several responses. From Buurtzorg's inception, Jos de Blok envisioned that the "BuurtzorgWeb" would be a critical piece in the company's self-managing puzzle. The alternative—attempting to centralize knowledge within a staff of experts—would most likely be less effective and more costly. Above all, it would undermine the sense of pride with Buurtzorg's nurses that they are the experts and collectively have invaluable knowledge to offer one another.

Trust versus control

With no middle management and little staff, Teal Organizations dispense with the usual control mechanisms; they are built on foundations of mutual trust. Zobrist has written a book outlining FAVI's practices that is subtitled: *L'entreprise qui croit que l'Homme est bon* ("The organization that believes that mankind is good"). The heart of the matter is that workers and employees are seen as reasonable people that can be trusted to do the right thing. With that premise, very few rules and control mechanisms are needed.

Before Zobrist sparked change at the company, it had, like most of its manufacturing peers still have today, intricate systems to exert control and ensure compliance. Workers clocked in and clocked out (white-collar employees were exempt from the system), and the hourly output of every machine was registered. Every minute a worker showed up late for work, and any output below the hourly target, would be recorded and lead to a deduction from the monthly paycheck. Shortly after taking over as CEO, Zobrist got rid of the clocks and the production norms with no warning (chapter 3.3 tells the story of how Zobrist shifted FAVI from Amber to Teal management practices). The management team he had inherited was aghast. This was a recipe for disaster! Productivity would collapse! Zobrist admits he checked the productivity numbers every day for a week after he had gotten rid of the control systems, not sure what would happen. He firmly believed in the power of trust and was hoping productivity would not decrease, but he had no guarantee his wager would pay off. It turned out that productivity didn't decrease but increased! When Zobrist saw the numbers, he inquired with the operators to understand what happened. When you operate a machine, they told him, there is an optimal physiological rhythm that is the least tiring for the body. In the old system, with the hourly targets, they had always intentionally slowed down. They gave themselves some slack in case management increased the targets. For years, operators had effectively worked below their natural productivity, at a rhythm that was more tiring and less comfortable for them—and less profitable for the company. Now they simply worked at their natural rhythm.

Another unexpected outcome: when time clocks were still around, workers used to leave their machines the minute the shift came to an end; they now regularly stay a few minutes or half an hour longer to finish the work they have started. When you ask them why, they say that their self-image has changed: they used to work for the paycheck; now they feel responsible for their work and they take pride in a job well done.

One administrative staff member, Ginette, had worked full time on maintaining the control system and calculating the pay deductions. Zobrist sat down with her and said *"Ginette, I can't imagine you can be happy in the role of the factory sentry, spending your days fining people. I apologize; I should have put an end to this earlier. ... Take the time you need to find yourself another job within FAVI. Your salary will stay the same."* Ginette talked to her colleagues and found out that reception really needed to be staffed in two shifts; clients increasingly expected their calls to be answered early in the morning and late into the afternoon. She had found herself a new job.

At FAVI, trust extends well beyond working hours and production norms. Keys to company cars are freely available at the reception. Any worker can decide to leave the factory floor, pick up a car, and drive to a supplier or a client, no approval needed (though the habit is to inform colleagues, should someone be interested in joining). There used to be a stock keeper in the stock room who would give workers tools and supplies only if they came with a signed request from a shift supervisor. Whenever he went for a break, the stock room would be locked. Now the stock room is always open; workers can pick up anything they need. They just need to submit an entry in a logbook for replacement orders. When a drill was stolen one day, Zobrist put up a flipchart in the stock room with the following message *"A drill was stolen. You know that as a matter of principle we would fire someone for stealing toilet paper. So it's a stupid thing to do, especially as no one was ever denied permission to borrow a tool for an evening or a weekend."* That was enough to put an end to the matter; no further items were stolen. Experience shows that such breaches of trust are exceedingly rare at FAVI, as well as in other organizations that have gone down the road of self-management.

> *I'd rather get burned now and then than to treat my employees like snakes. My colleagues are honorable men and women, and they prove it every day by their actions in a workplace where they're at liberty to run amok if they're so inclined. They're just not so inclined, that's all. The exceptions are so rare that to clamp heavy restrictions on the whole work force just to try to control the actions of the potential bad apples would be a colossal self-sabotage.*
>
> Stan Richards

When trust is extended, it breeds responsibility in return. Emulation and peer pressure regulates the system better than hierarchy ever could. Teams set their own objectives, and they take pride in achieving them. When a person tries to take advantage of the system, such as by not pulling his weight and slacking off, his team members will be quick to let him know their feelings. At FAVI, workers are well aware, from their weekly meetings with the sales account manager, what sharp competition they are up against from China. Nurses at Buurtzorg know their patients intimately and care deeply for their well-being. Teams at FAVI and at Buurtzorg don't need management or control systems to spur them on.

The energy of trust

When people work in small teams of trusted colleagues, when they have all the resources and power to make the decisions they feel are needed, extraordinary things begin to happen. If you care to listen, Zobrist can fill a night telling stories about the energy that self-management has unleashed at FAVI. One such story happened a few years after the factory had adopted the new practices. One Monday morning, Zobrist sensed that something was up with the group producing gearbox forks for FIAT, the Italian car manufacturer (which also owns Alfa Romeo and Ferrari and recently acquired Chrysler). The team was used to a steady order pattern: every Sunday night, a fully loaded truck would depart from FAVI in the north of France to FIAT in Italy. That Monday morning, colleagues from the team told him, "Can you believe it? We did two trucks!" Zobrist had no clue what they were talking about. They were quick to share the story: on Friday, while Zobrist was traveling and away from the factory, FIAT inquired whether they could make an exception and send over two trucks on Sunday night. The team came together, and after a bit of thinking and planning, decided to take on the challenge. They enlisted some volunteers from other teams and added three shifts on Saturday and Sunday. Exhausted but proud, they sent two full trucks out to Italy on Sunday night. It didn't cross their mind to inform the CEO or to seek permission. No one asked to be paid overtime; the team self-organized so as to recover the extra time they had put in over the coming weeks. Zobrist observes:

> *We have used rules and regulations … to make ourselves safe. But there is no safety in separation. … We find well-being only when we remember that we belong together.*
> M. Wheatley & M. Kellner-Rogers

> *Had we been organized like everybody else, that is to say, with a planning department that processes client orders, that planning department would certainly have concluded that FIAT's request was impossible. Or, if it had accepted the request, the operators would certainly have felt that the extra hours were forced upon them, rather than making of it a collective adventure.*[11]

Another day, an operator at the Volkswagen team noticed a quality problem on a part he was working on. He stopped the machine, and with a member of the quality team, sifted through all other finished pieces and works-in-progress. They found no other defective pieces. He chose nevertheless to discuss the incident with the Volkswagen sales account manager. Together, they decided to pick up the keys to a company car and go for the eight-hour drive to the German Volkswagen plant. Once there, they explained the reason for their impromptu visit and were allowed to inspect all similar parts FAVI had previously shipped. All items proved to be perfect, and no defect was found. The quality manager at Volkswagen was flabbergasted. Normally, a defective piece at a supplier leads to some official notification and legal paperwork in the best of cases; more likely, an operator might quietly try to cover up the problem, for fear of reprisals from management. This machine operator not only owned up to his mistake, but he also felt responsible for driving all the way to his client to personally make sure any possible problem was prevented!

> *Everything that is really great and inspiring is created by the individual who can labor in freedom.*
>
> Albert Einstein

These cases might seem extraordinary, but they testify to a spirit that can be found every day in self-managing organizations—at FAVI, Buurtzorg, and elsewhere. Ultimately, it comes down to this—fear is a great inhibitor. When organizations are built not on implicit mechanisms of fear but on structures and practices that breed trust and responsibility, extraordinary and unexpected things start to happen.

Projects

Sun Hydraulics, a 900-person-strong Florida-based global producer of hydraulic cartridge valves and manifolds, is another industrial organization thriving on self-management. Bob Koski, one of the two engineers who founded the company in 1970, wanted to create a "healthy, self-managed, and informal" organization, instead of what he considered "mostly a poisonous and disrespectful atmosphere of bureaucracy and intimidation" in the companies he had worked for previously.[12] Like FAVI, Sun has no quality control, scheduling, or purchasing departments. There are no standard production times, no time clocks, no piece rates. People work in natural clusters and self-organize to get their work done. The results have been spectacular here too. Sun Hydraulics, now a public company quoted on the NASDAQ stock exchange, has a stellar reputation for quality and service in the industry. The atmosphere on the shop floor and in the offices is unlike anything I have experienced in traditional manufacturing environments. In Florida, and throughout engineering schools in the country, people know that if you can land a job at Sun, you'd better take it! Financially, Sun's results are impressive too. In a highly cyclical industry, the company never took a loss in almost 40 years. In 2009, at the height of the financial crisis, its revenues were cut in half, and yet it posted a profit for the 38th consecutive year, even though it didn't lay off workers (it never has in any previous downturn either). In a normal year, its profit margins are off the charts[13] and it has been growing at double-digit rates since the 1970s.

Radically simplified project management

Sun makes a good illustration of another aspect: how projects are run in a self-managing environment. Sun is an engineering-heavy company. At any point in time, there are hundreds of engineering projects running in parallel, ranging from product modifications prompted by machine operators, custom-designed manifolds for clients, new cartridge valves to extend the line, or entirely new products the company is inventing. Running so many projects in parallel and getting them completed on time and within budget is a difficult feat for any organization. Prioritizing resources across all these projects can easily turn into a logistical and political quagmire. A whole industry has come into being, trying to help organizations get control of this complexity. Software systems help track all the projects with elaborate Gantt charts that calculate interdependencies and resource needs. Project and program managers are trained in specific methodologies to keep things under control. A major part of their job is to produce monthly reports and indicators to track progress, so that people higher up can understand the situation and make informed decisions.

> *As you've found out by now, you were not hired to fill a specific job description. You were hired to constantly be looking around for the most valuable work you could be doing.*
>
> Valve handbook for employees

At Sun Hydraulics, all of this is radically simplified. There is no management that wants to understand and control the complexity. Projects happen organically and informally. Engineers are typically working on several projects in parallel. They constantly rearrange their priorities, based on what they sense is the most important, most urgent, or most fun to do. Google has the famous practice of "20 percent time"—engineers are free to decide how to spend their Fridays. Sun and other self-managing organizations basically extend this to the whole week. There is no master plan. There are no project charters and no one bothers with staffing people on projects. Project teams form organically and disband again when work is done. Nobody knows if projects are on time or on budget, because for 90 percent of the projects, no one cares to put a timeline on paper or to establish a budget. A huge amount of time is freed by dropping all the formalities of project planning—writing the plan, getting approval, reporting on progress, explaining variations, rescheduling, and re-estimating, not to mention the politics that go into securing resources for one's project or to find someone to blame when projects are over time or over budget. When I discussed with Kirsten Regal, one of Sun's leaders, how little their meeting rooms seemed to be used, she quipped, "We don't waste time being busy."

Project prioritization

But then how are things prioritized? Who decides what should take precedence? "Things have a natural way of taking priority," one of Sun's engineers told me. At Sun, people have dropped the illusion that one person, however competent, could master all the information of such a complex system and heroically, from above, make the right call for hundreds of decisions that need to be made every week. Instead, they trust the collective intelligence of the system.

If the notion of trusting the collective intelligence of a system seems risky or outright foolish, think about this: the idea that a country's economy would best be run by the heavy hand of central planning committees in Soviet style has been totally discredited. We all know that a free-market system where a myriad of players pick up on signals, make decisions, and coordinate among themselves works much better. Yet for some strange reason, inside organizations, we still trust the equivalent of central planning committees. Self-management brings the principles that account for successful free-market economies inside organizations. "Things do fall through the cracks occasionally," the engineer conceded. But that is often to be welcomed as the outcome of a collective prioritization effort; the system simply roots out a project that doesn't seem promising or important after all. If it had been, someone would have picked it up. Contrast this with failing projects in traditionally run companies: they are often kept alive way too long; everyone knows they are doomed, and everyone also knows that once the project is finally axed, someone will carry the blame. In the hope that the blame will fall on someone else, everyone keeps a low profile.

FAVI relies on the same principle of prioritization as Sun. The factory was an eager and early adopter of Japanese manufacturing techniques; it masters continuous improvement like few others, a critical capability to survive and thrive in the low-margin automotive business. FAVI, you might not be surprised to hear, has no continuous improvement department and no lean production experts; these ideas are all embedded deeply within the teams. A very simple process is at work: whenever a team stumbles upon a problem or an opportunity, as happens every day, the issue is logged in a logbook. Anybody can volunteer to tackle an item by writing his or her initials next to the issue in the logbook. Typically, the two or three people that are most affected or interested decide to join forces and analyze the issue. If no one picks up a certain problem or opportunity, it probably means it is not important. Otherwise it will come up again, and someone will end up tackling it. Like at Sun, no one bothers with statistics, master plans, project management software, or reporting. There is a simple reminder mechanism: operators have asked a woman working in administration to go through the logs once in a while, and if there are items that have been open for more than three months, to remind people who had signed up to tackle the issue about their commitment. Teams have found this gentle prodding to be helpful.

Companies whose work involves lots of projects have started to rethink the physical architecture of their spaces. The office at Sun Hydraulics is a big open space with custom-designed cubicles that go only waist high. At a glance, people can see who is there and can overhear many conversations. It greatly improves collaboration, colleagues say: many problems that would initiate an email exchange or the scheduling of a meeting at another company are solved by people simply talking to each other over the low dividers.

Valve, a Seattle game-software company whose 400 employees work entirely based on self-management principles, has pushed the physical fluidity a step further. All employees have desks on wheels. Every day, some people will roll their desk to a new place, depending on the projects they join or leave. All it takes is unplugging the cables from the wall in one place and plugging them in somewhere else. The fluid way Valve runs projects (people vote with their feet) is physically reflected in the office space, in the form of ever-morphing clusters of desks huddling together to get work done. Because people move around so often, the company has created an app on its intranet to locate colleagues. It renders a map of the office in real-time, showing the spots where people have plugged their computers into the wall.

Scaling to tens of thousands of employees

Can such self-governing organizations scale beyond a few hundred or thousand coworkers? Can they go global? Applied Energy Services (AES), a global energy provider with headquarters in Arlington, Virginia, shows that self-management principles can work in all cultures and scale to an organization with tens of thousands of employees. From its founding in 1982, the company grew to 40,000 employees in the year 2000, operating power plants and power distribution grids in 31 countries on all continents—from Argentina to El Salvador, from Hungary to Kazakhstan, from Bangladesh to China, and from South Africa to Tanzania. The story of AES, incidentally, also highlights how a company can revert to traditional management under new leadership—a topic picked up in more detail in chapter 3.1. Today, unfortunately, not much is left of the self-managing structure and practices that AES pioneered.

The company was founded in 1982 by Roger Sant and Dennis Bakke. They had conceived the business plan for the company two years earlier while driving from Maryland to Washington, D.C. As Sant dropped Bakke at his house, he added, "And let's make it fun." Bakke, the driving force behind AES's innovative management practices, had spent years working in different departments of the federal government, which profoundly shaped his thinking about organizations. There, he learned that purpose was necessary to make work meaningful, but he also experienced the dispiriting nature of hierarchical organizations and staff functions:

> *As a line executive responsible for the Energy Conservation Program in the federal government ... I experienced the debilitating effects of "serving" central staff groups. It seemed as if I had 15 bosses. Each one of the offices was responsible for something I thought was essential to operating my program. ... People like me couldn't even testify before a congressional committee without an entourage of people concerned that I might say something related to their area of responsibility. As the executive of the program, I was not really trusted to operate it or speak freely about it. It was almost as if I didn't have a job. At best, my "line" job was about coordinating all the "staff" people who drifted in and out of my program.*[14]

Bakke recounts an earlier anecdote that explains how his view on work was shaped from early childhood—one of a strand of many experiences that would determine his vocation to create organizations that make work fun and fulfilling:

> *On this particular day, my mother had organized the evening work in her usual style. The kitchen was abuzz with activity. I was 16 years old and charged with cooking creamed peas for supper. My younger brother was carrying wood from the shed to the storage area next to the kitchen. Kenny's older sisters [Kenny and his sisters were foster children at the Bakke home] were clearing dirty cooking dishes and setting the table with dinner ware. .... No one was paying attention to Kenny. .... Suddenly the two-year-old ... picked up the spoon on his tray. "I want jobs, I want jobs, I want jobs," he chanted as he pounded his spoon.*
>
> *I think this little guy with a crooked smile and troubled past was saying, "I want to contribute. I can make a difference. I want to be part of the team. I'm somebody. I want to have fun working, too!" Over the years, I have reflected on that moment and come to believe that it captures the early and substantial influence Mom had on my concept of fun in the workplace. Somehow, she created an environment in which everyone was energized, not from fear of punishment or promise of reward, but from a desire to accomplish something positive. She had unbridled confidence in our ability to accomplish the tasks at hand. ... She gave us enormous freedom to work and make decisions. Somehow she made work so attractive that even an abused two-year-old wanted desperately to pitch in for the sheer joy and excitement of it.*[15]

Under Sant and Bakke, AES, a massive 40,000-employee organization, functioned in self-managing teams of 15 to 20 people. Believing that bad things start to happen when any site becomes too big, they also tried to limit the number of employees in a site to a maximum of 300 to 400 (15 to 20 teams of 15 to 20 people)—the natural limit, they felt, for colleagues to more or less put names and faces together and enter into a casual discussion with any colleague.

Like their counterparts at FAVI and Sun, teams at AES were responsible for decisions relating to all aspects of day-to-day operations: budgets, workload, safety, schedules, maintenance, hiring and firing, working hours, training, evaluations, compensation, capital expenditures, purchasing, and quality control, as well as long-term strategy, charitable giving, and community relations. Let me invite you to pause for a second, as you would be forgiven for having read through that long list of responsibilities too quickly. AES is an energy provider, operating thermal and hydroelectric power plants as well as electrical grids. This equipment is absolutely central to the lives of many people and businesses. Operating problems can lead to disastrous blackouts for the economy, and accidents to the loss of many human lives. And yet millions of customers throughout the world were supplied with energy produced by self-governing teams responsible for such crucial matters as safety and maintenance. With 40,000 people scattered across different continents, AES only had about 100 people working at headquarters in Arlington—hardly a number that could claim to control what was happening in faraway places like Cameroon, Colombia, or the Czech Republic.

And yet, it worked. A front-page article in the *Wall Street Journal* by reporter Alex Markels illustrates with a story how far teams at AES went with taking on responsibilities typically handled by headquarters:

> *MONTVILLE, Conn. — His hands still blackened from coal he has just unloaded from a barge, Jeff Hatch picks up the phone and calls his favorite broker. "What kind of rate can you give me for $10 million at 30 days?" he asks the agent, who handles Treasury bills. "Only 6.09? But I just got a 6.13 quote from Chase."*
>
> *In another room, Joe Oddo is working on J.P. Morgan & Co. "6.15 at 30 days?" confirms Mr. Oddo, a maintenance technician at AES Corp.'s power plant here. "I'll get right back to you." Members of an ad hoc team that manages a $33 million plant investment fund, Messrs. Oddo and Hatch quickly confer with their associates, then close the deal. …*
>
> *It sounds like "empowerment" gone mad. Give workers more autonomy in their area of expertise? Sure. Open the books to employee purview? Perhaps. But what good could possibly come from handing corporate finance duties to workers whose collective borrowing experience totals a mortgage, two car loans, and some paid-off credit-card debt?*
>
> *Plenty of good, says AES. … "The more you increase individual responsibility, the better the chances for incremental improvements in*

operations," argues Dennis W. Bakke, the company's chief executive and one of its founders. ... "And more importantly" he says "it makes work a lot more fun."

Is giving coal handlers investment responsibility risky? Mr. Bakke thinks not. He notes that the volunteer team in Montville does have a financial adviser, and they work within a narrow range of investment choices. They aren't exactly buying derivatives. What the CEO likes about the arrangement is that "they're changed people by this experience. They've learned so much about the total aspect of the business, they'll never be the same."[16]

Volunteer task forces

Scale changes surprisingly little in the structures and practices of self-management. Buurtzorg operates with 7,000 people in pretty much the same way as it did with a few hundred. Before it reverted to more traditional management practices, AES, with its massive size and geographical dispersion, operated in nearly identical ways to Buurtzorg, FAVI, or Sun Hydraulics. There is one element, though, in the toolbox of self-management that AES relied on much more than its smaller counterparts needed to: the use of temporary and permanent task forces.

With only around 100 staff in its headquarters in Arlington, Virginia, AES had no central maintenance or safety departments, no purchasing, no HR, and no internal audit departments. In a smaller company, like FAVI and Sun, when an issue arises in one of these areas, people can simply call a meeting, or delegate a specific coordinating role to a colleague. At AES, with 40,000 people scattered around the globe, that was no longer feasible. The company came up with the "80-20 rule": every person working at AES, from cleaning staff to engineer, was expected to spend on average 80 percent of their time on their primary role and make themselves available for the other 20 percent in one or more of the many task forces that existed around the company.

> *The reality is that centralized decision makers simply don't have enough information to manage the specifics of corporate life. But because centralization is an idea in good currency, corporations apply the model ... to solve almost every problem. In so doing, power is amassed at the very top, rigid hierarchies are developed, workers lose their freedom while productivity eventually slows down.*
>
> Bob Fishman

Take investment budgeting, normally the prerogative of finance staff at headquarters. At AES, everything happened in the field; every team established its investment budget once a year. Investment budgets would be added up at the plant level, sometimes running as high as $300 million in a year. When teams were satisfied with the consolidated budget for the plant, it was reviewed, together with those from all other plants, by a budget task force that would suggest possible changes and improvements (but didn't have power to enforce changes). That task force was staffed with a few people from headquarters with relevant expertise, but predominantly with people from local units with all sorts of backgrounds—a security guard could sit next to a technician and an engineer. Internal audits were performed in the same way, by volunteer task forces: each plant would be audited by colleagues from other plants. Task forces were put in place for topics as diverse as compensation, community service, environmental work, and corporate values.

AES found out that using voluntary task forces instead of fixed staff functions has multiple benefits. Employees find avenues to express talents and gifts that their primary role might not call for. They develop a true sense of ownership and responsibility when they see they have real power to shape their company. Dennis Bakke insists on another point: these task forces are formidable learning institutions. At any point in time, thousands of people would be involved in task forces, picking up technical and leadership skills from more experienced colleagues. It's a modern-day form of apprenticeship, scaled to a massive level. No classroom training could ever provide the amount of learning that was taking place day in and day out in the voluntary task forces.

No organization chart, no job description, no job titles

Amber and Orange Organizations come with organization charts. Boxes on the charts come with titles and job descriptions, which in turn come with an implicit expectation: people must adapt to the box they have been recruited or promoted into. Teal Organizations reverse the premise: people are not made to fit pre-defined jobs; their job emerges from a multitude of roles and responsibilities they pick up based on their interests, talents, and the needs of the organization.

The traditional tasks of a manager—direction-setting, budgeting, analyzing, planning, organizing, measuring, controlling, recruiting, evaluating, and communicating—are now scattered among various members of a team. A worker at FAVI, for example, might operate a number of different machines, be in charge of ordering supplies for his team, lead a number of continuous improvement actions, and be responsible for recruitment to his team. Except perhaps for recruitment purposes, no one bothers to write down a job description. Try giving the above person's job a name—is he an "operator-recruiter-supply coordinator"? Job titles and descriptions hardly do justice to unique combinations of roles, and they are too static to account for the fluid nature of work in Teal Organizations. Colleagues frequently switch and trade roles according to workload and preferences. A nurse at Buurtzorg whose patients suddenly require more care might ask a colleague to take over her role of team planner, for instance. For a while, some nurses might carry more than their fair share of management tasks for the teams and less at other times. Thinking in terms of granular *roles* instead of pre-defined *jobs* creates great fluidity and adaptability. People can give up one role and take up another without needing to go through the cumbersome and often political processes of appointment, promotion, and salary negotiation.

At Buurtzorg, teams are careful to keep management tasks somewhat spread out at all times. There is a risk, as some teams have experienced, that hierarchical practices creep back in when too many management roles are delegated to a single team member. Other organizations, like FAVI for instance, have one person on the team that holds most management roles for the team (FAVI calls them, rather unhelpfully, a "team leader," which might imply hierarchical power over their colleagues). The nature of work in the two organizations accounts for the different approaches. It's easier for a nurse to spend some time in between two patients on a management role than it is for machine operators to stop their machines. FAVI found it works best to have one person free to roam among the team and only operate a machine occasionally when a helping hand is needed. FAVI's team leaders act as coaches for their colleagues, as a clearinghouse for information, and as a point person when coordination is needed with other teams. This choice nevertheless carries a risk. Our cultural baggage of hierarchy is so strong that over time, team leaders could start behaving like bosses and become the primary decision makers on their teams. At FAVI, a simple but powerful relief valve exists, should a team leader find the taste of power too sweet: workers can choose at any moment to join another team. Team leaders have no meaningful way of coercing people into desired behavior; they certainly don't have the authority to fire people unilaterally. If they start to behave autocratically, people can simply walk away.

In most organizations, especially of the Orange sort, job titles are a currency for status. Like all currencies, job titles are subject to the law of inflation. In many companies, they seem to swell and multiply—there are vice presidents, senior vice presidents, executive vice presidents, junior or senior directors, and ever more types of chief officers. It is a common expectation, in the Orange worldview, that people will work hard to achieve the next promotion and a bigger title.

From the Evolutionary-Teal perspective, job titles are like honeypots to the ego: alluring and addictive, but ultimately unhealthy. We can quickly get attached to our job title if it carries social prestige, and we can easily fall into the trap of believing we "are" our job identity. And in a hierarchical system, it's all too natural to start considering that we are somehow above certain people and below others. Unsurprisingly, Teal Organizations mostly do without job titles.

Again, we have to be careful: it does not mean that everyone is equal, that all jobs are the same. Some roles have a rather narrow scope (say, the role of operating a certain machine or cleaning the office), while other roles take a broader perspective (for instance, the role of designing a new product line). In all organizations researched for this book, there is one person recognized for taking the broadest perspective, and usually that person is called the CEO, at least by the outside world (even though she doesn't hold the same prerogatives as a traditional CEO, a topic discussed in chapter 3.1). And there are certain sets of well-defined roles that people naturally give a name to—for example, the regional coaches at Buurtzorg or the team leaders at FAVI. But for the vast majority of employees, people don't bother trying to find the right label that would capture all the different roles they hold at any point in time. Thinking in terms of job titles is so ingrained in our culture's thinking, though, that for their family and friends, most people invent a job title for themselves that somehow captures what they do in the language of traditional organizations.

The organizations I researched didn't only drop job titles; almost all of them also decided to drop words like *employee, worker,* or *manager,* and replace them with something else—most often simply *colleague.* If we stop and listen carefully to the meaning carried by the words *employee, worker,* or *manager,* we end up wondering how we use them so freely in everyday life.

Outsiders, and sometimes even insiders, can find the absence of job descriptions and job titles confusing. Without boxes to put people into, the organization chart disappears and it's not always easy to know who is responsible for what. For that reason, many organizations elect to keep a log on their intranet where colleagues can indicate the roles they currently fill. This is the case, for instance, at Buurtzorg, where a function within the intranet helps nurses locate the relevant colleague if they have a question or want a tip from someone filling the same role.

It's hard to not think in terms of the traditional organization chart. Often during my research, I caught myself trying to figure out where in a traditional organization chart a person might fit, given her roles. It happened when I was talking to an engineer at Sun Hydraulics and asked him, "So you would be the equivalent of a plant manager in a normal company, right?" With just three words, he gave the best possible answer: "Yes and no." On the one hand, yes, he performs some roles a plant manager would. For instance, one of his roles entails exploring factory-wide improvement initiatives; another is sensing the atmosphere among colleagues at the plant and bringing up issues if the mood is low. He might take the lead on some large projects, say, the automation of a step in the manufacturing process. On the other hand, he has no profit-and-loss responsibility for the factory (or to be more exact, he has it to the same degree as everybody else); his job is not on the line if results are bad (everybody's job is); he cannot impose decisions; he has no privilege to hire or fire people. In that sense, he is not at all like a traditional boss.

Does this mean there are no bosses in a self-managing organization? Quite the contrary. Every role people take on is a commitment they make to their peers. They are not accountable to one boss; every one of their peers is a boss in respect to the commitments they made. And as we will see in the next chapter, which discusses the practices that bring self-managing structures to life, anybody can put on the hat of "the boss" to bring about important decisions, launch new initiatives, hold underperforming colleagues to account, help resolve conflicts, or take over leadership if results are bad and action is needed.

Self-managing students, teachers, and parents—a Teal school

Our schools today are probably further away from self-management than most other types of organizations. We have turned schools, almost everywhere, into soulless factories that process students in batches of 25 per class, one year at a time. Children are viewed essentially as interchangeable units that need to be channeled through a pre-defined curriculum. At the end of the cycle, those that fit the mold are graduated; castoffs are discarded along the way. Learning happens best, this system seems to believe, when students sit quietly for hours in front of all-knowing teachers who fill their heads with information. Children can't be trusted to define their own learning plans and set their own goals; that must be done by the teachers. But, really, teachers cannot be trusted either; they must be tightly supervised by principals and superintendents and school districts and expert commissions and standardized tests and mandatory school programs, to make sure they do at least a somewhat decent job.

This factory-like system seems increasingly out of date. More and more people are crying out for innovation in education and starting to experiment with curricula, technologies, and governance in schools. But is it possible to build a truly Evolutionary-Teal school? And what would it look like? A superb example can be found in the center of Berlin in Germany. The "ESBZ" is a grade 7-12 school that opened its doors in 2007 with more than a bit of improvisation. Just three months before the start of the school year, the city council had suddenly given a decrepit prefabricated building from communist times to a group of pesky parents who simply wouldn't let go of their dream. When the school year started, only 16 students were registered. A few months later, at the mid-year point, 30 more students had joined, mostly rejects and troublemakers other schools had expelled. Hardly a promising start for a new school. And yet today, only a few years later, the school has 500 students and attracts hundreds of principals, teachers, and education specialists from all over the country who want to study the ESBZ model.

The driving spirit of the school is Margret Rasfeld, a former science teacher and radical innovator, whom the group of parents recruited as principal from the other side of the country. The seed for the school was planted 20 years earlier, in an event that would profoundly change Rasfeld's outlook on children and education. In 1986, a few 8th-grade students she was teaching approached her to discuss the violence, bullying, and extortions that were taking place in their school. She said they were welcome to talk things out in the privacy of her home, if they wanted to. Sixteen students came. A week later there were 33. The teenagers were looking to her for answers; she didn't have any, but she helped them journey to find their own. In the process, she discovered a side of the children she had never seen before. She marveled at the courage, persistence, resilience, intelligence, and compassion students were finding in themselves and that the school had never evoked before. From then on, she was determined that education should do justice to children's true potential and true nature; she wanted to engage not only their minds, but their hands, hearts, and souls, too.

Fast-forward to the present at the beginning of a school day. As a visitor to ESBZ, even while still outside at the entry gate of the school, you can sense there is something different about the school. It has to do with the children's presence, the way they walk and interact. The students don't hang out at the gate waiting until the last minute to go in; they seem happy to walk straight toward their classroom. They sport an air of quiet determination and concentration, their mind already on some project. There is no adolescent posturing, no competition of cool. The school claims in its founding principles that all children are unique, that they all have talents to contribute, that they are valuable, valued, and needed. Somehow, the way these children walk into their school seems to say these are more than mere words; the students seem to have embodied the school's guiding principles in their very bodies, posture, and attitudes.

How are these principles translated in the school? First and foremost, children are given full responsibility for their learning. To a large degree, students teach themselves and each other. Adults are mostly mentors and coaches and only act as teachers in the traditional sense when needed. They offer encouragement, counsel, praise, feedback, and challenge. The responsibility for learning is firmly in the hands of the students.

It starts with the way basic subjects are taught—language, math, and science. For these subjects, the school has done away with frontal teaching. Subjects are divided into modules, and each module comes in oversized flashcards that the teachers have devised with theory, exercises, and tests. Students self-pace their learning. A student that struggles with math can choose to spend more time on the subject to come to grips with it and spend less time on another subject that comes easily. There are advanced elements in the modules that interested students can take but are not required to. Students learn on their own or form small groups when helpful. When they have questions, they inquire first among other students; only if their peers can't help do they turn to the teacher (whose

> *Teachers open the door.*
> *You enter by yourself.*
> Chinese proverb

time is thereby freed to provide in-depth individual coaching). Classes mix several grades—students from grades 7, 8, and 9 learn together. Children continuously toggle from being learners to being teachers. The older students in particular learn to help out the younger ones (which helps them review material they have learned in the past). Because learning is self-paced, ESBZ has become unusually inclusive. In every classroom, there are children with autism and with light or severe learning disabilities. Normally they would be relegated to a special needs school, but here they can simply work alongside other students at their own rhythm. The student body has an unusually broad spectrum of social backgrounds: 20 percent of students come from a minority background, and 25 percent are eligible for subsidized meals; roughly a quarter of the students come from the other end of the spectrum, from very privileged backgrounds.

Each student has a logbook, in which they record what they have accomplished. It's not a free-for-all. There are clear expectations of what is expected at the end of the year (students are free of course to go beyond the expectations when they are passionate about a subject, and many children choose to do so). Every child has a one-on-one meeting every week on Friday with their tutor-teacher. Together they discuss progress made during the week, problems that might have come up, and plans for the week ahead—and also, when relevant, emotional or relational topics that weigh on the child's mind. Through these weekly one-on-one discussions, teachers and students know each other on a much deeper level than in traditional schools. The children know: *Someone cares about me; someone is there to listen*. Twice a year, in a discussion with their tutor, students set themselves three goals for the upcoming months. For instance, Paul, a shy 13-year-old, set himself the goal of becoming more comfortable being seen by others. One of the things he wants to learn is to speak up more in public.

The self-paced learning of basic subjects takes the first two hours of the morning. A big chunk of the day is spent working on individual or collective projects with real-life implications. Some students redesign a part of their school building and then coordinate the actual renovations. Others might try to get the city council to adopt higher environmental standards. Students are encouraged to find out what matters to them, to aim high, to fail, to try again, and to celebrate their accomplishments. They learn that their voice matters, that they can make a difference, that others need them and that they need others.

All year long in grades 7 and 8, students spend two hours every Wednesday outside of school in a class called "Responsibility." In counsel with their tutor-teacher, the children find themselves an activity where they can make a meaningful contribution while learning at the same time. Paul, who wants to overcome his shyness, volunteered to teach chess at his former primary school. The chess class he had loved so much would no longer take place, he had heard, because the teacher was moving to another school. Paul was sad that other kids wouldn't enjoy learning chess the way he had. Suddenly it all made sense: Paul could teach chess; standing in front of a group of children fit with Paul's goal of learning to speak in public—and doing so in front of younger children would be an easier way to practice. All he needed to do now was convince the principal of his former school to let him have a go at it. Just like Paul, all students find a place that suits them. Some work in retirement homes, while others organize school plays in kindergartens. It all depends on their interests and learning objectives. Children experience what it's like to take initiative, to be needed, and to make a difference in other people's lives.

In grades 8, 9, and 10, students have a class called "Challenge" (the beautiful German word "Herausforderung" literally means "being called to grow from the inside out"). They are invited to delve into some inner potential that lies dormant. During the year, they organize and prepare for a special three-week session, where they, alone or in small groups, will challenge themselves to step out of their comfort zone. One group of four students prepared for a three-week survival camp deep in the woods, where they lived in a shelter they built and on food they gathered. Daniel, a 16-year-old extroverted youngster, found his challenge in a three-week silent meditation in a monastery. A music teacher challenged a group of children to do intense music practice eight hours a day for three weeks in an abandoned old farm. Other students biked through Germany together, with little money, having to ask for accommodation and food along the way. The experience is often taxing, but students rave about their accomplishments and the personal growth they experienced, confronting their fears and growing beyond them.

The most daring experiment with student self-management is currently underway. At the end of grade 12, students in Germany must pass a state exam; the grades they get determine what university they can apply to. The stakes are so high that grades 10, 11, and 12 at ESBZ have thus far relied on more traditional teaching-to-the-test methods than students and faculty would like. Could it be possible, students and faculty wondered, to completely redesign the curriculum of grades 10, 11, and 12 in accordance with the school's guiding principles, while still preparing students well for the state exam? This year, all students from those grades will work in an ambitious yearlong project to redesign these three grades. Experts in Design Thinking (a methodology developed by IDEO, a celebrated design firm) will help the children and faculty, in an intensive two-day design workshop, to develop an overall concept. Students and teachers will then work the rest of the year, with support from leading education experts, to turn the concept into concrete structures and practices. Students and teachers are effectively redesigning their own school.

Teachers at ESBZ self-manage too. Teaching is often a lonely profession; at ESBZ it is a team sport. Every class has two tutor-teachers, so all teachers work in tandem. Three classes form a mini-school—they share a floor with a small faculty room where the six teachers meet weekly. The mini-schools are effectively what teams are to FAVI, Buurtzorg, or AES—flexible units that can react quickly to the daily flow of issues and opportunities. On paper, the school has a traditional hierarchy (it is publicly financed, and with that privilege comes a mandatory structure consisting of a principal, two vice-principals, and a pedagogical director), but mini-schools can make almost all decisions without needing approval from the principal.

Parents also self-manage. The school was created under a special status—the city only pays 93 percent of the teachers' salaries; for the building and all other expenses, the city provides no funds at all. Parents have to close the gap with a contribution calculated on the basis of their income. To minimize the cost, parents have decided that they would each contribute three hours of time every month to the school. What they do and how they do it all happens based on self-managing principles. The building renovation team, for instance, regularly organizes big festive weekends where 50 parents get their hands dirty and renovate a few classrooms. Piece by piece, parents have created warm, colorful, and functional school premises in what a few years ago were rundown leaky buildings. After school hours, the premises now host workshops attended by hundreds of principals and teachers who want to understand ESBZ's magic. The workshops (as you might have guessed) are taught almost exclusively by students, not by teachers or by Margret Rasfeld, the founder and principal.

What is remarkable is that ESBZ enjoys no free pass. The school has to make do with the same amount of teacher hours as any other school in Berlin. Even with the parents' contribution, the school has a lower budget than public schools. Every school can replicate ESBZ's success, because more money or resources are not the decisive factor. All it takes, really, is to look at children, teachers, parents, and education with fresh eyes.

CHAPTER 2.3

SELF-MANAGEMENT (PROCESSES)

Self-organization is not a startling new feature of the world. It is the way the world has created itself for billions of years. In all of human activity, self-organization is how we begin. It is what we do until we interfere with the process and try to control one another.

Margaret J. Wheatley and Myron Kellner-Rogers

Self-management requires an interlocking set of structures and practices. The previous chapter dealt with the structural aspects of self-management—for example, how the pyramid makes way for teams and how typical staff functions can be embedded within the teams. Change only the structure, though, and you are left hanging in midair. With the pyramid gone, many of the most fundamental organizational processes need to be reinvented—everything from decision-making practices to information flow, from investments to performance evaluations and compensation processes. We need answers to some very basic questions: if there is no longer a boss to call the shots, how do decisions get made? Who can spend company money? How is performance measured and discussed? What prevents employees from simply slacking off? Who gets to decide who deserves a salary increase or a bonus? This chapter will explore each of these questions in turn.

Decision-making—the advice process

If there is no formal hierarchy, how are decisions made? Can anybody just make any decision? That sounds like a recipe for chaos. Are decisions then made by consensus? That sounds exhausting and impractical, certainly for organizations with hundreds or thousands of employees.

Almost all organizations in this research use, in one form or another, a practice that AES called the "advice process." It is very simple: in principle, any person in the organization can make any decision. But before doing so, that person *must* seek advice from all affected parties and people with expertise on the matter. The person is under no obligation to integrate every piece of advice; the point is not to achieve a watered-down compromise that accommodates everybody's wishes. But advice must be sought and taken into serious consideration. The bigger the decision, the wider the net must be cast—including, when necessary, the CEO or the board of directors. Usually, the decision maker is the person who noticed the issue or the opportunity or the person most affected by it.

With the advice process, any person can make any decision but must seek advice from affected parties and people with expertise.

Dennis Bakke recounts a story that exemplifies the advice process in action. One day Shazad Qasim, a recently hired financial analyst at AES, consulted with Bakke. He was intending to leave his role to go back to his native Pakistan and research the opportunity for electricity-generating capacity there on behalf of AES. Bakke remembers his reaction:

> *I told him I was skeptical. Several years earlier, Agency for International Development (AID) representatives from the U.S. Department of State had encouraged us to expand into Pakistan. We had told them that we hardly knew what we were doing in the United States, let alone a place like Pakistan. Besides, it ranked as one of the most corrupt countries in the world for doing business. The ethical standards at AES probably ensured that we would never get any business there.*[1]

Despite the CEO's recommendation, the advice process meant the decision was Shazad's. He decided to go to Pakistan, effectively creating a new position for himself as business developer, retaining his previous salary. Six months later, the former financial analyst invited Bakke to Pakistan to meet the prime minister. Two and a half years later, a $700 million power plant was running. In line with AES's principles, the decision that AES would invest $200 million of its equity wasn't made by Bakke or the board, but by Shazad and people with less seniority (who of course, given the amounts at stake, asked Bakke and the board for advice).

We often think that decisions can be made in only two general ways: either through hierarchical authority (someone calls the shots; many people might be frustrated, but at least things get done) or through consensus (everyone gets a say, but it's often frustratingly slow and sometimes things get bogged down because no consensus can be reached). The advice process transcends this opposition beautifully: the agony of putting all decisions to consensus is avoided, and yet everybody with a stake has been given a voice; people have the freedom to seize opportunities and make decisions and yet must take into account other people's voices. The process is key to making self-management work on a large scale. It is actually so critical that, at AES and other self-managing organizations, colleagues know that forgetting to uphold the advice process is one of the few things that can get them fired (we'll touch later on the topic of how someone can be dismissed in the absence of hierarchy).

It's interesting to hear Bakke elaborate on the many benefits of the advice practice: in his experience, it creates community, humility, learning, better decisions, and fun (notice how these align with values that are important at the Evolutionary-Teal stage):

> *First, it draws people whose advice is sought into the question at hand. They learn about the issues and become knowledgeable critics or cheerleaders. The sharing of information reinforces the feeling of community. Each person whose advice is sought feels honored and needed.*
>
> *Second, asking for advice is an act of humility, which is one of the most important characteristics of a fun workplace. The act alone says, "I need you." The decision maker and the adviser are pushed into a closer relationship. In my experience, this makes it nearly impossible for the decision maker to simply ignore advice.*
>
> *Third, making decisions is on-the-job education. Advice comes from people who have an understanding of the situation and care about the outcome. No other form of education or training can match this real-time experience.*
>
> *Fourth, chances of reaching the best decision are greater than under conventional top-down approaches. The decision maker has the advantage of being closer to the issue and … usually has to live with the consequences of the decision.*
>
> *Fifth, the process is just plain fun for the decision maker because it mirrors the joy found in playing team sports. … The advice process stimulates initiative and creativity, which are enhanced by wisdom from knowledgeable people elsewhere in the organization.*[2]

It might be interesting to note that AES, unlike Buurtzorg and some other organizations we are yet to meet, did not completely figure out how to work entirely on peer-based systems. It still had some pyramid-like "layers" in place—operators, plant managers, regional directors, the executive committee. And yet, the simple practice of the advice process transcended these layers. Whatever someone's place in the organization, he or she could initiate any decision. People "higher up" could not simply overrule these decisions based on hierarchical position. Everybody, including the executive committee and Dennis

Bakke (the co-founder and CEO), had to seek advice to make decisions. Bakke even pushed the board to play by these rules. Its members actively participated in decision-making when consulted by employees on important decisions through the advice process; beyond that, he felt they should not make any decisions themselves other than those mandated by law.

Avoid jumping to any hasty conclusions. The CEOs and other leaders of self-managing companies are anything but weak, hands-off leaders. Arguably, these CEOs and senior leaders are better informed and more influential than leaders invested with the powers of hierarchy. With the advice process, they are continually consulted regarding decisions by people from all corners of the organization. Information and decisions that reach them are not vetted and filtered many times over as they climb up the chain of command. In traditional organizations, senior leaders must do the hard work of integrating conflicting perspectives into a decision; because this process takes time, senior leaders become bottlenecks for decision-making. With the advice process, they can ask tough questions and give their opinions forcefully, but then move on to the next question; meanwhile, someone else will do the work of integrating different perspectives and advice.

> *The [advice] process is bottom-up, but it is not a loosey-goosey, anything-goes affair. It involves creativity, careful analysis, meticulous planning, and disciplined execution.*
>
> Dennis Bakke

There is no prescribed format for seeking advice. People might reach out to colleagues in one-on-one discussion, or convene the relevant group for a meeting. When large groups are affected by a decision, email or the intranet is often the best way to collect input. Buurtzorg, for instance, has a very active internal social network. When Jos de Blok, the founder and CEO, or anybody else, is contemplating changes that might affect a great number of coworkers (for instance, a decision about compensation), he simply puts out the issue and the proposed solution on the social network to collect colleagues' advice.

No, it's not consensus

The advice process is a simple form of decision-making that transcends both consensus and unilateral action. In some cases, more elaborate decision-making approaches might be applied. Buurtzorg's elegant integrative process (discussed on page 67) is one example, and we'll encounter another one later in this chapter when we discuss Holacracy's governance process. It is worth repeating that these decision-making processes work *without consensus*. I have noticed that for some reason, many people naturally assume that in the absence of bosses, decisions in self-management organizations will be made by consensus. And because they have been scarred by the paralysis and endless discussions that often come when people seek consensus, they are quick to dismiss self-management as a viable way to run organizations.

In principle, consensus sounds appealing: give everyone an equal voice (a value particularly prized in Green). In practice, it often degenerates into a collective tyranny of the ego. Anybody has the power to block the group if his whims and wishes are not incorporated; now it's not only the boss, but everybody, who has power over others (albeit only the power to paralyze). Attempting to accommodate everyone's wishes, however trivial, often turns into an agonizing pursuit; in the end, it's not rare that most people stop caring, pleading for someone to *please* make a decision, whatever it turns out to be. With the advice process, no one has power over anybody else. The process transcends the need for consensus by giving everyone affected a voice (the appropriate voice, not an equal voice), but not the power to block progress.

Consensus comes with another flaw. It dilutes responsibility. In many cases, nobody feels responsible for the final decision. The original proposer is often frustrated that the group watered down her idea beyond recognition; she might well be the last one to champion the decision made by the group. For that reason, many decisions never get implemented, or are done so only half-heartedly. If things don't work out as planned, it's unclear who is responsible for stepping in. With the advice process, the ownership for the decision stays clearly with one person: the decision maker. Convinced that she made the best possible decision, she sees things through with great enthusiasm, trying to prove to advice givers that their trust was well placed or their objections immaterial. While consensus drains energy out of organizations, the advice process boosts motivation and initiative.

Decision-making in times of crisis

Can the advice process be upheld in times of crisis, when swift and even harsh decisions might be needed—say, to lay off staff in a downturn or to sell parts of a business? Can we genuinely consult with a group of coworkers about laying them off? Perhaps an extreme situation calls for extreme measures; perhaps self-management needs to be suspended temporarily for the CEO to make a few necessary, top-down decisions. But then, how can workers maintain trust in their organization's self-management, if every now and again the CEO can decide to step in and make autocratic decisions? FAVI, Buurtzorg, and AES have all faced crisis moments. The graceful ways they found to deal with such situations can provide inspiration for other self-managing organizations facing a crisis.

No one would call Jean-François Zobrist, a bear of a man and former paratrooper, a softie. But when he was faced with difficult and critical decisions at FAVI, he readily admitted he needed help to find a good answer. More than once, on impulse, he went around the shop floor, asked everybody to stop the machines, climbed on a soapbox and shared his problem with all the employees, trying to figure out a course of action. The first major crisis under his leadership happened in 1990 when car orders plummeted in the wake of the First Gulf War. Stocks were piling up, and there simply wasn't enough work to keep workers busy. Capacity and costs needed to be reduced. There was one obvious solution: fire the temp workers. But at FAVI, no one was really considered a temp worker. For reasons related to labor laws in France, new recruits were hired as temp workers for 18 months before they were offered a full contract. Most of them were already considered full members of their teams. By firing the temps, FAVI would rescind its moral commitment to them, and it would lose talent it had invested in, with a recovery perhaps only a few months away. With many questions and no clear answers, Zobrist found himself on the soapbox and shared his dilemma with all employees in that shift (including the temp workers whose fate was being discussed). People in the audience shouted questions and proposals. One worker said, "This month, why don't we all work only three weeks and get three weeks' pay, and we keep the temp workers? If we need to, we will do the same thing next month as well." Heads nodded, and the proposal was put to a vote. To Zobrist's surprise, there was unanimous agreement. Workers just agreed to a temporary 25 percent salary cut. In less than an hour, the problem was solved and machine noise reverberated around the factory again.

Most leaders I know would consider Zobrist's approach extremely risky. Sharing their dilemma openly with everybody would make them feel so vulnerable that this course of action probably wouldn't even cross their mind. Indeed, no one could have predicted with certainty how employees would react to the news that their jobs were on the line. The gathering could have descended into chaos, with fear of layoffs pitting people against each other in heated exchanges. Zobrist had no preconceived idea, no script, for how to lead the discussion once he had shared the company's problem. He chose to trust—trust himself, trust employees, and trust the process.

> *I finally figured out that not every crisis can be managed. As much as we want to keep ourselves safe, we can't protect ourselves from everything. If we want to embrace life, we also have to embrace chaos.*
>
> Susan Elizabeth Phillips

Obviously, the safer option would have been to ask the head of human resources (HR) to discreetly work out a number of scenarios, confidentially convene the management team to discuss them, and hide the problem from the workers until a decision was ready to be announced. (In the case of FAVI, of course, Zobrist didn't have an HR director nor an executive team at hand, but he could have convened a few trusted advisors.) This method is the tried-and-true way leaders have learned to handle sensitive issues in organizations. Whether they realize it or not, this approach is driven by a leader's fear: fear that employees might not be able to handle difficult news; fear that the leader's legitimacy might be questioned if he doesn't call the shots; and fear that he might look like a fool if he discusses a problem before he has fully figured out a solution. Zobrist's ability to keep his fear in check paved the way for a radically more productive and empowering approach and showed that it is possible to confront employees with a harsh problem and let them self-organize their way out of it. In the right framework, it seems that the advice process can be upheld even in crisis situations, and a leader should think twice before reverting to top-down decision-making.

Buurtzorg faced a crisis in 2010 and mastered it using the advice process too. The young company was growing at breakneck speed when Jos de Blok heard that health insurance companies had threatened to withhold €4 million in payments to Buurtzorg, citing technical reasons (the more likely reason: the insurance companies wanted to signal to Buurtzorg that it was growing too fast at the expense of established providers). A cash crunch loomed. Jos de Blok wrote an internal blog post to the nurses exposing the problem. He put forward two solutions: either Buurtzorg could temporarily stop growing (new teams cost money at first) or nurses could commit to increasing productivity (increasing client work within the contract hours). In the blog comments, nurses overwhelmingly chose to work harder because they didn't like the alternative: slower growth would have meant saying no to clients and nurses wanting to join Buurtzorg. In a matter of a day or two, a solution to the cash problem was found (and after some time, the insurance companies eventually disbursed the withheld funds).

AES gives an example of how to suspend the advice process—as gracefully as possible—in times of crisis. In fall of 2001, after the terrorist attacks and the collapse of Enron, AES's stock price plummeted. The company needed access to capital markets to serve its high debt levels but found them suddenly closed. Swift and drastic action was needed to prevent bankruptcy. A critical question was: how many and which power plants would need to be sold off to raise the necessary cash? With 40,000 people spread around the world, Dennis Bakke, the CEO, could hardly convene everybody and stand on a soapbox like Zobrist at FAVI. And the problem was so complex that he couldn't simply send out a blog post with two alternatives, like Jos de Blok did at Buurtzorg.

Bakke chose a course of action that temporarily suspended the advice process in a way that nevertheless minimized the risk of undermining trust in self-management. He didn't work out a plan behind closed doors with his management team; instead, he publicly announced that top-down decision-making would be made during a limited time for a limited number of decisions, albeit critical ones. The advice process would remain in force for all other decisions. To investigate the best course of action and make the tough calls, Bakke appointed Bill Luraschi, a young and brilliant general counsel. Luraschi wasn't regarded as one of the most senior leaders nor as someone who would seek a leading role in the future. The signal was clear: the senior leaders of the organization were not looking to exert more power. Top-down decision-making would be handled by someone with no thirst for power, and it really would be temporary.

If the advice process needs to be suspended in times of crisis, these two guidelines can serve to maintain trust in self-management: give full transparency about the scope and timeframe of top-down decision-making, and appoint someone to make those decisions who will not be suspected of continuing to exert such powers when the crisis is over.

Purchasing and investments

Employees' power to make decisions using the advice process is perhaps most evident when it comes to spending company money. Most organizations put authorization limits in place. A frontline manager might be free to spend money up to $1,000 but require authorization from his bosses beyond that amount; a unit manager might have spending power up to $10,000 and a plant manager up to $100,000. Whatever the amounts, the purchase order must generally proceed through a central procurement department that coordinates the relationships and negotiations with suppliers.

In self-managing organizations there are no authorization limits and no procurement departments. An employee who needs a new $50 printer doesn't have to call the IT department, hope for a green light from his boss, and wait the days or weeks it takes for the printer to arrive. He can simply head down to Walmart and buy a printer. In principle, any person can spend any amount of money, provided he has sought the necessary advice before making the decision; the larger the purchase, the more people are typically involved in the advice process. At FAVI, Sun Hydraulics, and other self-managing organizations, workers rather than managers are in charge of purchasing the machines and equipment that they work with, even when they cost several hundred thousand dollars. They do the analysis, write up the necessary specifications, visit and negotiate with suppliers, and secure financing from the bank if needed. In hierarchical organizations, when engineers do the analysis and choose a machine model, workers often complain about the new machine and drag their feet when it comes to learning how to operate it. When they have chosen the model, there is no such resistance to change.

What about volume discounts? Surely money is left on the table if purchases are not pooled? As often, the answer is: trust people to make the right decisions within the framework of self-management. For items where volume discounts are too good to give up, colleagues who buy from the same vendor will choose to coordinate to maximize their buying power. At Morning Star, a tomato processing company we'll soon discuss in greater depth, colleagues noticed that lots of people were buying threadlocker, an adhesive that prevents nuts and bolts from accidentally loosening, in dozens of different formats and from different vendors. They were not only losing out on volume discounts, but the uncoordinated purchasing generated unnecessary bureaucracy because regulations in the food industry required workers to painstakingly track every threadlocker format in a Material Safety Data Sheet. At some point, a worker suggested that he could walk around the plant once a quarter and ask colleagues if they wanted to order threadlocker through him. A similar solution emerged for purchasing packaging materials, an area where volume discounts can quickly add up. When there is value in coordination, people simply start to coordinate.

What about standardization? It makes sense to buy computer or telephone equipment from the same or compatible vendors, for instance. Again, one can simply trust the advice process. A secretary buying herself a new computer, unless she is very well versed in hardware and software specifications, will likely seek advice from a knowledgeable party to ensure the computer will easily fit in with the rest of the IT equipment. In this case, there is no need for a central department to enforce standards. In more complex cases, when standards need to be specified, someone will step up and call together a group that will look into the matter and define the standards.

Explicit assumptions

Founders and leaders of self-managing organizations get asked the same question over and over again: isn't it risky and foolish to let people make decisions without top-down control, especially when money is involved? In their experience, it is less, not more risky, because better decisions get made. But the really interesting thing is that the choice between trust and control is seldom debated on a rational level. It's a choice that gets made based on deeply held, often unconscious assumptions we hold about people and their motivations. Several leaders of Teal Organizations have found it useful, therefore, to talk often and explicitly about the assumptions underpinning self-management and to contrast them with the assumptions made by traditional hierarchies.

When AES acquired a new power plant, Bakke would often introduce AES's management practices to the new group of colleagues by asking them what assumptions owners and managers of a typical factory hold about their workers. Here is how Bakke summarizes the assumptions workers generally feel bosses have about them:

- *Workers are lazy. If they are not watched, they will not work diligently.*
- *Workers work primarily for money. They will do what it takes to make as much money as possible.*

- *Workers put their own interest ahead of what is best for the organization. They are selfish.*
- *Workers perform best and are most effective if they have one simple repeatable task to accomplish.*
- *Workers are not capable of making good decisions about important matters that affect the economic performance of the company. Bosses are good at making these decisions.*
- *Workers do not want to be responsible for their actions or for decisions that affect the performance of the organization.*
- *Workers need care and protection, just as children need the care of their parents.*
- *Workers should be compensated by the hour or by the number of "pieces" produced. Bosses should be paid a salary and possibly receive bonuses and stock.*
- *Workers are like interchangeable parts of machines. One "good" worker is pretty much the same as any other "good" worker.*
- *Workers need to be told what to do, when to do it, and how to do it. Bosses need to hold them accountable.* [3]

These assumptions sound harsh when they are put into words, and yet they are the basis for the structures and practices we have in organizations today. If this view of employees is true, leaders are prudent to build in controls, rewards, and punishments; only a fool would trust workers to make decisions using the advice process. Because the assumptions are often implicit, or even held subconsciously, Bakke felt it was critical to make them explicit and then to define a different set of assumptions.

AES people:

- *Are creative, thoughtful, trustworthy adults, capable of making important decisions;*
- *Are accountable and responsible for their decisions and actions;*
- *Are fallible. We make mistakes, sometimes on purpose;*
- *Are unique; and*
- *Want to use our talents and skills to make a positive contribution to the organization and the world.*[4]

With this set of assumptions, self-management and the advice process make perfect sense; while control mechanisms and hierarchy are needless and demoralizing distractions.

Jean-François Zobrist often initiated similar discussions with workers and new recruits at FAVI to explain the rationale for self-management. One day, for training purposes, he wrote down the following set of assumptions:

The analysis of our organization chart in the 1980s [when FAVI was still run like any other factory] *reveals without a doubt that men and women were considered to be:*

- ***Thieves** because everything was locked up in storage rooms.*
- ***Lazy,** as their working time was controlled and every late showing punished by somebody … who didn't even care to inquire about the reasons for being late.*
- ***Not dependable** because all their production was controlled by somebody else who must not have been very dependable either because random controls … had been put in place.*
- ***Not intelligent**, as a "manufacturing engineering" department did the thinking for them.*

Zobrist and his colleagues defined three new assumptions that over time have become mantras inside the factory.

- ***People are systematically considered to be good.***
  (Reliable, self-motivated, trustworthy, intelligent)
- ***There is no performance without happiness.***
  (To be happy, we need to be motivated. To be motivated, we need to be responsible. To be responsible we must understand why and for whom we work, and be free to decide how)
- ***Value is created on the shop floor.***
  (Shop floor operators craft the products; the CEO and staff at best serve to support them, at worst are costly distractions)[5]

If you are familiar with management theory, you will have recognized the similarity between the statements from AES and FAVI and the Theory X and Theory Y that Douglas McGregor developed in the 1960s when he was a professor at MIT. He stated that managers hold one of two sets of beliefs concerning employees: some think employees are inherently lazy and will avoid work whenever possible (Theory X); others think workers can be ambitious, self-motivated, and exercise self-control (Theory Y).

Which set of assumptions is true? People can debate this topic endlessly. McGregor had a key insight that has since been validated time and again: both are true. If you view people with mistrust (Theory X) and subject them to all sorts of controls, rules, and punishments, they will try to game the system, and you will feel your thinking is validated. Meet people with practices based on trust, and they will return your trust with responsible behavior. Again, you will feel your assumptions were validated. Expressed in terms of developmental psychology, if you create a strong Amber-Orange structure and culture, people will end up responding in Amber-Orange ways; create a strong enough Teal context and people are likely to behave accordingly.

At the core, this comes down to the fundamental spiritual truth that we reap what we sow: fear breeds fear and trust breeds trust. Traditional hierarchies and their plethora of built-in control systems are, at their core, formidable machines that breed fear and distrust. Self-managing structures and the advice process build up over time a vast, collective reservoir of trust among colleagues.

Organizations routinely talk about their values and mission; Teal Organizations talk about something even more fundamental—their basic assumptions about human nature. This has to do, I believe, with the fact that self-managing practices are still countercultural today. Many of us hold deeply ingrained assumptions about people and work that are based on fear, assumptions that call for hierarchy and control. Only by shining light on these fear-based beliefs can we decide to choose a different set of assumptions. FAVI, AES, and others have found that when colleagues know and talk about the two sets of assumptions frequently, people shift their belief system. The risk that fear-based control mechanisms will creep in through the back door is minimized. Someone will speak up and say, "Wait a minute! Does this new process fit our assumptions? I think not."

Whatever fundamental assumption you hold about human nature, it will be validated by the response your behavior will evoke from people around you.

Internal communications

The way information flows illustrates how assumptions (conscious or unconscious) shape organizational practices. In most workplaces, valuable information goes to important people first and then trickles down to the less important. Sensitive information is best kept within the confined circle of top management. If it must be released more widely, it needs to be filtered and presented carefully from the best possible angle. The underlying assumption is that employees cannot be trusted; their reactions could be unpredictable and unproductive, and they might seek to extract advantages if they receive too much information. Because the practice is based on distrust, it in turn breeds distrust among people lower in the hierarchy: *What are the bosses concealing now?*

In Teal Organizations, there are no unimportant people. Everybody expects to have access to all information at the same time. It's a "no secret" approach that extends to all data, including the most sensitive. This information includes not only financial data, but also salaries or the performance of individual teams. At Buurtzorg, for instance, teams can see every month how their productivity compares to that of other teams. The data of other teams is not anonymized or averaged out. People are trusted to deal with good and bad news. There is no culture of fear, and so teams with bad results are not deemed to need the protection of anonymity. Teams that go through a difficult phase are trusted to own up to the reality of the situation and to search for solutions.

Why go to this extraordinary length and share *all* information? Three reasons make this practice compelling for self-managing organizations:

- In the absence of hierarchy, self-managing teams need to have all available information to make the best decisions.
- Any information that isn't public will cause suspicion (why else would someone go through the trouble to keep it secret?), and suspicion is toxic for organizational trust.
- Informal hierarchies reemerge when some people are in the know while others are not.

In the case of AES, a publicly traded company, the decision to share all information with all employees brought up unprecedented questions with the U.S. Securities and Exchange Commission, as Bakke recalls:

> *If everyone had access to financial data of the company, then every AES employee, even those working in faraway plants, would be classified as "insiders." Instead of 5 to 10 "insiders" at a typical company, AES had thousands. All were subject to "blackout periods" in which they could not trade the company securities. Fairly soon after AES stock began trading publicly, we asked our people if they would like to limit their access to information so that they would not be considered insiders and would be free to trade AES stock at any time. By an overwhelming margin, they chose to have full access to financial information and to remain insiders.*[6]

In practice, to avoid information getting distorted or lost as it spreads from one person to another, self-managing organizations use their intranet as a central repository where everybody can publish and retrieve information in real time. At Buurtzorg, all data concerning performance of all the teams is put on the company's intranet. A team that struggles in one area can identify a team in the neighborhood with outstanding results and ask for advice and best practices. At FAVI and at Sun Hydraulics, there are computer stations with open access throughout the shop floor so that machine operators can log in to consult data at any time.

All-hands meetings are another standard practice in many Teal Organizations. They are typically held when there is new and important information to share: quarterly results, the annual values survey, a strategic inflection point, and so forth. The information is not simply shared top-down—it is discussed and debated. There tends to be no script to the meetings. Questions can take the meeting in any direction; frustrations can be vented; accomplishments and people spontaneously celebrated. In these moments, more is at play than simple information exchange. At a deeper level, trust in the organization and its values is tested and reaffirmed. All eyes are on the people in senior roles. Will they be candid, humble, and vulnerable? Will they face rather than dodge difficult questions or criticisms? Will they involve the whole group in problem solving? If traditional companies rarely hold all-hands meetings, it is precisely because they can be unpredictable and risky. But in that very risk lies their power to reaffirm an organization's basic assumptions and to strengthen the community of trust.

> *If you empower people but don't give them information, they just fumble in the dark.*
> Blair Vernon

Of course, not all news is pleasant to hear. The practice of sharing all information puts everyone in the same situation as the CEO of a traditional organization. It forces people to grow up and face unpleasant realities. In the 2002 recession, Sounds True, a media publishing company we will meet in the next chapter, was for the first time in its history facing a difficult financial situation. Its founder and CEO, Tami Simon, remembers that some people were then experiencing the other side of total transparency:

> *There is a certain kind of anxiety introduced in an environment where people know all about the business and its accompanying uncertainties. In companies where the executive team acts like parents who withhold difficult information from workers, people are protected from this anxiety. But I think that approach gives people a false sense of safety. Here, employees may feel anxious about finances more of the time, but at least everyone knows where they stand.*[7]

Conflict resolution

How do self-managing organizations deal with conflict? What happens when people have substantial disagreement on the right course of action? Or when two colleagues rub each other the wrong way? In a traditional workplace, people would send up the dispute to a boss to settle the matter. In self-managing organizations, disagreements are resolved among peers using a conflict resolution process. This process is so fundamental to collaboration without hierarchy that many self-managing organizations train every new recruit in conflict resolution.

That is the case, for instance, at Morning Star, the company in this research that has fleshed out, perhaps better than any other, the processes required for effective self-management. Morning Star is the world's largest tomato processing company, located on the West Coast of the United States. It began in 1970 when Chris Rufer, at the time a recent MBA graduate, started a one-person truck-driving operation hauling tomatoes. Today, Morning Star harvests tomatoes, runs a 200-truck hauling business, and operates three state-of-the-art processing plants that produce over 40 percent of the tomato paste and diced tomatoes consumed in the United States. Chances are that if you live in the United States and you're not allergic to spaghetti sauce, ketchup, or pizza, you've enjoyed Morning Star's products many, many times.

Tomato processing is a highly capital-intensive business working to incredibly exacting standards. From the outside, the processing factories look very much like chemical plants—they are huge masses of interconnected steel pipes digesting hundreds of tons of tomatoes per hour. The business is highly seasonal; the company works with 400 colleagues (the word Morning Star uses for employees) in low season but employs 2,400 people during harvest time in the summer. All of these people operate entirely on self-managing principles. There are 23 teams (called Business Units), no management positions, no HR department, and no purchasing department. Colleagues can make all business decisions, including buying expensive equipment on company funds, provided they have sought advice from the colleagues that will be affected or have expertise.

The founding principles for Morning Star's way of operating were set early in its history. When the first tomato processing factory was built, Chris Rufer and the company's first employees met to define how they wanted to work together. They decided that two principles, two basic social values, should inspire every management practice at Morning Star: individuals should *never use force* against other people and they should *honor their commitments*. These principles are at the heart of the company's conflict resolution mechanism, a process that is described in great detail in the "Colleague Principles," a core document outlining Morning Star's self-managing practices.

The conflict resolution process (called "Direct Communication and Gaining Agreement"), applies to any type of disagreement. It can be a difference of opinion about a technical decision in a given situation. It can be interpersonal conflict. It can be a breach of values. Or it can be related to performance issues, when one colleague finds that another is doing a lousy job or not pulling his weight. Whatever the topic, the process starts with one person asking another to gain agreement:

- In a first phase, they sit together and try to sort it out privately. The initiator has to make a clear request (not a judgment, not a demand), and the other person has to respond clearly to the request (with a "yes," a "no," or a counterproposal).
- If they can't find a solution agreeable to both of them, they nominate a colleague they both trust to act as a mediator. The colleague supports the parties in finding agreement but cannot impose a resolution.
- If mediation fails, a panel of topic-relevant colleagues is convened. The panel's role, again, is to listen and help shape agreement. It

cannot force a decision, but usually carries enough moral weight for matters to come to a conclusion.

- In an ultimate step, Chris Rufer, the founder and president, might be called into the panel, to add to the panel's moral weight.

Since the disagreement is private, all parties are expected to respect confidentiality during and after the processes. This confidentiality applies of course to the two persons at the heart of the conflict as well. They must resolve their disagreement between themselves and are discouraged from spreading the conflict by enlisting support and building rival factions.

Several other organizations in this research rely on virtually identical conflict resolution mechanisms: first a one-on-one discussion, then mediation by a trusted peer, and finally mediation by a panel. At first, I was struck by what seemed like an extraordinary coincidence. Before engaging in this research, I had never encountered a company with an explicit conflict resolution mechanism, and here I stumbled upon several organizations that had come up with virtually identical processes. In discussions with people at Morning Star, I came to understand that this process is about more than simply managing the occasional workplace conflict. Conflict resolution is a foundational piece in the puzzle of interlocking self-management practices. It is the mechanism through which peers hold each other to account for their mutual commitments. In traditional companies, when one person doesn't deliver, colleagues grumble and complain but leave it to the person's boss to do something about it. In self-managing organizations, people have to step up and confront colleagues who fail to uphold their commitments. Morning Star and other self-managing organizations readily admit that this essential piece can be tricky to put in place and to maintain. The process is effective to the degree that there is a culture within the workplace where people feel safe and encouraged to hold each other to account, and people have the skills and processes to work through disagreements with maturity and grace. Freedom and responsibility are two sides of the same coin—you can't have one without the other (at least not for long). Holding colleagues accountable to their commitment can feel uncomfortable. A clearly outlined conflict resolution process helps people confront each other when needed.

Role definition and allocation

We discussed in the previous chapter how Teal Organizations have done away with rigid job descriptions and job titles. Instead, every colleague has a number of roles that he has agreed and committed to fulfill. How are these roles created? And how are people appointed to new roles? In most cases, it happens organically without much fanfare. Someone senses an issue or an opportunity that calls for a new role. Say the receptionist notices that clients often call to ask about technical data of certain products. Wouldn't it make sense to put the technical data on the website? The logical next step is to discuss the idea with relevant people from product development and after-sales services. Most likely someone will step forward and take on the role. In hierarchical organizations, with their silos and turfs, this question might spark lots of debates and meetings regarding which department the job belongs in, what budget and resources should be allocated, and on and on. Here, someone simply steps forward and takes on the role.

Depending on their company culture and the industry they work in, organizations can put different levels of formalism around the process of creating roles. At FAVI, AES, Sun, and Buurtzorg, the process is pretty informal; you might remember the story of Frank at FAVI who created his own role as idea scout, or that of Shazad at AES who chose to relocate to Pakistan to try to get a power plant going there. People simply follow the advice process: they bounce the idea off the relevant people that a role must be created (or modified or scrapped). Or they simply discuss it in a team meeting.

Formalized contracting

Morning Star has created a somewhat more formal process to define and allocate roles. Given the annual rhythm of the tomato business, roles at Morning Star are formally discussed and determined once every year. (Of course roles keep evolving during the year, and ad hoc discussions to agree on changes of roles take place regularly.) As a Morning Star colleague, you write a personal mission statement ("Personal Commercial Mission" in Morning Star's language) and spell out all of the roles you commit to in a document called *Colleague Letter of Understanding* (or simply CLOU). Roles at Morning Star are defined very specifically, so you might well hold 20 or 30 different roles (one might be *receiver of tomatoes at the unloading station,* another might be *trainer of seasonal whole peel sorters*). For each role, you specify what it does, what authority you believe you should have (act, recommend, decide, or a combination thereof), what indicators will help you understand if you are doing a good job, and what improvements you hope to make on those indicators.

Why this level of formality and granularity? At FAVI and Buurtzorg, colleagues don't bother to write down roles in such detail, nor to define performance indicators or targets for themselves. The nature of nursing at Buurtzorg requires constant shifting and flexibility, and so too does the type of small batch processing that happens at FAVI. Turning tomatoes into paste, in contrast, is one long continuous process. Trucks repeatedly dump in tomatoes on one side, and paste comes out in aseptic packaging on the other. In what is essentially a low-margin commodity business, the name of the game here is not flexibility but continuous improvement to increase efficiency by one or two more percentage points. In that context, it makes sense to define roles with great granularity and to track performance indicators very closely.

In a continuous process like Morning Star's, each person in the chain receives tomatoes or paste in some form from someone upstream and delivers them in another form to someone downstream. Therefore, colleagues at Morning Star chose to discuss the CLOUs, once written or updated, not in a team setting (which most self-managing organizations do), but in a series of one-on-one discussions with the handful of colleagues up and downstream that people interact with most. People discuss and negotiate what's written in each other's CLOU documents very seriously—they want to make sure that people upstream commit to supplying them with the right input, so that they can in turn deliver to people downstream what they committed to. The chart below shows a visual depiction of the web of commitments within the company. Each dot represents a person, and the lines connect people who are joined by a commitment made in a CLOU. Morning Star has no organization chart. If it had one, this would be it.

The real organization chart in any company is a spider web of informal relations. Unfortunately, we insist on forcing a pyramid structure onto this web, which distorts the natural flow of work.

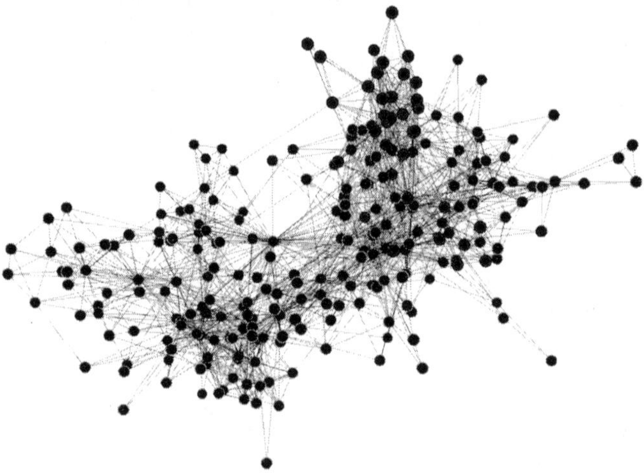

Web of commitments at Morning Star

Actually, one could argue that every organization's real structure looks like this: an intricate web of fluid relationships and commitments that people engage in to get their work done. Unfortunately, most organizations force a second structure, the one with boxes piled up in pyramid shape, on top of the first. No wonder it sits there so uneasily—it distorts more than it helps the real work going on in the web of relationships underneath.

Perhaps you noticed how many more lines there are in Morning Star's web than in a formal organization chart. The resulting structure weaves into a fabric that is highly resilient, like a spider web. Notice too how within such a system that there are no layers and thus no promotions. What happens is that people, as they grow in experience, take on roles with larger responsibilities and offload simpler ones to new recruits or more junior colleagues. People don't need approval from a boss to change roles, but consent from their peers. The implication is profound, as one Morning Star colleague expresses:

> *The temptation to not be ourselves and look good in the eyes of a boss is much diminished, as it is hard to constantly look good to a dozen colleagues. We just give up even trying to play that game.*[8]

In Teal Organizations, people don't compete for scarce promotions. You can broaden the scope of your work and increase your pay if your colleagues are ready to entrust you with new roles. They will grant you important roles if you've developed your skills and have shown yourself to be trustworthy and helpful. In Teal Organizations, there can be internal competition, but it's a healthy type. Chris Rufer uses a golfing analogy to explain:

> *When Jack Nicklaus was competing, was he concerned about becoming an executive senior vice president golfer? No. He knew that if he got good at it, he would achieve what everyone longs for: a sense of accomplishment. He also knew accomplishment would give him an income to enjoy the life he wanted. Moving up is about competency and reputation, not the office you hold.*[9]

Defining roles and governance within teams

At Morning Star, roles emerge from a series of one-on-one commitments, a practice that is well suited for an industry with a continuous process. In organizations where teams are the natural unit, Holacracy provides perhaps the most elegant process to define roles and help them evolve. Holacracy is not so much an organization as an *organizational operating model,* a brainchild of American entrepreneur Brian Robertson. In the 1990s, Robertson and two colleagues in the Philadelphia area founded and developed Ternary Software, which became a fast-growing software development company. The impulse for starting a new company was Robertson's deep dissatisfaction with organizations he had worked in:

> *I had gone through a several year period of just feeling like there was so much [in organizations] that was limiting our ability to express and to*

contribute everything we have to offer, that wasn't embracing ... our whole range of skills and talents, and wasn't allowing us to integrate together in the most effective way that I could envision or imagine. I wasn't quite sure how to resolve a lot of those things but it was really a spark of dissatisfaction that led to starting the software company: "My God there's got to be a better way, there's just got to be something better than this."[10]

Robertson and his two co-founders started experimenting relentlessly with any organizational practice that sounded promising. Where the ideas came from didn't matter—inspiration was found in places as different as agile software development, sociocracy, and David Allen's *Getting Things Done*. Anything that worked was kept; anything that didn't work was discarded. The almost daily new experiments with different organizational practices were taxing, as Robertson recalls:

I think there was [at Ternary Software] a real appreciation for the kind of culture where experimentation and change was embraced. However, the actual experimentation process at the level we engaged in to get to Holacracy was very taxing. Things would change under you: one day we are doing it this way, the next day we'd completely change something core, and the next day it's yet different and we're always running to catch up. The sense of lack of stability was huge, and for good reason: there wasn't much stability in our processes and methods because we were evolving them so damn quick. ...

There was a lot of pain in that organization from the continual experimentation. It would have been so much easier just to say "we are going to run this company in a conventional way"! To be very concrete, there was a 12 month to 18 month period where we went through five different salary systems, each one of which changed the way people were paid, changed the level of pay, changed the way pay was calculated. ... These were scary changes. Each system was better than the last, but that didn't change the impact of "oh my God everything is changing around here continually."[11]

In time, from the crazy experimentation was distilled a sophisticated and coherent set of structures and practices that Robertson calls "Holacracy." When Robertson hired a new management team and exited Ternary Software, he created HolacracyOne, a consulting and training firm dedicated to refining and spreading the practice of Holacracy in organizations. He often uses a computer analogy to explain what Holacracy is about:

Think about it as an operating system for an organization. Not a technology, not a piece of software, but a social technology. Your computer has an operating system ... [that] controls how communication happens, how power works, how applications share resources and information, the flow of work through that computer. Everything else is built on top of that operating system.

And likewise in our organizations today, we have an operating system that often goes unquestioned. Right now there is a bit of a monopoly on the organizational operating system market, so to speak. We pretty much have one way we use to structure and run a business, ultimately. There are some variations of course, but it really comes back to the same basic underlying structure for how power works and how work gets done in the company.[12]

Robertson and his colleagues at HolacracyOne have distilled a generic *minimum* set of practices they believe are needed to "upgrade the operating system."[13] All other practices are considered *apps* (that is, applications that run on top of that operating system, to keep with the analogy), which can be handled in many ways and need to be adapted to each company.

One of the core elements of Holacracy, which can be found in all Teal Organizations in this research, is to *separate role from soul,* to break the fusion of identity between people and their job titles. In holacratic language, people don't have a *job,* but *fill* a number of granular *roles.* Where Holacracy goes further than other organizations is in the elegant process through which roles are defined.

When someone senses that a new role must be created, or an existing role amended or discarded, he brings it up within his team[14] in a governance meeting. Governance meetings are specific meetings where only questions related to roles and collaboration are to be discussed, separate from the rumble and tumble of getting work done. (Everything that has to do with getting business done is discussed in what are called "tactical meetings" with specific meeting practices.) Governance meetings are held regularly—generally every month—and any member of a team can request an extra meeting at any point in time. They follow a strict process to ensure that everybody's voice is heard and that no one can dominate decision-making. A facilitator guides the proceeding. Anybody who feels a role needs to be created, amended, or discarded (called the *proposer*) can add it to the agenda. Each such governance item is discussed in turn and brought to resolution with the following process:

1. *Present proposal*: The proposer states his proposal and the issue this proposal is attempting to resolve.
2. *Clarifying questions*: Anybody can ask clarifying questions to seek information or understanding. This point is not yet the moment for reactions, and the facilitator will interrupt any question that is cloaking a reaction to the proposal.
3. *Reaction round*: Each person is given space to react to the proposal. Discussions and responses are not allowed at this stage.

4. *Amend and clarify*: The proposer can clarify the intent of his proposal further or amend it based on the prior discussion.
5. *Objection round*: The facilitator asks, "Do you see any reasons why adopting this proposal would cause harm or move us backwards?" Objections are stated and captured without discussion; the proposal is adopted if none surface.
6. *Integration*: If an objection is raised, the facilitator leads an open discussion to craft an amended proposal that would avoid the objection while still addressing the proposer's concern. If several objections are raised, they get addressed in this way one at a time, until all are removed.

With this process, every month a team will typically adapt, clarify, create, or discard one or several roles. The organization constantly adapts and corrects, based on problems and opportunities people sense. The process might sound formal, but people who use it report they find it deeply liberating. There is no need for corridor talk, for politics, for coalition building to get a change in roles. Anybody who senses the need for something in the organization to change knows that there is a place to take an idea and have it addressed. People who experience such a meeting for the first time are surprised at how dramatically efficient it is. It cuts through the sometimes endless, uncomfortable discussions we have when we deal with the sensitive topic of roles and responsibilities. In a single meeting, a number of changes of roles can be worked through, one after the other.

In essence, Holacracy's governance process is a variation of the advice process. In this case, it's not one person that integrates people's advice into a decision, but the team that does it as a whole. It ensures that no valid objection is overlooked, and it truly builds on the collective intelligence of a team. You might have noticed how similar Holacracy's governance process is to the one nurses use at Buurtzorg when they discuss important topics (see page 67). In both cases, the goal is to not to aim for a perfect and definite answer, but to find a workable solution and iterate quickly if needed. People don't wait for perfect answers to try out new arrangements and see how they fare. Roles evolve organically, all the time, to adapt to changes in the environment. Employees who are not used to such frequent change can find it taxing at first. Over time, most end up loving it. When there is only one promotion coming around every few years, people are ready to put up a fight for it. When every month there might be some changes to roles within the team, everybody is more relaxed. It's okay to sometimes forgo a nice role for a while. Nothing is written in stone; new interesting roles will come around.

Total responsibility

In hierarchical organizations, managers are responsible for delivering the numbers. Their area of responsibility is their turf. Just as they won't mess with somebody else's business, other managers had better stay out of theirs. In Teal Organizations, people have roles, which come with clear areas of responsibility, but no turfs. No part of the organization belongs to anybody. Many of the organizations researched for this book stress the opposite; they emphasize what Morning Star calls "total responsibility": all colleagues have the *obligation* to do something about an issue they sense, even when it falls outside of the scope of their roles. It's considered unacceptable to say, "Somebody should do something about this problem," and leave it at that; if you see a problem or an opportunity, you have an obligation to do something about it, and most often that "something" is to go and talk about it with the colleague whose role relates to the topic.

Holacracy has pushed this principle so far as to define explicit channels to make sure any "tension" (Holacracy's word for issues and opportunities[15]) that anybody senses at any time can get processed quickly and reliably. Depending on the type of issue, it can be brought to either a "governance meeting" or a "tactical meeting," each of which has its specific decision-making processes.[16] Everyone is invited to process any tension; "it's not my problem" is not an acceptable attitude.

Total responsibility can sound daunting, but the experience of Holacracy and Morning Star is that people grow to love it. People's concerns are no longer limited to their scope of responsibility; they can take the well-being of the whole organization to heart. Of course, not all team members cheer when a colleague comes and tells them they should consider doing something about an issue. But in a self-managing organization, people have roles, not turfs, and no one can formally shut out a colleague by saying, "This is none of your business."

Appointment process

In many cases, people's work evolves organically over time—they discard a few roles and take on another few. But sometimes there is a whole new "job" that opens up. Given Buurtzorg's explosive growth, every few months a new regional coach is needed. Or at Sun Hydraulics, a new role might open up in project engineering. Often, the appointment process is very organic; in time, a person emerges that team members entrust with the role. When Zobrist retired from his position as CEO of FAVI in 2009, one of the team leaders had emerged as a natural successor. No other team leader seems to have eyed the job; certainly, no one left in bitterness or disappointment. Leading up to the succession, there was no political jockeying and no infighting, and there was no settling of scores from the new leader after his appointment. The same is true of the other CEO transitions that took place in the organizations researched for this book. Perhaps it boils down to this: when employees are empowered to make all the decisions they want, the urge to climb the ladder recedes.

When everybody has the power to make decisions, the urge to climb the ladder recedes.

When needed, a more formal discussion process can be put in place. At Sun Hydraulics, for instance, when a new job is created or an existing job becomes available, an internal recruitment process takes place: candidates are interviewed by the colleagues who will work most closely with them. At FAVI, Zobrist instituted another nifty practice—a confirmation process. Every five years, he asked the team leaders to organize a vote in their teams to decide if he should stay on as the CEO of the organization. As we will discuss in chapter 3.1, it is critical that CEOs play by the same rules as everyone else, or self-management can unravel quite quickly. Zobrist of course expected his colleagues to speak up on the spot were he ever to behave autocratically. The formal vote was meant to remind workers that they have the power to make any decision, including removal of the CEO.

Trading roles

Because roles in self-managing organizations are defined granularly, it can be quite easy to trade roles within a team. A person that is very busy can ask colleagues to pick up one of her roles, temporarily or permanently. A team member that wants to learn a new skill can ask a colleague to trade a corresponding role toward that end.

To make it easy to trade roles across teams as well as within them, HolacracyOne has set up a company-wide *Role Market Place* (in holacratic language, this is an "app;" it's not part of the basic operating system). On the company's intranet is a file where colleagues can "rate" every role they currently fill, using a scale of -3 to +3:

- If they find the role energizing (+) or draining (-)
- If they find their talents aligned (+) or not (-) with this role
- If they find their current skills and knowledge conducive to (+) or limiting in (-) this role

Using the same scale of -3 to +3, people can also signal their interest in roles currently filled by other people. The market place helps people wanting to offload and people wanting to pick up roles to find each other more easily.

Talent management

In the last 20 years, it's become a general practice in large corporations to set up *talent management* programs. Managers throughout the company are asked to identify *high potentials,* which HR puts on special training tracks and provides with *stretch assignments* to prepare them for higher offices. *Succession planning* is another best practice in human resources—for every management position throughout the company, possible successors must be identified and groomed to be ready to take over. And then there is *career planning*. For every type of profile, HR should think through the best career paths that expose people to the right set of skills as they make their journey up the management ranks.

In self-managing organizations, leadership is distributed, and there are no leadership roles to prepare people for. None of the organizations in this research spends time on talent management, succession planning, or career planning. They have found that in a self-managing context, people naturally come across so many opportunities to learn and grow that senior leaders don't need to worry about people getting the right exposure. People who have freedom in their work are eager learners; they can be trusted to shape their own journeys. Careers in self-managing organizations emerge organically from people's interests, callings, and the opportunities that keep coming around in a liberated workplace.

Performance management at the team level

How does performance management work in a self-managed context? In Orange Organizations, it's the role of bosses to keep the pressure on employees and to prevent them from slacking off. Top management sets ambitious targets in the company's yearly budgets and mid-term plans, and these targets then cascade down the organization. It's part of a leader's role to always challenge subordinates to do more, to do it faster, to do it cheaper.

In self-managing organizations that have no managers to keep up the pressure, what prevents teams from getting complacent? The short answer: intrinsic motivation, calibrated by peer emulation and market demands.

The better question, though, might be: what makes us think that people need to be put under pressure to perform? Research shows that when people pursue a meaningful purpose, and when they have the decision-making power and the resources to work toward that purpose, they don't need pep talks or stretch targets.[17] Unfortunately, in many traditional organizations, people work under the opposite circumstances; they don't see much purpose in their work, and they feel restricted in their potential for self-expression by rules and bosses. No wonder they lose interest and must be pressured to give 100 percent. Imagine working as a nurse in a traditional Dutch neighborhood nursing organization: every morning, you receive a plan with 30 appointments with patients you don't know, put together by a planner you don't know. You are given exact time slots (10 minutes for an injection with the first patient, five minutes to change the compression stockings for the second patient, and so on). Patients are unhappy with you because you hurry them, and meanwhile you know that if you were to take more time, you'd have to explain yourself, because the time registration system keeps track of everything you do. The work is so mindless that you would be forgiven for wanting to slack off.

Now imagine what a day might be like working at Buurtzorg: you are part of a team that is known and respected in the neighborhood. You have made your own plan for the day. You will see 10 patients with whom you've developed a relationship. You know their life stories and medical histories. You might have met their children and neighbors and helped arrange a network to encourage your patients to regain more autonomy. You cheer when you see them making progress, and you stand by their side when they reach the end of their days.

People working in these conditions, Buurtzorg has found, don't need a boss to motivate them. More often than not, it's the other way around—nurses are so deeply engaged in their work that they must remind each other to set boundaries and not to let work overrun their private lives. More generally, experience shows that self-governing teams in pursuit of a meaningful purpose don't need prodding from above. If people stop working with enthusiasm and productivity drops, it is generally the symptom of a problem that needs addressing—for example, relational problems in the team or roles that need to be reallocated. Resolve the problem and spirits are restored.

When people have the decision-making power and the resources to work toward a meaningful purpose, they don't need pep talks or stretch targets.

People don't need pressure from above, but they still need to get a sense of whether they are doing well. Teal Organizations measure indicators like team results, productivity, and profit, just like other organizations—except that they mostly tend to do so at the level of teams or process steps, and they don't bother to measure individual performance (contrary to Orange Organizations that believe in individual incentives and therefore need individual metrics). The data is made public for all to see, creating emulation, a healthy form of peer pressure. When teams perform similar tasks—like the nursing teams at Buurtzorg or the automotive teams at FAVI—results are easy to compare. In a glance, a team in Buurtzorg can know if it is at the bottom or the top of the league in terms of, say, productivity. Teams at the bottom are motivated to improve out of pride; they don't need a boss to discuss how they could improve.

In traditional organizations, many people would consider such total transparency about results to be brutal. All depends on how information is handled. In Orange Organizations, bad results prompt fears (and good results provoke envy or suspicion). Who gets to see what data is a very touchy subject. In Teal Organizations, people know that information will not be used against them. No one needs to be protected from the facts, good or bad.

What about organizations where teams don't do comparable work? At Morning Star, teams engaged in "tomato sorting," "steam generation," or "packaging" don't share metrics that would help them compare themselves. To help teams nonetheless get feedback on their performance, the company has come up with an interesting practice: every year in January, teams present a self-evaluation to a group of colleagues, which comprises Chris Rufer (the founder and president) and anyone else who cares to join. They are expected to talk candidly about what went well and what didn't, how effectively they used company resources, and what they plan to do in the next year. It's not a superficial effort; each presentation lasts for a few hours, and teams can expect challenging, sometimes grilling questions from their colleagues. In the course of a month, all teams make presentations; teams that haven't performed well have received much input from their peers and know they have homework to do.[18] Morning Star's budget and investment cycle also offers another opportunity for peer review. Every year, each team presents its investment plans to a panel of peers for advice. Teams that are not performing well are likely to be challenged as to whether spending money is really the best way to fix their problems.

Individual performance management

In Teal Organizations, performance and outcomes are discussed foremost at the team level: *Are we collectively doing a good job contributing to the organization's purpose*? Most people nevertheless still look for feedback about their individual performance. Psychologists have come across an interesting phenomenon: a person put in a sensory-deprivation room (a so-called anechoic chamber, a room designed to dampen all sound and block out light) after only a short amount of time reports experiencing visual hallucinations, paranoia, and a depressed mood.[19] Put simply, without outside stimulus, we go mad. I believe something very similar happens when we are deprived of feedback related to our work. Our egos may be wary of feedback, but we are relational beings that thrive on honest feedback. I've seen organizations where no feedback is ever exchanged "go mad" because of it. People judge others behind their backs, only to wonder nervously what others might be saying when they have their backs turned. In places like these, every word, every silence, every raised eyebrow, is scrutinized for unspoken judgments.

Teal Organizations are high on trust and low on fears. Feedback in such environments feels less threatening, and most organizations in this research are places where colleagues exchange feedback frequently. In some of them, new recruits are trained in Marshall Rosenberg's Nonviolent Communication and in effective ways to give feedback. Of course, the advice process is a formidable feedback mechanism built right into the fabric of daily life in these organizations.

Because feedback is exchanged so freely, some organizations—FAVI, for instance—don't hold any formal appraisal discussions. But colleagues in most organizations in this research still see value in taking the time, once a year, to reflect on their performance at work. Of course, instead of a boss doing the appraisal, they put in place peer-based systems:

- At Morning Star, people receive feedback at the end of every year from each of the persons they have committed to in their CLOU.
- At AES, Dennis Bakke installed a beautiful practice of team appraisal with his closest peers. They got together once a year, often over dinner in one of their homes to make for a relaxed, informal setting. Every person in turn shared his or her self-evaluation. Other team members commented, questioned, or encouraged each other to reach a deeper understanding of their potential and performance.
- At Buurtzorg, the rules of the game (see page 70) simply stipulate that every year, each team is to hold individual appraisals within the team, based on a competency model that the team has designed. Each team decides what format it will use for their discussions. A team I spent time with decided to exchange feedback in subgroups of three colleagues. Everyone prepares a self-evaluation as well as feedback for the other two colleagues in the trio, so people can measure their self-perception against their colleague's perceptions.

Traditional performance evaluations can be dispiriting affairs. Often we don't recognize ourselves in the feedback because our boss only has a narrow view of our work (or sometimes because he tells us everything is all right, just to get the uncomfortable moment over with). With more input from more peers, we get a more meaningful reflection of our contribution. There is another reason why so many appraisal conversations feel lifeless: they tend to be very narrow discussions, sticking to some preformatted evaluation grid, neglecting to inquire into broader questions of the person's selfhood—their hopes, dreams, fears, yearnings, and sense of purpose in life. We will discuss in chapter 2.5 how a few simple questions can turn appraisal conversations into moments of joyful and soulful introspection (see page 183).

Dismissals

"What happens when someone does a lousy job, when someone needs to be fired?" is a question people often ask when they hear about self-management. If there is no boss, can low performers just hang on forever? What if someone is a pain and makes the workplace hell for others? Will he just be allowed to stay on? Self-managing organizations of course face such situations occasionally and have put processes in place to deal with them, processes that don't rely on a hierarchy but on peer-based mechanisms.

Before we go into these processes, though, let's start by saying that in practice, these cases prove to be surprisingly rare. In traditional workplaces where a job is a box in an organization chart, there is little flexibility: you are either a good fit for the job or you are not (in reality of course, you are probably a bit of both), and so you should either be allowed to stay in the job or asked to move on. In self-managing organizations, people can more easily customize a job for themselves at which they excel. A person with "performance issues" might shed one or several roles in which she fails to deliver and take up other roles that better match her skills, interests, and talents.

But some people just don't fit in, or they perform below what their colleagues expect of them. In a traditional organization, a boss or the HR department can decide to give them a bad review and to dismiss them for low performance, rather like a teacher has power to decide a child's future in the school. And so it's perhaps not surprising that people being dismissed react like children being told they failed to make it to the next grade—they feel like a failure, treated unfairly; they blame circumstances and nurture resentment. In this research, I encountered an interesting phenomenon: in self-managing organizations, it seems that almost universally, people choose to leave before they are dismissed. Only in the rarest cases is the company saying, "That's enough." How come? The dynamics of self-management give people natural clues that they might not be in the right place. At Sun Hydraulics, an engineer might notice that somehow little work comes his way—few colleagues spontaneously ask him to join their projects or solicit him for advice. At Buurtzorg, a nurse will feel in her interactions with colleagues that she doesn't fit the team, or that self-management doesn't suit her after all. There are currently 250 nurses joining Buurtzorg every month and 25 that leave each month, once they have been there for a while and realize it wasn't meant to be. Almost always, the departure happens by mutual consent, on a friendly basis.

> *Despite the American myth, I cannot be or do whatever I desire. … Our created natures make us like organisms in an ecosystem: there are some roles and relationships in which we thrive and others in which we wither and die.*
>
> Parker Palmer

This does not change the fact that on a personal level, the process can be painful. The self-managing context nevertheless helps people realize that no one is to blame; they are perhaps simply not meant for this particular work. How we react to an event such as a dismissal depends on our perspective on life. Remember: in a Conformist-Amber worldview, lifelong employment is the norm. A dismissal is therefore a deeply distressing event, a forced expulsion from an identity-giving community. In Achievement-Orange, it is often experienced as a traumatic blow to the sense of self-worth, and in Pluralistic-Green as a betrayal by the group. In Teal, we can hold the event more consciously: a door closes, perhaps painfully at first, in order for another door to open down the line that might bring us closer to our path in life. We can see it as an invitation to reflect on the real nature of our strengths and talents and discover what other work might better suit us. We learn, grow, and move on.

What about forced dismissals? Though rare, they do happen—for instance, when someone breaches the company values. In the absence of dominator hierarchy, the process is peer-based. At Buurtzorg, when one person has lost the trust of the team, the team tries to find a mutually agreeable solution. If that doesn't work out, the group calls in its regional coach or an external facilitator to mediate. In almost all cases, the presence of a mediator brings resolution. In some cases, the person and the team decide on some mutual commitments and give it another go. In others, after some deliberation, the person comes to see that trust is irrevocably broken and understands it is time to leave. If no agreement can be found, as a last chance to try to settle the matter, the team members can ask Jos de Blok, the founder, to mediate; in the rare cases where even that fails, they can ask him to put an end to the person's contract (legally, he is the only one who can do so).

> *In retrospect, I can see in my own life how the job I lost helped me find work I needed to do … how losses that felt irredeemable forced me to discern meanings I needed to know.*
>
> Parker Palmer

At Morning Star, the process is almost identical, except that it is initiated by an individual rather than a team (at Morning Star, people aren't embedded as deeply in teams). Morning Star views a dismissal as the final step in a conflict and therefore uses its conflict resolution mechanism to deal with the situation. The process starts when one person asks another to leave the organization. Suppose that someone finds that a colleague has fundamentally breached a company value (perhaps the person made an important decision without requesting advice from colleagues) or that a colleague is failing time after time to live up to his commitments, despite a number of previous attempts to improve the situation. She can initiate a conflict resolution process, asking her colleague to resign. The four-stage process kicks in:

- In a first phase, they have to sit together and try to sort it out. In the discussion, the person asked to leave can suggest ways to restore trust. Or perhaps he will come to see that he has irrevocably lost the trust of his colleagues and that he is better off looking for work elsewhere.
- If they can't agree on an outcome, another colleague is called in as mediator.
- If necessary, in a third step, a panel of colleagues is asked to mediate.
- As a last resort, Chris Rufer, the founder and president, is asked to join the panel.

People asked to mediate or sit on a panel take their role very seriously. Morning Star's principle of not using force against anyone is at stake. They are not a jury, passing a verdict on a colleague. Their role is to explore every possible way to restore trust in the relationship. The process can take a long time if needed. Only when the person who has been asked to leave sees that colleagues genuinely tried to find a solution, and that none could be found, will he come to accept that resignation is the reasonable outcome. Therein lies the power and legitimacy of the process.

How often do people leave Morning Star after such a process? No one knows. Because Morning Star views this as a private conflict between two persons, everyone is under the understanding of full confidentiality (as is always the case with the conflict resolution mechanism), and no one keeps statistics. But the process clearly does get used in practice: some of the more senior colleagues I've spoken to told me that they have been part of a handful of panels over the years. Having been part of such panels, they are keen advocates of the method. The discussions in the panel are never easy, they report, but they do help people reach fair and reasonable outcomes.

Compensation and incentives

What about compensation and incentives in Teal Organizations? Here again, they deeply question standard management practices and come up with different methods; these include the process to decide who deserves how much pay (people set their own salaries, with guidance from their peers), how people are incentivized (incentives distract people from their inner motivation, so we are better off without them), and what type of salary differences are deemed acceptable (people at the lower end of the scale should make enough to have their basic needs met).

Peer-based processes and self-set salaries

In the absence of bosses, the process to determine who gets to take home how much money must be peer-based. W. L. Gore, the company best known for developing Gore-Tex fabrics, pioneered self-management practices in the late 1950s. To decide on people's salaries, it asks each employee to rank, once a year, the colleagues they have worked with. HolacracyOne uses a similar ranking method. Once a year, coworkers fill out a survey for all their colleagues, consisting of only two questions:

- "This person contributes (much) more or (much) less than me." (On a scale of -3 to +3)
- "This person has a good basis to evaluate me." (On a scale of 1 to 5)

A simple algorithm crunches through the answers and groups colleagues into a few salary buckets. The more experienced, knowledgeable, and hard-working people land in the higher buckets that earn bigger salaries; the more junior, less experienced colleagues naturally gravitate toward buckets with lower salaries. The process is simple and easy to understand. It has the benefit of fairness. When it's not just one person (the boss), but all the colleagues we interact with informing the process, the resulting salary is likely to be a fairer reflection of our contribution.

Some organizations go a step further: they allow people to set their own salary. AES, under Dennis Bakke, experimented in certain areas with a radical version of a peer-based process. People set their own salary, using the advice process—they had to seek advice and recommendation from their peers around them. In that way, people were made fully responsible for assessing their own contribution and validating it in the eyes of the colleagues. Semco, a Brazilian group of companies operating in various manufacturing and service industries, has fared well for a great number of years with self-set pay.[20]

Morning Star has developed, to my knowledge, the most refined process: self-initiated pay with feedback from elected salary committees. If you work at Morning Star, then once a year, along with all your colleagues, you write a letter stating the raise in salary you believe to be fair for yourself and why. In an uneventful year, you are likely to stick with a cost-of-living adjustment. But if you feel you have taken on more challenging roles or made special contributions, you can choose a higher percentage. You back up the letter with the peer-based feedback you received from your CLOU colleagues (the people with whom you concluded one-on-one contracts a year earlier) and any relevant data on performance indicators you are responsible for. You then share your letter with a handful of colleagues that were elected into a compensation committee (there is one such committee in each of the company's four locations). The committee's job is to review all the letters it receives, calibrate them, and provide feedback. It might tell you that you've been too humble about your accomplishments and that you should consider going for a bigger raise. Or it might tell you that, in comparison to your peers, the salary increase you granted yourself seems on the high side. The committee has only advisory power. You can choose to take the committee's feedback into account or to keep the raise you had set originally, in which case the committee might choose to enter into a "Gaining Agreement" process with you[21]. Morning Star's experience is that people prove to be remarkably skillful at assessing a fair compensation for themselves. In any given year, roughly a quarter of people choose salary increases above the cost-of-living adjustment. Only a handful of people throughout the company receive feedback that they might have aimed too high.

In small organizations, the process can be simplified. All colleagues can come together for a meeting to discuss and honor their contribution and decide on the appropriate salary levels for every person in turn. Realize!, a four-person partnership in the field of organizational development consulting based in Amsterdam, the Netherlands, sets salaries in this way. (The company, which works with Holacracy's principles and practices, attracted some attention when two of its partners participated in the launch of a thought-provoking podcast series called "Waking up the Workplace.") Each quarter, the four partners come together for a much-anticipated discussion. The meeting starts with a traditional business update—discussing client activity, prominent events, and key figures for the last quarter. Then comes the beautiful (and sensitive) part: each partner in turn shares his perspective on his contribution during the last quarter, including work he has done, projects he has led, and support he has given to others. While one partner speaks, the others can chime in to add any unreported contributions, offer praise, or ask a critical question. When the group is done and feels that everyone's contribution has been heard and honored, each person pauses to reflect in silence about compensation. How could the earnings from the last quarter be shared among the partners in a way that reflects everyone's contribution? At some point, one partner breaks the silence with a proposal. Sometimes, the proposal feels just right and gets accepted on the spot. More often, it is a basis for a discussion: *I feel my contribution here or your contribution there deserves a higher recognition.* How exactly the cash will be split, the partners acknowledge, is ultimately not what this conversation is about. The discussion serves a higher purpose: making sure everybody feels his or her contribution is fully valued, that the inner and outer perspectives (what I know and what others perceive) are in sync. It is an exercise in openness, trust, and vulnerability. The four partners report that invariably they go into the discussion with some nervousness and leave the meeting with a deep sense of gratitude (and spontaneous collegial hugs) for being part of a partnership that operates from such deep levels of listening and trust.

No incentives, but company-wide bonuses

How people think about incentives is often directly linked to their worldview. Conformist-Amber holds that people should be paid according to their rank, with no performance incentives (a perspective unions embrace: "same work, same pay"). Achievement-Orange believes that people can be lured to work hard and smart if given the right individual incentives (a perspective shared by most organizational leaders today). Pluralistic-Green is uncomfortable with the competitive nature of individual incentives and high wage differentials. It prefers team bonuses to reward collaboration.

What about Evolutionary-Teal? It values intrinsic over extrinsic motivators. Once people make enough money to cover their basic needs, what matters more than incentives and bonuses is that work is meaningful and that they can express their talents and callings at work. For that reason, most of the organizations in this research have done away with incentives altogether. Almost all organizations studied here have abandoned the practice of individual incentives. Seen from an Evolutionary-Teal perspective, it's a rather sad image we have of people if we believe that their primary motivation is the size of the carrot we dangle in front of them. In his book *Drive*, Daniel Pink concludes from a great amount of research on the matter that in today's complex work settings, incentives are mostly counterproductive, reducing rather than enhancing people's performance. Yet, in the world of business, doing away with individual incentives is still rather revolutionary—sales people without sales targets and sales incentives? This process is what all the companies in this research have opted for. CEOs without bonuses and stock options? All but one of the organizations have done away with them.

Green Organizations often work with team incentives: teams that achieve outstanding results receive a bonus to be shared equally among all team members. Most organizations in this research have abandoned even that kind of incentive scheme. Instead, at the end of very profitable years, they choose to share some part of the profit with all employees (in some cases everyone receives the same fixed percent of base salary, in others everyone receives the same fixed amount).[22] At FAVI, for instance, all employees, regardless of their base salary, receive the same bonus when the profits are high. In 2011, everyone came home with an extra €3,000 ($4,000) at the end of the year.

Reduced compensation inequality

The dominant thinking in business today is Orange. *To achieve results, people must be motivated by individual incentives.* Orange has no problems if this results in large wage differentials, if these differentials are justified by people's merits and contributions. This thinking has created rather extraordinary wage inequalities in recent years. And, unsurprisingly, it has turned out to be a good deal for the leaders who advocate this practice: CNNMoney calculates that in 2011, the CEOs of Fortune 50 companies took home on average a staggering 379 times the median pay of employees in their company[23] (the multiple would be even higher when compared to the lowest paid employee).

From an Evolutionary-Teal perspective, the notion of meritocracy has, well, merit. But one person making a few hundred times the salary of someone else seems to stretch the boundaries. Most of the organizations researched for this book strive to reduce the salary differentials that are practiced in their industry—boosting lower salaries, while keeping higher salaries in check. From a Teal perspective, a particular point of attention is ensuring that the lowest paid employees make enough money to cover their basic needs (in keeping with Maslow's insight that people can only reach for self-actualization if their basic needs are met).

AES, like FAVI, eliminated hourly wages for operators and offered them fixed salaries. It erased the distinction between blue- and white-collar workers; all AES colleagues, including operators, were compensated based on the same principles. Dennis Bakke explains some of the consequences:

When we started this change in AES compensation policy, only 10 percent of our people worldwide were paid a salary. The other 90 percent received hourly wages and overtime. By the time I left in 2002, over 90 percent of 40,000 people in 31 countries were paid a salary, just like the company's leaders. It was a giant step in breaking down barriers between management and labor and in bringing us together as AES business people. On average, people were paid about the same amount of money as before but spent less time at their plants and offices. There was no reason to take four hours on a Saturday morning to make a repair instead of staying an extra hour on Friday evening to get it done. In most cases, employees took more responsibility, initiative, and pride in their work. The most important result was the self-respect that it engendered among AES people.[24]

RHD, a nonprofit we will meet in the next chapter, holds the principle that when there is room for salary increases, they should be disproportionately geared toward the lowest salaries first. The CEO's salary is capped to a maximum of 14 times the *lowest* salary in the organization. You can argue about the multiple—is it too high or too low?—but notice the clever twist RHD introduced by capping the highest salary not based on the *average* or *median* salary, as many Green Organizations have started doing, but on the *lowest*. It's now very much in the CEO's and the leadership's own interest to ensure that even the colleagues with the lowest qualification earn enough for a decent living. Next to this direct focus on entry-level salaries, RHD has set up a scholarship fund to offer staff members opportunities to pursue formal education and increase their earning potential. And it has instituted a companion currency, the *RHD Equal Dollar*, that allows lower-paid colleagues to increase their access to goods and services by trading with each other and with their local community.

Paying blue-collar employees salaries instead of hourly wages and capping CEO pay might sound revolutionary to some, but I wonder if the future will not bring even more profound changes. Today, salaries are determined in large part by the law of supply and demand. The organizations in this research have often done away with the pyramid, but a phantom pyramid still exists in terms of pay—people whose roles involve larger issues get paid more than people whose roles are more narrow. Some people argue that this is fair and desirable; those who contribute more to an organization's purpose should be paid more. Another perspective is that all colleagues are fundamentally of equal worth and that all work done with love and dedication is to be honored equally, be it strategic thinking or scrubbing the floors.[25] Perhaps people scrubbing the floors should be paid more, not less, if people find it a less desirable task. How we think about compensation is ultimately about much more than cash—it reveals much about our relationship to money, to scarcity and abundance, and to what we value in people and in ourselves. To what extent we will keep basing salaries on the law of supply and demand, as society as a whole transitions to a Teal perspective, is anyone's guess.

In summary—the structures, processes, and practices of self-management

Leading scientists believe that the principal science of the next century will be the study of complex, autocatalytic, self-organizing, nonlinear, and adaptive systems. This is usually referred to as "complexity" or "chaos theory" (the Teal equivalent to Orange's Newtonian science). But even though we are only now starting to get our heads around it, self-management is not a startling new invention by any means. It is the way life has operated in the world for billions of years, bringing forth creatures and ecosystems so magnificent and complex we can hardly comprehend them. Self-organization is the life force of the world, thriving on the edge of chaos with just enough order to funnel its energy, but not so much as to slow down adaptation and learning. For a long time, we didn't know better and thought we needed to interfere with life's self-organizing urge and try to control one another. It seems we are ready now to move beyond rigid structures and let organizations truly come to life. And yet self-management is still such a new concept that many people frequently misunderstand what it is about and what it takes to make it work.

Misperception 1: There is no structure, no management, no leadership

People who are new to the idea of self-management sometimes mistakenly assume that it simply means taking the hierarchy out of an organization and running everything democratically based on consensus. I hope it is clear by now that there is, of course, much more to it. Self-management, just like the traditional pyramidal model it replaces, works with an interlocking set of structures, processes, and practices; these inform how teams are set up, how decisions get made, how roles are defined and distributed, how salaries are set, how people are recruited or dismissed, and so on. The tables on pages 140-141 give an overview of the key practices of self-managing organizations and contrast them with the Orange equivalents that dominate today's thinking. Appendix 3 engages in a more detailed discussion of three types of self-managing structures encountered during the research and examines how certain industries or contexts can call for one type of structure rather than another.

What often puzzles us at first about self-managing organizations is that they are not structured along the control-minded hierarchical templates of Newtonian science. They are complex, participatory, interconnected, interdependent, and continually evolving systems, like ecosystems in nature. Form follows need. Roles are picked up, discarded, and exchanged fluidly. Power is distributed. Decisions are made at the point of origin. Innovations can spring up from all quarters. Meetings are held when they are needed. Temporary task forces are created spontaneously and quickly disbanded again. Here is how Chris Rufer, the founder and president of Morning Star, talks about the structure of self-managing organizations:

> *Clouds form and then go away because atmospheric conditions, temperatures, and humidity cause molecules of water to either condense or vaporize. Organizations should be the same; structures need to appear and disappear based on the forces that are acting in the organization. When people are free to act, they're able to sense those forces and act in ways that fit best with reality.*[26]

The tasks of management—setting direction and objectives, planning, directing, controlling, and evaluating—haven't disappeared. They are simply no longer concentrated in dedicated management roles. Because they are spread widely, not narrowly, it can be argued that there is *more* management and leadership happening at any time in Teal Organizations despite, or rather precisely because of, the absence of fulltime managers.

Misperception 2: Everyone is equal

For as long as human memory goes back, the problem of power inequality has plagued life in organizations. Much of the pervasive fear that runs silently through organizations—and much of the politics, the silos, the greed, blaming, and resentment that feed on fear—stem from the unequal distribution of power.

Interestingly, the interlocking structures and processes allowing for self-organization do not *resolve* the question of power inequality; they *transcend* it. Attempting to *resolve* the problem of power inequality would call for everyone to be given the same power (a notion consistent with the Green-Pluralistic worldview). Cooperatives, for instance, have sought in equal ownership a method to divide power equally. Interestingly, none of the organizations I have researched are employee-owned; the question of employee ownership doesn't seem to matter very much when power is truly distributed.

From an Evolutionary-Teal perspective, the right question is not: *how can everyone have equal power?* It is rather: *how can everyone be powerful?* Power is not viewed as a zero-sum game, where the power I have is necessarily power taken away from you. Instead, if we acknowledge that we are all interconnected, the more powerful you are, the more powerful I can become. The more powerfully you advance the organization's purpose, the more opportunities will open up for me to make contributions of my own.

Here we stumble upon a beautiful paradox: people can hold different levels of power, and yet everyone can be powerful. If I'm a machine operator—if my background, education, interests, and talents predispose me for such work—my scope of concern will be more limited than yours, if your roles involve coordinating the design of a whole new factory. And yet, if within what matters to me, I can take all necessary actions using the advice process, I have all the power I need.

This paradox cannot be understood with the unspoken metaphor we hold today of *organizations as machines*. In a machine, a small turn of the big cog at the top can send lots of little cogs spinning. The reverse isn't true—the little cog at the bottom can try as hard as it pleases, but it has little power to move the bigger cog. The metaphor of nature as a complex, self-organizing system can much better accommodate this paradox. In an ecosystem, interconnected organisms thrive without one holding power over another. A fern or a mushroom can express its full selfhood without ever reaching out as far into the sky as the tree next to which it grows. Through a complex collaboration involving exchanges of nutrients, moisture, and shade, the mushroom, fern, and tree don't compete but cooperate to grow into the biggest and healthiest version of themselves.

The problem of power inequality has plagued organizations since the dawn of time. Teal Organizations don't resolve *the problem, they* transcend *it.*

It's the same in Teal Organizations: the point is not to make everyone equal; it is to allow all employees to grow into the strongest, healthiest version of themselves. Gone is the dominator hierarchy (the structure where bosses hold power over their subordinates). And precisely for that reason, lots of natural, evolving, overlapping hierarchies can emerge—hierarchies of development, skill, talent, expertise, and recognition, for example. This is a point that management author Gary Hamel noted about Morning Star:

> *Morning Star is a collection of naturally dynamic hierarchies. There isn't one formal hierarchy; there are many informal ones. On any issue some colleagues will have a bigger say than others will, depending on their expertise and willingness to help. These are hierarchies of influence, not position, and they're built from the bottom up. At Morning Star one accumulates authority by demonstrating expertise, helping peers, and adding value. Stop doing those things, and your influence wanes—as will your pay.*[27]

So really, these organizations are anything but "flat," a word often used for organizations with little or no hierarchy. On the contrary, they are alive and moving in all directions, allowing anyone to reach out for opportunities. How high you reach depends on your talents, your interests, your character, and the support you inspire from colleagues; it is no longer artificially constrained by the organization chart.

Misperception 3: It's about empowerment

Many organizations today claim to be empowering. But note the painful irony in that statement. If employees need to be empowered, it is because the system's very design concentrates power at the top and makes people at the lower rungs essentially powerless, unless leaders are generous enough to share some of their power. In Teal Organizations, people are not empowered by the good graces of other people. Empowerment is baked into the very fabric of the organization, into its structure, processes, and practices. Individuals need not fight for power. They simply *have* it. For people experiencing self-management for the first time, the ride can be bittersweet at first. With freedom comes responsibility: you can no longer throw problems, harsh decisions, or difficult calls up the hierarchy and let your bosses take care of it. You can't take refuge in blame, apathy, or resentfulness. Everybody needs to grow up and take full responsibility for their thoughts and actions—a steep learning curve for some people. Former leaders and managers sometimes find it is a huge relief not having to deal with everybody else's problems. But many also feel the phantom pain of not being able to wield their former positional power.

> *At the moment power is shared … people feel needed and valued, because they are needed and valued.*
> Dennis Bakke

Many leading thinkers and practitioners in the field of organizational design focus their energy today on the question of how leaders can become more conscious. The thinking goes as follows: if only leaders could be more caring, more humble, more empowering, better listeners, more aware of the shadow they cast, they would wield their power more carefully and would create healthier and more productive organizations. Brian Robertson, the founder of Holacracy, put it well in a blog post:

> *We see attempts for leaders to develop to be more conscious, aware, awake, servant leaders that are empowering. … And yet, the irony: … If you need someone else to carefully wield their power and hold their space for you, then you are a victim. This is the irony of empowerment, and yet there is very little else we can do within our conventional operating system other than try our best to be conscious, empowering leaders.*[28]

If we can't think outside the pyramid, then indeed, as Robertson notes, the best we can do is try to patch up the unhealthy consequences of power inequality with more enlightened leadership. Pioneer Teal Organizations show that it's possible to transcend the problem of power inequality and not just patch it up. We can reinvent the basic structures and practices of organizations to make everyone powerful and no one powerless.

Misperception 4: It's still experimental

Another common misconception is that self-management might still be an experimental form of management. That is no longer true: self-management has proven its worth time and again, on both small and large scales and in various types of industry. W. L. Gore, a chemical manufacturing company best known for its Gore-Tex fabrics, has been operating on self-organizing principles since its founding in the late 1950s. Whole Foods, with its 60,000 employees and $9 billion in revenue, operates its more than 300 stores with self-governing units (the rest of the organization has more traditional hierarchical structures). Each store consists of roughly eight self-managing units, such as produce, seafood, and check-out (central services are run with a Green, empowered hierarchy).

The Orpheus Chamber Orchestra has operated since its founding in 1972 on entirely self-managing principles. The orchestra, with residence in New York's Carnegie Hall, has earned rave reviews and is widely regarded as one of the world's great orchestras. It operates without a conductor. Musicians from the orchestra make all artistic decisions, from choosing the repertoire to deciding how a piece ought to be played. They decide who to recruit, where to play, and with whom to collaborate.

Virtual and volunteer-driven organizations practice self-management on staggering scales. In 2012, Wikipedia had 100,000 active contributors. It is estimated that around the same number—100,000 people—have contributed to Linux. If these numbers sound large, they are dwarfed by other volunteer organizations. Alcoholics Anonymous currently has 1.8 million members participating in over 100,000 groups worldwide—each of them operating entirely on self-managing principles, structures, and practices.

I believe it is because we have grown up with traditional hierarchical organizations that we find it so hard to get our heads around self-management. Young people, on the other hand, who have grown up with the Web (variously referred to as Millennials, Generation Y, or Generation "F" for Facebook) "get" self-management instinctively. On the web, management writer Gary Hamel notes:

- *No one can kill a good idea*
- *Everyone can pitch in*
- *Anyone can lead*
- *No one can dictate*
- *You get to choose your cause*
- *You can easily build on top of what others have done*
- *You don't have to put up with bullies and tyrants*
- *Agitators don't get marginalized*
- *Excellence usually wins (and mediocrity doesn't)*
- *Passion-killing policies get reversed*
- *Great contributions get recognized and celebrated*[29]

Many organizational leaders and human resource managers complain that Millennials are hard to manage. Indeed, this generation has grown up in the disruptive world of the Internet, where people's influence is based on contribution and reputation, not position. Why would they want to put up with anything other than self-management in the workplace? Why would anyone else, for that matter?

Self-management

	Orange practices	Teal practices
Organization structure	• Hierarchical pyramid	• Self-organizing teams • When needed, coaches (no P&L responsibility, no management authority) cover several teams
Staff functions	• Plethora of central staff functions for HR, IT, purchasing, finance, controlling, quality, safety, risk management, etc.	• Most such functions performed by teams themselves, or by voluntary task forces • Few staff remaining have only advisory role
Coordination	• Coordination through fixed meetings at every level (from executive team downwards), often leading to meeting overload	• No executive team meetings • Coordination and meetings mostly ad hoc when needs arise
Projects	• Heavy machinery (program & project managers, Gantt charts, plans, budgets, etc.) to try and control complexity and prioritize resources	• Radically simplified project management • No project managers, people self-staff projects • Minimum (or no) plans and budgets, organic prioritization
Job titles & job descriptions	• Every job has job title and job description	• Fluid and granular roles instead of fixed job descriptions • No job titles
Decision-making	• High up in the pyramid • Any decision can be invalidated by hierarchical superior	• Fully decentralized based on advice process (or on holacratic decision-making mechanisms)
Crisis management	• Small group of advisors meet confidentially to support CEO in top-down decision making • Communication only when decision is made	• Transparent information sharing • Everyone involved to let the best response emerge from collective intelligence • If advice process needs to be suspended, scope and time of suspension is defined

Self-management

	Orange practices	Teal practices
Purchasing & investments	• Authorization limits linked to level in hierarchy • Investment budgets steered by top management	• Anybody can spend any amount provided advice process is respected • Peer-based challenging of team's investment budget
Information flow	• Information is power and is released on a need-to-know basis	• All information available in real-time to all, including about company financials and compensation
Conflict resolution	• (Conflict often glossed over, no conflict resolution practices)	• Formal multi-step conflict resolution practice • Culture restricts conflict to the conflicting parties and mediators; outsiders are not dragged in
Role allocation	• Intense jockeying for scarce promotions leads to politics and dysfunctional behavior • Silos: every manager is king of his castle	• No promotions, but fluid rearrangement of roles based on peer agreement • Responsibility to speak up about issues outside of one's scope of authority
Performance management	• Focus on individual performance • Appraisals established by hierarchical superior	• Focus on team performance • Peer-based processes for individual appraisals
Compensation	• Decision made by hierarchical superior • Individual incentives • Meritocratic principles can lead to large salary differences	• Self-set salaries with peer calibration for base pay • No bonuses, but equal profit sharing • Narrower salary differences
Dismissal	• Boss has authority (with HR approval) to dismiss a subordinate	• Dismissal last step in mediated conflict resolution mechanism • In practice very rare

CHAPTER 2.4

STRIVING FOR WHOLENESS (GENERAL PRACTICES)

A human ... experiences himself, his thoughts and feelings, as something separated from the rest. This delusion is a kind of prison for us, restricting us to our personal desires and to affection for a few persons nearest us. Our task must be to free ourselves from this prison by widening our circles of compassion to embrace all living creatures and the whole of nature in its beauty.

Albert Einstein

Historically, organizations have always been places where people showed up wearing a mask, both in an almost literal and in a figurative sense. Literally, we see this in the bishop's robe, the executive's suit, the doctor's white coat, and the uniforms at a store or restaurant, to name a few. The uniform signals a person's professional identity and rank. It is also a claim the organization makes on the person: while you wear this uniform, you don't fully belong to yourself. You are to behave and show up not as yourself, but in certain pre-determined, acceptable ways.

Along with the uniform comes a more subtle influence: people often feel they have to shut out part of who they are when they dress for work in the morning. They put on a professional mask, conforming to expectations of the workplace. In most cases, it means showing a masculine resolve, displaying determination and strength, hiding doubts and vulnerability. The feminine aspects of the self—the caring, questioning, inviting—are often neglected or dismissed. Rationality is valued above all other forms of intelligence; In most workplaces the emotional, intuitive, and spiritual parts of ourselves feel unwelcome, out of place.

Organizations are for the most part, in the true sense of the word, soulless places—places inhospitable to our deeper selfhood and to the secret longings of our soul.

What makes us leave so much of our selfhood behind when we go to work? There is a conspiracy of fears at play that involves employees as much as their organizations. Organizations fear that if people were to bring all of themselves to work—their moods, quirks, and weekend clothes—things would quickly dissolve into a mess. Armies have long known that people made to feel interchangeable are much easier to control. Employees, for their part, fear that if they were to show up with all of who they are, they might expose their selfhood to criticism and ridicule and come across as odd and out of place. It is deemed much better to play it safe and to hide the selfhood behind a professional mask.

> *You can measure an organization by the number of lies you need to tell to be part of it.*
>
> Parker Palmer

Wisdom traditions from around the world speak to this from a deeper level: at heart, we are all profoundly interconnected and part of a whole, but it's a truth we have forgotten. We are born into separation and raised to feel divided from our deeper nature, as well as from the people and life around us. Our deepest calling in life, these traditions tell us, is to reclaim wholeness, within ourselves and in our connection with the outside world.

This spiritual insight inspires Teal Organizations' second breakthrough: to create a space that supports us in our journey to wholeness. Extraordinary things begin to happen when we dare to bring all of who we are to work. Every time we leave a part of us behind, we cut ourselves off from part of our potential, of our creativity and energy. No wonder many workplaces feel somehow lifeless. In wholeness we are life-full. We discover in awe how much more life there is in us than we ever imagined. In our relationships with colleagues, much of what made the workplace unpleasant and inefficient vanishes; work becomes a vehicle where we help each other reveal our inner greatness and manifest our calling.

Self-management goes a long way toward helping us show up more fully. With no scarce promotions to fight for, no bosses to please, and no adversaries to elbow aside, much of the political poison is drained out of organizations. There is a phrase I heard many times in the self-managing organizations I researched: *here I feel I can fully be myself.* Without a boss looking over our shoulder, without employees to keep in line and peers that could turn into competitors, we can finally let our guard down and simply focus on the work we want to do. People in these organizations often use the archetypes of Parent-Child-Adult (from Eric Berne's Transactional Analysis) to describe how self-management opens the space for healthier ways to be at work. The bond between a boss and the subordinate often makes for an unhealthy parent-child relationship. In self-managing organizations, the system pushes us to behave in adult-to-adult relationships, whatever our differences in education, seniority, and scope of work. In a peer-based system, if we try to behave like a parent (or like a child for that matter), our colleagues will quickly let us know they won't have any of it.

Brian Robertson, the founder of Holacracy, sometimes uses another set of archetypes to talk about the power of self-management to shift relationships to a healthier level—helping us to move from Persecutor, Rescuer, Victim, to Challenger, Coach, Creator.

> *I've always appreciated the Karpman Drama Triangle model of Persecutor, Rescuer, Victim. We see it play out in organizations all the time, where people end up in this Drama Triangle pattern. ...*
>
> *I think it's a great frame to look at the effect of Holacracy. It's really difficult to maintain a victim stance in Holacracy. It's possible, but it's difficult, because the world keeps holding up a mirror to you, saying, "You can process your tensions. If you're choosing to be a victim, that is your choice, and perhaps a choice because you don't know how to do something else, but it's not because somebody else is persecuting you. It is your choice to stay in that pattern if you so choose." Which is a nice catalyst to shift someone over to a Creator side of "Oh, alright, let me bring a proposal, let me process a tension, let me do something to change the environment I'm in."*
>
> *Before Holacracy, it was easy for me to end up in a Persecutor role as I tried to lead an organization and get its needs met. ... Holacracy offers me a powerful alternative. ... Now I can be a Challenger. Now I can say, "Okay, well, what are you going to do? It's in your power. What's your next step?" I can ask questions, and I can challenge.*
>
> *There's a great story ... from Bernard Marie Chiquet, one of our licensees and Holacracy coaches, who talks about his own background with the Savior pattern. How easy it was for him in business to fall into that Savior/Rescuer pattern of trying to rescue others, and how Holacracy helps him shift to be a Coach, and say, "I'm done with rescuing," because in this environment, there are no victims that need to be rescued anyway.*[1]

Self-management greatly reduces the subtle levels of fear in organizations that prevent us from being ourselves. Some organizations, like Holacracy and Morning Star, focus clinically on self-management and feel little need to add other practices to encourage individual and collective wholeness. Other organizations find that even without hierarchy, being in a community of peers is hard. We all have personal histories and baggage we bring with us to the workplace. Perhaps the presence of others brings out a need to be liked. Or a desire to be perfect. Or to be seen as competent and successful. Or a need to dominate others. Or to be dominated.

Precisely in the difficulty of fully being ourselves, Teal Organizations see an opportunity. They create practices for people to support each other in their *inner work* while doing the *outer work* of the organization. Every time our fears get triggered is an opportunity to learn and grow into more wholeness, reclaiming aspects of ourselves that we have neglected or pushed into the shadows.

Inviting our humanity to work

Most of the practices to invite us into wholeness are surprisingly simple. And yet, we have grown so used to the narrow, almost aseptic places we call work that these practices can seem out of place in a professional context. Take the following practice of Sounds True, a Colorado-based business that disseminates the teaching of spiritual masters through audio and video recordings, books, and online seminars. In the early days, Tami Simon, the founder and CEO of Sounds True, brought her dog along to the office. When the business expanded and employees were hired, it didn't take long for some of them to ask if they too could bring their dogs to work. Tami couldn't think of a reason to refuse (other than the potential issue that has been taken care of with the rather loosely enforced "three poops and you're out" rule). Today it is not rare for a meeting to take place with two or three dogs lying at people's feet (currently the company has 20 dogs along with its 90 employees). Something special happens within the presence of dogs, colleagues noticed. Animals tend to ground us, to bring out the better sides of our nature. The simple practice of petting a dog tends to soothe us, to reconnect us to our body, and to calm down our spinning minds. And when it's a colleague's dog we pet, or a colleague that pets ours, we subtly build community. People found that the decision to open the company's doors didn't only allow in dogs, but more human life as well.

Something similar has happened at Patagonia, the outdoors apparel maker. At its headquarters in Ventura, California, the company hosts a Child Development Center for employees' children, from the tender age of a few months up to kindergarten age. Children's laughter and chatter are among the regular sounds at the office, coming from the playground outside, from children visiting their parents' desks, or from kids joining parents and colleagues for lunch at the cafeteria. It is not uncommon to see a mother nursing her child during a meeting. Relationships change subtly but profoundly when people see each other not only as colleagues, but also as people capable of the profound love and care young children inspire. When colleagues have just played with a baby over lunch, it's that much harder to fly at each other's throats when they sit in a meeting.[2]

Allowing dogs or children into the workplace is not earth-shattering. And yet in fifteen years of consulting and coaching, I haven't come across any organizations with such practices prior to these. It makes me wonder: how far have we gone in the madness of separation to find this so unusual? Of course, some will argue that animals and children might distract us from work. I have come to believe that something deeper is at play: we have found safety in showing up with just a narrow part of ourselves in the workplace. We might not at first like the thought of having babies or animals in the workplace precisely because it's so difficult, in their presence, not to show a whole different part of ourselves to our colleagues—a part that is deeply loving and caring.

Safe and open working environments

Yet underneath our fears, at the most fundamental level, a part of us aspires to wholeness. It longs to integrate our divided selves and to honor the truth of our soul. Why then is wholeness so hard to achieve and separation so easy to fall into? Showing up whole feels risky. We put out our selfhood for all to see, and expose this most treasured part of ourselves to potential criticism, ridicule, or rejection. Parker Palmer, the educator, writer, and activist, has explored throughout his life what it takes for us to seek and find wholeness in community.

> *What sort of space gives us the best chance to hear soul truth and follow it? … My answer draws on the only metaphor I know that reflects the soul's essence while honoring its mystery: the soul is like a wild animal.*
>
> *Just like a wild animal, the soul is tough, resilient, savvy, resourceful, and self-sufficient: it knows how to survive in hard places. Many of us learn about these qualities in the darkest moments of our lives when the faculties we normally depend upon utterly fail us—the intellect is useless, the emotions dead, the will impotent, and the ego shattered. But sometimes, way back in the thickets of our inner lives, we sense the presence of something that knows how to stay alive and helps us to keep going. That something, I suggest, is the tough and tenacious soul.*
>
> *Yet despite its toughness, the soul is also shy. Just like a wild animal, it seeks safety in the dense underbrush, especially when other people are around. If we want to see a wild animal, we know that the last thing we should do is go crashing through the woods yelling for it to come out. But if we will walk quietly in the woods, sit patiently at the base of a tree, breathe with the earth, and fade into our surroundings, the wild creature we seek might put in an appearance. …*
>
> *Unfortunately, community in our culture too often means a group of people who go crashing through the woods together, scaring the soul away. … Under these conditions, the intellect, emotions, will, and ego may emerge, but not the soul; we scare off all the soulful things, like respectful relationships, goodwill, and hope.*[3]

Crashing through the woods is how we have learned to be together in organizations. All it takes to scare the soul away is to make a sarcastic comment or to roll the eyes in a meeting. If we are to invite all of who we are to show up, including the shy inner voice of the soul, we need to create safe and caring spaces at work. We must learn to discern and be mindful of the subtle ways our words and actions undermine safety and trust in a community of colleagues.

Resources for Human Development (RHD), a Philadelphia-based nonprofit, provides a beautiful example of an organization that has strived, for more than 40 years, to create and maintain safe and open workplaces that invite people into wholeness. RHD was started in 1970 with a $50,000 contract to provide community mental health services in suburban Philadelphia. Today, its 4,600 staff provide services worth $200 million to tens of thousands of people in need through programs in 14 states that operate homes and shelters for the mentally ill, developmentally disabled, drug and alcohol addicted, criminally adjudicated, and homeless. They also operate outpatient mental health centers and serve troubled children in their homes and schools.

> *Showing up whole feels risky. We need spaces where we feel safe if we are to share with others our deeper selfhood, our gifts, our longings, and our concerns.*

RHD, like AES and FAVI, is explicitly founded on a number of basic assumptions about people and work—in the case of RHD, that 1) *all people are of equal human worth,* 2) *people are essentially good unless proven otherwise,* and 3) *there is no single way to manage corporate issues well.* Each of RHD's programs is run by a self-managing team, with an average of 20 and at most 40 to 50 people. Units, as these teams are called within RHD, are encouraged to develop their own sense of purpose, pride, and identity. Within the units, there are no job descriptions. Units are responsible for their entire operation, from defining a strategy to recruiting and purchasing, from budgeting to monitoring results. Central staff at headquarters is kept to a minimum. Specialist staff—for instance, the budget managers that support teams in financial matters or specialists in clinical review—can counsel teams, but the final decision is kept in the unit. At RHD, teams have a team leader (called "Unit Director"). Like team leaders at FAVI, Unit Directors have no power to impose decisions and cannot unilaterally hire or fire anybody.

"Above" the teams, there are no middle managers, but rather hub leaders that support a number of units in the same way that regional coaches at Buurtzorg support teams of nurses. Hub leaders expect to be kept informed of major existing or potential problems; they may advise or help, but the responsibility for resolving problems stays with the unit. Hubs have no business targets and are not responsible for their units' financial results. By design, units offering similar types of services are *not* regrouped within the same hub. One hub leader might support a residential care home for the mentally ill, a shelter for homeless people, and a service for troubled children. Robert Fishman, RHD's founder and CEO, explains the rationale: "Since no one person at the Hub level can know all this detail, the expertise needed to provide services remains decentralized, spread across a range of local managers. In this way, we avoid cookie-cutter uniformity and corporate blandness." It all makes for an incredibly vibrant and entrepreneurial organization. As one employee, Dennis, says:

> *The freedom started from the first day we were hired. Like most RHD employees, we weren't given job descriptions; instead, many of our job responsibilities were self-assigned and self-monitored. There were very few "oughts" or "shoulds." It was simply expected, though not necessarily stated, that we would do something constructive on behalf of others. And if we could be creative as well, it was never discouraged. In fact, it was celebrated. None of us take this for granted. At the drop of a hat we can tell the painful stories of friends who work in very different circumstances.*[4]

RHD is a remarkable success story. It has maintained a yearly growth rate of 30 percent on average since its inception more than 40 years ago. In all that time, while managing close to $2 billion in revenues, with 200 units in the field making autonomous decisions, it has never lost a contract due to fiscal mismanagement. But the numbers only tell part of the story. At the heart of RHD's success is the extraordinary care it provides every day to thousands of people in need. Here is one everyday story, recounted by Bob Fishman, RHD's founder and CEO, that captures what RHD is about:

> *This is the story about one of those "Friday-at-five" calls. The kind that come in when you're ready for the weekend—in this case, July 4th weekend—half out the door, and more than half tempted just to let that phone ring.*
>
> *The call was from a government administrator at wits' end. There was not a single bed available in Connecticut's entire Department of Mental Retardation system, he said, and no one was able to move any mountains before a holiday weekend. He had no idea what to do with a man who had just come into his charge, Rick, who was forty-five, developmentally disabled, in a panic, and without anyone to care for him after the unexpected death of his father. He was waiting in the Emergency Room of the hospital where his father had been having routine surgery. Could RHD-Connecticut do anything, anything at all, to help?*
>
> *No immediate solution presented itself to Paul, the Director of RHD-Connecticut. He was pretty sure, actually, that RHD's beds were full, just as the Department's were. Regardless of the uncertainty, however, regardless of the holiday, regardless of the time, Paul didn't hesitate. "Yes, of course, we will help." He wasn't a top executive, but he knew*

that as a Unit Director at RHD he had the power, as well as the responsibility, to make something happen.

Paul ... recalled that [he] had worked with Rick several years before ... "Rick could become violent and actually hit people or break things," Paul recalls. ... He had a dual diagnosis—he was both developmentally disabled and mentally ill. ... "It was clear that Rick would certainly be a challenge," Paul remembers, "but I thought the staff and the other residents could meet that challenge, especially if they were prepared."

Within a few hours after the phone call from the government, Paul had mobilized a team based at Sunset House, one of our family-like homes. ... The Sunset House team offers round-the-clock staff to serve for developmentally disabled people. On that Friday, Mary, the Sunset House nurse, called Rick's doctors and found a way to transfer his medication prescriptions to Sunset House—no easy task. Tracey, the House Manager, led the Sunset House team in moving quickly to dismantle the site's office and make it into a bedroom. The office was small, too small for the long term: for now it would do. ...

The residents were gathering that evening for a group event so Cassandra, RHD-Connecticut's Assistant Director, took the opportunity to tell them about Rick and his sadness at the death of his father. Cassandra and the residents talked about offering Rick a temporary home in what was the office, and that perhaps someday they could give him a permanent home at Sunset House, if they could renovate the garage. Not everyone was happy about the idea, but one resident after another agreed that it was important to help Rick out. ...

On the very same Friday that Paul got the initial call, Rick made the transition from the hospital to Sunset House. A staff member picked him up at the hospital and when Rick opened the front door, the residents gave him a big welcome. Paul remembers, "Rick grinned as he recognized me, took in all the smiling faces all around him, and cheerfully proclaimed, 'This is my new home.'"

"Sometimes," Paul recalls, "you know when you have done a good thing. And that day we did a really good thing."[5]

Fishman goes on to elaborate how RHD's basic assumptions have created a culture, practices, and decision-making mechanisms that allow small everyday miracles like this one to come about:

The vital interplay of RHD's values and delegation results in the success that is perfectly illustrated in Rick's story. Our first basic assumption, that all people have equal human worth, guided us in offering Rick a respectful and caring response to his desperate need. Our second basic assumption, that people are good unless proven otherwise, allowed our local Unit Director to work with government to solve a problem quickly and without a contract, with the expectation and the trust that we would get paid for it (we did). And our third basic assumption, that there is no single way to handle corporate issues well, gave us the flexibility we needed for everything we did. If we had tried to solve Rick's problem from the central office, we would not have had enough information either about Rick or the local unit to make wise decisions, or to avoid delays while we got up to speed; delays or missteps would have caused further misery to Rick and inconveniences to our governmental customer. Also the local staff group would have felt imposed upon, which is not a productive way to get a job done. …

RHD employees are not any different than the employees of other corporations; empowerment hasn't made people perfect. … What we aspire to do, and what we continue to achieve, however, is to manage status, power, and money according to our basic assumptions.[6]

Self-management is fundamental to RHD's extraordinary care; people need the freedom to decide in the moment how to best meet the needs of the people they care for. But another ingredient is just as important: the safe and open environment RHD has managed to create in the units and throughout the company, which helps people tap into their deepest humanity to bring out their care for others.

It is a challenge for any organization to create an environment where people feel safe to show up whole. It is even more so at RHD, whose very purpose is to deal, day in day out, with people experiencing difficult journeys in life—people who are mentally ill, alcoholic, ex-convicts, developmentally disabled, or homeless. In the midst of this testing environment, where verbal or physical violence can flare up quickly, RHD has distilled over time a beautiful set of practices to foster a safe and open working environment.

Ground rules for a safe environment

Fishman has written a book, together with his wife, about RHD's practices. In the introduction, he traces his calling to create a radically different type of workplace all the way back to his childhood:

Listening to my parents quarrel, and trying to understand why they repeatedly fought, absorbed many a night. This effort and its implications have shaped my thinking and my professional work for the past fifty years.

My parent's arguments always followed the same format: My mother insisted the she was right and that my father was wrong—and the bad one. When their fight reached a certain pitch, my father, a man of few words, angrily stomped out of the apartment, repeatedly demonstrating that he could leave her—and me.

By the time I was eleven, I figured out that neither she nor he was right—or bad. I couldn't side with either one. Later, my attention shifted to how my friends argued, and I realized that their complaints were also mostly trivial. It was the way they fought that was the problem. Without even knowing it, I began to practice peacemaking. … Looking back, I see that this was another step in what would become a lifelong effort to understand human relationships and find a better way to manage conflict. …

None of my teachers in college and graduate school seemed to have a vision of a healthy human relationship. They certainly taught me about relationships, but mostly I found myself studying hostile connections and the variety of ways people tried to find safety in the midst of the wars they created. Most people didn't see any way out. Why? I wondered. …

At work, I was exposed to supervisors who believed that their approaches to work problems were absolutely right. They had no doubt. And in order to make their favored solutions happen they acted like tyrants. It made no sense.

Slowly some answers emerged. I knew I needed to love and be loved—as do we all—and I knew I wanted to lead others in the search for better ways to work together. … RHD was conceived and developed as an experiment. Thirty-six years later, I'm clear that the experiment is about creating healthy workplace communities.[7]

Creating safe workplaces starts with raising everybody's awareness of the words and actions that create or undermine a safe working environment. Unfortunately, as Bob Fishman points out, we weren't taught this process in school. Teal Organizations spend significant time and energy training everybody in a number of ground rules that support healthy and productive collaboration. Several of the organizations in this book end up writing down these ground rules in a document. RHD, for instance, has developed over the years a beautiful and precisely worded *Bill of Rights and Responsibilities for Employees and Consumers.* The first two articles spell out RHD's objective of creating a safe environment and constructively managing conflict and anger. (Later articles deal with topics related to self-management.) The premise is maintained that conflict is inevitable, but that hostile behaviors are not:

This corporation has chosen to operate with several basic assumptions. One of those assumptions is that there are multiple "right" ways or paths we can follow in making decisions, thus there is no one "true" or "absolute" reality. Each person in a situation holds his/her own view of reality, and his/her own perspective about the most effective way to do things. This assumption allows us to recognize that conflict is inevitable and that people will disagree in the workplace. While conflict and difference (or disagreement) are to be expected, explosive or otherwise hostile expressions of anger are not acceptable in RHD.

As a member of the RHD community, it is important to be able to do two things:

- *a) Separate from our own need to be "right" in order to hear and respect others' realities and perspectives: and,*
- *b) Differentiate between thoughts (what's going on inside your head) and behaviors (what you do or say).*[8]

The document goes on to spell out in detail five unacceptable expressions of hostility. The first—*demeaning speech and behavior*—is described in the following terms:

> *Demeaning speech and behavior involves any verbal or nonverbal behavior that someone experiences as undermining of that person's self-esteem and implies that he/she is less than worthy as a human being. Such behaviors include, but are not limited to, name-calling, ridicule, sarcasm, or other actions which "put down" people. Demeaning a person with such physical behaviors as rolling one's eyes when the person speaks or otherwise negating her importance as a member of the community is also unacceptable. Anyone encountering such hostile behavior has the right and responsibility to surface it as an issue.*[9]

Other expressions of hostility—"negative triangulated messages," "threat of abandonment," "disconfirming the other person's reality," and "intimidation/explosion"—are defined in an equally precise manner.

Green Organizations have pioneered values-based cultures that, in one form or another, often include values such as integrity, respect, or openness. The detailed ground rules in Teal Organizations essentially take shared values to the next level. RHD is not an outlier in creating its detailed *Bill of Rights and Responsibilities*. Morning Star has documents called *Organizational Vision, Colleague Principles,* and *Statement of General Business Philosophy*; FAVI has its *fiches,* and Holacracy its *Constitution*. These documents provide a vision for a safe and productive workplace. They give colleagues a vocabulary to discuss healthy relationships, and they draw lines that separate recommended from unacceptable behaviors.

> *Ground rules take shared values to the next level. They spell out the mindsets and behaviors that foster or undermine a safe and healthy work environment.*

Practices to cultivate discussions about values and ground rules

Of course, it takes more than a document to bring values to life. Many organizations in this research have chosen to start right at the beginning: all new recruits are invited, as part of the onboarding, to a training session about the company values and ground rules, which helps to create common references and a common language across the organization.

Companies have found that beyond the initial training, there is a need for dedicated times to discuss the values and the ground rules to keep them alive. It can be done in a hundred ways; here are a few examples:

- *Values Day:* Many organizations hold a yearly company-wide values day where everybody is invited, through playful and/or introspective activities, to revisit the organization's purpose, values, and ground rules and inquire how they, individually and within their teams, live up to them. At RHD, for example, Values Day is a major event, with lots of fun, singing, and dancing. People celebrate and reaffirm their commitment to the company's extraordinary culture.

- *Values meeting:* Every two months, all RHD colleagues are invited to join the *values implementation meeting,* where people can bring up issues they have encountered with values in the workplace or suggest changes to the *Bill of Rights and Responsibilities*. The meeting is well attended. Bob Fishman, RHD's founder, makes a point to be present every time.
- *Annual survey:* Many organizations cultivate discussion about values and ground rules through an annual survey. At AES, for instance, a task force of volunteers devised a new set of questions every year and sent them out to the entire organization. Each unit had the obligation—it was one of the ground rules—to discuss the outcome of the survey, in whatever format it thought would be useful.

Reflective spaces

Wisdom traditions insist on the need for regular silence and reflection to quiet the mind and let truth emerge from a deeper part of ourselves. An increasing number of people pick up contemplative practices—meditation, prayer, yoga, walking in nature—and integrate these into their daily lives. Many organizations researched for this book have set up a quiet room somewhere in the office, and others have put meditation and yoga classes in place. This practice opens up space for individual reflection and mindfulness in the middle of busy days. A number of them go a step further: they also create *collective* moments for self-reflection through practices such as group coaching, team supervision, large-group reflections, and days of silence.

An organization that can show us, perhaps better than any other, how reflective practices can be integrated deeply into everyday life is a German company called Heiligenfeld. It is a fast-growing company with 630 employees running four mental health and rehabilitation hospitals in the center of Germany. It is the brainchild of Dr. Joachim Galuska, a medical doctor and psychotherapist. In the 1980s, he felt that more holistic approaches to therapy were needed to treat patients in mental hospitals; he wanted to add spiritual and transpersonal approaches to classical psychotherapy. He found that none of the existing hospitals he talked to seemed open to his vision. In 1990, he stumbled upon Fritz Lang, an entrepreneur and owner of a historic, if somewhat faded, hotel in Bad Kissingen. Together they decided to transform the hotel into a small 43-bed mental health hospital that would offer a holistic approach to therapy. The success has been overwhelming, with clients traveling in from all over Germany and other parts of Europe. Twenty years later, Heiligenfeld has become a network of hospitals with 600 beds, which most likely will keep expanding.

Dorothea Galuska, Joachim's wife and a therapist herself, shared with me a striking story of a patient treated at Heiligenfeld:

> *One day, I met a new patient who had been previously diagnosed with severe psychosis. The 55-year-old woman was suffering from depression and anxiety. She had never worked in her life and for a long time had been too anxious to leave home. In the discussion, I had a hunch. The woman might well be psychotic, but she seemed to have extraordinary intuitive powers. Could it be that she was anxious because she was overwhelmed by these powers and didn't know what to do with them? My hunch was confirmed at the end of the session. I was pregnant at the time, and the woman suddenly told me, out of the blue, "What a beautiful boy! What a pity he hasn't yet turned to be head-first." She was right on both counts, but how could she know?*
>
> *I recommended to her that she learn to master her psychic powers. She registered in a course with a renowned teacher. We helped her with her depression in the hospital, but the training proved the key to her healing. Today she is transformed. She has a thriving practice where she offers her talents to the world. What used to cripple her with anxiousness now provides her with meaning and income.*[10]

Not every patient's story is that remarkable, of course, but it illustrates what Heiligenfeld is about—a holistic perspective of mental health problems that can open avenues for healing unavailable to more narrow concepts of psychotherapy.

Heiligenfeld is an extraordinary place, and not just for patients; it is also an incredibly vibrant workplace, the recipient of a remarkable range of awards, among them "Best Workplace" in the health care sector in Europe.

Large group reflections

Among the great number of innovative management practices Heiligenfeld has introduced over the years, employees often credit one practice in particular for making the company an outstanding workplace. Every Tuesday morning, 350 employees come together for an hour and a quarter to engage in joint reflection. (Ideally, all employees would participate, but some colleagues need to stay with patients; the number of participants is also currently limited by the size of the largest available meeting room on the premises.)[11]

Every week, a new topic that is relevant at the moment and conducive to self-reflection is put on the agenda. Recent meetings have reflected on subjects as diverse as conflict resolution, dealing with failure, company values, interpersonal communication, bureaucracy, IT innovations, risk management, personal health, and mindfulness.

The meeting always kicks off with a short presentation to frame the subject matter. But the heart of the meeting happens in small groups engaged in self-reflection. Let's take the example of the topic "dealing with failure" to illustrate how this event plays out at Heiligenfeld. The short plenary presentation introduces ways to deal gracefully with failure—how new possibilities open up when we stop being judgmental about our failures; how from a higher place of consciousness we can view failure as life's invitation to expand our skills and awareness and grow into more of who we are.

After this short introduction, people shuffle their chairs around to create groups of six to 10 people. In the groups, people are asked to reflect on the topic—how they deal with failure in their lives, at work and at home, individually and collectively. Every group elects a facilitator who enforces a few ground rules to create a space where it's safe to explore, to be authentic and vulnerable. In the confines of the small group, helped by their colleagues' listening, people dare to dig deep and gain new insights about themselves and others. At some point, a microphone goes around the room and people who feel inclined to do so share what came up for them in the discussion. There is no scripted outcome to these meetings, no expected end product; everyone comes out of the meeting with his or her own personal learning. Often, collective insights emerge, as well as decisions and initiatives that are then carried out when people go back to work.

It's a time-consuming practice for sure—75 minutes every week for more than half of the company. But people at Heiligenfeld say the benefits far outweigh the costs. These large group meetings are like a company-wide training program on steroids; the whole organization grows its way through one topic after another, week after week (so much so that the company is about to shift to a biweekly rhythm—there simply aren't that many hot topics popping up anymore).

The common experience also fosters community and a common language beyond what can be achieved by any other practice I know of. Colleagues are exposed repeatedly every week to a space made safe by ground rules that invites them to truly be themselves. They learn to see each other in the light of their deep humanity, in the beauty of their strengths and vulnerability. The trust, empathy, and compassion that build up in the meeting expand well beyond the confines of the meeting room. These feelings start to permeate the whole organization. To approving chuckles in the room, an employee of Heiligenfeld stood up at the end of one of these Tuesday meetings and said, "You know, I wish I could have more Heiligenfeld at home, too!"

Team supervision

Working in teams, which is what most people do in self-managing organizations, invariably brings up tensions. We run into colleagues with different styles, preferences, and belief systems. We can choose, as most organizations do, to sweep the tensions under the rug. Or we can have the courage to confront them so as to grow individually and collectively. Heiligenfeld has developed a simple practice of team supervision. The company works with four external coaches who each have their domain of expertise (relationships, organizational development, system thinking, leadership). There are a number of time slots with the coaches every month that teams can sign up for. The recommendation is for every team to hold at least one session a year; on average teams hold two to four. In the discussion, with the help of the outside supervisor, colleagues can explore what a tension reveals about themselves and how they can grow to resolve it.

Peer coaching

Team supervision helps to deal with an issue that affects the whole team. Peer coaching uses the power of the team to help one specific team member work through an individual issue. At Buurtzorg, all nurses are trained in "Intervisie," a peer-coaching technique that originated in the Netherlands. A nurse that wrestles with a certain question can ask colleagues on her team to help her sort it out in a group coaching session. *How should she deal with a client that refuses to take life-saving medication? How can she help an elderly patient accept help from his children? How to say no to clients to protect herself from burnout?* Often, when a nurse struggles with one of these matters, it is because the question brings up a broader personal issue she hasn't worked through. In these cases, a peer coaching session can help. Some Buurtzorg teams allot an hour for peer coaching every month; other teams convene when a team member requests it.

"Intervisie," the process used at Buurtzorg, follows a strict format and ground rules to prevent the group from administering the all-too-common medicine of advice, admonitions, or reassurance. During most of the process, team members can ask only open-ended questions; they become fellow travelers into the mystery of the issue the person is dealing with. A safe space is created that invites deep listening, authenticity, and vulnerability—the necessary ingredients for inner truth to emerge. The goal is for the nurse to see the problem in a new light and discover her own solutions. It is at once a simple and beautiful process. Being respectfully and compassionately "held" by a group is for many people a new and unforgettable experience.[12]

Individual coaching

Offering individual coaching at certain stages of people's careers has become standard practice in many organizations today. Most often, it is reserved for senior leaders, stars on their way up, or underperformers on their way out. Not surprisingly, Teal Organizations expand coaching to all colleagues, whatever their role in the organization. RHD's coaching program goes one step further: it offers 10 free counseling sessions for employees and/or their families every year. No one else in the organization needs to be informed about the theme of the coaching and the theme must not be a professional topic. The program is built on the trust that if an employee is seeking support from an external coach, the topic must be important enough to be worth the money the company pays for it.

Silence

If we want to listen to the wisdom and truth of our souls, we need to find moments to slow down and honor silence in the middle of the noise and buzz of the work place. At Sounds True, a bell rings every day at 8:30 a.m. Employees can join a 15-minute group meditation or simply sit in silence at their desk for those minutes. At Heiligenfeld all new employees—therapists and cleaning staff alike—are taught to meditate as part of their onboarding. All mental-health patients are invited to learn to meditate too. There are several fixed group meditation sessions every week: some for employees only, others where patients are invited to join in too.

Four times a year, Heiligenfeld organizes a "mindfulness day"—a day that patients and staff spend in silence. Patients are invited to remain entirely silent (they wear a tag with the word "silence" to remind each other), while the staff speaks only when needed, in whispers (staff wear a tag with the word "mindfulness"). There are no talking therapy sessions that day. Instead, other forms of therapy take place—walks in the woods, painting, or creative activities, for instance. Information sessions help patients prepare for the day, and there are "emergency talking places" for patients who feel overwhelmed by the silence. "The majority of patients love the experience and many ask us to organize this more often," says Dorothea Galuska. "Roughly a third of the patients are confronted with some of their shadows and find the experience difficult. 'If silence was hard for you, you got lucky,' I tell them. 'People who've enjoyed it had a good day. But you've now got great material for therapy.'" It's also a day that employees look forward to. Collaborating in silence brings a special quality to relationships between colleagues. It requires a new level of mindfulness, listening not to what colleagues say, but to their presence, emotions, and intentions.

> *Silence in community is feared for the exact reason that makes this practice so powerful: without words to fill the space, we create an opening for deeper voices to emerge.*

Storytelling

In self-managing organizations as well as hierarchical ones, trust is the secret sauce of productive and joyful collaboration. But it's hard for trust to flourish when everyone is hiding, to some degree, behind a professional mask. We don't just lose productivity; at a deeper level, our humanity feels cheated by the shallow relationships we have when we don't engage with each other at levels that truly matter.

If we want workplaces of trust, if we hope for deep, rich, and meaningful relationships, we have to reveal more of who we are. It has become fashionable in many companies, when teams don't collaborate well, to call for a team-building event. Going bowling together can be a fun break from work, but such activities are generally "more of the same": they keep to the surface and don't really foster trust or community at any deep level. These events lack the essential element we have used to build community and create shared narratives since the dawn of time: the practice of storytelling. We have lost track of the power of stories to bring us together, and in the process, we have let communal relations dwindle and erode. We need to recover the power of storytelling, as author Parker Palmer tells us:

> *The more you know about another person's journey, the less possible it is to distrust or dislike that person. Want to know how to build relational trust? Learn more about each other. Learn it through simple questions that can be tucked into the doing of work, creating workplaces that not only employ people but honor the soul in the process.*
>
> *This is how to weave a fabric of communal relationships that has resilience in times of crisis, resourcefulness in times of need. It's a fabric that must be woven before the need or the crisis arrives, when it's too late for community to emerge in the stress of the moment. So let's make sure, in our language and in our practice, that we're building collegial communities around persons as well as tasks, around souls as well as roles.*[13]

Not surprisingly, Parker Palmer's Center for Courage & Renewal (CC&R) has explored how to integrate storytelling into organizational life. The nonprofit center creates soulful retreats to help teachers, doctors, clergy, and business leaders reconnect with their vocation and reunite *role and soul*.[14] It is a small organization—around 10 staff supporting a network of 200 trained facilitators who have hosted retreats for more than 40,000 teachers and other professionals during the last 10 years.

The center uses simple practices to weave storytelling into the life of the organization. For example, at a staff retreat, a question might find its way into the program that everyone gets two or three minutes to answer (but is always free to take a pass on). "Tell us about an elder who has been important in your life." "Tell us about the first dollar you ever earned." The practice is simple enough, and yet it allows people to lift a veil and share with colleagues a defining moment that has shaped them on their journey to selfhood.

A staff retreat is a natural occasion for storytelling. The recruitment of a new colleague is another one. The CC&R welcomes new personnel in a special meeting. Each existing team member brings an object that symbolizes a wish for the new colleague. In turn, they present the object and share their wish. The practice is a wonderful way to celebrate the newcomer and make him or her feel welcome. But in many ways, it serves existing team members as much as the newcomer, as they too get to know each other at a deeper level. Each wish is a story that reveals what the storyteller cherishes in the workplace and in their relationships with colleagues.

There is a similar practice at the CC&R for when a person leaves the organization. It's customary for team members to join together for a meal with the departing colleague. Everybody comes prepared with a personal story about that person's time with the organization. Of course, the stories are meant to celebrate the person who is leaving. But again, they reveal just as much about the storyteller—what he cherishes in other people, what touches him, what he prizes in relationships at work.

ESBZ, the grade 7-12 school in Berlin, has an extraordinary trust and community-building practice based around storytelling: the "praise meeting." Every Friday afternoon, the entire school—students, teachers, and staff—comes together for an hour in a large hall. They always start by singing a song together, to settle into community. All the rest of the time together is unscripted. There is an open microphone on stage, with a simple rule: we are here to praise and thank each other. For the next 50 minutes, students and teachers who feel called to do so stand up, walk up on stage, take the microphone, and praise or thank another student or teacher for something they did or said earlier in the week; then they go sit down again and someone else takes the stage. Every person at the microphone shares what is essentially a miniature story that reveals something about two people—the storyteller and the person being praised or thanked—in their struggles and in their glories.

> *Relationships change us, reveal us, evoke more from us. Only when we join with others do our gifts become visible, even to ourselves.*
>
> M. Wheatley & M. Kellner-Rogers

The storytelling erases boundaries between students and teachers. It's part of the human condition that everyone at some point feels down, confused, or stuck, and in need of help. And everyone has the gift of empathy, of finding ways to offer support, comfort, and friendship. It takes courage to stand up and praise others publicly, but in the school it has become standard practice. Students don't shy away from stories that are funny, touching, and heartfelt. Students and teachers credit this weekly session as the defining practice for the school's extraordinary spirit of learning, collaboration, and maturity.

Ozvision, a 40-person Japanese Internet company that has experimented a good deal with innovative management approaches, has two interesting practices involving storytelling. Every morning, people get together in their teams for a quick meeting called "good or new," a sort of check-in for the day. Within each team, a doll is passed around, like a talking stick, and whoever has the doll can share either something *new* (news from something they are working on, noteworthy news they might have read in the paper when commuting, or news from their private lives) or something *good,* simply some moving story they want their colleagues to know about, work-related or not. It's a beautiful practice that starts the day with a brief and joyful moment, a sort of ritual that says, *"Let's acknowledge that we are all here, as colleagues and as human beings."*

Ozvision's second practice of storytelling aims to foster a spirit of gratitude in the organization. Each employee can take one extra day off each year, called a "day of thanking." The employee receives $200 in cash from company funds that she can spend in any way she wants to thank someone special during that day. It can be a colleague, but it can also be a parent, a friend, a neighbor, or a long-lost but not forgotten primary school teacher. The only rule is that once she returns to work, she must share the story of what she gave and to whom and how the gift was received. Imagine what it's like to work at Ozvision. The company has 40 employees, so on average, colleagues there hear three or four such stories every month, often deeply personal stories where colleagues are willing to share three meaningful moments in their lives—when the seed for gratitude was planted, what they had come up with to thank the person, and how their gift and "thank you" were received.

Storytelling doesn't always rely only on words, as two rituals from Sounds True illustrate. Five years ago, a colleague there took it upon herself to organize an "Art Salon" on a Friday afternoon. Everyone was invited to share some artistic passion with his or her colleagues. Walls throughout the office were filled with photographs and paintings. A small stage was erected for people to perform. Some colleagues chose to sing (some songs composed about life in the company were particular hits), others juggled or danced tango. People enjoyed themselves so much that the salon has turned into an annual event. Tami Simon, the company founder, wasn't involved in setting up the first salon, but she sees that it has become an important element in the company culture:

> *I realized these events are saying to people, "You get to be a whole person. This part of you, it may not fit to do it as part of your job every day. ... But the fact that you can now juggle five balls is actually cool. And on a Friday afternoon, we want to sit back and have a glass of wine and watch you do this and acknowledge this part of you." That is part of what I think makes people feel [that] the wholeness of who they are is actually welcome. Because we do welcome it, we want to see it.*[15]

Another ritual at Sounds True is "Pajama Day." For reasons by now half forgotten, someone suggested they celebrate spring on a special note: everyone who wanted to join would share breakfast at the office ... in pajamas. The handful that showed up had so much fun during breakfast that they decided to keep their pajamas on at work the rest of the day. Since then, the event has taken place every year. Now 90 percent of the employees show up in pajamas, and a prize is given for the best outfit. (This year, a matching set of pajamas for master and dog shared the prize with a man who wore curlers in his hair along with a "short silky thing" that was not further explained to me.) It has become an event people look forward to and prepare for long in advance. In its own quirky way, "Pajama Day" is a storytelling event—every pair of pajamas is a story waiting to reveal something about the person who is wearing it: *What made you choose that outfit?* Holding up a professional mask at work is decidedly more difficult when everyone strolls around in funny sleepwear.

I find it interesting that neither the Art Salon nor Pajama Day were introduced by someone with a human resources role or by the CEO. In an atmosphere where people feel safe enough to be themselves, it seems that rituals such as these emerge spontaneously, because we all have a longing, deep inside, to be heard and seen in all of our humanity, the funny and the quirky as much as the serious and the responsible, and to create human connection from all these places.

Meetings

Meetings can bring out the best and the worst of human nature. In the best of cases, they can be places where the presence of others helps us listen in to our authenticity and voice what we really care about (what Parker Palmer calls "hearing each other into speech"). Unfortunately, more often than not, meetings in companies turn into playfields for the egos that push the souls into hiding. Nobody likes losing an argument in public or seeing his point of view dismissed in a meeting with colleagues. To feel safe, some people seek to dominate the proceedings and others withdraw.

Self-managing organizations have far fewer meetings, as we discussed in the previous chapters, and the absence of a boss takes some of the fears out of the room. But a group of peers can go "crashing through the woods" just as well. For that reason, almost all organizations researched for this book have instituted specific meeting practices to help participants keep their egos in check and interact with each other from a place of wholeness. Some are very simple, while others much more elaborate. At Sounds True, every meeting starts with a minute of silence (if you forgive the occasional sound of a dog curling up under the table) to help people ground themselves in the moment. Several of the companies in this research start meetings with a round of check-in and finish with a round of check-out. At check-in, participants are invited to share how they feel in the moment, as they enter the meeting. The practice brings participants to listen within, to reconnect with their body and sensations, and to grow the capacity for awareness in the moment. Naming an emotion is often all it takes to leave it behind and not carry it over into the meeting. It also allows participants to know where others are at. When needed, this practice helps clear the air. A participant might say, for instance, "I'm feeling tense, because I'm still puzzled by your reaction, Peter, to my email. I think we need to talk things out after this meeting." The round of check-out, at the end of the meeting, allows acknowledgement of the unspoken emotions in the room—the gratitude, excitement, ambition, frustration, or concerns that the meeting brought out. The practice encourages a culture of direct feedback and truth telling about the quality of the team's interactions.

At the Center for Courage & Renewal, meetings start with a short reading that one person prepared. After a few moments of silence, participants share thoughts the reading has sparked (no one is required to speak, and there is no going around the table, which can be another subtle form of crashing through the woods). Meetings often end with a moment of silence and time for closing reflections.

FAVI, for many years, had the practice of starting every meeting with all participants sharing a brief story of someone they had recently thanked or congratulated. The practice had a beautiful effect on the meeting: it created a mood of possibility, gratitude, celebration, and trust in other people's goodness and talents. Focusing on others and their accomplishments can also help people to shift their concern away from self-centered goals they might have come into the meeting with ("I need to get X out of the meeting") and reconnect with the broader needs of the organization. After a few years, this practice started feeling staid to people at FAVI, and was dropped. It might show up again, perhaps in another form; these practices must feel fresh and meaningful, not formal and staid.

FAVI has kept another interesting practice around meetings. All upcoming meetings are listed on the intranet so that anybody can invite himself or herself into any meeting to share a concern or an idea. Everyone can be in the know of what happens around the company, so no one feels excluded.

Heiligenfeld uses a combination of the previous practices, and adds a twist. Every meeting starts in one of three ways: a minute of silence; a minute of silence and a reading; or a minute of silence and a joke. The meeting moves forward with a ritual question: "Who is going to ring the bell today?" The volunteer takes possession of a pair of tingsha bells, two small hand cymbals that can make a beautiful, crystal-like sound. Whenever the person feels that ground rules are not being respected, or that the meeting is serving egos more than purpose, she can make the cymbals sing. The rule is that no one can speak until the last sound of the cymbal has died out—which takes a surprisingly long time. During the silence, participants are to reflect on the question: "Am I in service to the topic we are discussing and to the organization?" Colleagues are now so used to this practice that simply reaching out to the cymbals is all it takes to get a meeting back on track. (Reflecting on this practice, I realized that in many executive meetings in traditional corporations I've been invited to join over the years, people were speaking *only* from their ego. Had they used this practice, the only sound in the meeting would have come from the tingsha bells!)

Silence, a reading, check-in and check-out, praise, open invitation, hand cymbals—these are simple practices to keep egos in check and make meetings more productive. For meetings that promise to be particularly touchy, an external facilitator might be called in to join the group. RHD has a group of central facilitators that units can always draw upon; Buurtzorg teams can call in their regional coach; and the school in Berlin partners with outside facilitators that the mini-schools or the student council can call in when needed.

Some organizations go a step further: for certain meetings, they have adopted formal decision-making practices (see page 67 for an example from Buurtzorg and page 119 for an example from Holacracy). These mechanisms ensure that everybody's voice is heard and that no one can dominate the proceedings. Practical, workable decisions can be made quickly and efficiently even for touchy, complex subjects; cutting through the threat of endless discussions in pursuit of consensus. Holacracy, in particular, has refined these practices to a wonderful degree. As a side-benefit, Brian Robertson notes, meetings have become powerful settings for personal growth.

> *All of the meeting structures [in Holacracy] are designed to shine a light on our stuff, our projections, our ego … to make it all just visible, clear and transparent, not judge it but let it naturally dissolve.*
>
> *This is also one of the hard things about Holacracy. My experience is: people love Holacracy when it prevents somebody else's stuff, their ego, their frustrations, their fear, from jumping in and dominating the organization, from derailing the natural process of working together towards a purpose. Everyone loves Holacracy when it stops that process for someone else and hates it when it does it to them (Robertson laughs), and this is certainly my experience of living in it. … It holds up a mirror to me and shines a light on my own attachments, to my own stuff.*[16]

Because the discussion and decision-making mechanisms prevent people from bringing in their personal "stuff" into the meeting, they help people become aware of how often such stuff comes up in meetings.

Managing conflict

In most organizations, we have too much conflict sparked by the ego and too little conflict sparked by the soul. The soul's claims can be demanding: if we choose to listen, we often find it asks us to speak a truth that others might not like to hear. Deep inside, something in us hurts when we acknowledge how the organizations we work for harm our planet; how the schools in which we teach damage the children; how hospitals and retirement homes objectify patients and old people; how the farms that feed us mistreat animals and the earth. To bring about better organizations, we need to risk speaking the truth of our soul and learn to navigate the conflicts that might ensue.

The soul also calls us to speak out over more everyday matters, when our selfhood is at stake. It's easy in our relationships with colleagues to fall prey to our desire to please or to impress, to be liked, or to dominate. We easily intrude on others or let them intrude on us. Our soul knows the right boundaries, and sometimes it tells us we need conflict to set them in the right place. Without conflict, we can be over-accommodating or over-protective, and in both cases, we stop being true to ourselves when interacting with colleagues.

Too often we fear conflict. We have become so wary of conflicts of the ego that we neglect to engage in conflicts of the soul.

This research has revealed three types of practices Teal Organizations can put in place to help us bring up and deal with necessary conflicts in the workplace. The first type of practice around conflict management helps people bring tensions to the surface. It can be hard for someone to stand up to a colleague and say, "We need to talk." Some organizations create a space that helps lingering conflict among colleagues to surface. Here are some examples:

- At ESBZ, the school in Berlin, every class gets together at a fixed time each week to discuss and deal with tensions in the group. The meeting is facilitated by a student who enforces a number of ground rules that keep the discussion safe.
- At Heiligenfeld, once a year colleagues in every team rate the quality of their interaction with other teams. The result is a company-wide "heat map" that reveals which teams should have a conversation to improve their collaboration.
- RHD holds a bi-monthly "isms in the workplace meeting." Anyone feeling that the organization should pay attention to a specific form or occurrence of racism, sexism, or any other "-ism" can join the meeting. Of course, an act inspired by blatant racism should be confronted directly on the spot. The meeting is meant for more subtle forms of -ism. What if you notice that the organization as a whole tends to hire disproportionately more white than black people, or that women generally don't step into certain roles? There

is no obvious party to confront; everyone is called to find a solution. The "-isms meeting" gives time and space for introspection: where might we fall prey to our collective and unconscious prejudices? What should we do about it?

We have discussed the second type of practice in the previous chapter: spelling out a well-defined and thorough conflict resolution process (see page 112). Such a process is needed in self-managing organizations for peers to settle issues when there is no boss to act as referee. Having a clear process that everyone knows about also helps people raise issues. It's easier to ask someone to discuss a disagreement when we know there is a well-paved avenue that will get us unharmed to the other side.

A community is a place that can fight gracefully.
M. Scott Peck

But even that might not be enough. Morning Star says that conflict avoidance remains their major organizational issue. Making that first move to confront someone is hard. Some organizations, therefore, go one step further and train all their colleagues in interpersonal skills to enable them to deal gracefully with conflict. At ESBZ, all teachers are trained in Nonviolent Communication, and so are the students. At Sounds True, all colleagues have the opportunity to learn a simple three-step process for difficult conversation:

- Step 1: Here is how I feel.
- Step 2: Here is what I need.
- Step 3: What do you need?

The process has become so key to managing interpersonal dynamics at Sounds True that people *have* to engage with it, as Tami Simon explains:

> *When we first introduced this at the company, we had a COO that told me, "I don't want to talk with other people about how I'm feeling. That's not why you hired me. You hired me to run your operations, Tami. My wife has been trying to get me talking about my feelings for years unsuccessfully. Now I come into work and you are trying to get me to talk about my feelings?" I told him, "We are not going to be able to move forward emotionally, together as a group, if you can't talk about your feelings. You have to commit to this process." He ended up leaving the company. People have to be okay with having a conversation about how they are feeling, what they need, and listening to what the other person needs.*[17]

Wholeness sometimes calls for conflict. Organizations researched for this book demonstrate that conflict doesn't need to be bitter. Certain practices help people feel safe in raising issues and engaging in the ensuing discussion in ways that respect their own and other people's selfhood.

Buildings and status

We can learn much about an organization from simply looking at its office space. Churchill once said, "We shape our buildings, and thereafter they shape us." This is true of office and factory spaces, too—they subtly shape our thinking and behavior. Imagine the following situation: you've been appointed as CEO of a large organization. You have inherited from your predecessor a spacious, mahogany-paneled executive office that you access through a private elevator straight from your reserved parking space. Others meanwhile toil away in crammed cubicles. Unless you were born with an endless supply of humility, at some point the prestige of the job will become part of your identity. Probably unconsciously, you will start to rationalize the status difference by embracing the thought that somehow you deserve the corner office. At some level, you must be worth more than others. People might not always like it, but you are right to call the shots when needed.

Now imagine the luxurious corner office never existed, and that you, the CEO, simply work in a cubicle of your own, right next to your colleagues. How would that change your thinking, your relationships, your leadership style? It would certainly help you stay humble and connected and keep your ego in check.

The Teal Organizations in this research have formidable founders or CEOs—it takes inspired and courageous leadership to build organizations that are ahead of their time. But almost all of them have consciously decided to abandon status markers in and around the office. There are no fancy corner offices and no reserved parking spaces for executives. RHD's Bob Fishman talks about the bewilderment this can cause to first-time visitors coming to see him:

> *When people come to see the CEO—me—they often ask for the executive suite. "Really," the receptionist insists, "there is no executive suite. He sits right there by the window. And when he wants a private meeting space, he signs up for it like everyone else." And I've grown used to the visitors' well-meant, but unnecessary commiseration. "How can you do without the quiet? The privacy? I could never work that way!"*[18]

At FAVI, Jean-François Zobrist mischievously reversed status symbols to make a point when he set the revolution in motion: after refurbishment, the nicest toilets in the factory are now reserved for clients. Just somewhat less luxurious, but still worthy of a four-star hotel, are the toilets at the shop floor level. In comparison, the toilets closest to the offices of the engineers and white-collar workers are merely clean and functional.

Of course, it is not only status symbols that influence our thinking and behavior. The materials and design features typically used in office spaces might be easy to clean and maintain, but they are also bland and soulless. I don't know of any person who would decorate his home to look like the offices we work in. Most places of work insidiously signal that we are in a place somehow removed from normal life, and they call us to behave differently than we would in other environments. Does it need to be that way? Why don't we strive for offices that celebrate life, that are warm and full of textures, cherished objects, and comfortable sofas? The spaces we work in could give us a little help with bringing more of ourselves into the office.

Several organizations in this research have done precisely that. Sounds True doesn't only invite dogs into the office (see page 146). It has also installed a kitchen with a stove where colleagues can cook and share a meal over lunch. Since the dawn of time, we have evoked community by cooking and eating together. Tami Simon, the founder of Sounds True, talks about the surprise of the architect who was asked to plan for a stove. "Businesses have microwaves, not stoves," he told her. The absence of real kitchens in our organizations is a powerful revealer of how we think about our workplaces. They are transient and somewhat lifeless places, where we rent out our labor for a few hours, but not places we invest in, in the way we invest in our homes.

It doesn't need to be that way. At Buurtzorg, nurses are encouraged to decorate their small community offices to make them their own—there is no attempt at uniform branding across its hundreds of offices in the Netherlands. At RHD, units often lovingly decorate the residences and shelters that serve as both offices and homes for the people RHD welcomes. Again, no corporate guidelines, no common branding.

With the help of parents and students, ESBZ in Berlin has transformed the decrepit prefabricated building it inherited from the communist era. Classrooms are full of plants, there are benches close to the windows, cushions in the corners, and carpets on the floor. At FAVI, operators have decorated the shop floor with posters, plants, and aquariums. Each team has chosen a color and repainted machines in their area to make it feel homey. FAVI is still a noisy and greasy factory, but one that people have vested with some of their identity.

Nature is a great healer of the soul. When we are immersed in nature, we tend to slow down and find a deeper connection with ourselves and the world around us. It's no accident that monasteries in Eastern and Western traditions have often sought isolation in the middle of nature, or that today's corporate off-sites seek out places in nature to mark a break from work. For the same reason, some organizations in this research have tried to bring nature back into the workplace. All four of Sun Hydraulic's factories are located next to a lake. There are big decks where people can work, meet, think, or eat overlooking the water. I held more than one discussion on the decks while researching for this book, and there is no doubt to me that the peaceful presence of nature helped me ground my presence and the discussions I had at a deeper level. Sun Hydraulics has also brought nature *into* the building. There are thousands of green plants hanging everywhere from the factory ceiling, an unusual sight in a manufacturing environment. The joke at Sun is that the only person with a job title printed on her business card is the "plant manager"—the full-time employee looking after the plants.

When Sounds True was planning a new office building, the architects came to show the drawing to the employees. One woman asked if the windows could open. The architects said no: windows don't open in corporate buildings because that would interfere with centralized temperature control, and because windows that open are more expensive. Despite the tight budget, the architects were overruled and plans were changed. On a deeper level, the matter of windows opening or not is revealing about our relationship at work with nature and with ourselves. How far have we taken the madness of control when we seal ourselves off from even a breath of fresh air?

Environmental and social concerns

Nature has the ability to call forth wholeness in us. This also works in the other direction: when we feel whole within ourselves we can't help but feel a sense of connection to everything that surrounds us. The damage we do to the environment becomes more than an intellectual concern; we feel the pain and sorrow of nature's suffering within ourselves. The same holds true for social concerns: when we come from a place of wholeness, we feel compelled to do our share to heal our broken relationship with life in all its forms.

> *As long as Nature is seen as something outside ourselves, frontiered and foreign, separate, it is lost both to us and in us.*
>
> Sir Crispin Tickell

The organizations in this research have not yet reached the ultimate goal of zero waste, zero toxicity, and zero impact on ecosystems, but many have taken significant steps in that direction. AES, for instance, started planting millions of trees in the 1990s to offset the carbon footprint from its coal-fired plants, at a time when global warming was not yet center stage.

It's not so much in *what* they do, but in *how* they do it, that Teal Organizations have a different approach to dealing with their environmental and social impact. They look at the matter from a different angle. Instead of asking the question *What will it cost?* they start with the deeper, more personal question: *What is the right thing to do?* Only then follows the question, *How can we do it in financially acceptable ways?* Of course, not everything is possible, and trade-offs need to be made. But from an Evolutionary-Teal perspective, it all starts with inner rightness. Here is how AES expressed it in a public filing with the U.S. Securities and Exchange Commission when it offered stock to the public:

> *An important element of AES is its commitment to four major "shared" values [note: one of which is Social Responsibility, which triggered AES' decision to plant trees]. If the company perceives a conflict between these values and profits, it will try to adhere to its values—even if doing so might result in diminished profits or foregone opportunities. Moreover, the Company seeks to adhere to these values not as a means to achieve economic success, but because adherence is a worthwhile goal in and of itself.*

Often, the impact of doing what's right from an environmental or social point of view can't be fully assessed up front. How much will it *really* cost? What return, if any, could it generate? In many cases, the decision involves a leap of faith. A company particularly familiar with making such calls is Patagonia, the outdoor clothing designer. For years, it has been pushing the boundaries, venturing into uncharted territory to reduce its environmental footprint, sometimes in ways that seem small, sometimes truly significant, but always involving a risk to the bottom line. Here is one example as told by Yvon Chouinard, Patagonia's founder:

> *In the mid-nineties, we decided to change the packaging of our thermal underwear. We were using a thick, wraparound cardboard header inside a heavy Ziploc plastic bag. To get away from this packaging for the heavier-weight expedition underwear, we decided to go without any packaging at all and hang them up like regular clothing. As for the underwear made of lighter-weight material, we just rolled them up and put a rubber band around them. We were warned to be prepared for a 30 percent cut in sales because we were competing with companies that were extremely competitive with their packaging. One competitor, for example, put its product out in adorable sealed tin cans. We did it anyway because it was the right thing to do. The first year this practice kept twelve tons of material from being shipped around the world and eventually being discarded and duped into landfills, and it saved the company $150,000 in unnecessary packaging.*
>
> *It also brought us a 25 percent increase in thermal underwear sales. Since they weren't hidden away in a package and had to be displayed like the regular clothing, people could feel the material and appreciate the quality. And since they were displayed like the other clothes, we were forced to make our underwear look like regular clothing, to the point that now most Capilene underwear tops can be worn as a regular shirt, fulfilling our goal of making clothes that are multifunctional.*[19]

Looking back, Chouinard found that more often than not in Patagonia's history, risky bets have turned out to be profitable in the end. Most strikingly, Patagonia resolved in the summer of 1994 to replace all conventionally grown cotton with organic cotton by spring of 1996—a decision with an insanely fast timeline and wide-reaching implications. The raw material cost three times more, and the cotton product line was reduced from 91 styles to 66. It was a crazy risk. And yet Patagonia felt there was no alternative when it realized the full extent of the damage the cotton industry was doing to the world: cotton fields that covered only three percent of the world's farmland were responsible for 10 percent of the worldwide use of pesticide and 25 percent of the use of insecticides. Against all expectations, Patagonia's organic cotton program turned out to be financially beneficial. More importantly, it has convinced others in the industry to follow suit.

Many wisdom traditions affirm that when we act from deep integrity and align with what we feel called to do, the universe conspires to support us. Perhaps this helps to explain how Patagonia's bets so often work out. When acting from the Achievement-Orange paradigm, we often try to not get involved personally in difficult decisions; we try to get our selfhood out of the line of fire by staying scrupulously objective. We hope to settle difficult trade-offs by quantifying every conceivable aspect of future scenarios—and take the plunge only when the numbers show that the benefits outweigh the costs. To act from wholeness calls for more than rational decision-making alone; we must learn to combine the power of the rational mind with the wisdom of intuition and integrity—and dare to take the leap.

Wisdom traditions affirm that when we act from deep integrity, the universe conspires to support us.

Incidentally, none of the organizations researched for this book have developed accounting systems with multiple bottom lines—a finding that some people might find surprising. There is a school of thought that suggests we need accounting systems that track not just profit but also a firm's impact on people and the planet; how else could managers make trade-offs between these elements? The argument sounds reasonable, so how come none of the pioneer Teal Organizations use multiple-bottom-line accounting systems? I think the following is at play: multiple bottom lines may help to overcome the fixation on profits alone, but the concept is still rooted in Orange thinking, where decisions are informed only by quantitative trade-offs, by weighing costs and benefits. From an Evolutionary-Teal perspective, not everything needs to be quantified to discern a right course of action. Of course, there are valuable insights to be gained from measuring how a company's actions impact the environment and society (and for that reason, multiple bottom lines may well become a standard way of reporting in the future). But these pioneers seem to believe that, more than advanced accounting systems, we need integrity and wholeness to transcend the primacy of profits and heal our relationship with the world.

There is a second difference in the way Teal Organizations approach environmental and social practices, which stems from self-management. As employees, we may have genuine concerns about the environment and the communities we work in, but in traditional organizations, our concerns rarely translate into corporate actions. Too often we self-censor, too often we fail to fight for our concerns, for fear of being branded a dreamer, an activist, or a troublemaker. For that reason, environmental and social initiatives rarely bubble up from inside the organization; they almost always come mandated top-down. This is not to diminish the value of bold environmental targets set in recent years by CEOs of companies like Walmart or GE. But the truth is that the vast majority of people in these organizations—all the managers and front-line employees—don't feel empowered to act on their environmental concerns. This comes at a great cost to us and to the world. When it feels unsafe to speak our truth, we shut down our inner voice, we lose personal integrity, and we fail to set in motion changes the world is crying out for.

In Teal Organizations, power is decentralized; therefore, environmental and social initiatives can be initiated by passionate people joining forces from any place in the organization. AES's initiative to plant millions of trees to offset carbon emissions from its plants wasn't an idea championed by the CEO or someone at headquarters. An employee in a plant in Los Angeles was the one who pushed the idea. Of course, initially there was no budget for such expenses. Using the advice process, she peddled her idea with the persons she thought needed to be involved and tested with them the amount of money she thought the company should put into trees.

Another beautiful example comes from Patagonia. When the company moved its warehouse from Ventura, California, to Reno, Nevada, many colleagues decided to move too. They realized that Nevada has lots of wild country and federal land, but very little of it was designated and protected wilderness. Four employees took the initiative to make an inventory of land and decide which areas would most easily qualify. They talked to the leadership and said, "Look, if you continue paying our salaries and give us a desk, we think we'll have a wilderness bill within a couple of years." They built a broad coalition, went to Washington, and lobbied. As a result, 1.2 million acres of wilderness were protected for about 10 cents an acre. Other massive areas have since been added.

CHAPTER 2.5

STRIVING FOR WHOLENESS (HR PROCESSES)

> *We have developed speed but we have shut ourselves in. Machinery that gives abundance has left us in want. Our knowledge has made us cynical, our cleverness hard and unkind. We think too much and feel too little. More than machinery we need humanity; more than cleverness we need kindness and gentleness. Without these qualities, life will be violent and all will be lost.*
>
> Charles Chaplin (speech from the Jewish barber in *The Great Dictator*)

Striving for wholeness is no easy task. With every unsettling event, we are tempted to seek refuge in separation. Our soul goes into hiding and the ego takes over, doing what it feels it needs to do to make us feel safe. But it's a safety that comes at a cost: we now relate to others and ourselves with fear and judgment, no longer with love and acceptance.

In many wisdom traditions, the highest purpose in life is overcoming separation and reclaiming wholeness. The practices outlined in the previous chapter—explicit ground rules, conflict resolution processes, meeting practices, reflective spaces, office buildings—are all designed to create a space that is safe enough to reveal our selfhood, to venture into individual and collective wholeness. The pioneer organizations researched for this book found they couldn't stop there. They also reframed all of the key human resources processes—recruitment, onboarding, evaluation, compensation, dismissal—because too often the way we go about them in organizations today brings out fears and separation.

Recruitment

It is often during recruitment, even before a person has taken his first steps in the organization, that the lying starts. As candidates, we conform to who we think we ought to be in the eyes of an employer—in everything from our CV, the way we dress, our attitudes, and the questions we feel appropriate to ask or not to ask to the stories we choose to tell about ourselves. Employers, too, will often try to attract candidates by putting on a mask of their own. (A whole field of marketing called "employer branding" has emerged, which tries to lure not customers but job candidates with a positive spin about how great an employer a company is.) The recruitment process is often an uncomfortable dance of two partners wearing high heels to look taller, tight clothes to tuck the belly in, and so much make-up that you would not recognize them on a normal day.

Teal Organizations tweak the traditional recruitment process to allow both parties a better, hopefully more truthful look at each other. It starts with the fact that interviews aren't handled by human resources personnel trained in interview techniques, but by future teammates who simply want to decide if they would want to work with the candidate on a daily basis. Employees have no recruitment targets to make, and they tend to be much more honest about their workplace. After all, they will have to live with the consequences if they oversell the company to their potential new teammate.

> *I say beware of all enterprises that require new clothes.*
>
> Henry David Thoreau

Because team members doing the interviewing tend to be honest about the workplace, candidates feel invited to be honest too. This is critical, because every single organization in this research insists that a candidate's attitude is equally if not more important than her skills and experience. Is the person energized by the organization's values and by its purpose? Will the person thrive in a self-organizing environment? Will the person fit in? Employees want to engage with the real person, not the candidate that gives all the right answers.

Tami Simon, the founder of Sounds True, tells the following story about its particular culture and how people may or may not fit in:

> *One of the things I've found at Sounds True is in the first three months of employment a lot of the people don't stay. ... At Sounds True, people want to get to know who you are, they want you to be real, they don't want you to wear forty masks to work. It's like—will the real person please stand up? There is this sense of authenticity; who we are when we are not at work is who we are when we are at work. That's the kind of environment that's here and of course we try to screen for this and let people know before they take the job, and a lot of people go "Oh I'm totally ready for that. I'm interested in that, that's what I want." But then they come in and may or may not be comfortable actually working*

in that kind of environment where people when they stop in the hallway and ask "How are you doing?" actually mean it! How are *you doing?*[1]

Of course, skills and experience matter, but generally they take second place. Roles are so fluid that it makes little sense to hire somebody for one particular box. Organizations in this research have also found that when people are self-motivated, they can pick up new skills and experience in surprisingly little time. The real deal-breaker is someone who doesn't fit in, particularly, someone who is not suited for self-management, as an employee of AES explained:

[A bad hire is] someone who is a chronic complainer, who is not happy, who blames others, who doesn't take responsibility, who's not honest, who doesn't trust other people. A bad hire would be someone who needs specific direction and waits to be told what to do. A poor hire would be someone who wasn't flexible and who says, "It's not my job."[2]

Most organizations spend a lot of time during the recruitment process informing candidates about the values of the organization and what it's like to work there, so that people can decide whether they want to be part of it or not. Every potential hire at Morning Star gets thoroughly introduced to self-management during the interview process. At AES, candidates were invited to discussions about the organization's values and practices during the recruitment process. And in many of these organizations, a significant number of teammates interview the candidates—10 to 12 interviews is no rarity—providing ample time for both parties to feel each other out. It is, in essence, a two-way discovery process to answer one fundamental question: *Are we meant to journey together?*

Some organizations, such as FAVI, make extended use of the trial period for both parties to test whether the match works out. Zappos.com, an online shoe retailer, offers its new hires a $3,000 check if they have second thoughts and choose to quit during the four-week orientation. The idea is that everyone will be better off not staying in a marriage that isn't meant to be. Three thousand dollars is a lot of money for people working in call centers or moving boxes in fulfillment centers, which is what most Zappos employees do. It's a tribute to Zappos' outstanding culture that the percentage of people taking the money and leaving is only around one or two percent. Whenever the percentage of people taking the check draws too close to zero, Zappos increases the amount (it started with $100, then raised it to $200, and raised it again and again up to its current level). The practice, in essence, boils down to a real-life barometer of the health of the organization's culture. (Zappos.com is famous for its Green cultural practices described in the bestseller *Delivering Happiness*, written by CEO Tony Hsieh. The 1,500-employee company is currently making the leap to Holacracy, which will make it the largest holacratic organization to date.)

Onboarding

The onboarding process in many organizations today is rather basic. People might receive a few brochures about the company's history, mission statement and values, or there might be a two-hour session where some senior leader talks about these topics. But mostly, the first steps are often mundane: there are papers to sign, a desk and computer to find, and a password to be assigned in order to access the firm's network. Once ready to go, the new employee must try to box out some time in his supervisor's agenda to get some guidance on what to do. The first days are rarely productive; quickly the courtship of recruitment can feel like a romance from yesteryear.

Teal Organizations, in comparison, invest significantly more time and energy welcoming new colleagues. The first days and weeks are critical to making someone feel that she has come into a new and different workplace. At the heart of the onboarding process is some form of training that helps new recruits understand and navigate the new environment they joined. The training often touches, in one way or another, on the three breakthroughs of self-management, wholeness, and evolutionary purpose.

- *Self-management:* For people who join from traditional hierarchical organizations, self-management can be puzzling at first. A training program can help with understanding how it works, what is different and what stays the same, what skills are needed to thrive in such an environment, and so forth. At Buurtzorg, all new team members are trained in problem solving and meeting practices, so as to operate as a team without a boss to call the shots. Similarly, all new recruits at Morning Star attend a seminar on the basics of self-management. Particularly for people who were previously in leadership positions, the transition can be difficult. They have to learn to get things done without the blunt weapon of command and control. Getting some help to ease the transition is no luxury. Paul Green Jr., who heads Morning Star's Self-Management Institute, estimates that close to 50 percent of people who formerly had senior positions in other organizations (VP levels or above) end up leaving the organization after a year or two "because they have a hard time adapting to a system where they can't play God."
- *Striving for wholeness:* New colleagues are also trained in the assumptions, ground rules, and values that allow people to show up more authentically. The initial Buurtzorg training also includes techniques for conflict resolution and Nonviolent Communication. All new hires at Heiligenfeld go through six training modules that include topics like "self-mastery" and "dealing with failure."
- *Listening to evolutionary purpose*: Another central part of the onboarding revolves around the organization's purpose: *What is it*

and where does it come from? New colleagues are invited to reflect on their personal calling and how it resonates with the broader organizational purpose. How can the two support and nurture each other? Some founders and CEOs—such as Jos de Blok at Buurtzorg and Yvon Chouinard at Patagonia—find this module so significant that they choose to participate in every onboarding session.

Some organizations choose also to train everybody in frontline skills. At FAVI, the French automotive supplier, all engineers and administrative workers have been trained to operate at least one machine on the shop floor. The training is regularly put to good use: when orders must be rushed out, it happens that all hands get called on deck. White-collar workers come down from the office space on the first floor to man the machines for a few hours. It's a wonderful community-building practice. People in engineering and administrative roles work under the guidance of the machine operators. They witness first-hand how hard the work on the machines can be and how much skill it involves. At the end of the day, when the orders are out on time, colleagues share a sense of pride in the work accomplished.

At Sun Hydraulics, all new hires start with a "manufacturing tour," no matter what their future role will be; they learn to operate not just one, but several work stations. For hourly employees, the tour lasts for two to four weeks, and they work in four to six different areas. For salaried employees, it takes even longer: one to four months on the shop floor. Only then do they take on the roles they were hired for.

Why such a long induction? People at Sun believe it's critical to build relationships with other employees across the company to understand it from all angles. A self-managing environment provides opportunity to make things happen, to freely reach out to colleagues, to discuss change without going through a hierarchy of approvals. The more people you know, the more you understand the whole, the more you'll be able to come up with new ideas and turn them into reality. At Sun, it is not unusual that after the manufacturing tour, new hires end up taking up a role that wasn't the one they were hired for. They stumble upon a new interest or some urgent need and end up in a different place.

FAVI's onboarding process ends on a nice touch. New teammates who have gone through all the training modules of the first two months are asked to write an open letter to the group of colleagues they have joined. There are no instructions on what the letter should be about, so new hires often dig deep in their selfhood to find something worthwhile to say. The letters are, time and again, deeply touching accounts of gratitude and joy. Many blue-collar workers join FAVI scarred from past experience of mistrust and command and control. Joining an environment where they are considered trustworthy and where their voice counts is often a groundbreaking experience. For many machine operators, writing is not their preferred style of expression. Finding the right words for the letter can take a lot of effort, and the practice is akin to a ritual, a rite of passage into the community.

Training

Self-managing organizations naturally provide for exceptional learning opportunities. No one stops you from picking up a new role, from trying out new things. To the contrary, the more you are seeking to contribute, the more your reputation grows and the more people will turn to you for advice and help—and the more you will be trusted to take on new roles and launch new initiatives. Dennis Bakke says that "the design of the AES workplace somewhat accidentally created one of the finest educational institutions around"[3] because people were constantly learning by making decisions and seeking advice, working in voluntary task forces, picking up skills and knowledge that elsewhere would be concentrated in management and staff functions. An employee from Sun Hydraulics put it beautifully:

Self-managing organizations naturally provide for exceptional learning opportunities. No one stops you from picking up a new role.

> *A lot of good things get done here that could never happen in a more traditional company. ... We have so many free thinkers, gifted people who could have lived their whole lives without knowing they had the talents they've been forced to discover here. Sometimes I miss the security of knowing whether anyone recognizes what I do; whether I'm doing a good job or whether I'm offering all I can. But there's never an end to the opportunity to do new things.*[4]

Personal responsibility and freedom for training

The biggest change in regard to training is, of course, that employees are in charge of their own learning; there is no HR function that defines training programs and determines who can attend what training programs or at what point. Provided they use the advice process, employees can sign up for any training inside or outside the company, if they believe the costs can be justified. To make matters even simpler, several companies researched for this book have decided on a budget at the individual or team level to be used for outside training, no advice process needed. At Buurtzorg, for instance, a principle emerged that teams could spend three percent of revenue on training without needing to consult. They freely decide on their own training needs and look for the best provider—a medical supplier, a hospital department, or sometimes simply a pharmacist or another Buurtzorg team. Jos de Blok,

Buurtzorg's founder, comments on how this freedom allows nurses to react quickly:

> *A remarkably high number of colleagues get themselves trained in specific medical conditions and technical equipment so that they can assist new clients in the best possible way. From drug pumps to dialysis and breathing devices, they learn how the equipment works and must be operated so that the number of professionals that deals with any client stays low. Because colleagues don't need to ask if they can learn about something, their motivation to do so increases immediately. "It is as if I just woke up, because I start again to think of all sorts of possibilities," is what you often hear at Buurtzorg.*[5]

> *It's not the work of the organization to develop people, but people are given the opportunity to develop by doing the work of the organization.*
> Tom Thomison

As the word spreads that Buurtzorg's nurses can handle all sort of devices and techniques, doctors start prescribing treatment methods that improve their patients' lives—say, a drug pump for a person with chronic pain—that fall outside the limited standards handled by traditional nursing organizations.

Different categories of training

In traditional organizations, training programs tend to fall into two categories:

1. Training that helps employees progress along the career ladder—training for young talents, first time managers, managers of managers, senior leaders, and so on. Green Organizations in particular dedicate much time and money toward training to help new managers deal gracefully with power and delegate much of it to their subordinates.
2. Skill training, for example, courses on specific topics such as sales skills, financial analysis, or lean manufacturing.

In self-managing organizations, the first category disappears; there are no training programs to help people climb the career ladder. Instead, Teal Organizations offer two types of training rarely found in traditional organizations: training to establish a common culture, and personal development training. Skill training programs are still around, but are delivered with a twist—they are often led by colleagues rather than external trainers and are deeply infused with the company's values and culture.

Common training programs attended by all

In almost all the organizations I researched, there are a number of training sessions that every new hire attends, no matter what roles they will later take on, for instance, on topics such as Nonviolent

Communication, how to deal with conflict, and how to get things done without hierarchy.

A one-off training program is often insufficient, however, in helping someone unlearn previous habits and pick up new ones. These initial training modules are therefore expanded with follow-up training and workshops that are interwoven into daily life. At FAVI, Jean-François Zobrist used to chair a one-hour session every Friday morning, open to whoever wanted to join. The topic: An in-depth look at one of FAVI's core organizational tools. (FAVI calls them *fiches*, or index cards, as they are literally available in the form of index cards to employees.) These include the purpose of the organization, its values, its decision-making mechanisms, and lean manufacturing techniques. Formats used by other organizations include team coaching (to work through some upset), company retreats, purpose circles, and values days.

Employees become trainers

When it comes to in-house training, most of the organizations in this research stopped using external trainers. Classes are presented by colleagues who are passionate about the subject, and who tailor material to the language and culture of the organization. Typically, the courses go from the inside out: they help people connect with and discover who they are, and then find authentic ways to express their selfhood about the subject matter. Turning team members into trainers both saves on costs and boosts morale, as it gives them an opportunity to shine and be recognized for their expertise. ESBZ, the school in Berlin, relies heavily on this method. It recently stumbled on a powerful technique for students to improve in memorization. It has sent a delegation including both teachers and students to be trained as trainers. Who says that teachers need to do all the teaching? Why not train students to teach other students?

Job descriptions, job titles, and career planning

In the previous chapter, we saw that self-managing organizations do away with rigid job descriptions and job titles. Most people no longer have a single "job" that fits a generic description; instead, they fill a unique combination of roles. The practice comes with a wonderful side benefit: without a job title, it becomes that much harder to merge our identity, who we think we are, with the position we hold. This fusion is commonplace today. When we are asked what we do professionally, we all tend to answer, *I am a ...* (shift supervisor, head of sales, vice president of human resources). Part of us believes that is really *who* we are, and we start thinking and behaving accordingly. In the absence of job titles and job descriptions, we are more likely to see ourselves and others first and foremost as human beings that happen to put our energy into specific work roles during a period of time.

Teal Organizations also do away with job descriptions, and that comes with a side benefit too: we can't turn to the job description to tell us how we ought to work. We have to find within ourselves our own unique way to fill a role with life and meaning. Bob Fishman, the founder of RHD, illustrates this with a telling example:

> *RHD consciously does not use [job descriptions]. Instead, the assumption that people are essentially good leads us to believe that, once an employee has a general sense of the job, he or she will want to shape the way it is done. …*
>
> *Thelma, for instance, had already been working as a receptionist at our new outpatient clinic for many years when she asked me for a job description. … I felt, and so told her, that it was absurd for me to define the details of her work since she was already doing a quality job. One of her outstanding behaviors was the kindness with which she greeted our clients, brought them coffee, and made sure that the therapist took them into the therapy room in a timely manner. Delineating her kindness was impossible: words would never have done justice to her heartfelt warmth. Thelma already knew how to perform her job and a detailed job description, I believed, would have done her more harm than good. …*
>
> *There is no single way to define a job, and no supervisor has the answer to how another person's job should be performed. If … I imposed my view on her job, the corporation would, in effect, lose her special contribution—her way of managing the relationship between people. That would have been a great loss.*[6]

Thelma's story shows how, at first, having no job titles and no job descriptions can feel uncomfortable for many of us—we like to know what is expected of us. The absence of a job title and job description forces us to search within ourselves for a personal, meaningful way to define who we are and what we can contribute. There is no preset template to conform to, no pre-given label that can shape our identity. It is another great paradox of Teal Organizations: on the one hand, they invite us to dissociate soul from role—who we are from what we do. And, in a beautiful paradox, this allows us to fill our role with more of our true identity. With no job description, with no one telling us how to do a particular job, we might as well do it from our own selfhood, and infuse it with our unique personality and talents.

Commitment, working hours and flexibility

In traditional organizations, when it comes to working hours, people fall into one of two camps. There are those (often at the lower levels of the pyramid) that work a fixed set of hours, and those (often in higher positions) who come and go when they want as long as they achieve certain outcomes. In practice, both of these arrangements prove demeaning.

Imposing fixed working hours is based on the premise that people are resources, a set of arms or brains hired for a specific amount of time. It assumes that work is essentially uninteresting and people interchangeable; it assumes that people will stay around only for as long as they are paid to. And it assumes that people at lower stages in organizations can't be trusted to set their own goals and work until they reach them. Teal Organizations start from the premise that even for routine work, people have a sense of pride and want to do a good job. At FAVI and at Sun Hydraulics, people stopped clocking in and out, and no one controls working hours. The working day is still divided into shifts, which is roughly the time colleagues are expected to spend on the shop floor, but it happens that operators stay on to finish a job even when the new shift has arrived.

In most organizations, the higher-ups have no fixed working hours; they are trusted to have self-discipline and work until the job is done. But implicitly, the expectation goes further: there is an unspoken assumption that people in managerial positions should put their commitment to work above any other commitment in their lives. An increasing number of people feel that they are always "on," always reachable, and must put other important commitments in their lives second (or at least give the impression of doing so). I know few executives who would dare to cancel an important meeting for their child's school play or because a good friend needs their help. The few that do feel they need to invoke some false pretext. We work in corporate cultures that invite us to disown some of the things we care most about.

If we want to be authentic and whole at work, we must learn to speak up about other important commitments in our lives. We must stop pretending that work will always trump them in all circumstances. A simple practice can help: at regular intervals, have a meeting where colleagues discuss how much time and energy, at that moment in their lives, they want to commit to the organization's purpose. HolacracyOne has put such a practice in place. Tom Thomison, one of HolacracyOne's co-founders, explains the rationale:

> *What we are striving for is each partner making a conscious choice about how much time and energy they are willing to commit to help the organization move towards its purpose. And that gives us a conscious way of holding and recognizing that we as humans have multiple endeavors that interest us and that enliven us, and we are choosing how much of our time and energy to focus on this particular focus. So without prejudice, we look at each individual colleague and ask: "How much focused time and energy are you bringing to this endeavor?"*[7]

Morning Star has a similar practice: each colleague indicates in his CLOU his *work schedule commitment*. A person might indicate, for example, 40 to 45 hours off-season, and 50 to 55 hours in high season (when tomatoes are harvested and processed). Because colleagues discuss their CLOUs, they know about each other's commitments.

When someone needs to dedicate more time to a private commitment, the structure of small, self-managing teams helps in providing flexibility. At Buurtzorg, if a nurse wants to reduce her working hours—perhaps because she has a sick parent to take care of herself—the team will reshuffle existing clients and temporarily take in fewer new clients. An operator at FAVI who was having a house built brought the topic up with his team. To be on site with the builders, he wanted to switch to the night shift. Would a colleague from the night shift be willing to swap shifts for a four-month period? An arrangement was quickly found—the request didn't need to go through a formal HR process or receive manager approval.

Sometimes finding a solution is not that easy. During high season at Morning Star, all hands need to be on deck—the continuous tomato-processing operation can't be slowed down or stopped because one colleague wants more time off. If someone wants to reduce working hours, they are expected to find a solution to uphold the commitments that they have made. This expectation is the flip side of having no centralized HR or planning function. You can't simply file a request with HR and then let them worry about solving the issue. You have full liberty to find a solution, but until you have found one, you are bound to your previous commitments. In practice, colleagues tend to go out of their way to help you. They know that in turn, people will help them when they need flexibility. It results in a culture where colleagues chip in for each other, and where people dare to ask for help when something important is going on in their private lives.

Feedback and performance management

Most of us naturally want to receive feedback on our contribution at work. We want to know: Was our work helpful? Was it worth the effort we put into it? And yet, most organizations find it exceedingly difficult to create a culture of feedback. Often, people take good work for granted or simply say, "Great job!"—a rather unspecific form of feedback. And for negative feedback, we tend to dance around the issue, often waiting until the next formal appraisal discussion to bring up the topic. No wonder annual appraisals are, in many companies, the most awkward moments of the year. As employees, we go into these meetings in two minds. On the one hand, we hope our contributions will finally be acknowledged; on the other, we fear negative feedback might have built up over time because so much tends to be left unsaid during the year. In their book *Accountability*, Rob Lebow and Randy Spitzer write:

> *Too often, appraisal destroys human spirit and, in the span of a 30-minute meeting, can transform a vibrant, highly committed employee*

into a demoralized, indifferent wallflower who reads the want ads on the weekend. … They don't work because most performance appraisal systems are a form of judgment and control.[8]

I believe Lebow and Spitzer are right; consciously or unconsciously, all too often we use feedback to try to mold other people into how we believe they should be. There is no faster way to make a soul go into hiding. And yet, it doesn't need to be like that. If we approach appraisal discussions from a different mindset, we can turn them into moments where our contributions are celebrated and recognized, where, without judgment, we inquire truthfully into what isn't going so well: places where our knowledge, experience, talent, or attitude fall short of what our roles require. And we can inquire into even deeper questions: *What do we truly long to do? What is our offer to the world? What are our unique gifts? What holds us back? What could help us step more boldly into the life that wants to be lived through us?*

In chapter 2.3 (page 123), we have seen that Teal Organizations put the responsibility of performance management foremost at the team level. Individual feedback and appraisals are given not by a boss, but by peers. This process is helpful, but not enough to ensure that performance management becomes a time of inquiry and celebration, rather than judgment and control. Three additional practices can help.

The first is simply to approach feedback with the ancient insight shared by all wisdom traditions. We can approach the world from one of two sides: from a place of fear, judgment, and separation; or from one of love, acceptance, and connection. When we have difficult feedback to give, we enter the discussion uneasily, and this pushes us to the side of fear and judgment, where we believe we know what is wrong with the other person and how we can fix him. If we are mindful, we can come to such discussions from a place of care. When we do, we can enter into beautiful moments of inquiry, where we have no easy answers but can help the colleague assess himself more truthfully. Bringing this kind of mindfulness to discussions is something we can learn, something that can be taught. Simple practices can help too: we can start feedback sessions with a minute of silence or any other personal ritual that helps us tune in to love and care.

> *People must feel safe to be honest about themselves and towards others. Only then can we use the strength of everyone and prevent people from doing things that they don't really know how to do or don't want to do.*
>
> Jos de Blok

The second practice flows out of the first. We must learn the language of the heart. We've been told that we should assess other people as objectively as possible. That's a tragic mistake. Assessments are never objective (at best we can say they are culturally grounded, if many people share the same assessment), but nevertheless we often believe that they are. We turn our subjective impressions into "truths" about a person; no wonder they resist our feedback. Rather than cloaking ourselves in objective detachment, we must get involved. We must learn to speak in "I" language, to share how we have been inspired, touched, puzzled, hurt, frustrated, or angered as a result of what the other person has said or done. Feedback given that way is not an objective evaluation, but a joint inquiry. We offer a peek into our own inner world so as to help the other person better understand the impact of their behavior. The more we open up, the more we invite our feedback partner to do the same.

The third practice requires that we change the nature of the discussion in performance evaluations. Most appraisal discussions attempt to take a seemingly objective snapshot of a person's abilities—resulting in a series of scores on predefined performance criteria, a sort of balance sheet of strengths and weaknesses. What a disheartening way to sum up a person! What if we changed the discussion? Instead of a snapshot, we can choose a wide-angle perspective. Let's look at a person's current roles at work in the broader light of her life's journey, her potential, hopes, and calling. This can't be done on a scale of one to five, or from "below average" to "exceeding expectations." We need to make it personal, call forth stories, celebrate achievements, and explore the learning behind our failures. This will also naturally help us to go from stating ("I see you as a three on the criterion of 'following through'") to inquiring ("Where do you see yourself going?").

It doesn't need to be complicated. The Center for Courage & Renewal, with its 10-person staff, only recently introduced yearly performance discussions. It shunned the usual practice of assessing people with a rating scale on some performance criteria. Instead, the center simply framed a few questions that turned the appraisal into a moment of joint exploration:

Lauds:

- *What has gone really well this year that we might celebrate?*

Learning:

- *What has been learned in the process?*
- *What didn't go as well or might have been done differently?*
- *How do we "take stock" of where things are now compared to where we thought they might be?*

Looking forward:

- *What are you most excited about in this next year?*
- *What concerns you most?*
- *What changes, if any, would you suggest in your functions?*
- *What ongoing professional development will help you to grow in your current job and for your future?*
- *How can I be of most help to you and your work?*

Setting goals:

- *When you think about your work in the year ahead, what specific goals will guide you?*[9]

In a similar vein, Bob Koski, the founder of Sun Hydraulics, suggested four simple statements for the yearly appraisal discussions:

1. *State an admirable feature about the employee.*
2. *Ask what contributions they have made to Sun.*
3. *Ask what contributions they would like to make at Sun.*
4. *Ask how Sun can help them.*[10]

You might have noticed that in this four-question framework there is no place allotted for negative feedback, for telling a person what they could do better. Does this mean that colleagues should pretend that everybody is perfect, that no one needs to be told what they could improve in? Of course not. But such feedback should be given on the spot, all year round, and not left unsaid, waiting for the appraisal discussion at the end of the year.

The annual feedback at Sounds True gives us an example of how the three changes—coming from a place of love and care, speaking subjectively, and changing the questions—can come together to turn appraisal discussions into moments of true inquiry and celebration. There are three steps in the performance appraisal process at Sounds True:

1. In a first phase, as an employee, you reflect on your own performance and aspirations based on a list of questions to trigger the thinking.
2. Colleagues add to that picture by giving you feedback. This wonderful team-based practice starts with a minute of silence during which your colleagues close their eyes and try to hold you in their heart, to let go of any form of judgment and offer feedback from a place of love and connection. One after the other, each colleague (typically six to 12 people, including people from other teams who work closely with you) takes the seat in front of you and gives you the gift of answering two questions: "What is the one thing I most value about working with you?" and "What is one area where I sense you could change and grow"? A note-taker transcribes the answers to the questions from your colleagues on a large piece of paper that he hands over to you when the round is done. The experience at Sounds True is that people feel held very lovingly in the process, and tears of gratitude for being so deeply understood are not unusual.

3. In a third phase, you reflect on the input and deepen your thinking in discussion with a colleague. (At Sounds True, which still has a hierarchical structure, this colleague is your manager, but in a self-managing structure it can take place with a trusted peer.) "What do you take away from the discussions? What did you learn? What do you want to pay attention to in the future? Where do you feel called to go?"

Examples such as these show that feedback mechanisms and annual appraisals don't need to be dispiriting, lifeless affairs. With the right presence and the right questions, we can turn them into rituals of celebration and inquiry into our selfhood and calling.

Dismissals and layoffs

Wisdom traditions say that there is no such thing as failure; there are only invitations to learn and grow. To realize (or to be told) that we aren't cut out for a particular job is life's way of saying, "You've just been given a gift (albeit one that doesn't come gift-wrapped, and that can feel painful at first)." Inquire into what happened for insights into what you're *not* meant to do, what you're *not* meant to be. Look deeper still, and you might find a new road opening up and leading you where your talents are calling you. Colleagues can do much to support a person in that phase (see page 126 for more about peer-based dismissal processes). Even a dismissal can be an opportunity to extend love and compassion. Held in that way, it becomes much easier for a person to explore why a job might not have fit his talents or calling, and where and how to look for work he is called to do.

Beyond individuals being asked to leave a company, there is the question of collective layoffs for economic reasons. I believe we need to make a distinction between *temporary* and *structural* overstaffing. I find it interesting that not a single organization in this research has laid people off during times of downturn. Self-managing organizations are exceedingly flexible and accumulate little overhead; therefore, they weather downturns much better than traditional organizations. FAVI and Sun Hydraulics, for example, have both withstood severe recessions with revenue decreases of 30 to 50 percent without layoffs. In some cases, colleagues agreed to share the pain and take temporary pay cuts (chapter 2.3 tells one such story regarding FAVI; see page 103). From a Teal perspective, it would be improper to lay off colleagues when the overstaffing is only temporary, just to bolster profits for a few months.

The case is different when the overstaffing is structural. AES has faced this case dozens of times: the power plants it bought in Eastern Europe, Asia, Latin America, and Africa were frequently tremendously overstaffed. In many cases, governments that previously owned them used these facilities to create artificial jobs. After making the acquisition,

AES swiftly reduced the number of employees. This can sound surprising: how can a progressive company, like AES was at the time, lay off hundreds of people? Here is Dennis Bakke's perspective on the matter:

> *The right size of a workforce is equal to the number of people needed to make the workplace fun. Having too many employees demoralizes colleagues and causes turf battles. A very astute AES plant manager in Northern Ireland told me that arguments over turf are good indicators that the facility has too many people. No one worries about who does what when there is enough work to go around.*
>
> *My belief that business should not carry unneeded employees does not mean that they should be given pink slips and hustled out the door. Departing employees need time to make the transitions to new work. Organizations should be generous with severance arrangements. We encountered overstaffing almost every time we made an acquisition. One of the first things we did after acquiring a business was to set up a generous and voluntary severance program. Only rarely were individuals asked to leave.*
>
> *In Panama, AES created a loan fund for employees who took the severance package. A year later, I traveled to a celebration lunch with former employees who had left the company. Seventy-one new businesses had been started by these former employees, most of whom tapped the AES loan fund. Even with generous voluntary severance arrangements, the changeover from a company you know to one you don't can be traumatic. I strongly believe that these difficult transitions are a necessary evil that forces employees and organizations to adjust to a dynamic world. Part of the joy of work is learning new roles and taking on new responsibilities. Job security is attractive gift wrapping, but seldom is there anything of lasting value inside.*[11]

Maintaining jobs artificially makes no sense from an Evolutionary-Teal perspective. We value job security, but ultimately it is a notion inspired by fear. It neglects the fundamental truth that everything changes; it dismisses the possibility of abundance—that a person whose talents are wasted in an overstaffed organization will find a better way to express his gifts where they are needed.

Life is continuously unfolding; dismissals and even layoffs can be part of that unfolding, although they are comparatively rare in self-managed structures. Organizations in this research show us that we don't need to reduce dismissals to cold, contractual transactions. We can welcome the emotions and the pain. And when they have abated, we can start inquiring into the deeper meaning, the message that life wants us to hear, the new road we might be called to travel on.

In summary—practices and processes supporting wholeness

Wholeness and separation, love and fear, these are the great dichotomies all wisdom traditions have explored. In most organizations today, we seek separation for the safety we believe it provides. We retreat into a world of judgment, where we distance ourselves from others and from ourselves. We wear a mask, sometimes for so long that even we ourselves come to believe the mask is who we are. In the workplace, this mask is often mental, rational, masculine, self-centered. We cut ourselves off from our emotions, our intuitions, our body, our feminine side. We don't heed our inner voice, our longings, our calling, our soul. We neglect our capacity for connection and compassion, for love for ourselves, for others, and for all life that surrounds us. At first, we feel safe. Only gradually do we come to feel the emptiness and the pain of separation.

In the last two chapters, we have explored a great number of simple practices that Teal Organizations can put in place to help us reconnect with our inner wholeness. At first, we can feel vulnerable when we bring more of who we are into our own awareness and into the community of our colleagues. But once we do, it is as if life has switched from black and white to full color: it becomes rich, vibrant, and meaningful. It makes business sense too. Workplaces where we feel we can show up with all of who we are unleash unprecedented energy and creativity. The tables on pages 190-191 summarize the main practices related to wholeness encountered within the pioneer organizations researched for this book.

Wholeness

	Orange practices		Teal practices
Buildings	• Standardized, soulless professional buildings • Abundant status markers	➡	• Self-decorated, warm spaces, open to children, animals, nature • No status markers
Values and ground rules	• (Values often only a plaque on the wall)	➡	• Clear values translated into explicit ground rules of (un)acceptable behaviors to foster safe environment • Practices to cultivate ongoing discussion about values and ground rules
Reflective spaces	-	➡	• Quiet room • Group meditation and silence practices • Large group reflection practices • Team supervision and peer coaching
Community building	-	➡	• Storytelling practices to support self-disclosure and build community
Job titles & job descriptions	• Job titles are identity-giving status markers • Prescriptive job descriptions	➡	• Absence of job titles compels oneself to find deeper sense of identity • No job description to allow selfhood to shape roles
Time commitment	-	➡	• Honest discussion about individual time commitment to work vs. other meaningful commitments in life
Conflicts	-	➡	• Regular time devoted to bring to light and address conflicts • Multi-step conflict resolution process • Everyone trained in managing conflict

Wholeness

	Orange practices		Teal practices
Meetings	• (Many meetings, but few meeting practices)	➡	• Specific meeting practices to keep ego in check and ensure everybody's voice is heard
Environmental and social initiatives	• Money as extrinsic yardstick: *Only if it doesn't cost too much* • Only the very top can begin initiatives with financial consequences	➡	• Integrity as intrinsic yardstick: *What is the right thing to do?* • Distributed initiative taking, everyone senses the right thing to do
Recruitment	• Interviews by trained HR personnel, focus is on fit with job description	➡	• Interviews by future colleagues, focus is on fit with organization and with purpose
Onboarding	• (Mostly administrative onboarding process)	➡	• Significant training in relational skills and in company culture • Rotation programs to immerse oneself in the organization
Training	• Training trajectories designed by HR • Mostly skill and management training	➡	• Personal freedom and responsibility for training • Critical importance of culture-building training that everybody attends
Performance management	• Aims to establish objective snapshot of past performance	➡	• Personal inquiry into one's learning journey and calling
Dismissal	• Dismissal mostly a legal and financial process	➡	• Caring support to turn dismissal into a learning opportunity

CHAPTER 2.6

LISTENING TO EVOLUTIONARY PURPOSE

Life wants to happen. Life is unstoppable. Anytime we try and contain life, or interfere with its fundamental need for expression, we get into trouble. …

Partnering with life, working with its cohering motions, requires that we take life's direction seriously. Life moves toward wholeness. This direction cannot be ignored or taken lightly. People do not respond for long to small and self-centered purposes or to self-aggrandizing work. Too many organizations ask us to engage in hollow work, to be enthusiastic about small-minded visions, to commit ourselves to selfish purposes, to engage our energy in competitive drives. … When we respond with disgust, when we withdraw our energy from such endeavors, it is a sign of our commitment to life and to each other.

M. Wheatley and M. Kellner-Rogers

Few business leaders have become living legends. Jack Welch is one of them. Under his leadership, General Electric (GE) has achieved extraordinary financial success. In many ways, GE and Jack Welch are poster children of Orange Organizations and Orange leadership—pushy to the point of ruthlessness, clever, and highly successful. After he retired, Welch wrote a book that distills his lessons in management. The title of the book has only one word, but it speaks volumes about the fundamental drive of Orange Organizations: *Winning*. Welch's book is emblematic of a whole genre of business books that promise readers they will learn the secrets to make their company successful, increase profit, gain market share, and beat the competition. The implied promise, of course, is that these secrets will also make the readers personally successful, helping them beat their colleagues in the race to the very top where wealth and fame await the winners.[1] Something is notably absent in these books: the purpose organizations serve. What makes "winning" worthwhile? Why do organizations exist in the first place, and why do they deserve our energy, talents, and creativity?

The primacy of "winning" over purpose goes a long way in explaining why the "mission statements" that organizations define often ring so hollow. These statements are supposed to provide employees with inspiration and guidance. Try the following experiment: ask someone, anyone, working for an organization to tell you what that organization's mission is. When I ask, I nearly always get a blank stare in return. Sometimes people scratch their heads, mumbling half-baked sentences, trying to remember what it is. CEOs don't pass the test any better than middle managers or frontline workers. People have become cynical about mission statements because in practice they don't drive behavior or decisions. Executives, at least in my experience, don't pause in a heated debate to turn to the company's mission statement for guidance, asking, "What does our purpose require us to do?"

So if the collective purpose isn't what drives decision-making, what does? It is the self-preservation of the organization. The fear-based nature of the ego in Red, Amber, and Orange predisposes leaders and employees to see the world as a dangerous place with competitors everywhere trying to steal their lunch. The only way to ensure survival is to seize every opportunity to make more profit and to gain market share at the expense of competitors. In the heat of the battle, who has time to think about purpose? Sadly, this fear-based fixation on competition plays out even when the self-preservation of the organization is not in doubt. In organizations that are somewhat shielded from competition (for example the military, public schools, and government agencies), the fearful ego still seeks safety, this time in internal competition; managers fight for the self-preservation of their units in turf wars with other units, to secure more funding, talent, or recognition.

With the transition to Evolutionary-Teal, people learn to tame the fears of their egos. This process makes room for exploring deeper questions of meaning and purpose, both individually and collectively: *What is my calling? What is truly worth achieving?* Survival is no longer a fixation for Teal Organizations. Instead, the founding purpose truly matters. In many of the organizations researched for this book, the overarching purpose is not only a statement on a plaque at the reception desk or in the annual report, but an energy that inspires and gives direction. The shift from self-preservation to purpose also transforms a number of key organizational practices: how the strategy is developed,

> *When we quit thinking primarily about ourselves and our own self-preservation, we undergo a truly heroic transformation of consciousness.*
>
> Joseph Campbell

how budgets are established and followed, how targets are set, how products are developed and sold, and how employees are recruited and suppliers chosen, among others.

Competition, market share, and growth

In my research, as I listened to leaders of Teal Organizations and as I read their annual reports and internal documents, something struck me: competition is not mentioned anywhere. Orange Organizations are obsessed with competition, and here the very notion of competition seems to have vanished. Where has it gone?

The answer is surprisingly straightforward: when an organization truly lives for its purpose, there is no competition. Anybody that can help to achieve the purpose on a wider scale or more quickly is a friend, an ally, not a competitor. Take Buurtzorg: its purpose—to help sick and elderly patients live a more autonomous and meaningful life—is paramount, so much so that Jos de Blok, its founder, has documented and published Buurtzorg's revolutionary ways of operating in great detail, to *invite competition to imitate him.* He accepts all invitations from competitors to explain his methods. He and a colleague are deeply involved as advisors to ZorgAccent, a direct competitor, and don't ask to be compensated for it. From an Orange perspective, this attitude makes no sense. Buurtzorg's breakthrough organizational innovations are its equivalent to Coca-Cola's secret formula: a competitive advantage that should be locked up in a vault. But from an Evolutionary-Teal perspective, the defining purpose is not Buurtzorg's market share or Jos de Blok's personal success. What matters is patients living a healthy, autonomous and meaningful life. Prompted on the subject, de Blok told me:

> *Evolution as survival of the fittest has inhibited our observation of coevolution. There is no hostile world out there plotting our demise. We are utterly intertwined.*
>
> M. Wheatley and M. Kellner-Rogers

> *In my perspective, the whole notion of competition is idiotic. It really makes no sense. You try to figure out how you can best organize things to provide the best care. If you then share the knowledge and the information, things will change more quickly.*

And in a nice wink to the abundance of life, he added:

> *But even when I take the perspective of Buurtzorg as an organization, I believe very strongly the more open you are about what you do, the more advantages come back to you. If you are open, people will receive you in friendlier ways.*[2]

Indeed, Buurtzorg's journey has been surprisingly smooth, considering that it steamrolled its market. In the seven years since its founding,

60 percent of neighborhood nurses and clients in the country deserted established players to join Buurtzorg. There should have been acrimonious reactions. Somehow they didn't come.

Market share, from an Evolutionary-Teal perspective, is only relevant when comparing with other organizations that operate from an old paradigm. Buurtzorg is actively helping competitors, but if they don't shun the old model of fragmented care, it doesn't mind taking over clients. Patagonia tries to help the whole industry raise its environmental standards. In the meantime it's happy if customers shop with Patagonia instead of a competitor using polluting fiber and toxic dyes.

Growth, in the same vein, is only an objective insofar as the purpose can be manifested on a larger scale, but never an objective in itself. Remember, for instance, that Buurtzorg actively helps patients build a network of support with their families, friends, and neighbors. It basically tries to make itself irrelevant in patients' lives as quickly as possible, which it does very successfully: a 2009 study showed that Buurtzorg's patients get released from care twice as fast as competitors' clients, and they end up claiming only 50 percent of the prescribed hours of care. Buurtzorg's core strategy—helping patients become healthy and autonomous—in fact comes down to pursuing less growth, not more. Similarly, Patagonia is famous for having run full-page ads reading, "Don't buy this jacket." The ads were part of its "Common Threads Partnership." Patagonia reckons that many of us in the developed world have enough clothes in our closets to keep us warm for a lifetime. And yet we keep buying new clothes, which are environmentally harmful to produce and will end up in a landfill. The Common Threads Partnership takes a serious stab at *reducing* (making clothes that last longer), *repairing* (Patagonia repairs clothes for its customers), *reusing* (the company resells your used clothes on eBay or in their stores' Worn Wear section), and *recycling* (you can return your old clothes to Patagonia and they recycle them). Will this initiative harm Patagonia's growth in the short term? Yes. Every repaired and every reused jacket is one less jacket bought. Will it increase its growth in the long term, through higher customer loyalty? Perhaps. But Patagonia's decision wasn't driven by forecasts and financials. The company chose the path its purpose called for. That path could have resulted in lower sales revenue, which Patagonia would have been ready to swallow.

> *It's an ethical imperative for neighborhood nurses to make themselves irrelevant.*
>
> Jos de Blok

The paradox, of course, is that while they don't have Orange's obsession with growth, Buurtzorg, Patagonia, and the other organizations surveyed in this research have fantastic growth records. Teal practices unleash tremendous energies; when these energies meet a noble purpose and a deep hunger in the world, how could anything but growth ensue?

Profit

Shareholder value has become the dominant perspective of Orange Organizations. It states that corporations have one overriding duty: to maximize profits. In many countries, this perspective is legally binding; management can be sued for decisions that jeopardize profitability. Under the spell of shareholder value, public companies focus relentlessly on the bottom line. Profits and losses are forecasted month-by-month, quarter-by-quarter, and every element that could increase or reduce the bottom line is analyzed and analyzed some more.

The for-profit organizations researched for this book have a different perspective on profit. Profit is necessary and investors deserve a fair return, but the objective is purpose, not profit. Several of the organizational founders used the same metaphor: profit is like the air we breathe. We need air to live, but we don't live to breathe. Tami Simon, the CEO of Sounds True, gives a definition of a business's purpose that is as simple as it is beautiful:

> *We have this idea about business—everything we do has to help us make more money, be more productive or whatever. But that's not my view of business. My view of business is that we are coming together as a community to fill a human need and actualize our lives.*[3]

In Teal Organizations, profits are a byproduct of a job well done. Philosopher Viktor Frankl perhaps captured it best: "Success, like happiness, cannot be pursued; it must ensue, and it only does so as the unintended side-effect of one's personal dedication to a cause greater than oneself." This idea is another great paradox: by focusing on purpose rather than profits, profits tend to roll in more plentifully.

A few of the founders of organizations in this research didn't set out to create a business at all, initially. Their pursuit of a purpose happened to take the shape, at some point, of a business; in a very literal sense, purpose came before profits. Yvon Chouinard, the founder and owner of Patagonia, was probably one of the people most unlikely to become a business founder, until he stumbled on the purpose that would turn into a $540 million company employing 1,350 people.

As a kid, he spent every free minute outdoors—rock-climbing, diving, and training hawks for hunting. A misfit in school, Chouinard remembers that the classroom was mostly "an opportunity for me to practice holding my breath, so that on weekends I could free-dive deeper to catch the abundant abalone and lobster off the Malibu coast." When he left school, he lived with no income, finding shelter in shacks on the beach or near the mountains, hopping on freight trains in pursuit of the next climb or dive. In 1957, he bought a used coal-fired forge from a junkyard and taught himself blacksmithing to make his own climbing pitons. When a few friends asked him to produce pitons for them, he found a way to sustain his simple lifestyle. For years, he would fabricate pitons in the winter months, making just enough money to spend April to July on the walls of Yosemite, devote the summer to the mountains of Wyoming, and then go back to Yosemite in the fall until snow fell in November. He wouldn't have been considered a businessman by anybody, least of all himself. Now, as the owner of a multimillion-dollar company, he has turned into one, but he hasn't lost sight of the lights and shadows of the profession:

> *Speaking personally, I want my films to make money, but money is just fuel for the rocket. What I really want to do is to go somewhere. I don't want to just collect more fuel.*
>
> Brad Bird, director of *The Incredibles* and *Ratatouille*

I've been a businessman for almost fifty years. It's as difficult for me to say those words as it is for someone to admit to being an alcoholic or a lawyer. I've never respected the profession. It's business that has to take the majority of the blame for being the enemy of nature, for destroying native cultures, for taking from the poor and giving to the rich, and poisoning the earth with the effluent from its factories.

Yet business can produce food, cure disease, control population, employ people, and generally enrich our lives. And it can do these good things and make a profit without losing its soul.[4]

Chouinard's defining experience as a businessman came as he climbed up a mountain in 1970.

After an ascent of the Nose route on El Capitan, which had been pristine a few summers earlier, I came home disgusted with the degradation I had seen. The repeated hammering of hard steel pitons, during both placement and removal in the same fragile cracks, were severely disfiguring the rock. Frost [his friend and partner in the forge] and I decided we would phase out the piton business. ... Pitons were the mainstay of our business, but we were destroying the very rocks we loved.[5]

Chouinard and Frost found an alternative to hard steel pitons: aluminum chocks that can be wedged by hand and leave the rock unaltered. Two years later, Chouinard edited his first product catalog, and within a few months, the piton business was done; chocks sold faster than they could be made. Yvon Chouinard stumbled upon a need of the climbing world when he found a way for the activity he and others loved not to create environmental damage.

For Tami Simon, purpose came before business too:

I'm kind of a strange person in a certain way. I dropped out of college because I didn't feel like I actually could be myself in an academic environment. ... I felt that in the academic environment I was being asked to pose as somebody who had answers to questions when instead I had experiences that I wanted to explore more deeply. ... I went into a deep internal process where I prayed extremely hard and the prayer had to do with being of service. ... The way I was thinking as a 20-, 21-year-old college dropout was, "Could I please be given the opportunity to take the talents that I have and all the gifts that I have been given by a very supporting and loving family and terrific opportunities for higher education ... and give back in some way?" ... The prayer was, "God, I'm willing to do your work. Please show me what it is. Please just show me what it is."

This phrase "willing to do your work" was very important to me because I didn't want to be willful. I didn't want to insist that it had to go my way. At the same time I didn't want to be will-less where I was simply waiting in a coffee shop to be discovered. ...

I feel like Sounds True, this business, came to me as a 21-, 22-year-old as a gift and as a kind of covenant with the universe, a kind of bond where I said, "I'll serve you. I'll work really hard," and the other side of it was, "You'll be supported, you'll be shown, doors will open, you'll meet the people, opportunities will happen." It's this sense of a cosmic agreement that ... I could help distribute spiritual teachings from different wisdom traditions from around the world. And I could do it with sincerity and devotion. That was my outlook from the beginning. It was never really about me per se. I wanted to be myself, I wanted to be authentic, and I wanted to make a contribution.[6]

Decision-making through listening to evolutionary purpose

On what basis do Teal Organizations make important decisions, if not based on trade-offs related to profit and market share? By *listening in* to the organization's purpose. This is new vocabulary in an organizational setting. Achievement-Orange thinks of organizations *as machines,* and machines have no soul, no direction of their own. In that perspective, it's the role of the CEO and his leadership team to decide what the machine must do. In Evolutionary-Teal, an organization is viewed as a *living system,* an entity with its own energy, its own identity, its own creative potential and sense of direction. We don't need to tell it what to do; we just need to listen, partner with it, join it in its dance, and discover where it will take us.

> *At the heart of every organization is a self reaching out to new possibilities.*
> M. Wheatley & M. Kellner-Rogers

Brian Robertson, the founder of Holacracy, uses the term *evolutionary purpose* to indicate that organizations, just like us, have a calling and an evolutionary energy to move toward that calling:

What is the organization's identity? And what does it want? ... The metaphor is like the parent-child journey: ... we recognize our child has its own identity and its own path and its own purpose. And just because

I might be really excited at the idea of my child being a doctor, that doesn't mean I get to project that on my child. There is a harmful, co-dependent process when I do that. We've learned as parents that the healthy parent's journey is a differentiation process, and ironically that differentiation of parent and child allows each to have their own autonomy and identity more fully, which then allows a more conscious integration where we are in relationship and interconnect, but it's a relation of peers, of equals. …

It's us humans that can tune into the organization's evolutionary purpose; but the key is about separating identity and figuring out "What is this organization's calling?" Not "What do we want to use this organization to do, as property?" but rather "What is this life, this living system's creative potential?" That's what we mean by evolutionary purpose: the deepest creative potential to bring something new to life, to contribute something energetically, valuably to the world. … It's that creative impulse or potential that we want to tune into, independent from what we want ourselves.[7]

Buurtzorg provides an interesting illustration of Robertson's assertion. The company was created not only out of frustration with the way neighborhood nursing companies in the Netherlands had fragmented a noble profession into a series of senseless tasks. It grew out of a new, much broader perspective of neighborhood care. The purpose of care is not to inject medication or change a bandage; it is to help people have rich, meaningful, and autonomous lives, to whatever degree is possible. Within this broad definition, Buurtzorg keeps evolving, keeps moving to where it feels called.

Recently, for instance, one team in the countryside developed a new concept: a boarding house for patients, to offer the patient's primary caregiver a break. With most patients, Buurtzorg provides medical care, but someone else—often the patient's husband or wife, sometimes a patient's child—is really the primary caretaker. It is not unusual for the husband or wife, often elderly as well, to be exhausted by the constant care the patient needs, sometimes 24 hours a day. If the strain becomes too much, the caregiver can fall sick too. *Wouldn't it be wonderful,* one team of nurses thought, *if we could have a place where we could take in our patients for a day or two, or even a week—a sort of bed and breakfast and lunch and dinner and care—so that their primary caretaker could take a break and rest?* One of the nurses had inherited a small farmhouse in the countryside. Together, the team transformed it into a Buurtzorg boarding house.

At a recent company retreat, the team presented its concept to all of its colleagues. Now time will tell if this concept catches on, if other teams feel called to create boarding houses. Here is what makes Buurtzorg's approach to this potential extension of its purpose fasciating: there is no one at Buurtzorg, not even Jos de Blok, the founder, who makes the call in the name of the company to say, "Yes, this fits Buurtzorg's purpose, so we will create dozens of boarding houses and here is the budget we will allocate," or "No, this is not within the scope of Buurtzorg. Let's not pursue this." The idea of boarding houses will run its own course. If it is meant to be, if it has enough life force, it will attract nurses to make it happen and carry Buurtzorg into a new dimension of care. Otherwise, it will remain a small-scale experiment.

Interestingly, Buurtzorg never wrote down its purpose in the form of a mission statement. Jos de Blok and others talk about the purpose all the time. But they find that keeping it oral keeps it alive, and prevents it from becoming constraining. To use Robertson's term, it allows the purpose to be *evolutionary*, to keep evolving.

Now you might argue that it's easy for Buurtzorg to listen in to its purpose. There is an obvious purpose in caring for sick and old people (even though other neighborhood nursing companies in the Netherlands have lost track of it). But what about organizations that manufacture car parts, make tomato paste, or sell shoes? Is there really a higher purpose that these organizations can tap into?

I believe the answer is yes. From the perspective of *organizations as living entities*, any organization has its own soul, its own life force. The real question is: do we listen hard enough to hear the purpose? Take FAVI, the French brass foundry that sells components that go into electric motors, faucets, and gearboxes. Obviously, it's not hard to define a meaningful purpose for its business: faucets put the gift of running water at our fingertips. Gearboxes go into cars that bring us the gift of freedom to go where we please. Yet somehow, justifying the organization's purpose on its downstream activity feels a bit constructed. These might be the purposes of a faucet maker or a car manufacturer. But what about FAVI?

> *With age, I feel more clearly and distinctly … how ridiculous is anything that does not have its own meaning, its own soul, anything that is not imbued with love.*
>
> Marc Chagall

Early on in his tenure as CEO, Jean-François Zobrist invited all the factory employees to a meeting to figure out the organization's *raison d'être*. The soul searching was prompted by a proposed order that came out of the blue from a French car manufacturer. Could they, within a year, supply not only a gear fork, but a full gearbox? This single order would be larger than all of FAVI's existing business. Many people thought it was too risky. Zobrist felt the decision could not be made without inquiring into the purpose of the organization. In keeping with his style, he involved the whole company, in meetings with subgroups of 15 people at a time on Friday afternoons. He showed up at the meeting with no agenda and no process; he trusted that his colleagues would somehow self-organize in these meetings, reconvening every

Friday if needed, until they had answered this most fundamental question: what is our purpose?

After much discussion, when the obvious but superficial ideas had been discarded, the answer emerged with clarity. FAVI has two reasons for existence, two fundamental purposes: the first is to provide meaningful work in the area of Hallencourt, a rural area in northern France where good work is rare; the second is to give and receive love from clients. Yes, *love*, a word rarely heard in the world of business, a word few would expect in a blue-collar manufacturing environment. At FAVI, it has taken on real meaning. Operators don't just send products to their clients, they send products into which they have put their heart. A few years ago, around Christmas time, an operator at FAVI molded excess brass into a few small figurines of Santa and of reindeers. He added the figurines into the boxes of finished products, rather like kids put a message in a bottle they throw out to sea, imagining that someone, somewhere, would find it. Other operators have since picked up on the idea and at random times of the year add brass figurines into their shipments, as little tokens of love to their counterparts working on assembly lines at Volkswagen or Volvo, who will find the figurines when they unpack the boxes.

> *Most of us are tempted by power, money, and fame. When our mission is to serve others, we don't think as much about ourselves. Channeling our energy toward worthy pursuits is infinitely more effective in governing behavior than draconian compliance programs.*
>
> Dennis Bakke

Practices to listen in to evolutionary purpose

If we accept that an organization has its own energy, its own sense of direction, and that our role is to align with it rather than direct it, how do we find out where it wants to go?

Sensing

The simplest answer: do nothing special. Let self-management work its magic. There is a word that often comes up with Teal pioneers: *sensing*. We are all natural sensors; we are gifted to notice when something isn't working as well as it could or when a new opportunity opens up. With self-management, everybody can be a sensor and initiate changes—just as in a living organism every cell senses its environment and can alert the organism to needed change. We cannot stop sensing. Sensing happens everywhere, all the time, but in traditional organizations, the information often gets filtered out. Only the signals sensed at the top are acted upon, but unfortunately these signals are often distorted and far removed from reality on the ground. Holacracy's Brian Robertson uses a powerful analogy to talk about organizations filtering people's ability to sense their environment:

A transformative experience [happened] for me when I nearly crashed an airplane. I was a student pilot, and shortly into a solo flight my "Low Voltage" light came on. Every other instrument was telling me "all is well," so I ignored it, just like we do in organizational life all the time, when one lone "instrument" (a human) senses something that no one else does. Ignoring a key instrument proved to be a very bad decision when flying an airplane and helped catalyze my search for organizational approaches that didn't suffer from the same blindness—how can an organization fully harness each of us [as] human instruments, without "outvoting the low-voltage light"?[8]

A story can help illustrate how this works in practice. Two nurses on a Buurtzorg team found themselves pondering the fact that elderly people, when they fall, often break their hips. Hip replacements are routine surgery, but patients don't always recover the same autonomy. Could Buurtzorg play a role in preventing its older patients from falling down? The two nurses experimented and created a partnership with a physiotherapist and an occupational therapist from their neighborhood. They advised patients on small changes they could bring to their home interiors, and changes of habits that would minimize risks of falling down. Other teams showed interest, and the approach, now called Buurtzorg+, has spread throughout the country.

The two nurses sensed a need, and with the power of self-management acted upon it. Self-management helped the idea to spread. Any team interested in Buurtzorg+ can sign up for a training event that teaches them the basics of how the concept works and how to create such a partnership in their neighborhood. In a traditional organization, the low-voltage light might well have been ignored. Who knows whether their idea would have made it through the layers of management to reach the committees that have the authority to sign off on and fund such an initiative? And even if top management had endorsed the idea, a top-down decision to implement Buurtzorg+ countrywide might have felt like an imposition to the teams, who might have resisted the initiative or dragged their feet.

In a self-managing organization, change can come from any person who senses that change is needed. This is how nature has worked for millions of years. Innovation doesn't happen centrally, according to plan, but at the edges, all the time, when some organism senses a change in the environment and experiments to find an appropriate response. Some attempts fail to catch on; others rapidly spread to all corners of the ecosystem.

Practices in the spiritual realm

We are all naturally gifted sensors, but we can increase our capacity to sense with practice. Meditative or spiritual practices, in particular, can help us distance ourselves from self-centered needs and tap into broader sources of wisdom. Tami Simon, the founder of Sounds True, has found that spiritual practices have helped her develop her intuitive capacities, which she believes serves her well in her business, as she told Judi Neal, an academic focusing on spirituality in the workplace:

> *"Intuition is basically my entire existence," Tami states. She studies with a meditation teacher named Reggie Ray. Reggie's teacher taught him how to "read the signs" and Reggie passed these teachings on to Tami.*
>
> *"It's an art form and an indigenous survival skill. If you were on a hunt, you would watch for the tracks. That's how we pick projects. We read the signs. How many people are talking about it? How many requests do we get for a particular author? And what are our inner feelings about the project? That's very important, too."*
>
> *The company "reads the signs" for internal issues as well. ... One exercise that Tami finds useful for tapping into inspiration is a visualization exercise. She describes the process: "You visualize yourself going into the center of the Earth to tap into fresh waters and bring them to the surface. It's weird; totally new ideas just emerge. The visualization calms down the chatty mind and creates the space for vision to come forward."*[9]

Meditative practices and guided visualization tap into non-ordinary states of consciousness to bring to light insights that might not be available to the conscious mind in an ordinary waking state. For many employees, even of Teal Organizations, tapping into non-ordinary states of consciousness can feel like stretching the boundaries, and I've encountered few such practices during the research for this book. And yet, as people operating from Evolutionary-Teal in general become quite comfortable with and interested in transrational ways of knowing, I believe it's a reasonable assumption that such techniques might one day find their way into organizational settings.[10]

The empty chair

A simple, less esoteric practice to listen in to an organization's purpose consists of allocating an empty chair at every meeting to represent the organization and its evolutionary purpose. Anybody participating in the meeting can, at any time, change seats, to listen to and become the voice of the organization. Here are some questions one might tune into while sitting in that chair:

- Have the decisions and the discussion served you (the organization) well? How are you at the end of this meeting?
- What stands out to you from today's meeting?
- In what direction do you want to go? At what speed? Are we being bold enough? Too bold?
- Is there something else that needs to be said or discussed?

Heiligenfeld's use of small hand cymbals in meetings (see page 163) essentially boils down to the same. Whenever a person makes the cymbals sing, people are asked to reflect on the question "Am I in service to the topic we're discussing and to the organization?"

Sounds True has built a variation of the empty chair method into a New Year's ritual, where colleagues at the beginning of the year bless the office building for the year to come.[11] At the end of the ritual, colleagues sit together in silence and listen in to what Sounds True, the organization, wants from them for the year to come. Everyone who wants can share with the group what they have heard.

Large group processes

The empty chair can be used on a day-to-day basis, even for relatively minor decisions. When an organization faces a major inflection point, there are a number of beautiful, more elaborate processes that can help large groups of people to listen in jointly to their organization's purpose and sense of direction. These processes include Otto Scharmer's "Theory U," David Cooperrider's "Appreciative Inquiry," Marvin Weisbord and Sandra Janoff's "Future Search," and Harrison Owen's "Open Space." These processes are non-hierarchical and self-organizing. They often bring the "whole system" into the room: all colleagues of an organization, whether a few dozen, hundreds, or thousands, come together for a working session of one or several days. Clients, partners, and suppliers can be invited to join, to add their perspective to the inquiry. Each of these processes comes with its particular format, but they have one thing in common: they achieve the unlikely feat of giving everybody a voice (even when thousands of people are involved), while at the same time channeling these voices toward a valuable collective outcome.

These large group techniques can energize organizations in a way that top-down strategies cannot. Something extraordinary happens when a vision emerges collectively, with everybody in the room. People make a personal, emotional connection with the image of the future that emerges. And they take charge of implementing the vision: project teams emerge on the spot, based on people's interests, skills, and talents. Strategy is no longer the domain of a few minds at the top, and implementation is no longer a mandate given to a few program managers. A whole organization is mobilized to sense into the future and help that future unfold. (Chapter 3.3 gives an illustration of a two-day Appreciative Inquiry summary; see page 279.)

Heiligenfeld uses such large group meetings at regular intervals to sense into its future. From one such session, the vision emerged of bringing Heiligenfeld's holistic approach to mental illness to families with children and adolescents. Wouldn't it be wonderful if patients could be treated together with their close family members, in a way that would specifically address and honor the family ties in the therapy? A year later, Klinik Waldmünchen opened, a new mental health hospital specifically dedicated to therapy for families.

There is of course one prerequisite: leaders must be willing to surrender their power to the group. Once the process is underway, their voice has the same weight as anybody else's, not more. They can no longer control or steer the outcome in a specific direction. They must trust that the collective sensing of the group will come up with better answers than they could on their own. It takes humility, courage, and trust for a leader to surrender power in that way. Few leaders in large organizations today are ready to go down that path. Top-down strategy is, at least for now, the safe option for a leader wanting to stay in control (despite the evidence from experience as well as academic research that top-down change projects fail in great numbers).

Outside prompting

Many people have come to experience that when they follow their calling, life seems to bring up all the right opportunities at just the right time. The same seems to be true at the organizational level. When a company is clear about its purpose, the outside world comes knocking at its door with opportunities. Sometimes it feels as if it isn't only people inside the organization sensing where it wants to go, but people from the outside, too.

Buurtzorg provides a fascinating case in point. By now, people from all sorts of backgrounds get in touch with Jos de Blok and others in the organization to explore ideas that could shape where Buurtzorg might go next. De Blok and his colleagues accept these meetings and listen with open minds. When the discussion seems promising, they set up experiments and see what happens. There are no committees, no stage-gate processes, no set budgets. It really is that simple: discussions take place and things evolve from there. What is meant to happen will happen.

When a company is clear about its purpose, the outside world comes knocking at its door with opportunities.

Buurtzorg has, for instance, been approached by nurses and health care administrators from many countries in Europe and beyond. One team has started caring for patients in Sweden as of 2012, and there is serious interest coming from the United States, Switzerland, Belgium, England, Scotland, Canada, Japan, China, and Korea to start up teams there, too. There is not much effort involved for Buurtzorg in the Netherlands, other than to sit in a few meetings to listen, sense if things are meant to happen, and to provide support to those wanting to start Buurtzorg teams abroad.

Buurtzorg has also set up a unit called "Buurtdienst" (literally, "neighborhood services") that helps people such as Alzheimer's patients handle domestic chores. Working with the same structure of small teams, it has grown to 750 employees in two years. The organization has also been approached by youth workers. In 2012, the first two teams of

"Buurtzorg Jong" (literally, "Buurtzorg Young") have sprung up to work with neglected or delinquent children. The teams combine social workers, educators, and nurses, working with children and their families in their home, in collaboration with the police, schools, and family doctors. The teams self-organize like teams of nurses, and they hope to pull off the same trick: overcoming the fragmented nature of how social services are traditionally delivered and the high overhead costs of today's providers.

Exploration is ongoing to create "Buurtzorg T," bringing therapeutic care to people's homes in the early stages of mental illness. The therapists that approached Buurtzorg believe this type of care could prevent a substantial amount of placement in mental health hospitals.

Buurtzorg is also in talks to create small-scale community living units for older people, as an alternative to large, impersonal retirement homes. Exploration is also underway to think about the future of hospitals. In the pursuit of economies of scale, hospitals have grown into massive, bureaucratic, and often soulless institutions. What would a radically different concept look like, with small, networked units spread throughout neighborhoods of a city? In all of these cases, Buurtzorg reacts to outside stimulus and tries to sense what is meant to be.

Strategy as an organic process

The way Teal Organizations think about purpose turns the typical strategy process on its head. In traditional corporations, strategy is decided at the top. It's the domain of the CEO and the management team (supported in large corporations by a strategy department, a Chief Strategy Officer, or outside consultants). At regular intervals, a strategy process produces a thick document that sets out a new direction. The plan, and the change projects to put them in place, are then communicated top-down to the organization, often with some "burning-platform" message: we need to change, or else ...

In Teal Organizations, there is no strategy process. No one at the top sets out a course for others to follow. None of the organizations I have researched had a strategy in the form of a document that charts out a course. Instead, people in these companies have a very clear, keen sense of the organization's purpose and a broad sense of the direction the organization might be called to go. A more detailed map is not needed. It would limit possibilities to a narrow, pre-charted course.

With the purpose as a guiding light, everyone, individually and collectively, is empowered to sense what might be called for. Strategy happens organically, all the time, everywhere, as people toy with ideas and test them out in the field. The organization evolves, morphs, expands, or contracts, in response to a process of collective intelligence. Reality is the great referee, not the CEO, the board or a committee. What works gathers momentum and energy within the organization; other ideas fail to catch on and wither.

Product offering and marketing

Businesses have become highly sophisticated at slicing and dicing customers into segments based on their conscious and unconscious needs, preferences, and buying behaviors. For each customer segment, they will carefully position their products and brands to make themselves attractive. Increasingly, in our mature, consumerist markets, companies must create new needs, often playing cleverly on our secret fears and vanity. "Buy this and you will feel good about yourself." "Buy this and others will like you." "Buy this and you will be successful."

In comparison, Teal Organizations' approach to marketing is almost simplistic. The organizations simply listen in to what feels like the right offering. There are no customer surveys and no focus groups. Essentially, marketing boils down to this statement: *This is our offer. At this moment, we feel this is the best we can possibly do. We hope you will like it.* In a strange paradox, Teal Organizations go about filling a need of the world not by tuning in to the noise of the world (the surveys, the focus groups, the customer segmentation), but by listening within. *What product would we be really proud of? What product would fill a genuine need in the world?* These are the kinds of questions people turn to in Teal Organizations to define new products. It's a process guided by beauty and intuition more than analytics. Sounds True could sell many, many more books and recordings if it were to publish titles in the "Three-Step Guide to Bliss" segment of the market. But that has never been an option for Sounds True, which considers that such offerings add more confusion to people's lives than clarity.

> *When I die and go to hell, the devil is going to make me the marketing director for a cola company. I'll be in charge of trying to sell a product that no one needs, is identical to its competition, and can't be sold on its merits. I'll be competing head-on in the cola wars, on price, distribution, advertising and promotion, which would indeed be hell for me.*
>
> Yvon Chouinard

This approach works in the nuts and bolts world of manufacturing as well as it does for spiritual teachings. In the 1990s, Zobrist and a few colleagues at FAVI became fascinated with the following idea: foundries always produce alloys, because pure copper cannot be molded into a shape. What if FAVI could, somehow, do the impossible—shape industrial products made of 100 percent pure copper? They started tinkering. Would there be a market for such products? They had no idea, but they didn't care to commission a market study. Pure copper has some properties, like electrical conductivity, that alloys don't have; such a property must have a purpose. What really got them excited was not the market they might discover. They were excited by the beauty of the seemingly impossible: to shape pure copper. After two years of tinkering, they succeeded. And as they had imagined, a market came knocking at their door. Pure copper rotors have interesting properties in electrical motors, now an important business for FAVI.

The Orange approach to product development is predominantly a left-brain process: it focuses on technical features, stage gates, and costs of manufacturing. Evolutionary-Teal also invites the intuitive power of the right brain. With the help of a Japanese professor, Shoji Shiba, FAVI has adopted a product development process that explicitly factors in emotions, beauty, and intuition. How this can play out is illustrated by another experiment FAVI pursued a few years later. Metallurgists have long known that copper has antiseptic properties. *It's a shame,* people at FAVI thought, *that this property isn't put to use in products.* A team started tinkering with antimicrobial copper equipment for hospitals. A prototype soon gave promising results, but Zobrist was bothered by its color. The reddish color of copper evokes the faded world of old 19th-century sanatoriums, he found. Zobrist asked the project team if they could make a prototype with a silver-colored alloy, to give it the shine of stainless steel we associate with modern equipment. The team scoffed: this simply made no sense. The added material for the alloy would make the copper lose its antiseptic properties. Zobrist knew he had no ground to stand on. But he was possessed by a deep aesthetic and intuitive sense that it was worth pursuing. He managed to persuade the team into giving it a try. To everybody's surprise, and for reasons still unclear, the silver-color alloy not only kept the copper's antiseptic properties, it enhanced them. A new market opened for FAVI.

> *When I am working on a problem, I never think about beauty ... but when I have finished, if the solution is not beautiful, I know it is wrong.*
> Richard Buckminster Fuller

Planning, budgeting, and controlling

Teal Organizations' approach to planning and budgeting departs quite radically from what is considered best practice in traditional management thinking. Instead of trying to *predict and control* (the goal behind all planning and budgeting practices), Teal Organizations try to *sense and respond.* Brian Robertson from Holacracy uses a powerful metaphor to contrast the two approaches:

> *Imagine if we rode a bicycle like we try to manage our companies today. It would look something like this: we'd have our big committee meeting, where we all plan how to best steer the bicycle. We'd fearfully look at the road up ahead, trying to predict exactly where the bicycle is going to be when. ... We'd make our plans, we'd have our project managers, we'd have our Gantt charts, we'd put in place our controls to make sure this all goes according to plan.*
>
> *Then we get on the bicycle, we close our eyes, we hold the handle bar rigidly at the angle we calculated up front and we try to steer according to plan. And if the bicycle falls over somewhere along the way ... well, first: who is to blame? Let's find them, fire them, get them out of here.*

And then: we know what to do differently next time. We obviously missed something. We need more upfront prediction. We need more controls to make sure things go according to plan. …

Our underlying management paradigm today is based on trying to predict and control. And the challenge with that: it often gives us more illusion of control than real control. And we do want *real control. Holacracy tries to bake into the core of the organization a paradigm shift to a steering modality we call dynamic steering, which is based not on predict and control, but on sense and respond.*

When you are actually riding a bicycle, steering is not something you do once upfront; it's something you do in continuous flow, with micro increments all the time, and you do it consciously, you do it based on opening your eyes, taking in data in multiple ways. You've got your balance, your heading, you've got your senses fully at play by staying present in the moment, sensing your reality and consciously choosing your response at every moment. It's not directionless, you still have a purpose pulling you forward, and in fact you are more likely to maintain control towards expressing your purpose by being conscious and present in every moment.

The deep challenge here: it requires letting go of our beautiful illusion of control, our comforting illusion of control. The illusion that we've done our job as leaders: we've done all the analysis, we've got the plan, things are going to go according to plan, we are in control. It's a much higher bar, and a much scarier standard to let go of those illusions, to get clear on purpose and to stay conscious and present in every moment.[12]

FAVI uses another metaphor that hints at the same underlying paradigm shift. The traditional practice in organizations, says FAVI, is to look five years ahead and make plans for the next year. FAVI believes we should think like farmers: look 20 years ahead, and plan only for the next day. One must look far out to decide which fruit trees to plant or which crops to grow. But it makes no sense to plan at the beginning of the year the precise date for harvest. As hard as we try, we cannot control the weather, the crops, the soil; they all have a life of their own beyond our control. A farmer who would stick rigidly to plan, instead of sensing and adjusting to reality, would quickly grow hungry.

What does this mean in practice for organizations? How can they learn to *sense and respond*?

Workable solutions, fast iterations

The paradigm of *predict and control* naturally prompts us to look for perfect answers. If the future can be predicted, then our job is to find the solutions that will reap the best results in the future we foresee. Predictions are valuable in a *complicated* world, but they lose all relevance in a *complex* world. Jean-François Zobrist at FAVI found insightful metaphors to explain the difference. An airplane like a Boeing 747 is a *complicated* system. There are millions of parts that need to work together seamlessly. But everything can be mapped out; if you change one part, you should be able to predict all the consequences. A bowl of spaghetti is a *complex* system. Even though it has just a few dozen "parts," it is virtually impossible to predict what will happen when you pull at the end of a strand of spaghetti that sticks out of the bowl.

Making predictions gives us a comforting sense of control. But the reality is that organizations and the world we live in have become *complex* systems. In such systems, it becomes meaningless to predict the future, and then analyze our way into *the best* decision. When we do, out of habit, we only waste energy and time producing an illusion of control and perfection. Teal Organizations make peace with a complex world in which perfection eludes us. They shoot explicitly not for the *best possible decision*, but for a *workable solution* that can be implemented quickly. Based on new information, the decision can be revisited and improved at any point.

> *In complicated systems, we can try to figure out* the best *solution. In complex systems, we need* workable *solutions and fast iterations.*

These principles are at the heart of lean manufacturing and agile software development, two approaches that have revolutionized their respective fields. Holacracy's governance process and Buurtzorg's decision-making process show that they can be embedded in all departments of an organization. In both cases, if there is a workable solution on the table—"workable" meaning a solution that nobody believes will make things worse—it will be adopted. Decisions are not postponed because someone thinks more data or more analysis could result in a better decision. The decision can be reviewed at any time if new data comes up or someone stumbles on a better idea.[13] Coming back to the analogy of the bicycle: instead of trying to calculate the perfect angle, the rider gets on the bike straight away, starts with an angle that seems about right, and then keeps adjusting to get to the destination.

Companies that work this way, that make many fast iterations instead of a few mighty leaps, progress much faster and much more smoothly toward their purpose. No energy is wasted figuring out the supposedly best decision; no time is wasted waiting for more data and more certainty before making decisions. Just as important, when decisions are small and we are used to revising them often, it also becomes much easier to correct a decision that proves mistaken. (Whereas when we have invested much effort in defining *the best* solutions, we become attached to them and stick with them much longer than needed when things don't turn out as planned). In the end, paradoxically, we feel safer in a world where we give up the illusion of control gained from predicting the future and learn to work with reality as it unfolds.

No targets

Teal Organizations don't set any top-down targets. You might remember that sales people at FAVI have no targets to reach. From an Evolutionary-Teal perspective, targets are problematic for at least three reasons: they rest on the assumption that we can predict the future, they skew our behavior away from inner motivation, and they tend to narrow our capacity to sense new possibilities.

Life is so complex, and events and circumstances change so fast, that setting a target is mostly guesswork; a year after it has been set, a target is in most cases just an arbitrary number—either so easy to reach as to be meaningless or so challenging that people must take shortcuts to meet the number, actions that will hurt the company in the long run.

Targets also skew our behavior. In many companies, there is an open secret: managers make sure to spend any budget left at the end of the year, sometimes on pretty meaningless expenditures. They fear their funding might be cut the next year if it appears they didn't need all their budget this year. Sales people who reach their yearly target early (say, in September) stop selling until January. They fear that next year's target will be increased if they overshoot this year's target. Without targets, these games disappear. People are free to tap into their inner motivation to simply do the best job they can.

In self-managing organizations, people can choose to set themselves targets when they find it useful—rather like a hobby runner who spurs herself on by extending her goals. At FAVI, operators set themselves target times to machine their pieces, and they monitor their performance against that target. Colleagues at Morning Star set themselves targets for their part of the process, to stimulate continuous improvement. They measure indicators, compare them to the self-set targets, analyze root causes, and experiment with new ideas. These targets are mostly set at a local level, for one machine or one process step, where the outcomes can be predicted with some certainty.

But even with self-set targets, we need to be careful not to focus too narrowly on the target only. We need to stay open to the unexpected, the new, the signs that a different future might want to unfold that we hadn't imagined when we set the target. Targets, well understood, are like maps that guide toward one possible future. They become problematic when we cling to the road we had set out on even after circumstances have changed and a new road seems more promising. Margaret J. Wheatley and Myron Kellner-Rogers put it well:

> *Life is intent on finding what works. ... The capacity to keep changing, to find what works now, is what keeps any organism alive.*
> M. Wheatley & M. Kellner-Rogers

> *[In] an emergent world ... we can no longer stand at the end of something we visualize in detail and plan backwards from that future. Instead we must stand at the beginning, clear in our intent, with a*

willingness to be involved in discovery. The world asks that we focus less on how we can coerce something to make it conform to our designs and focus more on how we can engage with one another, how we can enter into the experience and then notice what comes forth. It asks that we participate more than plan.[14]

Simplified budgets, no tracking of variance

Many traditional organizations go through a painful budgeting cycle every year. In a bottom-up fashion, functional teams and business are asked to provide data and predictions for the next year. Top management then pores over the aggregated results, and more often than not, finds them lacking in ambition. In a top-down manner, bosses tell business units to up their predictions. Sometimes a few more rounds are needed, until numbers are reached that top management is satisfied with. By that time, people at the frontline have lost all faith in the numbers they had to submit (unless they were cunning enough to hide some sources of revenue and savings from the higher-ups). From that moment on, the budget is owned by the CFO, who will track the difference between plan and reality month after month. Managers that fall short are called in to justify why they didn't make the numbers. This process triggers painful discussions that suck much energy into explaining the problem away, blaming bad market conditions or a neighboring unit.

> *If you want to make God laugh, tell him your plans.*
> Woody Allen

The pioneers researched for this book take a simpler approach:

- Budgets are established only if some forecast is needed to inform an important decision. At FAVI, for instance, teams make rough monthly predictions for the year to come, to secure contracts for raw materials. Otherwise, many of these companies don't create any budget at all. Sun Hydraulics makes no budget (unless the board demands one, in which case a rough one-page budget is put together). Teams in Buurtzorg don't do any significant purchasing or investments, so they don't bother with budgets either. At the aggregate level, Buurtzorg makes a simple projection of its expected cash flow to get a sense of how many new teams it can allow to start up; new teams can take up to a year to break even, and Buurtzorg wants to make sure it doesn't go bust if too many new teams get started at the same time.
- If a budget is established, there is no tweaking from above. Whatever numbers the teams forecast become the budget. In some companies, peers challenge each other's budgets, but no one can force a team to change their numbers. For example at Morning Star, units present their budget and investment plans to a budget task force, composed of volunteers from all parts of the business, that can challenge the numbers, and offer opinions and suggestions. AES used to have a similar process.

- Budgets are used to make decisions, not to control performance. Companies like FAVI or Morning Star that put together budgets have found that there is no value in tracking differences between forecast and reality; they don't waste energy doing it.

In its management manifesto, FAVI captures the thinking about budgets in a provocative statement: "In the new way of thinking, we aim to *make money without knowing how we do it*, as opposed to the old way of *losing money knowing exactly how we lose it*." FAVI is privately owned and doesn't need to report to outside shareholders. The case of Sun Hydraulics shows that this budget-free approach is possible even for a publicly listed company, as Allen Carlson, the CEO, explains:

> *I never worry about the future. It comes soon enough.*
> Albert Einstein

> *After our IPO in January 1997, we had to get better at predicting our numbers. … The market penalized us when we missed one quarter in '99 after we adopted a new manufacturing system. We said, "Look, we can't predict what's going on in the economy, and we have no idea what our orders will look like a year from now. … We don't run this business by the numbers. The numbers will be doing what the numbers will be doing; we can just give you a good picture of what the next quarter will bring. So, we got away from making annual projections and started just doing quarterly forecasts. … We know our performance in the long run will be a result of just doing the right things every day.*[15]

Most business leaders would feel naked without budgets and forecasts. I put this question to Carlson: *How do you deal with having no forecasts to compare people's performance to? For instance, how do you know if the guys in Germany (where Sun has a plant) were doing a good job last year, if you have no target to compare against?* His answer came shooting out of the barrel:

> *Who knows? Who cares? They are all working hard, doing the best they can. We have good people in all the places around the world and if I need that sort of scorecard I probably got the wrong person. That's just the way we operate. … If I'm the head of sales of Sun in the US and you ask me what is the forecast, I have no clue! How could I generate one anyway? … At the end of the day, there is so much outside of your control. … It's impossible to predict the unpredictable.*[16]

Change management

Earlier in this chapter, we discussed how Teal pioneers never talk about competition. Here are two other terms I have not encountered even once during the research: *change* and *change management*. This is rather extraordinary, when we come to think of it! Every manager knows that making change happen in an organization is hard. Change is one of the most frustrating, and therefore most widely discussed, problems of management today. A whole industry of experts and consultants in change management has sprung forth to support managers in the trying journey of change. In the pioneer Teal Organizations in this book, however, change seems to happen naturally and continuously. It doesn't seem to require any attention, effort, or management. What is going on here?

In the machine paradigm of Orange, organizations are viewed as inanimate, static systems—a collection of boxes that stack up in a pyramid structure. Static systems don't have an inner capacity for change. Force must be applied to the system from the outside. Change in that worldview is not a fluid, emerging phenomenon, but a one-time movement from point A to point B, from one static state to another.

Change in this worldview is an unfortunate necessity. We try to minimize the need for change by predicting and controlling the future. We seek to plan the surprises out of life. We pray that reality stays within the boundaries of the budget and the strategic plan. When it doesn't, we often bury our head in the sand; we can't imagine that reality will be so cruel as to make our plans irrelevant. When we put our head up again, and we notice that the world around us has changed while we stuck to plan, we are frightened by what we see. We now have to make up for lost time and force change to happen.

> *People don't resist change. They resist being changed.*
>
> Peter Senge

The change will be painful, we tell ourselves, but once we reach point B, everything will be fine again. In the meantime, we need to redesign the organization like we redesign a machine, moving people around to fit the new blueprint. Not surprisingly, people resist being moved around. To overcome resistance, organizations often feel compelled to play on fears, telling frightening stories of how a hostile, competitive world threatens their survival if nothing changes.

In a world where organizations are self-managing, living systems, we don't need to impose change from the outside. Living systems have the innate capacity to sense changes in their environment and to adapt from within. In a forest, there is no master tree that plans and dictates change when rain fails to fall or when the spring comes early. The whole ecosystem reacts creatively, in the moment. Teal Organizations deal with change in a similar way. People are free to act on what they sense is needed; they are not boxed in by static job descriptions, reporting lines, and functional units. They can react creatively to life's emerging, surprising, non-linear unfolding. Change is a given, it happens naturally, everywhere, all the time, mostly without pain and effort.

If your organization has started to adopt Teal practices, the way it deals with change can reveal how far it has come. If change is still a concern, a topic of discussion, take it as an invitation to inquire among your colleagues: *Where are we still stuck in the machine paradigm? How can we help the organization express itself fully as a living system?*

Customers, suppliers, and information flow

When an organization takes its purpose seriously, it can't limit its concern to the boundaries of the organization. It will naturally embrace suppliers and customers in its quest to manifest the purpose.

Patagonia, for instance, will only work with garment suppliers with impeccable environmental practices; RHD will favor suppliers that maintain a high standard of integrity in dealing with their employees. Suppliers are chosen not just based on price and quality, but also on their alignment with the organization's purpose.

Teal Organizations often reach out to their customers, too, to involve them in their purpose. We discussed earlier in this chapter how Patagonia calls upon its customers to extend the lifecycle of their clothes by having them repaired, reused, or recycled. The RHD "-ism committee" not only teaches RHD's staff ways to recognize and deal with overt and covert forms of racism, sexism, or other forms of –ism. It has also started teaching some of the residents in its homes and shelters these social skills. Only by enlisting its customers can RHD truly live out its purpose to help people live lives of autonomy, dignity, and respect.

Stepping beyond the boundaries of the organization to enlist support from suppliers and consumers is not always comfortable. It requires that the organization state publicly and clearly what it stands for, what it believes in, and what it requests from its suppliers and consumers. Not all suppliers welcome the scrutiny, and consumers can be turned off by an activist stance. Perhaps more uncomfortable still: when purpose is paramount, it would be inconsistent to be open about the purpose to outsiders but secretive about *how* the organization is pursuing that purpose. Often we are secretive not only for competitive reasons, but also simply because we fear embarrassment if we opened up our inner ways of working to outside scrutiny. But from a purpose perspective, we have much to gain by opening up to outsiders who can help us with feedback and expertise. Patagonia has gone that route with its "Footprint Chronicles," an initiative aiming to provide total transparency to the outside world about its supply chain. Casey Sheahan, Patagonia's current CEO, explains the journey the company took and its unexpected consequences:

> *About four years ago, we took what was a traditional Corporate Social Responsibility report and we put everything online and it's called the Footprint Chronicles. ... We actually took video cameras, we took tape recorders and still cameras into the factories. We told our factories: we intend to show our customers where everything is made, how it's*

made, what the conditions are like, what the impact of transportation and water usage is on the overall carbon footprint. The Footprint Chronicles talks about the good, the bad, and the ugly of everything we make. It's tracking about 40 styles right now, which represent hundreds of our overall styles in our annual seasonal output.

The factories at first, like all of us, were reluctant to go down this path of total transparency. But ... what happened was that customers, biologists, and efficiency experts would give us ideas about how to do a better job of manufacturing and shipping apparel, providing that information to us via email. It became a really exciting exchange, given how interactive the web is and how immediate it is. We learned a lot.

It was just a new way of thinking about transparency that had before been, "Well gosh, I can't talk about this stuff, I can't open the kimono on what's going on in my business. Someone might attack me and get angry." But it's turned out that the more honest and open and candid we are with what's going on, the more our customers are wanting to engage with us in our efforts to be a better global citizen.[17]

I believe we will increasingly witness companies choosing a radical level of honesty when dealing with outside parties that can help their purpose materialize. With fewer ego-fears, there is less need for PR polish, less urge to hide failures. Outsiders can be granted a deep view inside the organization, in all sorts of ways. Clients can participate in workshops to listen in to the purpose; all-hands meetings can be streamed live over the Internet (a regular practice at Zappos.com, for instance); or, like Patagonia, companies can choose to film their key production processes and publish them online. HolacracyOne has developed an intranet-type software called Glassfrog that captures people's roles and accountabilities, the structure of the organization, meeting notes and metrics. Traditionally this kind of data is deemed sensitive and restricted to employees of the organization. HolacracyOne has chosen to put everything online. Anybody from the outside can look at who holds what responsibility, read the latest meeting notes, or take a peek at the company's internal numbers.

Purposeful mood management

Organizations, like the human beings they comprise, have moods.[18] I know of organizations, or units within them, that live in a mood of resignation; others that exude fear and resentment; and yet others that brim with ambition. Psychology, neuroscience, and ancient wisdom traditions all teach us in their own way how powerfully moods and emotions can limit—or increase—what we can achieve. Under the spell of frustration, we are predisposed to give up, to abandon. Anger predisposes us to strike back, to seek revenge. A mood of ambition sets us up to shoot higher, to go for it.

Moods determine what is possible: every mood predisposes us to a particular course of action, and closes us to many others. Consciously managing the mood of an organization is therefore one of the most potent (yet often overlooked) tools that can help us to achieve—or fail to achieve—a collective purpose. As with purpose itself, we should be careful not to project our individual wishes onto the organization. Our personality might tend toward certain moods more than others—for instance some people prefer a playful, exuberant atmosphere at work, while others prefer a more serious, focused mood. The question, of course, is: What is the mood that would best serve the organization at this moment in time so as to achieve its purpose? It might well be playfulness or concentration, but perhaps it is something else altogether—a mood of prudence, joy, pride, care, gratitude, wonder, curiosity, or determination.

Say you sense that gratitude is called for. Gratitude is a powerful emotion. We declare that we are satisfied. We can drop our search for more; in this moment, we have everything we need. Out of that fullness, other emotions naturally bubble up. We tend to get in touch with joy and generosity, and we treat others with love and care.

If this mood is so powerful, how can we nurture it consciously in the workplace? We need to invent practices that evoke the mood:

- FAVI, for a number of years, had a beautiful practice of gratitude and celebration: every meeting in the company started with a round where each participant in turn shared a brief story of someone they had recently thanked or congratulated (see page 163).
- Remember Ozvision's practice of the "day of thanking" (see page 161)? Every employee gets an extra day off and an envelope of $200 in cash to spend in any way they want to express their gratitude to somebody who has been important in their life. When they come back to work, they share the story of what happened that day with their 40 colleagues. Over time, these stories weave a powerful mood of gratitude.
- The Friday afternoon "praise meeting" at ESBZ, the school in Berlin, also works to foster a mood of gratitude (see page 160). Every small story of kindness, courage, care, or professionalism told at the microphone is a thread woven into a rich tapestry of gratitude that has become key to the school's exceptional learning culture. Faculty meetings have now integrated the same practice: they always start with a round of praise.
- BerylHealth, a Texas-based company that provides call center and other services to hospitals, has come up with a variation of the school's practice. Instead of physically coming together, a mass email chain always erupts at some point on Friday afternoon (hence the name the practice has taken: "Good Stuff Friday"). One colleague sends an email to the entire workforce recognizing and thanking a colleague or another department for something that

happened that week, or simply to share some good news. The first email invariably triggers a whole avalanche of thanking and recognition. The practice builds community and closes the week in a spirit of appreciation and gratitude.[19]

Individual and organizational purpose

Individual and organizational purpose go hand in hand. One needs the other to flourish. Most of today's organizations are primarily concerned with self-preservation and the bottom line, hardly a good setting for people to explore their calling. In such a setting, employees also view work in terms of self-preservation—as a way to get a paycheck that pays the bills. In contrast, when colleagues are invited to listen in to their organization's purpose, they are likely to wonder about their personal calling too: *Does the organization's purpose resonate with me? Is this a place I feel called to work? What do I really feel called to do at this moment in my life? Will this place allow me to express my selfhood? Will it help me grow and develop?*

When the individual and organizational purpose enter into resonance and reinforce each other, extraordinary things can happen. When work meets vocation—an encounter that theologian Frederick Buechner described as "the place where your deep gladness meets the world's deep hunger"—we often feel overcome with grace. It feels like we have grown wings. Working from our strengths, everything feels effortless and we feel productive like rarely before.

Recruitment, training, and appraisal discussions are times that lend themselves naturally to exploring the junction of individual and collective purpose. Take recruitment. The previous chapter suggested that, in their recruitment process, Teal Organizations look at three types of fit: fit with the role (the traditional skill and behavioral interview), fit with the organization (its values and self-management practices), and fit with its purpose. Fit with the purpose cannot be explored meaningfully without touching on personal purpose, too. Here are some questions that can be weaved into the recruitment discussions:

> *Our deepest calling is to grow into our own authentic selfhood, whether or not it conforms to some image of who we ought to be. As we do so, we will not only find the joy that every human being seeks—we will also find our path of authentic service in the world.*
>
> Parker Palmer

- What is your sense of your life trajectory? How could working here fit with what you sense you are called to be and to do in the world?
- What aspect of the organizational purpose resonates with you? What unique talents and gifts could you contribute to the organization's journey?

Ultimately, both parties are trying to answer one simple, fundamental question: *Do we sense that we are meant to journey together?*

The discussion triggered by these questions can reach substantial depth and help both the prospective candidate and the organization learn more about themselves; recruitment becomes a process of self-enquiry as much as a process of mutual assessment. Many Teal Organizations report that their recruitment process and decisions can take significantly longer than usual. They sometimes accept to grow more slowly, keeping a posting open until they find a person that fits not only the job opening but also the organization and its purpose.

Questions that came up in the recruitment process can be explored again during annual performance discussions. Heiligenfeld, the German network of mental health hospitals, includes two wonderfully simple questions to prompt such a discussion in the yearly appraisal process:

- Is my heart at work?
- Do I sense that I am at the right place?

Questions about our purpose and calling are simple to ask but can be difficult to answer. Organizations can support individuals in their self-reflection through individual coaching or workshops that can tap into techniques like storytelling or guided visualization to help them discern what their path in life may be.

Most organizations today feel that they are in business to get stuff done, not to help people figure out their calling (and in these soulless organizations, many people would be reluctant to explore subjects as intimate as one's personal calling). Yet individual and organizational purpose go hand in hand. It's at the juncture where organizational purpose and individual calling start to resonate with and reinforce each other that truly extraordinary things happen. The more clarity there is around what the organization is called to do, the more people can enter into resonance with it. And the more people know about their calling, the more they can contribute to the organization's energy to do its work in the world.

> *Organizations could accomplish so much more if they relied on the passion evoked when we connect to others, purpose to purpose. So many of us want to be more. So many of us hunger to discover who we might become together.*
>
> M. Wheatley & M. Kellner-Rogers

Listening to evolutionary purpose—in summary

It's not only Jack Welch's business book that promises "winning." Take any of the most influential business best sellers of the last 20 years—*The Seven Habits of Highly Effective People, In Search of Excellence, Built to Last, From Good to Great, Competitive Advantage*—and the very titles of the books reveal what most leaders today believe to be the primary objective in business: being successful, beating the competition, and making it to the top.[20] With that perspective, profit and market share are the name of the game. It's the essence of the shareholder model: the manager's duty is not to serve some purpose in the world, but to maximize shareholder value.

More recently, we've seen the emergence of a new perspective, the *stakeholder model*, which insists that companies have to answer not only to investors, but also to customers, employees, suppliers, the local community, the environment, and others. An organization's leadership must mediate between the often-conflicting needs of stakeholders, so that everybody is satisfied in the long run. A number of highly successful companies like Whole Foods and Southwest Airlines are vocal advocates of this more balanced perspective. Viewed from an evolutionary perspective, the (Pluralistic-Green) stakeholder model is a clear step up from the more narrow (Achievement-Orange) shareholder model. But the organization is still viewed as an entity that we humans need to steer, so that it can serve all stakeholders.

The next step—the Evolutionary-Teal perspective—views the organization no longer as property, not even shared property in service of its different stakeholders. The organization is viewed as an energy field, emerging potential, a form of life that transcends its stakeholders, pursuing its own unique evolutionary purpose. In that paradigm, we don't "run" the organization, not even if we are the founder or legal owner. Instead, we are stewards of the organization; we are the vehicle that listens in to the organization's deep creative potential to help it do its work in the world.

This perspective is so profoundly new and different that we probably cannot yet fully comprehend all its implications. For instance, how can anyone "own" an organization, or some shares of the organization, if we see it as an energy field or a life form of its own? Today, investors own organizations. We might have to invent new legal frameworks that give investors their proper place, while respecting the autonomy of the organization.

There is certainly more to be learned and understood, but the pioneer organizations researched for this book give us a solid set of practices toward listening in to the evolutionary purpose of an organization. The tables on pages 223-224 give a quick summary of these practices, contrasting them with the dominant (Orange) perspective in the field of management today. Ultimately, granting organizations their own evolutionary impulse can be a tremendous relief. We don't need to foresee the future to devise a perfect strategy, we don't need to force change to happen, we don't need to make detailed budgets and kick ourselves when we don't meet the numbers. We can partner with life and listen in to what wants to come about. In *A Simpler Way*, Margaret J. Wheatley and Myron Kellner-Rogers put it well:

> *Work is love in action.*
>
> Peter Caddy

It's a strange place for us to be, this self-organizing world. ... We don't have to be the organizers. We don't have to design the world. ... We could give up our belief ... that all forms of organization are our responsibility, that it's a difficult, arduous task to ... to make something manifest. We could give up our belief that nothing happens without us. The world knows how to create itself. We are its good partners in this process. Or we can be.[21]

	Orange practices		Teal practices
Concept of purpose	• Primary purpose is organizational self-preservation (whatever the mission statement says)	➡	• Organization seen as a living entity with its own evolutionary purpose
Strategy	• Strategic course charted by top leadership	➡	• Strategy emerges organically from the collective intelligence of self-managing employees
Decision-making	• (No practices to listen to the purpose; self-preservation against competition is the key driver of decision making)	➡	• Practices to listen into the organization's purpose: – Everyone a sensor – Large group processes – Meditations, guided visualizations, etc. – Responding to outside prompting
Competition	• Competition is the enemy that energizes action	➡	• The concept of competition is irrelevant • "Competitors" are embraced to pursue purpose
Growth and market share	• Key drivers of success	➡	• Significant only inasmuch as they help achieve purpose
Profit	• Leading indicator	➡	• Lagging indicator: will come naturally when doing the right thing
Marketing & product development	• Outside in: customer surveys and segmentation define the offer • Client needs are created if necessary	➡	• Inside out: offer is defined by purpose • Guided by intuition and beauty

	Orange practices		Teal practices
Planning, budgeting, & controlling	• Based on "predict and control" • Painful cycles of mid-term planning, yearly and monthly budgets • Stick to plan is the rule, deviations must be explained and gaps closed • Ambitious targets to motivate employees	➡	• Based on "sense and respond" • No or radically simplified budgets, no tracking of variance • Workable solutions and fast iterations instead of searching for "perfect" answers • Constant sensing of what's needed • No targets
Change management	• Whole arsenal of change management tools to get organization to change from A to B	➡	• ("Change" no longer a relevant topic because organizations constantly adapt from within)
Suppliers and transparency	• Suppliers chosen based on price and quality • Secrecy toward the outside world is the default position	➡	• Suppliers also chosen by fit with purpose • Total transparency invites outsiders to make suggestions to better bring about purpose
Mood management	-	➡	• Conscious sensing of what mood would serve the organization's purpose
Individual purpose	• (It's not the organization's role to help employees identify their personal calling)	➡	• Recruitment, training, and appraisals used to explore juncture of individual calling and organizational purpose

CHAPTER 2.7

COMMON CULTURAL TRAITS

Culture is a little like dropping an Alka-Seltzer into a glass. You don't see it, but somehow it does something.

Hans Magnus Enzensberger

The previous three chapters have focused on organizational structures, systems, processes, and practices—the tangible aspects of Teal Organizations. This chapter discusses the less visible but equally powerful aspect of *organizational culture*. The term is generally used to refer to the assumptions, norms, and concerns shared by the people of an organization. A simpler way to put it is: culture is *how* things get done, without people having to think about it. It's something in the air that visitors pick up on when they walk the hallways of an organization. Often we can't pinpoint anything in particular, and yet everything is revealing to some extent—for example, how offices are decorated, what people talk about at the water cooler, the jokes they make, how people with big and small jobs interact, how people deal with good and bad news. Bob Koski, the co-founder of Sun Hydraulics, called it the *character* of an organization:

> *I judge the character of an organization in two ways. To gauge its short-term health, I listen for what kind of humor—dark, lively, or absent—appears throughout the organization and notice if people line up to leave as soon as the bell rings at the end of the day. To assess its long-term quality or strength, I wonder how well it can heal itself from injury. Does it enable people to take risks so they can develop the self-confidence that allows healing? Is there a practice of comforting? Are there big objectives? Does it foster a corporate culture of trust and questioning, even though questioning can be a sign of distrust?*[1]

Koski's questions point to the power of organizational culture. In subtle but very real ways, culture makes or breaks organizations, makes them thrive or stumble. Numerous academic studies have established the powerful link between culture and results, and yet in the Achievement/Orange machine paradigm, many still dismiss culture as "soft" stuff. In the machine paradigm, the "hard" stuff is what matters—whether the complex organizational machinery is set up to function properly. Wondering about soft stuff is somehow incongruous—who worries about the inner life of cogs? Leaders operating from Orange often seem perplexed when a perfect plan they worked out is derailed by people's behavior (communication problems, conflicts, resistance to change, for example).

Because we are human beings and not cogs, assumptions, norms, and concerns play a critical role in our behavior. Take an organization where people share the assumption that information must be communicated freely. Compare it to another where people believe that information is power and should be shared only on a need-to-know basis. Obviously the two organizations won't achieve the same outcomes. Or picture an organization where it's accepted practice to blame others and complain behind their backs. Compare it to another with the shared norm that people own their accountabilities and work out differences one-on-one. It's easy to guess which of the two provides a more productive and pleasant workplace.

Leaders looking at the world through Pluralistic-Green lenses often take the opposite perspective. To them, culture is the ultimate asset, the alpha and the omega of corporate success. In Green's metaphor of organization as a family, everything is personal and relational. In that perspective, few things are more critical—and deserving of investment in time and money—than to ensure that the family has a healthy rather than a dysfunctional family culture.

How culture, systems, and worldviews interact: the four quadrants

Which side of the argument has got it right, then? Is it best to rely on the tangible elements of structure or the intangible substance of culture? The answer has profound implications for leaders, and yet this question is often discussed without much grounding. Ken Wilber's *four-quadrant* model can provide a solid basis for this discussion through a few simple yet powerful distinctions. Wilber, the founder of Integral Theory, uncovered a profound truth about the nature of reality: any phenomenon has four facets and can be approached from four sides. To understand it well, we should both look at it objectively from the outside (the tangible, measurable, exterior dimension) *and* we should sense the phenomenon from the inside (the intangible interior dimension of thoughts, feelings, and sensations). We must also look at the event in isolation (the individual dimension) *and* look at the event in its broader context (the collective dimension). Only when we look at all four aspects will we get what Wilber calls an *integral* grasp of reality.

Wilber's insight, applied to organizations, means that we should look at 1) people's mindsets and beliefs; 2) people's behavior; 3) the organizational culture; and 4) the organizational structures, processes, and practices. (Incidentally, this is what this book does for Teal Organizations: mindsets, beliefs, and behaviors are discussed in chapter 1.3 and 3.1; organizational systems in chapters 2.2 through 2.6; and organizational culture in this chapter.)

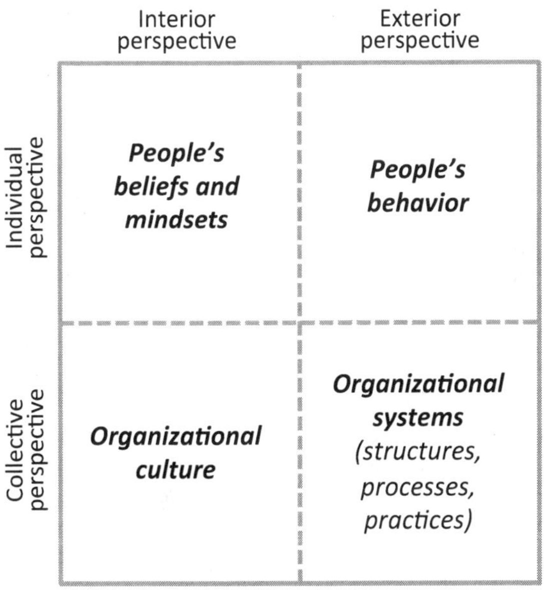

Wilber's four-quadrant model applied to organizations

A practical example can help us better understand the model. Let's take the common (Orange) belief that people are motivated by money and recognition. Leaders who hold such a belief (upper-left corner) will naturally put in place incentive systems that match their belief: people should be given ambitious targets and a lofty bonus if they reach them (lower-right quadrant). The belief and the incentives will likely affect people's behavior throughout the organization: people will behave individualistically; they will be tempted to cut corners if needed to make the numbers (upper-right quadrant). And a culture will develop that esteems great achievers above team players (lower-left corner).

	Interior	Exterior
Individual	**Beliefs & mindsets** *People are motivated by money and recognition*	**Behavior** *Individualistic behavior, people cut corners to make the numbers*
Collective	**Organizational culture** *Culture of internal competition, individual achievers valued above team players*	**Structures, processes, practices** *Top-down target setting, individual incentives*

The four-quadrant model shows how deeply mindsets, culture, behavior, and systems are intertwined. A change in any one dimension will ripple through the other three. Yet very often, we don't grasp the full picture. Amber and Orange only see the "hard" measurable outer dimensions (the right-hand quadrants), and neglect the "soft" inner dimensions (the left-hand quadrants). Green's breakthrough is to bring attention to the inner dimensions of mindsets and culture, but often the pendulum swings too far the other way. Green Organizations tend to focus so much on culture that they neglect to rethink structure, processes, and practices. (Edgar Schein, one of the academic pioneers in the field of organizational culture, once said, "The only thing of real importance that leaders do is to create and manage culture," a typical example of that extreme school of thought.) Companies like Southwest Airlines or Ben & Jerry's keep many of the systemic elements from traditional hierarchical structures (the lower-right quadrant), but also put in place a culture (lower-left quadrant) that asks managers to behave in non-hierarchical ways, to be servant leaders who listen to their subordinates and empower them.

Hierarchical structures with non-hierarchical cultures—it's easy to see that the two go together like oil and water. That is why leaders in these companies insist that culture needs constant attention and continuous investment. In a hierarchical structure that gives managers power over their subordinates, a constant investment of energy is required to keep managers from using that power in hierarchical ways. Stop investing in culture, and the structurally embedded hierarchy is likely to take the upper hand.

Self-managing structures transcend the issue of culture versus systems. Inner and outer dimensions, culture and systems, work hand in hand, not in opposite directions. Power is naturally distributed and there is no need to invest time and effort to prod middle managers to "empower" people below them. If managers have no weapons, there is no need to invest in a culture that keeps people from using their weapons. This is the experience that David Allen, of *Getting Things Done* fame, had when he adopted Holacracy in his consulting and training firm, the David Allen Company:

> *As we've distributed accountability down and throughout the organization, I've had much less of my attention on the culture. In an operating system that's dysfunctional, you need to focus on things like values in order to make that somewhat tolerable, but if we're all willing to pay attention to the higher purpose, and do what we do and do it well, the culture just emerges. You don't have to force it.*[2]

Does this mean, then, that culture is less relevant in Teal Organizations? Brian Robertson gives an eloquent answer: Culture in self-managing structures is both *less necessary and more impactful* than in traditional organizations. Less necessary because culture is not needed to overcome the troubles brought about by hierarchy. And more impactful, for the same reason—no energy is gobbled up fighting the structure, and all energy and attention brought to organizational culture can bear fruit. From a Teal perspective, organizational culture and organizational systems go hand in hand, and are facets of the same reality—both are equally deserving of conscious attention.

The culture of Teal Organizations

Is there a specific culture that all Teal Organizations share? The research shows that Teal Organizations can have greatly different cultures, but a number of cultural elements tend to be present in all of them.

The context in which a company operates, and the purpose it pursues, calls for a unique, specific culture. Let's contrast, for instance, the culture of RHD with that of Morning Star. RHD's central office is as quirky and colorful as any you are likely to have ever seen. Picture a few interlocking former warehouses converted into one giant open office space. The walls are painted in bright orange, but you can see the bright color only in those places where there are no oversized photographs of RHD's customers, paintings from some of the mentally ill patients it serves, or posters employees have put up featuring quotes or community activities they organize. The waiting area for visitors consists of a few chairs in the middle of this vibrant craze, next to a small pond where rather eccentric-looking plastic ducks proudly float in place of the goldfish that perhaps once swam there.

The contrast with Morning Star's offices in their factories and headquarters couldn't be starker. Everything there exudes quality and tidiness. Walls are painted white, paintings are elegantly framed, and papers are pinned only on the intended message boards.

The two companies work in very different contexts, which helps explain the very different culture reflected in their office buildings. RHD's vibrant central office reveals a culture where people are encouraged to accept other people's quirkiness as much as their own. RHD's purpose is to help people with such issues as mental diseases, mental disabilities, homelessness, and substance addiction build better lives for themselves. Central to achieving that purpose is the ability of employees to offer their consumers a caring, nonjudgmental presence. It helps if people don't define each other in binary categories—the *normal* employees and *not-so-normal* customers—and if instead *everyone* is seen as unique and quirky, whether employee or customer. Morning Star, on the other hand, operates in the food industry, with exacting standards of hygiene. A crazy, buzzing environment like RHD's would be anathema there. In the factory, things must be spotless, so that any problem in the process becomes immediately apparent, and that ethos pervades office spaces as well.

An organization's purpose and context determine the culture it needs. And yet some cultural elements are common to Teal Organizations in general.

Context and purpose drive the culture that is called for in an organization. But beyond the unique culture of each company, there are a number of common traits linked to the developmental stage of an organization. All Amber Organizations, to one extent or another, value the following of orders as part of their culture; a norm that loses its meaning in self-managing Teal Organizations. Below are some of the commonly shared cultural elements—norms, assumptions, concerns—I have encountered in the pioneer organizations studied for this book, elements that also seem consistent with the Evolutionary-Teal worldview. The list is neither exhaustive nor prescriptive, but it can provide food for thought.

Self-management

Trust

- We relate to one another with an assumption of positive intent.
- Until we are proven wrong, trusting co-workers is our default means of engagement.
- Freedom and accountability are two sides of the same coin.

Information and decision-making

- All business information is open to all.
- Every one of us is able to handle difficult and sensitive news.

- We believe in the power of collective intelligence. Nobody is as smart as everybody. Therefore all decisions will be made with the advice process.

Responsibility and accountability

- We each have full responsibility for the organization. If we sense that something needs to happen, we have a duty to address it. It's not acceptable to limit our concern to the remit of our roles.
- Everyone must be comfortable with holding others accountable to their commitments through feedback and respectful confrontation.

Wholeness

Equal worth

- We are all of fundamentally equal worth.
- At the same time, our community will be richest if we let all members contribute in their distinctive way, appreciating the differences in roles, education, backgrounds, interests, skills, characters, points of view, and so on.

Safe and caring workplace

- Any situation can be approached from fear and separation, or from love and connection. We choose love and connection.
- We strive to create emotionally and spiritually safe environments, where each of us can behave authentically.
- We honor the moods of ... [love, care, recognition, gratitude, curiosity, fun, playfulness ...].
- We are comfortable with vocabulary like care, love, service, purpose, soul ... in the workplace.

Overcoming separation

- We aim to have a workplace where we can honor all parts of us: the cognitive, physical, emotional, and spiritual; the rational and the intuitive; the feminine and the masculine.
- We recognize that we are all deeply interconnected, part of a bigger whole that includes nature and all forms of life.

Learning

- Every problem is an invitation to learn and grow. We will always be learners. We have never arrived.
- Failure is always a possibility if we strive boldly for our purpose. We discuss our failures openly and learn from them. Hiding or neglecting to learn from failure is unacceptable.
- Feedback and respectful confrontation are gifts we share to help one another grow.
- We focus on strengths more than weaknesses, on opportunities more than problems.

Relationships and conflict

- It's impossible to change other people. We can only change ourselves.
- We take ownership for our thoughts, beliefs, words, and actions.
- We don't spread rumors. We don't talk behind someone's back.
- We resolve disagreements one-on-one and don't drag other people into the problem.
- We don't blame problems on others. When we feel like blaming, we take it as an invitation to reflect on how we might be part of the problem (and the solution).

Purpose

Collective purpose

- We view the organization as having a soul and purpose of its own.
- We try to listen in to where the organization wants to go and beware of forcing a direction onto it.

Individual purpose

- We have a duty to ourselves and to the organization to inquire into our personal sense of calling to see if and how it resonates with the organization's purpose.
- We try to imbue our roles with our souls, not our egos.

Planning the future

- Trying to predict and control the future is futile. We make forecasts only when a specific decision requires us to do so.
- Everything will unfold with more grace if we stop trying to control and instead choose to simply sense and respond.

Profit

- In the long run, there are no trade-offs between purpose and profits. If we focus on purpose, profits will follow.

Supporting the emergence of an organization's culture

How does an organizational culture emerge, and what makes one culture more powerful than another? In most companies, the culture simply reflects the assumptions, norms, and concerns of the organization's founders or leaders, with all their lights and shadows.

From an Evolutionary-Teal perspective, an organization is a living organism with its own life force, and it should be allowed to have its own autonomous culture, distinct from the assumptions and concerns of its founders and leaders. Everyone should be invited to listen in to the culture that best fits the organization's context and the purpose it pursues (for instance using large group processes that were described in the previous chapter; see page 155). When there is clarity as to the culture that is most supportive of the organization's context and purpose, the question becomes: how can a group of people consciously bring about that culture? Wilber's framework provides a simple answer: to shape the culture (the lower-left quadrant), you can pursue three avenues in parallel:

- Put supportive structures, practices, and processes in place (lower-right quadrant)
- Ensure that people with moral authority in the company role-model the behavior associated with the culture (upper-right quadrant)
- Invite people to explore how their personal belief system supports or undermines the new culture (upper-left quadrant)

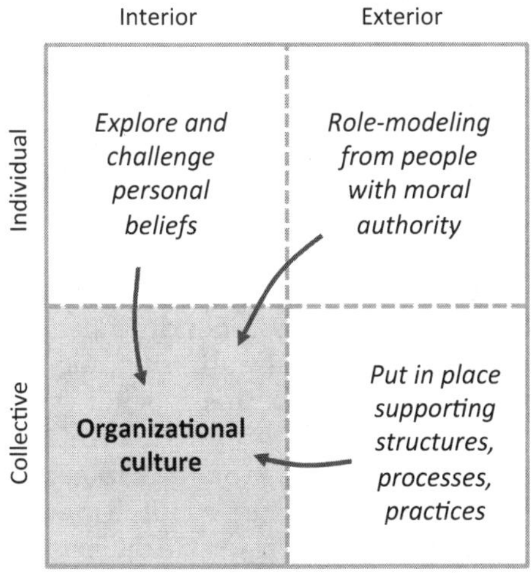

As an illustration, let's assume you feel your organization calls for a mood of gratitude and celebration.

- You can try to put in place recurring practices (lower-right quadrant) that evoke a mood of gratitude and celebration, such as, for example, ESBZ's "praise meeting" (see page 160) or Ozvision's "day of thanking" (see page 161). Maintain these practices for a few months and the company will develop a culture where people feel it is natural to praise and thank each other spontaneously.
- You can call on the company's most respected figures—the people that others look up to—to double down for a while on thanking their colleagues and celebrating effort and achievements.
- You can also hold workshops where people explore how they personally relate to gratitude and celebration. Some people naturally thank and praise colleagues, without even thinking about it. Others don't—thanking or celebrating people might feel awkward to them, perhaps because they grew up in a family

where such things weren't spoken about, for example. Coaching can help uncover limiting beliefs that hold people back from engaging with others in gratitude and celebration.

In summary, what is the place of organizational culture in Teal Organizations? With self-managing structures and processes in place, and with practices to pursue wholeness and purpose, culture becomes both *less necessary* and *more impactful*. The culture of the organization should be shaped by the context and the purpose of the organization, not by the personal assumptions, norms, and concerns of the founders and leaders. In self-managing structures, chances are this happens naturally and organically because everyone, not just the people at the top, participates in sensing what is needed. If there is a sense, however, that an organization's culture needs to further evolve, colleagues can dedicate time, possibly using a large group process, to listen in to the culture that the context and purpose call for.

While many aspects of the needed culture will be unique to the organization, some characteristic elements of the Evolutionary-Teal stage of development are likely to emerge. Teams can refer to the list provided earlier in this chapter to stimulate reflection.

There are three ways to help put new cultural elements in place: through practices that support corresponding behavior, through role-modeling by colleagues with moral authority, and by creating a space where people can explore how their belief system supports or undermines the new culture.

Philosophically, Teal's breakthrough is to give all four quadrants their due—culture, systems, mindsets, and behavior. Previous paradigms focused on the "hard" dimension at the expense of the "soft" or vice-versa. It's a safe bet to assume that the future belongs to organizations where "hard" and "soft" work hand in hand, and reinforce each other in service of the organization's purpose.

Part 3

The Emergence of Teal Organizations

CHAPTER 3.1

NECESSARY CONDITIONS

Today, there is almost too much focus on leadership, mainly because it is widely thought to be the key to economic success. In fact, the degree to which a leader can actually affect technical performance has been substantially overstated. ...

On the other hand, the importance and impact of moral leadership on the life and success of an organization have been greatly underappreciated.

Dennis Bakke

What are the necessary conditions for creating a new organization with Evolutionary-Teal principles, structure, practices, and culture? Or to transform an existing one? Are there some critical ingredients without which we don't need to bother trying? The research behind this book suggests that there are two—and only two—necessary conditions, in the following two spheres:

1. **Top leadership**: The founder or top leader (let's call him the CEO for lack of a better term) must have integrated a worldview and psychological development consistent with the Teal developmental level. Several examples show that it is helpful, but not necessary, to have a critical mass of leaders operating at that stage.
2. **Ownership**: Owners of the organization must also understand and embrace Evolutionary-Teal worldviews. Board members that "don't get it," experience shows, can temporarily give a Teal leader free rein when their methods deliver outstanding results. But when the organization hits a rough patch or faces a critical choice, owners will want to get things under control in the only way that makes sense to them—through top-down, hierarchical command and control mechanisms.

These two conditions are the only make-or-break factors. No other parameter is critical to running organizations within the Evolutionary-Teal paradigm:

- The *sector of activity* doesn't seem to matter. There are successful pioneers in the for-profit and nonprofit sectors, in health care, manufacturing, retail, food processing, service industries, and others.
- The principles and practices can be adopted by *small and large organizations* alike. Case examples researched for this book range from hundreds to thousands to tens of thousands of employees.
- *Geography* and *cultural backgrounds* seem to not matter much either. AES's self-management practices took root in all the plants it acquired. Research has shown that the developmental stages of human consciousness are relevant across cultures, and AES's case seems to bear this out.

The only make-or-break factors are the worldview held by the top leadership and by the owners/board of the organization. That is still a tall order. What about those businesses, nonprofits, schools, hospitals, government agencies, and other entities where these conditions are not in place? Can a middle manager put Teal practices in place for the department he is responsible for? When I am asked this question, as much as I would like to believe the opposite, I tell people not to waste their energy trying. Experience shows that efforts to bring Teal practices into subsets of organizations bear fruit, at best, only for a short while. If the CEO and the top leadership see the world through Amber or Orange lenses (Green's tolerance allows for more hope), they will consider the Teal experiment frivolous, if not outright dangerous. They might allow it for a while until they understand what is going on. But ultimately, the pyramid will get its way and reassert control. In the process, the energy that was invested often turns into bitterness and cynicism. I wish I could offer more hope. But I simply haven't come across a single example of a unit, plant, or department that has operated to any degree with Teal practices for a substantial amount of time to show otherwise. And while the experiment lasted, the people in those units often had to fight, again and again, with the big bosses outside of their unit to defend their unorthodox ways of operating.

So what can middle or senior managers do in these situations? Obviously, you can try first to convince the CEO and the leadership team that Teal practices are the way to go, by sharing case stories, organizing company visits to existing Teal Organizations, and so on. Unfortunately, I'm not very hopeful about this avenue either. What you are trying to do is get these leaders to adopt an Evolutionary-Teal perspective. From all we know, climbing the developmental ladder is a complex, mysterious, spiritual process. It happens from within and cannot be imposed on somebody from the outside, not even with the best of arguments. I regularly come across coaches and consultants who try to prove with hard numbers that adopting Green or Teal practices will deliver a good return on investment—effectively using Achievement-Orange language to sell Green or Teal. I've never seen it work—the leaders listen with interest until they understand what practices are involved and how much control they would have to relinquish.

So if the leadership isn't ready, what can you do? I believe that *vertical* transformation (from Amber, Orange, or Green, to Teal) is a lost battle; but that still leaves *horizontal* transformation as an option—for example, from an unhealthy to a healthy form of Orange. Orange Organizations can be vibrant and innovative places where management by objectives gives people room to maneuver and to express themselves; or they can be stressful, lifeless places constrained by a thicket of rules, procedures, budgets, and targets. As a middle or senior manager, you can foster an environment that is as healthy as possible for your department within the Orange context. Let's take target-setting as an example: abolishing targets within your unit altogether (in the way Teal Organizations do) will raise red flags all around the organization. But you can amend the target setting process in ways that stay within acceptable bounds. Instead of top-down targets, you can ask individuals or teams working "under" you to define their own targets. If, once summed up, the self-set targets fall short of expectations from above, you don't need to be the one raising the targets. Ask team members to get together and determine, in a peer-based process, which targets could be raised. If the team functions well, you don't even need to be part of the meeting. Let them come up with the best solution on their own—after all, the targets will be theirs. Creating a healthy version of the existing, dominant paradigm, like in this example, has a much higher chance of succeeding, and the example could easily spread from your unit to the entire organization.

TOP LEADERSHIP

Let's dig deeper into the first of the two necessary conditions. The general rule seems to be that the level of consciousness of an organization cannot exceed the level of consciousness of its leader. The CEO must look at the world through an Evolutionary-Teal lens for Teal practices to flourish. There are several examples of organizations that have operated with Teal practices and then quickly reverted to traditional management approaches when a new CEO came in who saw the world from an Orange perspective.

You might have noticed a major paradox: CEOs are both much less and much more important in self-managing organizations compared to traditional ones. They have given up their top-down hierarchical power. The lines of the pyramid no longer converge toward them. They can no longer make or overturn any decision. And yet, in a time when people still think about organizations in Amber, Orange, and Green ways, the CEO has an absolutely critical role in creating and holding a Teal organizational space. But beyond creating and holding that space, paradoxically, there is not much a CEO needs to do; he can let the self-organizing, emerging nature of Evolutionary-Teal take over.

A good deal of literature has been written on the mindful, authentic, and humble characteristics of Teal leadership, which I will not try to summarize here. Nearly always, the backdrop of that literature is a traditional (Amber/Orange/Green) organization, and it examines questions such as: how can Teal leaders bring more mindfulness into hierarchical structures? How can they create more conscious, healthy cultures? I want to discuss a different question that this literature hasn't yet examined: *What are the roles of a CEO in a Teal Organization?* The case examples show that the roles of the CEO are radically different when the organization runs on Teal principles and practices, rather than traditional ones.

The general rule seems to be that the level of consciousness of an organization cannot exceed the level of consciousness of its leader.

One role remains the same: the CEO is often the public face of the company to the outside world. Suppliers, big clients, and regulators often want to deal with the "head" of the organization, and the CEO often (but not necessarily) takes on that role. But as for the rest, most of the other responsibilities traditionally held by the CEO simply fall away—there are, for example, no targets to set, no budgets to approve, no executive team to run, no top-down strategies to devise, no disputes to settle, no promotions to decide on.

On the other hand, the research into the pioneer organizations suggests there are two new and critical roles a CEO needs to play: *creating and maintaining a space for Teal ways of operating* and *role-modeling of Teal behaviors*. Beyond that, the CEO is a colleague like any other, who can sense what's needed, get involved in a project, and make decisions using the advice process. I keep using the term CEO for lack of a better alternative ("The space holder, role model, and public face"?), but I realize how misleading the term can be, as it inevitably evokes the image of the commander sitting at the top of the pyramid.

Holding the space

Teal operating principles run deeply against the grain of accepted management thinking, and so a critical role of the founder/CEO is to *hold the space* for Teal structures and practices. Whenever a problem comes up, someone, somewhere, will call for tried-and-proven solutions: *let's add a rule, a control system; let's put the issue under some centralized function; let's add a layer of supervision; let's make processes more prescriptive; let's make such decisions at a higher level in the future.* The calls can come from different corners—one time it's a board member who will call for more control, another time a colleague, a supplier, or a client. Over and over again, the CEO must ensure that trust prevails and that traditional management practices don't creep in through the back door.

Let's take a practical example: the tendency in organizations to create rules and policies. Avoiding rules and policies is no easy feat. We have grown up with a deeply held assumption that control mechanisms make us safe. No matter how many corporate scandals keep happening in organizations full of control mechanisms, we hold on to this assumption. Whenever something goes wrong, whenever a colleague makes a stupid decision or abuses the system, there will be loud cries to put control systems in place to prevent the problem from happening again. And for that reason, over time, most large organizations end up with expense policies, travel guidelines, dress codes, company car policies, client entertainment policies, supplier agreement procedures, vacation policies, mobile phone and IT policies, email and Internet usage policies … and the list goes on and on. Of course, a policy is useful only if it is enforced, so some department is given authority to impose some paper trail for compliance and to hand down punishment in case of infringement.

Trust is so countercultural that it needs to be defended and reaffirmed every time a problem arises. At RHD, one such instance involved Maria, who had managed RHD's company cars for many years. She was a likeable woman, with a dry, quick-witted sense of humor. Everyone was shocked when it appeared she was involved in fraud. She had given one of the company cars to her son who had left home for college. Two days later, she was dismissed. But the story doesn't end there. Some people called for more controls: *Isn't it unwise to let people deal with company assets or spend company money without any supervision?* In such cases, it is often the role of the CEO to make sure the company stands firm on its principles and assumptions, as Bob Fishman, RHD's founder, explains:

> *RHD's culture is vulnerable. … Someone like Maria, who steals from us, makes it a little less likely that we will trust each other. That makes RHD a little less safe for the rest of us. … Because her behavior exposed RHD's vulnerability to this kind of theft, it raised certain questions within the office: Were other employees also using corporate property for personal use? Should management set up a system to check the location of all corporate cars weekly or daily? Should we ask all unit directors who manage cars across the country to attest in writing that the cars are not being used for personal business?*
>
> *The danger was, and is, that Maria's theft could lead to a change in RHD's culture. … It's very easy to reduce the level of trust that fills RHD with life and creativity.*
>
> *The essential question is: Should we respond to one instance of corporate theft by lowering the bar of trust, and in so doing treat 3,000 people as though they too might be thieves? Should we let one employee's*

bad judgment have an even greater impact on the corporate culture by creating procedures that reflect distrust? ... Many administrators in corporate America would say yes to those questions. They would call it "facing reality." At the root of this position is the all-too-common assumption that people cannot be trusted. ...

At RHD, we say "no" to lowering our level of trust. Besides protecting the entity called the corporation, we must also protect a culture that's based on our belief in the worth, dignity, and honesty of each employee. In the end, RHD did not lose any money. Maria returned the car. All of which brings us to this essential fact: RHD has managed $1.433 billion in government funds over the past 36 years, and we can identify only about $325,000 in corporate theft that was perpetrated by individuals. That's a loss factor of .00023.[1]

Similar calls for more controls have occurred in all organizations in this research. You might remember the story of the stolen drill at FAVI (see page 81): when a drill disappeared from the supply room one day, some people called for the supply room to be locked again. Jean-François Zobrist simply put up a flipchart in the supply room stating how stupid it was to steal a drill. Anybody could take home a drill for a day when needed, but stealing it could lead to immediate dismissal. Zobrist reacted in a similar fashion on the day where a female colleague reported that a drawing of a penis had appeared on a wall in the women's bathroom. Some people called for an investigation. In his customary cheeky style, Zobrist put up a flipchart in front of the women's bathroom and wrote on it: "There is among us a slightly mad person who feels the need to make sexual drawings for his sanity. Please make your drawings on this paper in the future and not on the bathroom walls." In both cases, the problem disappeared without investigation and without control mechanisms.

There are thornier cases, of course. Several CEOs of pioneer organizations told me the most difficult pressures to deal with come from the outside world. When a large client insists it will only do business with you if your shipments are signed off on by your head of quality assurance, can you avoid creating such a function? How do you deal with industry standards and certifications that require hierarchical flow of authority? Enterprise software packages are designed for siloed and hierarchical organizational structures; costly and cumbersome contortions are sometimes needed to adapt their architecture to the reality of self-managing teams. In all these cases, the easy way out would be to reinstate, at least partially, some hierarchical process. Experience shows that time and again, a creative solution can be found to uphold the Teal way of functioning, but it requires energy and dedication.

Of course, in a self-managing organization, everyone can and should step up, like the CEO, to uphold Evolutionary-Teal principles and practices. But not everybody needs to view the world through Teal lenses. That is the magic of organizations: their processes can lift up employees to adopt behaviors from later stages of consciousness that they might not yet have integrated at an individual level. If many people in an organization have grown to a Teal perspective, there are that many more people who can hold the space. But ultimately, if everyone else fails to do so, that task falls back on the CEO. Perhaps the day will come where most or all colleagues in an organization have embraced the Evolutionary-Teal stage of development; then the CEO's role of holding the space will not be needed any longer. Until that happens, this role remains essential.

Role-modeling Teal's three breakthroughs

The founders and CEOs of self-managing organizations don't have hierarchical power, but they often carry much moral authority. Each of the founders and CEOs I spoke to during this research was keenly aware that his or her presence, words, and actions carried particular weight. People look up to them and wonder: *Is he for real? Can we trust him? Does she play by the same rules as everyone else? Is she authentic? Can I be myself in his presence?* For good or bad, the behavior a CEO models ends up shaping the organization in profound ways. If they are keen to see their organizations work along Teal practices, they need to role-model the behavior associated with the three breakthroughs of self-management, wholeness, and purpose.

Role-modeling self-management

First and foremost, founders and CEOs of Teal Organizations must accept that their power is severely limited by the advice process. It doesn't matter how strongly they are convinced about their point of view; they cannot make a decision without consulting people affected by the matter and people with relevant expertise. This is a tall order. Put yourself in the shoes, for instance, of Chris Rufer, the successful founder and president of Morning Star. He started the company more than 20 years ago, driving a truck to haul tomatoes. Today, Morning Star is the biggest tomato processor and transporter in the world. The company has been so profitable that it didn't need outside investors to finance its growth. Rufer owns 100 percent of the company and he is its sole board member. And yet, as the founder, president, and owner of the company, it is not proper for him to make any decisions that meaningfully affect other people on his own without consulting them.

Bob Fishman, who founded RHD in 1970 and has been its CEO throughout its growth to a 4,000-person organization, admits he still finds this difficult:

> *As soon as our [first] mental health clinic opened, the employees and I began to examine our values, write them down, and translate them into*

the behaviors we would follow. And I began to realize the ramifications of these values for me in corporate life. It struck me that even though I was the founder, the "boss" of this corporation, adhering to these values meant I wouldn't be able to impose a corporate directive—even when I was sure it was the right thing to do. This was a huge challenge. It still is.[2]

It is unreasonable to expect anyone to be perfect. Founders and CEOs will not role-model the new paradigm faultlessly, all the time. But paradoxically, the occasional mistake can reinforce rather than undermine self-management. An interesting example comes from Buurtzorg when Jos de Blok once rather carelessly stepped over the advice process. The topic was overtime. Nurses' workloads can fluctuate quite strongly and unexpectedly, depending on the health of their clients. At some point, Jos de Blok noticed that in certain teams the workload was unevenly spread among nurses. Some were paid significant overtime, while others did less than their contracted hours, a financially detrimental situation for Buurtzorg. De Blok posted a message on the intranet blog asking nurses to discuss within their teams how they could better balance the workload across colleagues. Meanwhile, overtime would only be paid out if the team as a whole worked more than their contracted hours. The blog post drew a host of comments. Most were along the line of, "We recognize this is a difficult question. It's important we think this through. But the way the decision was made not to pay out overtime is not the way we do things at Buurtzorg." Within hours, de Blok responded with a message that acknowledged that his decision was mistaken; he should have consulted the nurses before making such a decision. Overtime would be paid out as before. He suggested volunteers create a workgroup to look into the issue of how to best deal with overtime. The issue sparked by de Blok's first blog post self-corrected in just a few hours, as often happens in self-managing organizations. The incident reaffirmed rather than undermined the advice process.

Even as they follow the advice process, founders and CEOs must also be careful with the way they initiate actions. Take the case, a few years ago, when Bob Fishman felt the moment was ripe for RHD to consider serving the imprisoned adult population. The normal course of action would be for the CEO to assign the project to a trusted person, and then ask for periodic reports. Instead, Fishman sent out an invitation to the entire workforce asking interested people to join him in a meeting to explore the topic. Ten people showed up. After a fruitful discussion, they selected among themselves a "point person" to take the lead on the initiative. From there, the project took on a life of its own. Fishman had to accept that the group could take the project in a direction that would be different from the one he would have chosen if he had kept tight control.

Fighting the inner urge to control is probably the hardest challenge for founders and CEOs in self-managing organizations. Over and over again, they must remember to trust. An interesting example comes from AES's early days. Dennis Bakke recalls a moment where one of his colleagues proudly demonstrated the IT system of the very first power plant AES had started operating:

> *On his desk, he had a computer that had the control panel for the plant. "Dennis, I can essentially watch and control the operations from here. I can get one for you as well, and we can add all the new plants as they go commercial." I told him not to bother and suggested he get rid of his as well. This kind of centralization can have a major negative effect on the workplace.*[3]

I find this example instructive because it is subtle. Self-management thrives on total information transparency. What is wrong with the CEO having real-time access to the performance data of all the plants? Nothing in principle (as long as the same data is supplied to everyone else too). But self-management implies that teams monitor their own performance and don't need other people to tell them to get their act together. In a subtle but very real way, teams' psychological ownership is undermined when they know the CEO can look over their shoulder in real time to monitor their performance.

Fighting the inner urge to control is probably the hardest challenge for founders and CEOs of self-managing organizations.

The most subtle, and perhaps most demanding, change for a founder or CEO in a Teal Organization is to leave behind the sometimes addictive sense that others need you to make things happen. Holacracy's Brian Robertson admits it has been a challenge for him to accept that in his self-managing company everybody, not just the CEO, gets to be a hero:

> *When I first became an entrepreneur and a CEO, I realized how addictive that role was. You get to be a hero every day. There is nothing that feels quite so good as to come in and save the day and have that "everything rests on you and your shoulders" feeling.*
>
> *One of the challenges and opportunities of Holacracy is: now I get to be a hero just like I did before, but now everybody else gets to be a hero too. Instead of me saving the day for everyone else, for a bunch of mostly powerless folks who are looking at my leadership to pull them forward, now everybody gets to lead their role ... while nobody gets to be a hero and save the day for others. That's an interesting struggle. It removes some of the addictive quality of power, of being that guy at the top ... and yet ... how great is that for the organization when it's full of heroes instead of resting on just one at the top.*[4]

Role-modeling wholeness

There is little chance that people will take the risk of showing up with the fullness of who they are if the founder or CEO is hiding behind a professional mask. In his or her own unique way, each of the founders and CEOs of the companies I researched carry strong moral authority. They can invite their colleagues into wholeness by acting from wholeness themselves. Tami Simon, the founder and CEO of Sounds True, gives the example of bringing depth to check-ins at the beginning of meetings:

> *Check-ins can have different levels of depth to them. People can check in and say, "Yeah, I'm doing great, everything is fine." I find you need someone in the room who will go to a deeper level inside themself. You can have some of these tools, but if you don't have people who are bringing the depth of themselves to it, nothing changes. It doesn't take very many people; it can take just one or two. I'm always willing to be that person.*[5]

CEOs that role-model virtues such as humility, trust, courage, candor, vulnerability, and authenticity invite colleagues to take the same risks. When Jos de Blok decided to change the principle for calculating overtime without seeking advice and then publicly acknowledged his mistake, he turned a blunder into a public display of vulnerability and humility. Jean-François Zobrist showed similar humility at FAVI when, from the top of a soapbox, he told his assembled colleagues he didn't know how to solve a thorny problem and he needed their help (see page 103).

These stories reveal another beautiful Teal paradox: vulnerability and strength are not in opposition, but polarities that reinforce each other. At Heiligenfeld, the German network of mental health hospitals, there is a wonderful story of how Joachim Galuska, the co-founder and CEO, defused a touchy matter in a playful way. A few years ago, Galuska chose a top-of-the-line Jaguar as his company car, which sparked some chatter among colleagues who felt that such a display of opulence didn't fit the company culture. When the leasing period was over, in a playful wink, Galuska acknowledged he knew about the chatter all along: he bought the car and donated it to the organization. Heiligenfeld had an existing gratefulness practice where colleagues thanked each other with written thank-you notes. Every week, one of the recipients of a thank-you note is chosen randomly and gets to enjoy the Jaguar, washed and with a full tank, for a week. Fifty-two times a year, the Jaguar changes hands and is driven by a different colleague. It has become a symbol of Galuska's willingness to acknowledge feedback, as well as an expression of life lived from abundance and joie-de-vivre. (This particular expression of abundance has been used to the fullest; the

Jaguar is about to reach the end of its life cycle and will soon be decommissioned).

Role-modeling listening to purpose

One way that leaders show humility is by reminding themselves and others that their work is in service of a purpose that transcends them individually. When we put energy, time, and talent into our work, we naturally hope that our efforts will be successful and be acknowledged. What Teal leaders recognize—but need to remind themselves and others of—is that personal and collective success are both wonderful when they come as a consequence of pursuing a meaningful purpose, but that we should be careful not to pursue success as a goal in itself, careful not to fall back into competitive drives that serve our ego and not our soul, that serve the organization but not its purpose.

> *Focus on higher purpose seems to be precluded when a leader is deeply rooted in ego because the currency of the ego is fear; how can a leader be available to lead others in a conscious way if they are busy defending a fractured ego?*
>
> Sarah Morris

This is not about being *self-less* at work. In some religious and spiritual traditions, the road to salvation is through spirit alone; it requires that we distance ourselves from our sinful incarnate natures. Because of this cultural background, a common misunderstanding suggests that we can pursue a higher purpose only when we are *self-less*, when we distance ourselves from our personal needs and aspirations. To avoid being full of ourselves (in service of our ego), we must strive to be self-less in service of a higher purpose. Teal paradoxical thinking invites us to transcend this either-or dichotomy: we can be both fully ourselves (rather than full of ourselves), *and* be working toward achieving an organization's deeper purpose. We don't need to reject parts of ourselves to be in service. It's just the opposite: we are at our most productive and joyful when *all* of who we are is energized by a broader purpose that nourishes our calling and our soul.

The simplest and most powerful way for CEOs to role-model the pre-eminence of purpose is to ask questions:

- Every decision offers the opportunity to ask the question: *What decision will best serve the organization's purpose?*
- When a change of role is discussed, it begs the question: *How will this role serve the organization's purpose?*
- A new client or supplier can trigger the question: *Will working with this client/this supplier further the organization's purpose?*

Every time leaders ask these questions, they remind themselves and their colleagues that we don't need to impose a direction onto the organization. Work will be more joyful and more effective when we partner with the organization's sense of direction, when we listen to what its purpose wants to manifest in the world.

For the rest: a colleague like any other

In large, traditional organizations, most CEOs have crazy agendas, meetings booked back-to-back, all day long, often weeks in advance. In meeting after meeting, they are asked to first digest an endless stream of written memos and slide decks as background information for all the decisions they need to make or approve. It can hardly be otherwise: in pyramidal organizations, any decision that requires someone to see the big picture must be made at the top.

This all changes radically with self-management. Much of what gobbles up the agenda of company founders or CEOs falls away in Teal Organizations. There are no more executive meetings, no steering committees ... there are hardly any fixed meetings at all. When I met Allen Carlson, the CEO of Sun Hydraulics (a publicly listed company), I asked him if he would show me his agenda for the week. He had only four meetings planned in that entire week, two of which were with me.

So what do CEOs in Teal Organizations do then? you might wonder. The two specific roles we discussed—holding the space and role-modeling behaviors—consume some of their time. As for the rest, like any other colleague, they can take on roles that help manifest their company's purpose. They can participate in a project; lead an initiative; participate in recruitment; mediate conflicts; or meet with clients and regulators. Whatever roles they choose, they have to add value, like everyone else, or their colleagues won't entrust them with the roles for long.

Most of the CEOs that I know in traditional companies would find it awkward, to say the least, to have to prove their worth for the roles they fill. They are used to claiming whatever roles they feel they need or want to pick up. This is one of the reasons that hiring a CEO or other leaders with seniority and experience from the outside is a tricky proposition for self-managing organizations. Sun Hydraulics has developed an interesting way to bring in experienced leaders nevertheless. When Bob Koski—the co-founder and long-time CEO—was nearing retirement, Clyde Nixon, a long-time business acquaintance and CEO of a competitor, was looking for a new job. Koski invited Nixon to join Sun for a year to "wander around and see what he thought he could do." Nixon was given no role and no title. Could he find ways to add value to the organization and be embraced by existing colleagues? He did, and a year later, it was decided that he would take over the presidency from Koski.

Nixon's succession, twelve years later, happened in similar fashion. Allen Carlson had risen through the ranks at a large industrial firm when he was hired by Sun for his marketing expertise. Quickly, Carlson realized the organization didn't need a marketer. It had plenty of orders, but the company wasn't shipping on time. Carlson found himself spending most of his time pleading with customers to cancel just their order, but not the relationship. The urgent need was to fix delivery times in manufacturing, not to market the products better. Carlson felt the best thing was to look for a marketing role in another firm somewhere else, but Nixon suggested that Carlson, while looking for another job, get involved in manufacturing to try to improve the situation. Carlson started working with people in operations; a whole new manufacturing system was adopted, which involved disbanding the scheduling department, and Sun started shipping on time. Carlson got so involved that he never found time to look for another job. Having made himself a reputation for getting things done using self-managing methods, even in an area where he had no prior expertise, he became the new CEO when Nixon retired three years later.

Leadership with the advice process

The roles that founders and CEOs of Teal Organizations pick up tend to concern some of the broadest questions in the organization. *Should we launch a new product line? Should we move offices, or build a new factory? Should we introduce a new compensation system?* Those kinds of questions affect large groups of colleagues, sometimes every single one.

In traditional organizations, CEOs make such decisions in top-down fashion, and then rely on managers to cascade the decision downwards. In Teal Organizations, they must abide by the advice process, which implies that a very large group of people be consulted. How can that be done? In small organizations, CEOs can simply walk around and talk to their colleagues—a practice used by Zobrist at FAVI, for instance. When organizations grow into the hundreds or thousands and have dispersed geographical locations, walking around is no longer a viable option. At Buurtzorg, for instance, thousands of nurses are scattered around the Netherlands—there is no way Jos de Blok or anyone else can simply walk by and discuss a decision with everyone affected. And yet the advice process requires that people be consulted.

De Blok found an answer both simple and powerful. He has turned his blog on Buurtzorg's intranet into a leadership instrument. He writes posts regularly, straight from the heart, without PR polish (as you might expect, there is no communications department at Buurtzorg). Given the respect he enjoys in the company, his posts are widely read. One morning when I met him, 1,900 nurses had already read a post he had written from his home the previous night. By the end of the day, most of the 7,000 nurses had read the post. De Blok's messages can go in any direction, from the pragmatic and practical to the speculative and inspirational. He shares directions the company could take, decisions he feels are needed, or simply a nice encounter he has had during the day that epitomizes what Buurtzorg is about. Within hours, the posts evoke dozens, sometimes hundreds, of comments. It quickly becomes apparent if the post resonates with colleagues or if it brings out mixed reactions. In both cases, the post helps the entire group of colleagues grow in awareness about how they assess current reality and future possibilities.

The blog posts also allow for fast decision-making. When de Blok has a decision in mind that affects a great number of people, he shares his thoughts in a blog post and invites colleagues to react. If their comments signal agreement, the decision is made within hours; if debate ensues, the proposal is amended and floated again. If it appears that the decision is not yet ripe, a workgroup is set up to refine the proposal.

Leadership by blog post requires a degree of candor and vulnerability that few CEOs in traditional organizations would feel comfortable with. Once a post is published, there is no going back. Critical comments and rebukes are public for all to see; they cannot be erased and cannot be ignored. The blog post is like an impulse given to the organization; what the organization does with the impulse is beyond the CEO's control.

What seems risky when looked at through a traditional lens looks wonderfully efficient from an Evolutionary-Teal perspective. A blog post you write from the comfort of the sofa in the evening at home can turn into a decision the next afternoon, endorsed by thousands of people in the organization. An idea or concern about where the industry is going? Write a short post, and you get to know how the organization reacts. If people disagree with your thought, you have lost 15 minutes of your time ... but gained a new insight into what the organization thinks. When we think of how decision-making happens in large organizations today (the PowerPoint decks that need to be written, the lengthy steering committee and executive meetings where decisions get debated, followed by top-down communications where every word is weighted), we can only marvel at the efficiency of leadership by blog post.[6]

A different way to look at the CEO's role

In his book *The Living Organization*, Norman Wolfe suggests an insightful distinction between three types of energy fields in the workplace: *Activity*, *Relationship*, and *Context*. With *Activity*, he refers to the energy of action, the "what we do and how we do it." *Relationship* refers to the energy brought to the interactions; what we say, how we say it, how we relate to each other. *Context* in turn is the energy of meaning and purpose, of connection with a larger whole.

In the machine paradigm, *Activity* is all there is. It is no surprise, then, that leaders in traditional organizations naturally focus their energy on the *Activity field*, the problem solving, decision-making, troubleshooting, and so forth. In my experience, most of them view the field of *Relationships* as a necessary evil, an area they need to invest some time in, because sometimes interpersonal frictions threaten to slow down the machinery. The energy field of *Context* is often outside of their conscious focus altogether.

Founders and CEOs of the pioneer organizations researched for this book start from the opposite end. Their most critical role—holding the space—has entirely to do with the energy field of *Context*. Role-modeling Teal leadership crosses over into both *Context* and *Relationships*. Leaders spend the rest of their time in roles of the *Activity field*. But even when they focus on Activity—say they argue passionately for their point of view when consulted by a colleague during the advice process—they try to be mindful of the *Context* and the *Relationship* field at the same time: how their arguing supports or undermines the Teal breakthroughs of self-management, wholeness, and evolutionary purpose.

When I spent a day with Jos de Blok in the small headquarters of Buurtzorg, I was profoundly struck by something I had already noticed at some level when I spent time with other organizations researched for this book, but had not yet put into words: how much simpler life can be in Teal Organizations! Remember, Buurtzorg is a 7,000-person organization growing at breakneck speed. In seven years, it has gone from having 0 percent to 60 percent of the market share in neighborhood nursing in the Netherlands. The organization is venturing out in many new directions, from international expansion to youth services, psychiatric home care, and small community living. You could expect an organization struggling with growth and complexity. Instead, there are only 30 people working at headquarters, none of who seems particularly stressed or overworked. The building exudes an air of quiet concentration. I spoke with Jos de Blok for several hours, and at some point I realized we hadn't been interrupted once in all that time. No urgent phone calls, no assistant coming in and whispering into the CEO's ear because something important or urgent came up that needed his attention. Everything seems to unfold so easily it verges on the magical.

> *Go confidently in the direction of your dreams! Live the life you've imagined. As you simplify your life, the laws of the universe will be simpler.*
>
> Henry David Thoreau

The distinction of *Context, Relationship,* and *Activity* gives a way to frame the magic. When the energy field of *Context* is healthy and powerful, *Relationships* are healthy and powerful too. And then, what in other circumstances causes time and energy to be wasted in the field of *Activity* simply disappears. Nothing stands in the way of getting work done. In many companies, it feels like people are trapped in a rat race. Buurtzorg and other companies conjure a different image: it feels like they have grown wings and fly gently but powerfully toward their destination. With the right *Context* and *Relationships*, there really is a much simpler way to run organizations.

BOARD AND OWNERSHIP

There is a second necessary condition for an organization to operate from Evolutionary-Teal: not only must the CEO see the world through Teal lenses; the board needs to see it that way too.

In both for-profits and nonprofits, boards have the power to appoint and remove the CEO. Board members who view the world through any other lens are unlikely to tolerate Teal structures and practices for long because they simply make no sense to them. Sooner or later, they will appoint a CEO who operates from Amber or Orange to get things back under control.

The composition of the board is therefore a matter that company founders need to take seriously. RHD's board comprises a handful of people who are all deeply committed to RHD's principles, some serving since RHD's founding. It wasn't that way from the start at Buurtzorg: at first, de Blok had chosen people for their expertise (say, legal or financial) but found they were not in tune with Buurtzorg's way of operating. Over time, one by one, they were replaced with new board members who understand and support what the organization is about. Morning Star and Heiligenfeld are 100 percent owned by their founders. FAVI is family owned, and so far at least, the owners are supportive of its unusual ways of operating. Sounds True has only one angel investor, a person who put money into the business primarily because he believes in the company's purpose of disseminating spiritual wisdom.

There are two organizations researched for this book that pioneered new ways of operating, but then reverted to traditional management practices. In both cases, this happened because the board didn't see the world in the same way as the founder and pulled the plug.

Eckart Wintzen founded BSO/Origin, a software-consulting firm, in the Netherlands in 1973. In the following 20 years, he grew the company to 10,000 people, setting up shop in 18 countries in Europe, South America, and Asia. The company's structure consisted entirely of self-managing units, with virtually no headquarters and no staff functions. In 1994, the company established a joint venture with a Business Unit from Philips that took majority ownership of BSO/Origin two years later. As Wintzen recounts a decade later in a book, two worlds clashed:

> *I [became] a board member and gave powerful speeches to leave the system in place. But unfortunately—but not surprisingly given the perspective they came from—my colleagues from Philips on the board pronounced the word "unacceptable" regularly and forcefully. In the eyes of Philips it was a "deadly sin" to give people the authority to hire personnel or even just give away tickets for a musical. I believe that once we literally shouted over the issue until our faces turned red. Two worlds collided, one of strict financial procedures combined with "check, check, double check" with one of "have trust, have trust."*[7]

In a matter of mere months, as traditional management practices were brought back in, Wintzen saw the company he founded 20 years earlier lose its mojo.

AES, the energy generation and distribution powerhouse co-founded in 1982 by Roger Sant and Dennis Bakke, provides a similar story. Under Sant's leadership as CEO until 1994, and then with Bakke at the helm, it grew from a two-person firm into a global energy producer employing 40,000 people in plants located in more than 30 countries around the world. AES became a Wall Street darling after it was publicly listed in 1991. For years, while the company was going from success to success, the board members were supportive of AES's radically decentralized and trust-based decision-making. And yet as Bakke suspected, "Most board members loved the AES approach primarily because they believed it pushed the stock price up, not because it was the 'right' way to operate an organization."[8]

In 1992, an unexpected problem confirmed Bakke's suspicion that most board members were still firmly rooted in a command-and-control perspective. That year, not long after AES became public, a colleague informed Bakke that nine technicians at the AES plant in Shady Point, Oklahoma, had falsified results of water testing and sent inaccurate data to the U.S. Environmental Protection Agency (EPA). No harm was actually done to the river into which the water was discharged, and the fine the EPA ultimately imposed was small. But when an internal letter where Bakke shared the news with all of his colleagues was picked up by the press, investors overreacted and AES's shares plummeted by 40 percent. In an instant, Bakke remembers, board members as well as some of his senior colleagues were ready to throw self-managing principles overboard:

> *After the stock price dropped, the nature of our response changed dramatically. We became panicky, and our emphasis shifted from disclosure to damage control. Much or our attention turned to reassuring our shareholders. A host of lawyers descended on the plant to "protect the assets." ... Several of our most senior people and board members raised the possibility that our approach to operations was a major part of the problems. It was as if the entire company were on the verge of ruin. They jumped to the conclusions that our radical decentralizations, lack of organizational layers, and unorthodox operating style had caused "economic" collapse. There was, of course, no real economic collapse. Only the stock price had declined. In addition, one of our senior vice presidents did a presentation to the board suggesting that "Protecting our Assets" rather than "Serving Electrical Needs" should be the top goal of the company. What he meant was that we should follow a defensive strategy, led by a phalanx of lawyers, in order to avoid legal, environmental, and regulatory wrangles. There was also discussion of adding a new layer of operating vice presidents between me and the five plant managers we had at the time. ... Under pressure from lawyers and because of an understandable loss of confidence, the [Oklahoma] plant had decided to return to a "proven" approach to running industrial*

facilities. Back came shift supervisors, an assistant plant manager, and a new environmental staff department reporting to the plant manager (to make sure water treatment employees did the right thing). These steps increased our staffing level at the plant by more than 30 percent.

During this time I felt under-appreciated and uncertain about how much support I had among board members, who seemed to like our values only because they generated good press and were popular among employees. I felt I was alone in fighting for our values because they were intrinsically right.[9]

This event triggered an exhausting six-month period where Bakke held what seemed like endless conversations with board members. At the end of it, he just managed to keep the board's confidence and stay in his role. While the board thought that he had pushed things too far, he came to the opposite conclusion: the new principles weren't yet anchored firmly enough in the company. He was determined, in his own words, "to challenge every organizational design and every system either in place or proposed" for consistency with AES's basic assumptions. Over the next 10 years, Bakke focused his energy on embedding self-management deeply within the organization. By his own account, he succeeded at one level but failed at another: employees became champions of "Joy at Work," as Bakke called AES's management practices. But at the board level, Bakke was less successful:

I had several clues that my campaign to win over my board colleagues had been ineffective. ... Even while some board members were telling shareholders that they loved "giving up power," I could see that they found it difficult to give advice rather than make decisions. In addition, board members often suggested I tone down the "rhetoric" concerning our shared values and purpose, especially when writing the company annual letter and in meetings with shareholders.[10]

When the dotcom bubble burst in 2001, AES's share price, which had peaked at $70, began to slide. After the 9/11 terrorist attacks it fell lower, to $26. In October, when Enron declared bankruptcy, the stock of all energy providers fell through the floor in a mood of panic—AES's stock hit a low of $5. AES's leadership had made some decisions in the previous years that proved risky and mistaken when the economy crashed. Much of the company's growth was financed with debt on the belief that "debt is cheaper than equity," which was true until the debt financing collapsed. AES had also begun operating some "merchant plants" in the late 1990s, facilities that sold electricity to the spot market without long-term contracts, leaving it more vulnerable to swings in the price of electricity.

AES's self-management practices could hardly be blamed for the stock price decline: the decisions that proved risky in hindsight had not been made by some out-of-control renegades, but had been discussed and agreed upon at board level. But it didn't matter; fear took over among board members, who called for a major reorganization of the company and for centralizing all important decision-making. Scores of lawyers, consultants, and advisors were hired to give the board further control over the company. Employees, meanwhile, were still devoted to AES's decentralized way of operating, and to Bakke, who embodied it. Finding themselves in a bind, the board decided not to replace Bakke but to bring in a co-CEO whose instructions Bakke was asked to carry out. With opposite perspectives on almost every matter, their collaboration proved extremely difficult. Nine frustrating months later, Bakke resigned. Without him, the new leadership was free to impose tried-and-proven management recipes in place of the self-managing practices that AES had started pioneering 20 years earlier.

The stories of AES and BSO/Origin illustrate that Teal organizational practices are vulnerable when investors and board members don't share in the paradigm. Viewed through Conformist-Amber or Orange lenses, the Teal structures and practices stand out as foolish or even dangerous. In good faith, board members feel it is their duty to protect the organization (and themselves) with traditional, control-based mechanisms.

In the case of for-profit companies, this means that founders need to be careful who they invite to invest in their companies. In today's legal systems, shareholders are the owners of their organizations and can impose the organizational paradigm—Red, Amber, Orange, Green, or Teal—that fits their worldview. That leaves two choices to founders wanting to grow a Teal Organization: If possible, they can strive to do without external investors, financing their growth through bank loans and their own cash flow, even if it means slower growth (a route taken by Morning Star, Heiligenfeld, and FAVI); or they need to carefully select equity investors who have integrated a Teal perspective (a route Tami Simon chose for Sounds True).

Especially in critical moments, board members will look to appoint leaders who share their worldview, who look at problems and solutions from the same angle.

Limiting legal frameworks

In today's corporate world, shareholders own their company, and as owners can freely choose what to do with it. From a Green perspective, they are but one of many stakeholders, and their powers should be limited by the say given to other stakeholders (employees, customers, suppliers, local communities, and the environment). From an Evolutionary-Teal perspective, their power should not be limited, but transcended by the organization's purpose. The more shareholders, just like all other stakeholders, agree to listen to the company's purpose and to follow its sense of direction, the more likely a healthy return will be generated from their investment.

It is too early to say how such a view, which challenges a fundamental assumption of the capitalist system, could one day be integrated into legal frameworks. Some experiments are underway. Holacracy, for instance, has drafted a *constitution* that a board can adopt and that henceforth becomes binding, even to future shareholders. It gives shareholders a legitimate say in matters related to finance, but prevents them from unilaterally imposing a strategy, or from reverting the organization to traditional management practices. Holacracy has done the legal footwork to make its constitution fit within US corporate law, and it is currently adapting the constitution to legal systems in other countries. Only a handful of organizations have adopted the holacratic constitution at the time of writing. While there isn't yet much experience with how the constitution works in practice, it looks like a promising avenue toward transcending the shareholder perspective into one where the evolutionary purpose is central.

Another initiative called B-Corporation has been getting some attention recently. B-Corporations are for-profit companies that explicitly include a social or environmental purpose. Patagonia, the outdoor apparel maker, was the first Californian company to adopt the B-Corporation status at the beginning of 2012. By the time of writing, laws have been passed in 11 US States, including California, Illinois, and New York, and 16 more states are working on similar legislation. In for-profit companies as we know them (the so-called C-Corporations), the organizations' directors have a fiduciary duty to the shareholders, and to the shareholders only. They face the prospect of civil claims if they stray from their fiduciary duties by taking environmental or social concerns into account at the expense of shareholders. The duty of directors of B-Corporations is extended to include non-financial interests, such as social benefit, concerns of employees and suppliers, and environmental impact. To put it in different words, where C-Corporations are based on the (Orange) notion of shareholder value, B-Corporations stem from the (Green) concept of stakeholder perspective. In B-Corporations, a special provision requires at least two-thirds or more of the votes on the board for changes of control, structure, or purpose. These provisions offer some protection to entrepreneurs who wish to raise capital but fear losing control of their business's social or environmental mission.

As society as a whole transitions towards Teal, I believe we will see many more legal experiments along the line of Holacracy's constitution and B-Corporations. In the final chapter of this book, I speculate about an even more profound change: Could it be that in a Teal society, we would no longer think in terms of *ownership*, but in terms of *stewardship*? Such a shift would have profound implications in terms of legal ownership of organizations. Only time will tell if and how such a scenario will play out. For now, initiatives such as B-Corporations and Holacracy's constitution provide interesting avenues for leaders wanting to ground their organizations in a legal framework more agreeable to a Teal perspective.

Necessary, but not sufficient

Having a CEO and a board that "get it" are necessary, but not sufficient, conditions. There is a common belief in organizational development circles that if we could only get leaders to be more enlightened, all would be well. That notion is too simplistic; enlightened leaders don't automatically make for enlightened organizations, unless they also embrace structures, practices, and cultures that change how power is held, how people can show up, and how the organization's purpose can express itself. (Using Integral's four-quadrant model, it's easy to see that changing only the top two quadrants and leaving the bottom two unchanged only gets you halfway.) In a blog post, Deborah Boyar, one of HolacracyOne's employees, contrasts her experience there with other settings where leaders were likely equally or more enlightened, but the structures were not:

> *I was first drawn to Holacracy through a sense of frustration at repeated cycles of coming together with like-minded people who shared aspirations to transform culture in meaningful ways. Gradually, yet inexorably, I found myself becoming annoyed, paralyzed, or ultimately defeated by the limits of our collective capacity to manifest even a fraction of the noble aims that had initially magnetized our collaboration. Regardless of what was accomplished, it became increasingly painful to keep participating due to my dismay, disappointment, and disbelief at how interpersonal politics and painful meetings throttled the flow of effective action, and drained both my own human capital and that of my friends.*
>
> *Again and again, I was stunned at the gap between personal development and organizational capacity. These failed experiments appeared in many different contexts of my life, and were extremely confusing, because each iteration involved people who already got along well as friends, shared similar worldviews and goals, and had the best of intentions. Not only did I personally live through many such upheavals, but as the wife of a well-known spiritual teacher who works with other well-known spiritual teachers, I also witnessed similar cycles play out in their lives—and I considered most of them much better equipped than I to weather these storms. Yet even they, the "most highly developed," got swept away and even drowned at times in the familiar struggles over power, authority, and productivity.*
>
> *I gradually developed a layer of cynicism to protect myself from the hurt, anger, and sadness I carried from these flawed attempts to organize*

in service of a higher purpose. How could so many wonderful people, with so much talent and so many skills, fail to break through this morass of politics and personality? I concluded that this phenomenon was just another manifestation of our flawed humanity, and of the disjunction between what we can envision and what we can manifest. I determined that my expectations were too high, and decided I needed to cultivate more patience, humility, and refine my interpersonal skills. I worried about having a bad case of "Boomeritis"—wanting everything to come immediately and easily without putting in the necessary effort over time. Though much of this may still be true about me, it still doesn't take away the profoundly liberating alternative I've discovered through practicing Holacracy, and especially through becoming a partner of HolacracyOne.

Joining HolacracyOne has been utterly catalytic on all levels of my being. Playing politics is not necessary or useful in this system. Instead, I am expected to notice and process tensions I encounter—not to pretend they don't exist or sweep them under the rug. There is no pressure for me to be like other people. I'm very different, and that's valued. I don't have to develop, but it's happening. I don't have to be perfect, but I'm improving. I'm clear how authority is held in the roles I fill, and where I need to interface with other roles and incorporate their input—and when I'm not, I bring that tension to Governance [the meeting where governance issues get processed]. Things get done around here, without drama, and with clarity and regenerative creativity. The esprit de corps *is very positive and sustaining—not because we're uniquely optimistic, but because the system in which we operate is healthy and liberates our energies to flow and function. I feel I've entered a healthy family structure—again, not because the "family members" are particularly psychologically intact; like me, they are very human—but because our practice of Holacracy sources our interactions to arise in a clear space, free of baggage and politics.*

In the neuroscience of human development, there's a lot of interest these days in secure attachment. It's something that children develop when they are raised in a family where they can express themselves, be heard, have appropriate limits set as they develop, and respect the space and limits of others. At HolacracyOne, I'm becoming securely organizationally attached. It's a profoundly healing psychological as well as organizational experience. I feel more real, grounded, and incarnate. I feel inspired to focus and accomplish more than I ever have. I feel empowered to make decisions, and invited to get support around doing so. I feel totally lit up by the aim I am serving.[11]

CHAPTER 3.2

STARTING UP A TEAL ORGANIZATION

Whatever you do or dream you can do—begin it.
Boldness has genius and power and magic in it.
Johann Wolfgang von Goethe

Perhaps as you read this book you are about to start a new business, nonprofit, school, hospital, or foundation, and you are wondering how to bake Teal yeast into the dough of the organization from the start. (If you run an *existing* organization and are wondering how to transform it along Teal lines, the next chapter addresses that question more specifically.)

Starting a new organization can be exhilarating, but it's also sheer hard work. Here is the good news: it seems that operating on Teal principles from the start can make for a smoother ride.

In a way, in the very early stages, all startups tend to be pretty informal, self-organizing efforts. But when the organization grows, every so often it goes through a painful molt, and adds another layer of structure, hierarchy, and control. In comparison, Teal Organizations adapt and grow continuously, fluidly, and organically.

Experience also shows that it is easier to start out from Teal, rather than transforming an existing structure with its history and baggage from previous paradigms. Starting with a clean slate, you can listen in to the organization's purpose and shape the culture, the practices, the people you recruit, and other factors, accordingly. Here are some of the obvious questions to listen in to:

- If for a moment you try to take yourself (your wishes, your dreams) out of the equation and listen to the budding organization, what is the purpose that it wants to serve?
- What shape does the organization want to take?
- At what pace does the organization want to grow?
- Is the organization best served by you being a single founder or by several co-founders? Which other co-founders are meant to join you?

The presence and consciousness that you bring as a founder will affect the level of consciousness at which the organization operates. One of the best ways you can serve the project, therefore, is to spend a fair share of your energy reflecting on the presence you bring to bear, your lights and your shadows, through whatever means work best for you: feedback from peers and friends, mentoring, coaching, reading, meditation, personal and spiritual development, and so on.

Choosing the right co-founders—if there are co-founders—is a critical decision for any startup, but it is even more so here. It is not only important that they bring the right skills and that the interpersonal chemistry works. If you want the organization to run on Evolutionary-Teal principles, the degree to which its purpose resonates with them and their readiness to embrace Teal ways of operating are two additional critical factors to add to the list. Be ready to spend significant time discussing these topics. The depth at which you explore these questions will set a standard for the type of conversations you will henceforward consider normal in the organization. Effectively, you are shaping the culture of the organization before it has even started.

As soon as the co-founders or the first hires are on board, you will have to make some choices about the structure of the organization, and about the practices and processes to use. Who can make what decisions? Who can decide to spend company money? Will people have individual targets to achieve? Will people receive a bonus if they achieve them? Who evaluates whom? How are disagreements handled? Who ultimately calls the shots?

Each of these questions can be answered from Conformist-Amber, Achievement-Orange, Pluralistic-Green, or Evolutionary-Teal. In the very early days, start-ups tend to be quite informal—all information gets shared, all important decisions get debated by the team. But if you are not on the lookout, traditional management practices can quickly creep in, because for most of us, this is all we have ever known. If you believe the organization should run along Teal principles, it requires that whenever the need for a new practice or process arises, you are conscious that you have hit a fork in the road: you can go with traditional management practices, or you can explore Teal ways of operating. It might be helpful if all the early team members are familiar with the concepts outlined in this book. Even better: try to set aside time with the early team—perhaps as much as two or three days—to jointly sense the practices you want to adopt for the new organization. The tables summarizing the different Teal practices for self-management, wholeness, and evolutionary purpose on pages 140-141, 190-190 and 223-224 (see also Appendix 4 for a different view) can help you in your exploration.

Sometimes I am asked which of these practices are most critical when starting an organization. My response: there is no prescriptive, one-size-fits-all shortlist of practices that would fit the bill for every startup. Your organization's purpose and context will call for some unique priorities. As always, the answer is: start by listening for what you sense is called for. That being said, some practices stand out as natural candidates that any founding team should at least consider. They stand out in my mind because they are relevant from day one, and because they have some foundational qualities—they create a fertile ground that will help other Teal practices take root easily later on, when the organization grows and calls for more explicit structures and processes.

Overarching assumptions and values

Because these are early days for Teal, most of the organizational practices you choose will be deeply countercultural. Expect people to question your choices and tell you that your choices are foolish! Organizations researched for this book found that debates are much more fruitful when they don't stay at the level of arguing for or against a certain management practice, but when they take place at a deeper level, discussing the often hidden assumptions underneath the practices. You will probably make your life much easier if you articulate the assumptions you hold about people and about work. Here some examples to provide food for thought:

- RHD, you might remember, has defined for itself the following three basic assumptions: *people are of equal human worth; people are essentially good, unless proven otherwise; there is no single way to manage corporate issues well.*
- Morning Star's way of operating is founded on two core principles: *individuals shall work together with no use of force or coercion; individuals shall keep commitments.*
- FAVI has articulated three basic assumptions: *people are systematically considered to be good (reliable, self-motivated, trustworthy, intelligent); there is no performance without happiness; value is created on the shop floor.*

A practical tip: explore the assumptions *with your team,* not on your own. And as a first step, start by uncovering the unspoken assumptions behind the traditional hierarchical organizational (Amber/Orange) model: workers are lazy and untrustworthy; senior people have all the answers; employees can't handle difficult news; and so forth. Many people find this exercise eye-opening. When they realize what a sad set of assumptions underlies traditional management models, they are eager and energized to define a more positive set of assumptions.

Whatever alternative set of assumptions you define will serve two functions. First, it will make it easier for you and your colleagues to explain why you've chosen to operate using practices that defy conventional management. Second, the assumptions can serve as touchstones for every new practice or process you consider introducing; they will make it easier for anybody in the organization, even the most junior colleague, to speak up and say, "I wonder if what we are doing is in line with our basic assumptions?"

Three practices related to self-management

If you want to bake self-management into your organization right from the start, the first question to consider is: Do you want to take on an existing set of practices?—If yes, Holacracy is the most natural candidate, as it is documented and there are consultants, facilitators, and trainers who can help you. Or do you want to develop your own set of structures and practices? If you choose the latter, there are three practices you should consider from day one:

- *The advice process* (see page 99): From the start, make sure that all members of the organization can make any decision, as long as they consult with the people affected and the people who have expertise on the matter. If a new hire comes to you to approve a decision, refuse to give him the assent he is looking for. Make it clear that nobody, not even the founder, "approves" a decision in a self-managing organization. That said, if you are meaningfully affected by the decision or if you have expertise on the matter, you can of course share your advice.
- *A conflict resolution mechanism* (see page 112): When there is disagreement between two colleagues, they are likely to send it up to you if you are the founder or CEO. Resist the temptation to settle the matter for them. Instead, it's time to formulate a conflict resolution mechanism that will help them work their way through the conflict. (You might be involved later on if they can't sort the issue out one-on-one and if they choose you as a mediator or panel member.)
- *Peer-based evaluation and salary processes* (see pages 123 and 129): Who will decide on the compensation of a new hire, and based on what process? Unless you consciously think about it, you might do it the traditional way: as a founder, you negotiate and settle with the new recruit on a certain package (and then probably keep it confidential). Why not innovate from the start? Give the potential hire information about other people's salaries and let them peg their own number, to which the group of colleagues can then react

with advice to increase or lower the number. Similarly, it makes sense right from the beginning to choose a peer-based mechanism for the appraisal process if you choose to formalize such a process. Otherwise, people will naturally look to you, the founder, to tell them how they are doing, creating a de facto sense of hierarchy within the team.

Four practices related to wholeness

As a founder, your presence, the way you show up, will determine to a large extent how comfortable other people feel to show up with all of who they are. The more you self-disclose, the more authentic, the more vulnerable, the more honest you are about your strengths and weaknesses, the safer others will feel to do the same. This might all come naturally to you. In any case, when starting an organization, certain practices might help you and others ground yourselves in more wholeness. Four particular practices lend themselves to being introduced very early on:

- *Ground rules for safe space* (see page 151): To show up fully in the presence of others, we must feel it is safe to do so. Many organizations find it helpful to define a set of values and to translate them into concrete behaviors that are either encouraged or declared unacceptable in the community of colleagues. This is often best captured in a document, such as RHD's *Bill of Rights and Responsibilities*, or Morning Star's *Colleague Principles*. Some startups will find it important to draft a full version of such a document early on, based on experiences both good and bad from previous organizations they worked in. Others will write such a document chapter by chapter, whenever an incident triggers a new topic to be added. Whatever way you choose, make sure it is not written by a single person (not even you, if you are the founder), but stems from a collective effort (and it might be helpful to ask one or several volunteers to take on the role to keep it alive).
- *The office or factory building* (see page 167): Office buildings are often drab, soulless places. They unconsciously tell us: *This is a work setting where you are expected to think and behave in certain conditioned ways.* Why not, from the start, make the work setting colorful, inviting, warm, and quirky, in whatever ways fit the organization's culture and purpose? Spend a day or a weekend as a team planning and re-decorating the space. Go wild—forget any preconceived notions of what a workplace *should* look like. It will help colleagues remember that this place is special, and that they, like the building, are welcome to show up in their own unique way.

- *Onboarding process* (see page 176): The onboarding process is critical in making new members feel welcome and in conveying how this place works. What is the ideal experience for new hires in their first hours, days, and weeks at work? What foundational training should everybody that works in the organization experience? Self-management, deep listening, dealing constructively with conflict, creating a safe environment, some frontline skills ... ?
- *Meeting practices* (see on page 162): In the early days of an organization, people tend to meet often to align with and update one another. To prevent the typical meeting syndromes—egos showing up, some people's voices drowned out by others—you can integrate a meeting practice that invites people into wholeness. It can be as simple as starting with a minute of silence or a round of thanking, but you can also choose a structured decision-making process, such as those practiced by Holacracy and Buurtzorg.

Two practices related to purpose

If you put your energy into founding a business, a nonprofit, a school, or a hospital, then in all likelihood the organization's purpose resonates deeply with your own life trajectory. Share your passion and your story, with your team in particular, and with everyone possible. The more you do, the easier you make it for others to reflect on and define their own relationship with the organization's purpose.

For some founders, the purpose seems so self-evident that they focus all their energy on getting stuff done; they forget to talk about the *why*, the deeper purpose behind everyone's efforts. There is another pitfall at the opposite end of the spectrum: some founders evangelize about the purpose in a way that gives the impression that they are the only ones who can legitimately define it and talk about it.

The healthy relationship is one where as a founder you see, from the start, the organization as having a life and purpose of its own, distinct from your own wishes and desires. For a short time, you might be the main person to articulate it, but as soon as other people join you, they should be able to sense the broader purpose just as well and find their unique way to relate to it and express it. Two practices can help:

- *Recruitment* (see page 219): The recruitment process offers a beautiful opportunity to help potential new hires explore in depth in what unique ways the organization's purpose resonates (or doesn't) with their own calling and longings. These can be wonderfully deep, sometimes moving conversations. And perhaps the candidate might, even before joining the organization, offer a perspective of where he feels the organization might be called to go.

- *Empty chair meeting practice* (see page 204): The "empty chair" is a simple practice you can introduce from day one. At the end of every meeting (or at any moment during the meeting), someone from the team can sit in the empty chair that represents the organization's purpose and listen in, for instance, to the question: *Has this meeting served the organization well?*

CHAPTER 3.3

TRANSFORMING AN EXISTING ORGANIZATION

A radical inner transformation and rise to a new level of consciousness might be the only real hope we have in the current global crisis brought on by the dominance of the Western mechanistic paradigm.

Stanislav Grof

Most of the organizations researched for this book started experimenting with alternative management practices from the day they were founded, but a handful among them used to operate along the Amber/Orange paradigm before transforming to Teal. FAVI used to be an exceedingly hierarchical and control-minded factory before Jean-François Zobrist shook it up. AES is a special case: from the start, it operated on pioneer practices, but in its massive growth in the 1980s and 1990s, it acquired dozens of traditionally run power plants, which all successfully transitioned to adopt Teal management practices. And then there is HolacracyOne, a consultancy specializing in bringing self-management practices to existing organizations.

These are only a handful of organizations, but I believe their experiences offer some critical insights and food for thought for leaders contemplating a transition in the way their organizations operate. I have no doubt that in the future, as more organizations transition to Evolutionary-Teal, we will refine our understanding of what it takes to help organizations make the leap.

So, if you are part of an existing organization, what can you do to help it adopt Teal structures and practices? First, you need to check whether the two necessary conditions discussed in chapter 3.1 are present:

1. Does the CEO "get it?" Does she see the world through Teal lenses? Is he personally excited about the idea of running the organization based on Teal principles?
2. Do the members of the board "get it" and support it?

If the CEO is not on board, it is not worthwhile for anyone to put his time and effort in the project. (Instead, you can put your energy into a "horizontal" transformation toward a healthier form of the existing paradigm.) If the CEO is eager to begin, but the board is not aligned, your company is in for a difficult ride, because worldviews will collide. Your best bet, then, is to try to see if over time you can get supportive board members to replace existing ones. I would not bet on the chances of persuading existing board members of your perspective through the power of argument, for the same reason discussed in chapter 3.1 about CEOs.

If the two critical conditions are in place, there is good news: there are many roads that lead to a Teal Organization, and experience seems to indicate that if the CEO is persistent, he will get there one way or another. But where to start? What to focus on at first?

Living organizations change in increments, so rather than changing everything at once, it can make sense to start with only one of the three breakthroughs of Teal Organizations (self-management, wholeness, or evolutionary purpose) and to introduce the others over time. Obviously the three reinforce each other. For instance, when an organization self-manages, people take initiative at all levels all the time, allowing the organization to move toward its purpose without the need for top-down strategy setting. So focusing on one breakthrough may evoke change to some extent in other areas. But aiming to adopt all three breakthroughs at once might nevertheless push the organization beyond its natural rhythm of change.

> *Re-examine all that you have been told ... dismiss that which insults your soul.*
>
> Walt Whitman

Try listening to what best suits the organization's needs. Perhaps purpose needs to be explored first, because once all colleagues resonate with it, they will have energy for self-management and wholeness. Maybe the right thing to do is to start with wholeness, as a way to build sufficient trust and community for people to accept change in the other dimensions. Or it could be that the hierarchy needs to be broken down first. Only you and your colleagues can sense where it's best to put the initial focus.

Introducing self-management

The leaders who introduced self-management into existing organizations all shared the same insight with me: they received a very different response from middle-senior managers and those in staff functions than they did from frontline workers. Expect the same when you bring self-management into your organization

People at lower levels in the hierarchy warm to self-management quickly. Most of those who had previously been given very little power and room for decision-making will relish the freedom to shape their work in the way they see fit. Many Teal Organizations insist it is critically important to recruit the right people, those who will thrive in a self-management model; and yet cases like FAVI, AES, and others show that even without prior selection, a large proportion of *any* group of workers will warm to self-management and often become vocal advocates. Dennis Bakke recounts how every time AES took over a factory somewhere in the world, people told him self-management wouldn't work there:

> *My colleague Roger Naill and I often teamed together on visits to AES plants around the world, especially to meet with people at facilities recently acquired by AES. ... When it was time for questions and comments, invariably one of the first statements we heard was, "This sounds very interesting, but it won't work here because ..." ... We heard: "This is a communist country," "This is a developing country," "We have been here too long to change," "This is not America," "There is a union here" ... Roger Naill and I would share a knowing smile from across the room when these objections to the AES approach were recited. We had learned that if we were persistent and were able to install AES-style leaders in these organizations, the objections would usually melt away. ...*
>
> *The experience [of transforming dozens of] operations around the world taught me some valuable lessons. Most people will flourish in a liberated workplace. Age, sex, educational background, political inclination, union membership, color or ethnic background, and even IQ have little effect on whether someone will come to love and succeed in this kind of workplace.*[1]

There are exceptions, of course. Some people have been so scarred by years of command and control that they can't seem to adjust to life without a boss. Self-management is demanding: people have to take responsibility for their actions and their relationships; they are no longer shielded from unpleasant news and difficult trade-offs; there is no manager to hide behind or to pass the buck to. People who cannot adjust to the responsibility that comes with the freedom of self-management often choose to leave for a traditional, hierarchical employer.

Psychological ownership

Even though most people end up thriving under self-management, the transition can take time. In most companies, people at the lower levels are accustomed to being told what to do. They don't need to worry if the company is making or losing money or about threats and opportunities in the market: if results are bad or change is needed, someone from above will step in and make decisions. Self-management, on the other hand, relies on widespread "psychological ownership," as scholars call it. Everybody, not just a few at the top, is vested in his or her work, the organization's purpose, its culture, its results, its reputation, and so on.

Developing a feeling of psychological ownership is a process; it doesn't appear overnight just because people are given freedom to self-manage. I've noticed that some leaders believe that employees, once freed from rules, budgets, and managers, will somehow spontaneously start firing on all cylinders. That might happen if employees already feel a strong sense of psychological ownership. If they don't, I wouldn't bet much on it. When people have little emotional investment in the organization and in its purpose, when employees consider work as a burden to be minimized, then don't be surprised that given freedom, they take the freedom but not the responsibility. If people worked for years in a system that essentially relied on targets and pressure from above to prevent them from slacking off, then slacking off is exactly what might happen when bosses and targets are removed all of a sudden.

If you sense that there is little psychological ownership, then you need to think carefully and creatively about the journey that could help your colleagues develop an emotional investment in their work, the organization, and its purpose and achievements. In chapter 2.3, we discussed how in self-managing organizations, people don't abuse their freedom because of the intrinsic motivation that their work and the organization's purpose inspire in them; peer emulation and pressure from the market can play a part, too, in helping people operate at the top of their game (see page 123). Each of these elements could be important in the journey to help colleagues cultivate psychological ownership.

- *Purpose:* If there is no clarity around the purpose of the organization, or if that purpose doesn't feel inspiring, this area might need to be addressed before switching to self-management (ideas about how to do this are discussed later in this chapter).
- *Emulation:* How could colleagues feel emotionally invested in their work and their achievements towards a purpose? Here is one idea: challenge teams to make a plan, set themselves targets, and prepare an investment budget. Let teams know upfront that there will be a big event where they present their plans to one another (Morning Star's Business Units do this once a year). At the end of the event, hold a vote (say each team votes for the three teams with the best plans); teams need to be given sufficient time to prepare well so they can shine in front of their peers. In small companies, there might be too few teams to turn the presentation into a gentle competition. In that case, the team(s) could present their plan to the owner or the board. Upfront, they know that the

owner/board will only agree to switch to self-management (and effectively surrender their top-down power) if they are sufficiently impressed with the teams' presentations. Whatever the method, the presentations don't really matter as much as the preparation phase. It's in the team room that people's emotional investment grows, as they debate their plans and targets and start dreaming about what is possible and what is realistic. In the course of several meetings, in all likelihood, the early enthusiasts win over those who are warier.

Another way to create emulation comes with information transparency. If there is a common metric across teams, such as productivity at Buurtzorg, then simply publishing teams' results on a monthly basis can do the trick. No team likes to rank at the bottom of the list for long. At some point, the team's antibodies will kick in: if a team does poorly, it means that something isn't working out, that work is probably unpleasant. There comes a point when someone from within the team will speak out and force change to happen in one way or another.

- *Market pressure*: At FAVI, the team supplying a specific automobile maker, say, Volvo, hears every week from the teammate responsible for sales what order Volvo placed and the price the competition is quoting. The link to the customer is so direct that team members know if they don't stay on their toes, their job might be on the line, not because someone high up decides to fire them, but simply because customers will stop ordering. In organizations like FAVI and Buurtzorg, where all, or almost all teams, are customer-facing, pressure from the market provides a natural incentive to pick up responsibility for self-management. In organizations that have a longer process (as is the case, for instance, with Morning Star or AES's power plants) the effect is less powerful, as one team's high or low performance doesn't directly translate to the customers but is averaged out in the performance of all the teams.

One condition needs to be in place before starting out on a journey to foster people's emotional investment in their work and the organization: they have to trust the leader that wants to introduce self-management. In most places, workers have become instinctively distrustful of change efforts that senior leaders want to sell them. If you impose self-management practices from above on distrustful workers, they are likely to take the freedom but refuse the responsibility, and you end up with a company headed for failure.

People will follow you as a leader only when word gets around that you are somehow different, that you truly care, and that they can trust you even when you are about to do the craziest thing: to relinquish your own power. At FAVI, Zobrist launched the first step of his revolution only one year after he had joined the company. During that time, he was on the shop floor every day, talking with operators, asking questions, showing real interest. When he was asked questions in return, in his maverick style, he spoke his mind freely about things he felt needed to change. In the process, operators came to trust the man and his intentions.

Whenever AES acquired a new power plant, three or four leaders from existing plants were sent in to take over key positions. One of them would become the plant director. (Remember that having a "CEO" who gets it is a necessary condition, and a plant director of a remote unit is a CEO of sorts.) Like Zobrist, they wouldn't bring in self-management practices right from the start. These new directors waited awhile, for frontline workers to see that something was different about their leadership style, that their intentions could be trusted. It was often after only a year, sometimes two, that they would introduce AES's self-management practices in full.

Middle and senior management

Most senior and middle managers, as well as people in staff functions, will view the transition to self-management as a threat (at least at first). Don't expect them to embrace self-management with hoorays. In the best of cases, they will lose only their hierarchical power. More likely, they will have to find themselves a new job within the organization or outside it, because their function will disappear altogether. FAVI, for instance, used to have up to five levels of hierarchy; today it operates with only the CEO "above" the self-managing teams. Unsurprisingly, people whose power and jobs are at stake (and for whom the new practices often make no sense) tend to oppose the changes passionately. Expect their resistance to be the hardest nut to crack in your organization's transition.

> *The central question you are likely to face when adopting self-management practices is how to deal with resistance from middle and senior management, as well as staff functions.*

FAVI and AES can offer some insights into ways to handle that situation gracefully. At FAVI, Zobrist had been hired externally as the new CEO, with a four-month overlap period with the departing CEO. Zobrist knew that two bosses can be a recipe for disaster. He suggested his predecessor stay fully in charge during the overlap. For four months, Zobrist made no decisions. All he did was wander around and talk to people, to get to know them and the organization. One day he had an epiphany of sorts: he noticed a worker, a sheet of paper in hand, waiting in front of the supply room's locked door. Zobrist asked him what he was waiting for. The worker needed new gloves. The procedure required that he first get his superior to sign a document attesting that the old pair of gloves was worn out and that a new pair was needed. Now, with the signed paper in hand, he had to wait for the supply manager to unlock the supply room, and in exchange for the paper, hand him a new pair of gloves. Zobrist was puzzled. Why did the supply room need to be locked? Couldn't the workers be trusted? He ran some numbers in his head. The time the machine stood still because the operator had to comply with the procedure cost the organization *ten times* the price of the pair of gloves.

In that moment, Zobrist realized the problem was not just with the supply room. The lack of trust was everywhere. It was in the time clocks that required workers to clock in and out at the beginning and the end of the day. It was in the role of quality controllers who checked whether workers had done their jobs properly. It was in the five levels of management that separated the CEO from the workers. It was in the architecture of the building, in the window from his office that allowed him to overlook the entire factory. It was in the variable pay system that punished people for late arrivals and poor productivity.

For a few months after taking over, Zobrist tried to engage his executive team in discussions to break down some of these mechanisms but met strong resistance. Nine months after he had taken on the full CEO role, on the last working day of the year, just before the Christmas break, he decided to change tactics. He assembled the entire workforce in a corner of the factory. Standing on top of a few boxes, he shared that the way people were controlled in the company felt disgraceful to him. After the holidays, there would be no more time clocks at the factory entrance. The variable pay system would be replaced with a fixed salary—no more pay deductions to try to control people. The supply room would be unlocked and everybody would be trusted to take out the supplies they needed and to log what they took out for reordering purposes. Finally, the managers' canteen would be closed; everybody would have lunch together.

At that stage, the cadre of managers had turned pale and the audience was deeply silent. He added:

> *How will we operate in the future? To be perfectly honest, I don't know. I'm convinced that you deserve for us to work together differently, but I don't have an alternative model. I suggest that, together, we learn by doing, with good intentions, common sense, and in good faith.*[2]

Coming back from the holidays, the managers complained loudly to Zobrist. How would they keep people in line, now that some of their carrots and sticks had been taken away? Zobrist made it clear that there would be no turning back. He let them in on the next step he had in mind: teams would self-manage. Obviously, this would mean there would be no more need for supervisors and managers, and some of the staff functions would fall away too. He told people that no one would be fired: he suggested they take their time, look around, talk with workers, and find or create themselves a useful role. Their salaries would not be cut, whatever role they would take on. If they found no role of interest, or if they preferred taking on a managerial position in another firm, they would receive a fair exit package. In the end only one person, a former sales manager, left the company. Several people were close to retirement and found tasks to bridge the year or two they had left. The fact that FAVI started to grow significantly helped others find themselves new roles.

FAVI's story is instructive in several ways. There is, of course, an irony in the CEO imposing self-management in a last act of top-down decision-making. But if we look carefully, we can see that Zobrist wielded his power with precision, limiting himself to the smallest possible decision. He didn't define and impose a reorganization plan. He didn't decide how managers and staff functions would be reappointed. Neither did he decide who would stay and who would leave. Within the constraints he set (there would be no more management roles), he let people find the best path forward for themselves and for the factory. Granted, for many former managers, this was a difficult time in their careers, at least temporarily. In the end, many flourished in their new roles; they found a weight had been lifted from their shoulders now that they no longer needed to pressure subordinates to behave and to perform, nor to stay in the good graces of their superior.

The power plants taken over by AES in different parts of the world were just as hierarchical as FAVI, if not more. The plant in Kazakhstan, for example, used to have ten layers of hierarchy. In nearly all cases, when AES closed the acquisition, it would offer a generous severance package to invite middle managers to seek a job elsewhere; there simply weren't going to be enough roles going forward for the plethora of managers the plants used to employ. Like FAVI, AES spelled out how it wanted to run the plants going forward, and then gave people the means, through a generous package, to decide on their own future. They could either find a role within the organization that added value, or seek work elsewhere. AES reports the same experience as FAVI: Former managers who decided to stay often ended up relishing the environment without hierarchy. Middle managers in particular, who were often squeezed between the people they need to keep in line and the orders from the top, felt the sky suddenly cleared when hierarchical relationships became a thing of the past.

How to deal with middle/senior managers and colleagues in staff functions is in all likelihood the most challenging issue you will face in a transformation to Teal. Another key question will be determining the structure that might be most appropriate for your organization: Will it be self-managing teams, like Buurtzorg or FAVI? A structure based on individual contracting, like Morning Star? Holacracy's structure of nested teams? The industry you work in, the type of work you do, is likely to call for one type of structure over another. Discussing the respective merits of the structure types would take us too long here, but if you want to delve deeper into the matter, you can turn to Appendix 3, which addresses the differences between these models and the questions you can ponder with your team to discover which structure best fits your needs.

A third point relates to timing: how do you introduce self-management practices? Do you do it in one go, in big-bang fashion? Or progressively? How much (or rather how little) do you need to impose, and what can you let emerge organically? Of course, there is no one-size-fits-all answer to these questions. Every organization is on a unique journey, calling for a unique approach. Nevertheless we can distinguish between three broad types of approaches, a framing you might find helpful as you ponder the journey of your organization. I call them *creative chaos, bottom-up redesign,* and *pre-existing template.*

Creative chaos

In this approach, the CEO decides in top-down fashion, with the old powers vested in their role of CEO, to take out an essential lever of power. Take out a key staff function like the planning department, or a layer of management—for example, the first line supervisors. Or, like Zobrist did at FAVI, remove a key management tool, like the punch clocks and the variable pay system through which supervisors could control the machine operators. Chaos will ensue, which is what you hope for. This approach requires you to trust that the powers of self-organization will master the chaos (and master it fast enough for clients—and the organization's purpose—not to be affected too much in the transition). If you feel that employees already have psychological ownership over their work and the organization, and if frontline workers trust you, chances are they won't let this opportunity pass them by. They will rise to the occasion and self-organize their way into a future where they can express their power and talents. Even if you sense that psychological ownership is only patchy, you might still try to take the gamble, particularly if everything else you've tried to get middle and senior management on board has failed, as was the case for Zobrist at FAVI.

Bottom-up redesign

Another, less drastic, avenue is to invite everyone in the organization to design the future of the organization together. Get the group to determine what new structure makes most sense to replace the pyramid and what new practices will be introduced (for example, the advice process, transparent information, and peer-based evaluation). The more people you can involve, the better. Large-group techniques like Appreciative Inquiry, Future Search, or Process Design make it possible to harness the wisdom of everyone in the organization, even when there are hundreds or thousands of employees. Bringing in an experienced facilitator to support you in preparing and running such an event is certainly no luxury.

This method requires favorable conditions: frontline employees who trust you enough to be willing to explore the idea of self-management, and middle and senior managers who, despite their opposition, won't sabotage the effort. There is much you can do to prepare the ground. The more employees understand already up front what self-management is and how it can make their lives at work exciting and meaningful, the easier it will be. Talk about it, bring in a speaker, get people to visit a self-managing organization, hand out copies of this book or other books mentioned in the bibliography, and so on. AES used plant visits to great effect. Union leaders of newly acquired plants would be invited to spend a few days with an existing AES plant and experience "Joy at Work," as it called its management practices. Union leaders always returned to their plants as vocal advocates for the new way of doing things. When it comes to middle and senior management, as well as staff functions, it might be wise to give them some clarity about their future prospects before the collective design effort begins. If their current roles disappear, what can they do to find another role within the organization? If they don't find a new role that interests them, or if they choose to leave, what will the company do to help?

Pre-existing template (switch day)

A third approach consists of implementing an existing and proven set of self-managing practices. Holacracy is a natural candidate in this case. It is an elegant and interlocking set of practices for self-management that was pioneered originally with Ternary Software but has now been turned into an "organizational operating system" ready to be adopted by other organizations. There is a constitution that spells it all out; there are detailed meeting and decision-making practices; there are licensed consultants who can train you and your colleagues in the practices as well as facilitate meetings while you get used to the system. Adopting an existing set of practices like Holacracy can make the transition much smoother and faster. You benefit from accumulated insight gained by people who have put innovative practices to the test and refined them over and over again.

To get going with Holacracy, you need to define a starting structure of nested circles, and you must determine a switch day where the new structure, practices, and processes take effect and the old cease to exist (typically the day the organization's founder or CEO adopts Holacracy's constitution). The starting structure doesn't need to be perfect in any way—to keep things simple it can even mimic the old hierarchical structure to start with. Through the holacratic governance process, the structure will evolve organically and adapt to what best fits the context and the purpose.

Of course, you can also seek inspiration from other sources. Morning Star's "Self-Management Institute" has started to give two-day training courses to respond to requests from people wanting to learn about its practices. Buurtzorg has published extensively about its structure and practices (albeit only in Dutch so far) and is open to collaborating with people from abroad who are active in the health care sector. In general, self-managing organizations are happy to share their insights and practices with people seriously committed to adopting such practices in their organization.

When an already self-managing company acquires a traditionally run organization, it of course has an existing template for self-management in-house. To save time and to ensure consistency, people can choose not to reinvent the wheel and instead just invite the acquired entity to adopt the existing set of self-management practices. AES provides an interesting insight: the company chose to operate on the same set of practices—such as the advice process and peer-based budgeting—in all plants throughout the world. However, AES didn't standardize *the way* newly acquired plants adopted these practices. It found that the cultural background and the collective history of each plant called for a unique, specific approach. In some cases, AES practices were introduced gradually. In other cases, some of these changes were regrouped into a formal switch day, for instance on the ceremonial day when workers signed new contracts. In keeping with its philosophy, AES made it a point to invite blue-collar workers to switch from hourly wages to fixed salaries; in some plants, it was decided that the day workers signed their new contracts would become a day of celebration, a day that also marked when the plant would adopt the full package of AES's self-management practices.

Introducing practices related to wholeness

In all likelihood, introducing practices related to wholeness should be an easier process compared to the switch to self-management, for at least two reasons:

- With the switch to self-management, you can expect resistance from people who will lose their power or even their current job functions. When it comes to practices related to wholeness, some people might be uncomfortable at first, but if you invite people gently into these practices and don't force them, you are unlikely to face real opposition. As more and more people start dropping their professional masks, even those uncomfortable at first will most likely join in and realize they enjoy bringing more of themselves to work.
- Whereas self-management consists of interlocking practices (if you take the boss out, you need new processes, for example, to handle conflict, channel information, decide on roles and salaries), when it comes to wholeness you can introduce practices in the order and at the speed you feel best suits the organization.

There are two types of approaches you can take (or combine) in introducing practices around wholeness—gradual or more comprehensive.

Gradual introduction of wholeness practices

You can choose to introduce the practices related to wholeness gradually, one at a time, whenever it seems most relevant. You can start, for example, by suggesting a certain meeting practice in the meetings you attend (a round of check-in, a round of thanking, a minute of silence ...), and if people warm to the practice, advocate that it be generalized throughout the company. When the time of the year for performance evaluations comes up, you can suggest changing the format to turn the discussions into more of a personal inquiry into one's learning journey and calling. Or if you foresee hiring many new people, it might be the right time to rethink the onboarding process.

Before you try to bring in any of these practices, openly espouse and role-model what it's like to drop the professional mask and show up as fully as possible at work. Then speak about wholeness, and *why* you think wholeness is important in the workplace. Your colleagues are more likely to embrace these practices if they understand the underlying motive. Stories are always more powerful than arguments, especially when they are personal stories: *Why are you passionate about creating an organization where people relate more wholly with each other? Why is it important in your own life?* You can also link the topic of wholeness to the organization's purpose. Why does the organization's purpose need us to show up whole? There are many studies in the medical field, for instance, that show that the health of patients improves or deteriorates in meaningful ways depending on the relationship with their doctors and nurses. There are studies that show that the level of trust in schools (among teachers, between teachers and children, between parents and teachers) is the variable that most strongly determines academic outcomes.[3] Think about the purpose of your organization, and you are likely to find a clear and compelling connection between more wholeness and more purpose.

If you tell your story about wholeness with passion and authenticity, it will take root within the organization. Some people will tell you that your story resonates with them. Turn them into advocates. Ask them what practices they think could be introduced, and then let them take the lead. If there is a practice that you think needs to be introduced, see if someone else would want to take on leadership. If many people champion these practices, they will permeate the organization more quickly and more deeply.

Comprehensive introduction of wholeness practices

You can also invite the whole organization jointly to reflect upon wholeness and together design concrete practices to incorporate wholeness into day-to-day work. There are many large group approaches (Appreciative Inquiry, Future Search, Open Space, and others; see page 205) that make it possible to do this with hundreds or even thousands of employees at the same time. If you haven't had the chance to participate in such large group processes, you might find it hard to imagine how it's possible to do anything productive with such large groups. With these methodologies, there is no top-down control, but some process rules evoking the group's collective intelligence achieve the seemingly contradictory: through the power of self-organizing, everyone gets involved, everyone's voice counts, and yet very tangible outcomes are produced. When people listen in to what's most meaningful to them, and find out that their colleagues share in their deepest concerns, enormous energies are set free in the organization.

A fictive but realistic example might help to give a sense of how such a process can unfold. Let's imagine you work in a 500-employee factory that has recently switched to self-management. The transition has not been without challenges; people's attitudes still often betray some hierarchical thinking. You sense that inviting people to be more fully themselves could help them step more confidently into their freedom and responsibilities.

For two days, the machines will stop. You invite all 500 people to gather in a big warehouse for a two-day offsite event to delve into the question, "How can we really be ourselves at work?" using a technique called Appreciative Inquiry. (Some companies, of course, like hospitals or call centers, cannot simply shut down their entire operation; others are spread in different locations with different time zones. There are clever ways to design a process in which everybody can participate in successive shifts).

A group of 10 volunteers, assisted by an external facilitator, has prepared the program. Most colleagues have heard about the topic through the invitation, but don't really know what to expect. As people stream into the warehouse on the first morning, they are invited to sit down randomly at one of 70 round tables with eight chairs scattered around the room. The facilitator briefly explains the goal of the first morning: inquire as to what wholeness means for each colleague in the room and ask why it might be important for them personally and for the organization as a whole. Without further ado, people are asked to group into pairs and interview each other with the following questions:

- *Remember a time where you felt you could really be yourself at work, where you didn't need to act or look the part in any way. Tell me about it.*
- *How did you feel at the time?*
- *At that time, did you sense a difference in your relationships with your colleagues (and possibly with your clients, your wife or husband, your children)? What was the atmosphere like?*

- *Did being fully yourself change anything about your work? Did you feel more productive, more innovative, more ...? Tell me about it.*
- *Can you think back and try to remember what conditions were in place that helped you to be fully yourself at work?*

These paired interviews bring up hundreds of meaningful stories that in many cases people have not shared before. Colleagues discover new facets of one another and start to see each other in a new light.

When people are finished interviewing each other in pairs, they are asked to share the punch line of their story briefly again, this time with the group of eight people sitting around their table. When they are done, a microphone gets handed around the room and volunteers can raise their hand to share their story with the whole room. In just two hours, every colleague has heard many personal accounts of what wholeness can mean in the workplace—first from themselves and their interview partner, then from the six other people at the table of eight, and finally from a few stories within the group at large. Coming into the room in the morning, many colleagues were wondering what this topic of wholeness was about. Through collective storytelling, the topic has now become personal, meaningful, and relevant.

Before lunch, participants zoom in on the last question from the interview—*What conditions were in place that helped you to be fully yourself at work?*—in groups of eight around each table. They try to find common factors that allowed wholeness to emerge. After a while, a microphone is again handed around the room to volunteers from different tables to list the conditions they identified. Many tables have identified similar conditions (for instance, trust, absence of judgment, fun, knowing each other, having a common goal). While people speak into the microphone, an artist captures the key words that come up in a huge improvised drawing on a wall. In front of everybody's eyes, a picture emerges of the kind of workplace that invites people to be whole.

After lunch, colleagues dive deeper into the "dream" of a future where everybody can show up whole. Back at their tables of eight, they are asked to reflect on the following topic:

> *You fall into a deep sleep. You wake up five years from now, and when you come back to work, you are amazed at what you see. All the people in our company seem to be fully at ease with themselves and with their colleagues, brimming with enthusiasm and energy. Nobody wears a mask or pretends to be someone he is not. Everybody is using his or her talents to the fullest and seems incredibly alive.*
>
> *With the colleagues around your table, discuss what you see, what you hear, what you smell, what you sense. When a common picture has emerged in your group, find a way to communicate it to the rest of us—in whatever way you want: a skit, a story, a picture, a song, a poem ... but not a bullet point list!*

The room starts to buzz with energy, loud voices, and laughter. Two hours later, the facilitator asks a dozen volunteer groups to come up on a stage and present their vision of a future of wholeness to their colleagues. Some performances are funny, some are touching, some are clumsy, some are almost professional. Every time a team presents, a new picture of a desirable future is woven into the collective consciousness. During the presentations, the artist picks up on the team's skits to create another oversized mural of the collective dream of a wholesome future.

The next morning, participants are asked to gather in the same teams of eight people to pick up the thread from the previous day. Each team is invited to define two to three initiatives that could turn the vision they had imagined the previous day into reality. Very concretely, what could be done to create a context where people can show up whole? After half an hour, the microphone makes its way around the room and each team in turn shares its initiative with the whole group. The artist creates yet another mural capturing the roughly 100 initiatives, large and small, that teams have put forward. Now it's time to prioritize. All participants receive three sticky dots and are asked to place the dots next to the initiatives that most inspire them on the artist's mural. When everybody is sitting down again, the facilitator helps the group assess the results. Twenty ideas have gathered the majority of sticky dots, and in discussion with the group, the facilitator realizes they fall into five clusters:

- Ideas to create opportunities for people to get to know each other at a deeper level. (The more we know each other, the easier it is to be ourselves.)
- Initiatives to define a set of values and guidelines for interacting with each other in a safe space.
- Ideas to bring fun into the workplace—fun being a great way to drop the all-too-serious professional masks.
- Personal and professional training on topics related to wholeness.
- Changes to the layout and feel of the offices and/or factory floor.

When participants return after a break, 20 flipcharts (one for every idea) have been put up along the walls of the room. The facilitator invites people to vote with their feet by standing next to the flipchart with the idea they would be most energized to work on. Once groups have formed around flipcharts, the facilitator asks people to introduce themselves, if they don't already know each other, to their new teammates. The teams are quickly put to work: they are asked to come up with a "provocative statement"—expressing what the future will look like when their initiative is successfully implemented. It must be expressed in the present tense, using everyday language, and it must be bold.

After lunch, each team shares its provocative statements with two neighboring teams for instant feedback. When they have integrated the feedback, the teams are asked to engage in action planning and role allocation. Again, at regular intervals, the facilitator asks the teams to present their work to other groups for feedback, to help them incorporate collective wisdom in quick iterations. Finally, when teams have crafted their plans, allocated roles, and decided on their next steps, they are asked to think about one last question: *What promise do they feel ready to commit to in front of their entire group of colleagues?* The microphone is handed from group to group. "Here are the things we commit to do. This is what you can expect to see happening in our workplace in the next few weeks."

Time has come to close the day and the offsite. Everybody takes a seat around the tables. The topic of the two days has been wholeness. Does anybody want to share anything from the event that stood out to him or her? After some silence, a first person asks for the microphone: a woman shares that after all the stories she has heard from her colleagues, she now sees them, and the organization, in a whole new light. A few people highlight the tremendous energy they sensed in the self-organizing working sessions. The last person to share, before it's time to call it a day, hits a resounding chord in the room: it's a man from the finance team who shares that he now realizes how painful it has been all these years to try to appear as someone he was not, and how happy he is at the thought that from now on he will simply try to be himself at work.

As people go home, there is a sense that something profound has changed. The theme of the offsite—showing up more fully at work—has already been put into practice during the two days. People have shared hundreds of personal stories, and the more they heard other people open up, the more they have felt at liberty to open up themselves. In their skits, poems, and songs, they have taken risks and shown their funny, clumsy, or quirky sides. They have developed a common vocabulary and imagery around wholeness. Even the initial sceptics sense that something important has happened; this is not just "soft" stuff, there are now 20 initiatives ready to be launched that will embed wholeness into daily practice.

Introducing practices related to evolutionary purpose

Before we talk about practices to make evolutionary purpose central to people's work in the organization, let's make sure there is no misunderstanding. This is *not* about crafting a probably soon-forgotten mission statement. ("We strive to be the premier producer of widgets in the country, exceeding our customers' expectations, providing exciting opportunities to employees, and delivering superior returns to shareholders.") Here is the part many people find tricky to grasp at first: from an Evolutionary-Teal perspective, it's not about what you think the organization *should be* or *should do* (this is how we are used to thinking about it in the machine paradigm, because a machine must be instructed what to do). Instead, it's all about you and your colleagues getting a sense of the unique purpose your organization wants to manifest in the world. It's about looking at your company as a living organism with a soul and a purpose of its own. Can you listen in to what the organization *wants to be*? Can you, in the words of Holacracy, dance with the organization's "evolutionary purpose"?

Listen in whatever ways seem most appropriate to you. It could be as simple as a meeting where people listen in silence and wait for something to emerge. Or you could use specific methodologies—Theory U or Appreciative Inquiry, for example—to lead you step by step toward uncovering the creative impulse of the organization. Perhaps the answer will surface in just one session. Or perhaps it will be a journey of six months, a year, or longer, before it emerges with clarity. The more people join you in this process, the more ears are present to listen. And colleagues who have been part of the listening will feel a personal connection with the purpose that emerges and they will champion its pursuit.

Deep inside, everybody longs for work that serves a purpose in the world. Practices that put purpose at the heart of decision-making are likely to be embraced wholeheartedly, however unfamiliar they feel at first.

Once you sense that you understand what your organization's purpose calls for, the next challenge is to embed it in everyday conversations and to use it to inform decision-making. As a leader, you can play your part by talking about the organization's purpose over and over again, in daily conversations, in emails, and in meetings. Share why it's important to you personally. Ask people what it means to them. When colleagues discuss an important decision, refer them back to the purpose. You can advocate the practice of the empty chair in meetings. You can help change the conversation about competition, market share, growth, or profit. (There is no competition when it comes to manifesting the purpose; growth and profits are not goals, but merely indicators at the end of the day of your collective efforts toward the purpose.) You can use existing or new communication channels to spread the word—blog posts, a column in the internal newsletter, posters in meeting rooms, and clients invited to share their story in all-hands meetings, among many other methods. And you can take the initiative (or even better, suggest someone else take the initiative) to embed the purpose into recruitment, onboarding, and yearly evaluation processes.

When the purpose has taken root, when it resonates with colleagues and becomes part of everyday conversations, you can suggest some of the bigger changes discussed in chapter 2.4, such as reviewing the marketing and the product development processes. If you have already transitioned to self-management, you can also switch from *predict and control* to *sense and respond*—get rid of targets and scale back the budget and planning processes to the minimum you need.

Of the three breakthroughs of Teal, in all likelihood these practices related to purpose should be most easily embraced by colleagues in your organization. At first, the notion that the company has its own creative impulse and sense of direction might take some getting used to for some people. But deep inside, everyone longs for work that is purposeful and meaningful, so most people are likely to join in with their heart and soul.

This chapter has, I hope, given you some food for thought about your organization's journey to embrace Evolutionary-Teal ways of operating. The experiences of FAVI, AES, and Holacracy show that in practice, the transition is unlikely to be orderly and linear. It will be iterative in nature, at times difficult, and at times exhilarating.

One more suggestion: if you play a central role in the transformation, try to be as mindful as you can about your own presence. *What is it that others will consciously or unconsciously pick up from your presence? What fears, what desires, what needs drive you?* Consider asking somebody, outside or inside the organization, to be a mirror and to help you be mindful. The more trusting, loving, caring, but also the more clear-minded and determined you come across, the easier the transition will come about.

There is another extraordinary lesson that FAVI, AES, Holacracy, and others offer: if a CEO truly wants the shift to happen, and offers the right presence, it *will* happen. There may be initial resistance to self-management structure and practices, especially from senior and middle managers. But expect, too, that a majority of people, if they understand and trust the CEO's intentions, will rise to the unique opportunity to join in the rebirthing of their organization.

CHAPTER 3.4

RESULTS

The ideology of leadership and management that underpins large-scale human organizations today is as limiting to organizational success as the ideology of feudalism was limiting to economic success in the sixteenth and seventeenth centuries.

Gary Hamel

Penguins are strange, funny creatures. Their legs somehow too short for comfort, they don't walk as much as totter, their whole body falling sideways onto one foot and then sideways again on the other, their wings sometimes gesticulating to maintain balance. We could be forgiven for wondering how evolution produced such clumsy animals. But when penguins jump from land into water, it's a different story. They are unusually gifted swimmers; fast, agile, and joyful under water, they can swim more than 4,000 miles on the energy of a gallon of petrol (2,000 kilometers on a liter). No human machine comes close in terms of efficiency.

The penguin is an apt metaphor, I believe, for the power of context. The environment we operate in determines how much of our innate potential we can manifest. Every time humanity shifted to a new stage of consciousness, the new organizational model it developed—first Red, then Amber, then Orange, then Green—allowed more of our talent and potential to unfold. Today we are at a crossroads again. Despite the unprecedented prosperity and life expectancy that modern organizations have provided us with over the last hundred years, I have the sense that in these organizations, we humans still totter somewhat clumsily like penguins on land—our talent and potential constrained by the many ills of corporate life: politics, infighting, bureaucracy, silos, breakdowns in communication, resistance to change, and so forth. The pioneer organizations in this research reveal that with a different context, work can come to feel as fluid, joyful, and effortless as life in the water for penguins.

In the past, every shift to a new organizational model brought a quantum leap in organizational performance. Could this be the case again with Teal? Can Teal Organizations, like the metaphor of the penguin suggests, swim faster and further than similar organizations which run along Amber, Orange, or Green lines?

Before we try to answer the question, let's first pause and explore where the question comes from. In some ways, the question stems more from Orange than from Teal. Most business books today promise they will help their readers achieve better outcomes ("the secret recipes to boost your revenue, profit, and market share!"). This book would probably sell many more copies if such a claim were a central part of its message and not addressed only here, in one of the very last chapters. Keep in mind that, as we discussed in chapter 1.2, *extrinsic* motivators drive people in all stages prior to Evolutionary-Teal. For Orange, success is often measured in terms of money, profit, and status.

In Teal, people switch to *intrinsic motivation*—doing what feels right in relation to inner values and assumptions. This was confirmed to me in my discussion with founders and CEOs of the pioneer companies researched for this book: they didn't experiment with new management methods in the hopes of reaping more success. The driving force to invent a new organizational model stemmed from an inner imperative to make a difference, to work in an environment they liked, to act in accordance with their worldview. The traditional way of running organizations simply doesn't make sense to them; it infringes on their values and their own deeply held assumptions about the purpose of work and how people can relate to each other. Making money for themselves or the organization was never the key motivator. With hindsight, though, they are all convinced that the new models they devised turned out to be radically more productive. This is not to say, of course, that effectiveness in Teal does not matter; it just matters for a different reason. When we are pursuing a purpose that we find deeply meaningful, we want to be effective! From that perspective grounded in purpose, the question of whether Teal Organizations can indeed provide yet another breakthrough in terms of results is of real interest.

There are two other reasons why this question matters. For one thing, leaders setting out to create Teal Organizations in a world where Teal is still only emerging will face strong headwinds. They will be told *ad nauseam* that their choices are risky or even outright foolish. Some reassurance that other pioneers have fared well (and even exceedingly well) could give some welcome peace of mind. And if we look at the issue not from the perspective of one organization, but from that of society at large, the matter takes on real urgency. Einstein famously said that we cannot solve a problem using the same consciousness that created it. If that is true, then we won't be able to deal with the impending crises brought by modernity (global warming, overpopulation, depletion of natural resources, collapse of ecosystems) with organizations molded in modernity's thinking. Our best hope for a sustainable future might well rest on the notion that we can access radically more powerful ways to solve today's big problems.

Anecdotal evidence

The research for this book doesn't provide the grounds, in statistical terms, to prove or disprove the claim that Teal Organizations will deliver another leap in overall human performance. For one, such claims are always methodologically fraught: *Who do you select as Teal Organizations? Who is in the control group? How can you factor out all the elements other than the organizational model (strategy, technology, market conditions, talent, luck, and so on)?* And most crucially: *How do you define success? Profitability, market share, or increase in share price?* Those are straightforward to measure, but from a Teal perspective, not very relevant. For Teal, the interesting question is: *To what extent do the organization's accomplishments manifest its purpose?* This is the kind of variable that resists being reduced to a single measurable number.

I'm afraid that an academic framing to the question is, for practical reasons, so difficult to establish that any academic claims in the field would be questionable at best. We will have to trust anecdotal evidence and personal experience to provide an answer. The sample size of a dozen organizations researched for this book does not allow us to make sweeping conclusions in that regard, but it nevertheless provides meaningful anecdotal evidence that Teal Organizations can achieve spectacular outcomes.[1] The first company we discussed in this book was Buurtzorg, the Dutch neighborhood nursing organization, so let's circle back there again. One of Buurtzorg's most striking features is its massive growth. The organization expanded from a team of 10 employees when it was created in 2006 to 7,000 by mid-2013, employing two-thirds of all neighborhood nurses in the country. In what before was a stable competitive market, nurses have literally deserted traditional providers to join Buurtzorg. (The trend continues unabated. At the time of writing, Buurtzorg receives 400 applications every month from nurses who want to jump ship.)

Financially, Buurtzorg does fantastically well too. In 2012, it generated surplus funds (what we could call "profit" if Buurtzorg wasn't a nonprofit) of around seven percent of its revenue. This is remarkable, because its explosive growth is costly: every new team costs the organization €50,000 before it breaks even. If we look only at mature teams, Buurtzorg has a double-digit surplus margin—due mostly to its low overhead costs and its high productivity. When growth slows down, this nonprofit will be highly "profitable," giving it the means to possibly start disrupting other fields of health care.

From Buurtzorg's perspective, what truly matters is the quality of the care. Growth and a solid bottom line are meaningful inasmuch as they help the organization reach more people. And the medical outcomes of the care it provides to the people it serves are spectacular. Chapter 2.2 mentioned some of the results from an Ernst & Young study:

- Because it helps its clients become autonomous, Buurtzorg requires on average close to *40 percent fewer hours* of care per client than other nursing organizations (which is ironic when you think that other nursing organizations have come to time treatment "products" in minutes, whereas Buurtzorg's nurses take time for coffee and to talk with patients, their family, and neighbors).
- Patients stay in care only *half as long*.
- Hospital admissions are reduced by *one third*, and when a patient does need to be admitted to the hospital, the *average stay is shorter*.
- The savings for social security are considerable. Ernst & Young estimates they would be just below €2 billion in the Netherlands if all home care was provided in Buurtzorg fashion. Scaled to the US population, this would represent $49 billion—not too shabby if you consider that home care is only a fraction of total health care costs. What if hospitals were run that way?

In surveys, clients and doctors rate the service given by Buurtzorg significantly above that of other nursing organizations.[2] And nurses rave about their organization, too. Buurtzorg was named "Employer of the Year" in the Netherlands for the second time in a row in 2012. Every time a patient and a nurse come together in a relationship that honors the timeless human connection of care, a small miracle happens. Buurtzorg found the recipe to make that miracle happen, day in and day out, on a massive scale.

FAVI, the French brass foundry, had 80 employees when it started its transition to Evolutionary-Teal ways of operating in the 1980s. It has since delivered rather well on its purpose to create meaningful industrial employment in the underprivileged northeastern part of France where it is located. All its competitors in Europe have shut their doors and moved production to China; FAVI not only bucked the trend, but has expanded to more than 500 employees today. Its financial results are outstanding too. FAVI's primary business is in the cutthroat automotive industry, where it competes with Chinese suppliers. And yet it pulls off the feat of paying its workers salaries significantly above market rate (in a typical year, workers receive a profit share that gives them 17 or 18 months' worth of salary) and still make, year in and year out, an after-tax profit margin of five to seven

> *So much of what we call management consists in making it difficult for people to work.*
> Peter Drucker

percent. It has also proved extraordinarily resilient in times of recession. When the 2008 financial crash turned into an economic downturn, FAVI's revenue declined by a whopping 30 percent in 2009. True to its style, it avoided layoffs and still managed to achieve a 3.3 percent net profit margin in the midst of the crisis. In 2012, demand for its automotive products crashed again, this time by 22 percent, and yet FAVI finished the year with a 12 percent cash flow margin.

Another measure of success: FAVI is famous with its clients for its impeccable product quality and trustworthiness. Since the mid-1980s, it hasn't been late on a single order it shipped. A story from a few years back illustrates the pride workers have in their track record. One day, because of a technical glitch, one of FAVI's mini-factories produced items that, once the long truck drive was factored in, would reach the customer a few hours later than the promised delivery time. The team hired a helicopter to deliver the pieces on time. A few hours later, a puzzled client who saw a helicopter land on its premises called Jean-François Zobrist, FAVI's CEO, to tell him that there were still items in stock, and the helicopter really wasn't needed. Zobrist answered that the helicopter might look like an extravagant expense, but it was a statement members of the team made for themselves, about the commitment and the pride they place in their work. That was worth every penny of it.

> *Ego is the invisible line on your P&L.*
> D. Marcum and S. Smith

It would take too long, and would ultimately become tedious and redundant, to highlight the achievements of all the other companies in this research in the way I have for Buurtzorg and FAVI. But what is true for them is just as true for RHD, Sun Hydraulics, Heiligenfeld, Morning Star, and the others. These companies seem to fire on all cylinders at the same time. They provide a space in which employees thrive; they pay salaries above market rates; they grow year in and year out, and achieve remarkable profit margins; in downturns, they prove resilient even though they choose not to fire workers; and, perhaps most importantly, they are vehicles that help a noble purpose manifest itself in the world.

There is one striking paradox I want to highlight: These companies are highly profitable, despite the fact that they seem to be, from an Orange perspective at least, quite careless about profits. Remember that they don't make detailed budgets, they don't compare budgets to actuals at the end of the month, they don't set sales targets, and colleagues are free to spend any money they deem necessary without approval from above. They focus on what needs to be done, not on profitability, and yet this results in stellar profits. Take Morning Star: it operates in the thin-margin commodity market of tomato processing. And yet it has been so profitable that it has financed its growth from a single-truck operation to the biggest tomato processor in the world entirely from its own cash flow and bank loans, without any capital injection. Heiligenfeld also self-financed its growth into a network of mental health hospitals through profits alone. Sun Hydraulics generates gross margins in the range of 32 to 39 percent and net income margins from 13 to 18 percent—margins we are more likely to associate with a software firm than a manufacturing firm.

All this evidence is anecdotal and doesn't claim statistical validity; yet it shows, beyond a reasonable doubt, that Teal Organizations can achieve results that are at least on par with the best traditionally run organizations. A leader embarking on a Teal journey with his organization is not taking a foolish risk, despite what people might say. There is good reason to claim the opposite: that by embracing Teal structure and practices, leaders can shoot for outcomes that would otherwise be hard to achieve. Whether these breakthroughs can propel us to a more sustainable future on a societal level, only time will tell, of course.

Drivers of breakthrough performance

What can explain the spectacular outcomes of the pioneer organizations researched for this book? There are different ways to approach the question. We can of course point to the three breakthroughs of Teal Organizations: 1) Power is multiplied when everybody gets to be powerful, rather than just a few at the top (self-management); 2) Power is used with more wisdom, as people bring in more of themselves to work (wholeness); and 3) Somehow things just fall into place when people align their power and wisdom with the life force of the organization (evolutionary purpose).

Another way to look at the same question comes from reasoning in terms of energy, because everything in life ultimately comes down to energy. The shift to Evolutionary-Teal structures, practices, and cultures liberates tremendous energies that previously were bottled up, unavailable. And with the shift to Teal, these energies get harnessed and directed with more clarity and wisdom toward productive ends. This perspective can help us articulate some of the concrete drivers that explain these organizations' spectacular outcomes.

Liberating previously unavailable energies

- *Through purpose*: Individual energies are boosted when people identify with a purpose greater than themselves.
- *Through distribution of power*: Self-management creates enormous motivation and energy. We stop working for a boss and start working to meet our inner standards, which tend to be much higher and more demanding.
- *Through learning*: Self-management provides a strong incentive for continuous learning. And the definition of learning is broadened to include not only skills but the whole realm of inner development and personal growth.

- *Through better use of talent*: People are no longer forced to take management roles that might not fit their talents in order to make progress in their careers. The fluid arrangement of roles (instead of predefined job descriptions) also allows for a better matching of talent with roles.
- *Less energy wasted in propping up the ego*: Less time and energy goes into trying to please a boss, elbowing rivals for a promotion, defending silos, fighting turf battles, trying to be right and look good, blaming problems on others, and so on.
- *Less energy wasted in compliance*: Bosses' and staff's uncanny ability to create policies generates wasteful control mechanisms and reporting requirements that disappear almost completely with the self-management.
- *Less energy wasted in meetings*: In a pyramid structure, meetings are needed at every level to gather, package, filter, and transmit information as it flows up and down the chain of command. In self-managing structures, the need for these meetings falls away almost entirely.

Harnessing and directing energy with more clarity and wisdom

- *Through better sensing*: With self-management, every colleague can sense the surrounding reality and act upon that knowledge. Information doesn't get lost or filtered on its way up the hierarchy before it reaches a decision maker.
- *Through better decision-making:* With the advice process, the right people make decisions at the right level with the input from relevant and knowledgeable colleagues. Decisions are informed not only by the rational mind, but also by the wisdom of emotions, intuition, and aesthetics.
- *Through more decision-making*: In traditional organizations, there is a bottleneck at the top to make decisions. In self-managing structures, thousands of decisions are made everywhere, all the time.
- *Through timely decision-making*: As the saying goes, when a fisherman senses a fish in a particular spot, by the time his boss gives his approval to cast the fly, the fish has long moved on.
- *Through alignment with evolutionary purpose*: If we believe that an organization has its own sense of direction, its own evolutionary purpose, then people who align their decisions with that purpose will sail with the wind of evolution at their back.

There is yet another way to make sense of the achievements of Teal Organizations: they are fueled not by the power of human will, but by the much greater power of evolution, the engine of life itself. Evolution is a formidable process that brings forth unfathomable beauty and complexity not through a grand design, but by means of relentless, small-scale, parallel experimentation. Evolution is not a top-down process.

Everybody is invited, and is needed, to contribute to the whole. Every living entity in the ecosystem of life—every cell, every sentient being—senses its environment, enters into harmony with others, and explores new avenues. Solutions are quickly iterated; what doesn't work is quickly discarded, and what works spreads quickly throughout the system. Life inexorably calls for more life, more beauty, more complexity, more order within the chaos. We can travel so much farther when we partner with life, when we are not trying to impose our will.

> *What is difficult or impossible in one paradigm is easy even trivial in another.*
>
> Joel Barker

Thus far, we have run organizations on rigid templates, fearing evolution's messy and uncontrollable nature. Perhaps we are getting ready for the big leap. Ready to give up our attempts to control life and channel it into the narrow plans we have drawn up for it. Ready to open the doors of life. Ready to invite evolution, the most powerful process life has ever released, to propel our collective endeavors.

CHAPTER 3.5

TEAL ORGANIZATIONS AND TEAL SOCIETY

The only thing we know about the future is that it will be different. Trying to predict the future is like trying to drive down a country road at night with no lights while looking out the back window. The best way to predict the future is to create it.

Peter Drucker

In the past, with every change in consciousness (from Infrared to Magenta, to Red, to Amber, to Orange, and to Green) the very foundations of human society shifted: the techno-economic base (from hunting and gathering to horticulture, to agrarian, to industrial, to post-industrial); the social order and political governance (from bands to clans, to proto-empires, to feudal civilizations, to nation states, to supranational bodies); the religious/spiritual order (from the world of spirits to institutionalized religion to secularism). For instance, with the shift to Amber, humanity accessed feudal agrarian civilizations and institutionalized religion. And with Orange came the Scientific and Industrial revolutions, as well as liberal democracies, the nation-state, and secularism. Most likely, as we shift to an Evolutionary-Teal society, we can again expect fundamental changes to the economical, technological, political, and spiritual bases of human civilization.

Some academics have devised methodologies to measure a person's stage of development. Their samples indicate that the percentage of people relating to the world from an Evolutionary-Teal perspective is still rather small, at around five percent in Western societies. And yet, if we believe there is a direction in evolution, that consciousness is geared to ever more complexity, then the time will come when a large share of society will have shifted to Teal.

But for now, we live in a world where people see mostly through Amber, Orange, and Green lenses. The organizations featured in this research are pioneers in the true sense of the word, blazing a path in new, uncharted territory. They give us a glimpse of what is likely to come. Writing about Teal Organizations today is somewhat like writing about automobiles in 1900 based on the early models of Daimler, Benz, and Ford. Already then, discerning minds could see that future would belong to cars, as their models were already in many ways superior to the horse-and-carriage alternatives. But as the number of cars grew, a dynamic unfolded that brought changes to the basic infrastructure of society (think asphalt roads, highways, gas stations, suburbs, and malls) that in turn influenced the way automobiles were designed (think longer ranges, protection from wind and rain, better suspensions, and crash safety.) Could the same be true for Teal Organizations? If or when society moves to Teal in greater numbers, could the Teal organizational model evolve further, beyond what pioneers are able to do today?

Speculating about the future is tricky terrain, and I would probably do well to heed Drucker's words that "the only thing we know about the future is that it will be different," but I find the temptation hard to resist. I believe that at least in two particular areas—shareholdership and boundaries—there are fairly solid grounds to suggest that the Teal organizational model will evolve beyond the way it is described in Part 2 of this book.

What an Evolutionary-Teal society might look like

Many thinkers—futurists, economists, ecologists, mystics—have taken a stab at predicting how society might (have to) evolve. Some base their projections on trends already at work (for instance, resource depletion), others on what we know of the worldview and behaviors of people acting from an Evolutionary-Teal perspective (say, a new attitude toward consumerism). The predictions range from the fairly certain to the much more speculative; and then there are what Donald Rumsfeld called the "unknown unknowns," which might interfere with even the most reasonable forecasts. For now, let's stick with the most reasonable and widely shared predictions. What might a future Teal society look like?

> *More and more people understand: this is not a crisis, but the end of a cycle.*
> Jean-François Zobrist

Zero-growth, closed-loop economies

Increasingly, people accept the once controversial notion that the future calls for a society with no economic growth. A planet with limited resources cannot host unlimited growth (Kenneth Boulding, the economist, mystic, and peace activist, once quipped, "Anybody who believes exponential growth can go on forever in a finite world is either a madman or an economist"). It's not just oil and gas that will run out at some point, however deep we dig for them. We are depleting essential minerals just as fast, and sometimes faster. For instance, predictions are that we will run out of known reserves of silver in 12 years, zinc in 15, and nickel in 30.[1] We are getting short on land and fresh water, but we nevertheless continue to pollute much of both. Due to lack of an alternative, it's a safe bet to assume that society (and thus Teal Organizations) will have to operate near the ideal of a closed-loop economy with zero waste, zero toxicity, and 100 percent recycling.

> *At present, we are stealing the future, selling it in the present, and calling it GDP.*
>
> Paul Hawken

Alternative consumerism

Zero economic growth does not mean no growth. The tragedy of our times is that we've mistaken prosperity with growth. Teal societies might have zero or even negative GDP growth but be much richer emotionally, relationally, and spiritually. In all these domains, we can pursue growth and never worry about hitting a wall.

Given all we know about people operating from the Evolutionary-Teal perspective, we can safely predict that a Teal society will look back and find today's consumerism mindless. Many of today's product adver-tisements are pitched at our ego fears: buy this product and you will become popular, successful, and good-looking. When people are driven by internal more than external motivators, it is fair to assume that many of these products will no longer have a market. I find the following exercise fun as well as insightful: when I walk through a mall or sit through advertisements on TV, I sometimes ask myself the question, "Which of these products will still be around in a Teal society"? If you play the game, you might find the answers surprising. (I certainly find them ironic, as advertising and malls might well be among the casualties.) In the shift to Teal, whole industries are likely to disappear, helping us reduce our ecological footprint. And we are likely to witness the emergence of growth in other domains of activity, such as in the "high touch" services tending to our physical, emotional, and spiritual well-being.

Rebirthing of existing industries

A new worldview will also transform some of the most fundamental human activities—the way we grow food, educate children, care for the sick, and impart justice, to name a few. Intensive agriculture will yield to some form of advanced organic farming practices. In the field of education, our current narrow definition of knowing (analytical, left-brain) will likely yield to a more holistic approach where learning includes the realms of body, emotions, relationships, nature, and spirit. Schools and universities, which today mold students through uniform, factory-like batch processes, will in all probability be completely reinvented in a way that every learner co-creates his or her unique learning journey. It's fair to assume that hospitals and medical practices will change in fundamental ways, as they integrate a more soulful perspective on health care and integrate the best of traditional and alternative practices. What about the judiciary and the prison system, currently still very much stuck in Amber, when not in Red? What would a Teal justice system look like, where failure does not call for punishment, but for reparation and an invitation to grow?

Alternative monetary systems

Our current interest-bearing form of money needs continuous growth in order to sustain value. Many forward-thinking economists believe that a society with zero economic growth will have to invent new types of currencies that bear no or negative interest (some of which are already being experimented with on small scales). The monetary system is so fundamental to the way we deal with life today that I find it hard to wrap my head around the prediction that we might one day operate with an entirely different type of currency. What will society and the economy look like if money bears no interest? Or if interest was negative, if money was losing value when not being used? With the Evolutionary-Teal stage, fear of scarcity gives way to trust in abundance. Does this mean we might enter a world where, at an individual level, we discontinue stockpiling wealth to protect us from future misfortunes? Can we imagine a society where we would feel safe not because of the assets we have stashed away, but because of trust in a solid tapestry of communal relations, knowing that we will look out for each other when there is a need? Could it be that the economic system will lend us a helping hand in not worrying about the future and in living truly in the present?

> *Authentic abundance does not lie in secured stockpiles of food or cash … but in belonging to a community where we can give those goods to others—and receive them from others when we are in need.*
>
> Parker Palmer

Stewardship

The notion of ownership, one of the pillars of the Red, Amber, Orange, and Green societies, might be reexamined in Teal. In a closed-loop economic world, does it still make sense for an individual or an organization to own land, raw materials, or even something as mundane as a machine? A machine is made of all sorts of valuable raw materials that were extracted from the earth and refined using a good deal of energy. Yet more energy and human ingenuity were needed to shape it into a productive piece of equipment. Can a factory simply decide to throw it in a dump or let it rot away in some dusty corner when it no longer needs it? Can the factory really claim to *own* the machine? I'm not suggesting we will return to the days of clans and tribes where assets were held in communal ownership. In evolution, the answer is rarely found in reverting to past formulas. But we might invent some concept that transcends both collective and individual ownership. Perhaps it will be based on the concept of stewardship. A factory might have exclusive rights to the use of a machine for as long as it puts it to good use. This right comes with the duty to maintain the machine, and if it's no longer needed, to ensure it gets transferred, even at some cost, to another custodian that finds productive use for it again.

Global communities

The future price of energy is a big unknown. Humanity's astounding growth and prosperity since the Industrial Revolution has been fueled by cheap coal, oil, and gas. Unfortunately, we have become so addicted to fossil fuels that we will soon have burnt our way through them. All in all, in only 200 years, we will have used the energy reserves that were built up through fossilization over several *hundreds of millions* of years. Some people trust that human ingenuity will come up in time with a breakthrough that keeps energy flowing plentifully and cheaply (such as nuclear fusion or radically more productive ways to capture wind, solar, or geothermal power). Others foresee a future with much higher energy costs. In that case, economic activity and food production will largely relocalize because we won't be able to afford transportation, and manual labor will be needed again on a broader scale. Communal life, which gradually eroded with the advent of the (Achievement-Orange) industrial society, might be reinvented anew, both to respond to energy imperatives and in response to Teal's yearning for deep and meaningful relationships. In parallel, through existing technology (the Internet and social networks) and perhaps through technology yet to be developed (universal and instant translation? Augmented reality videoconferencing? Telepathy?), we might interact with people far away without the need for traveling; friendships and interest networks might become truly global. In a strange paradox, society in the future could turn out to be at the same time much more local and much more global.

> *Community doesn't just create abundance—community is abundance. If we could learn that equation from the world of nature, the human world might be transformed.*
>
> Parker Palmer

The end of work as we know it

Since the beginning of the Industrial Revolution, machines gradually replaced the muscle power of human laborers and horses. We are now entering a new wave of job destruction and creation that is having an impact not just on routine work, but also on cognitive and creative tasks. A tipping point seems to have been reached at which advanced robotics and artificial intelligence (including machine-learning, language-translation, and speech- and pattern-recognition software) are beginning to render even many middle-income jobs obsolete.

Travel agents have already largely been replaced by automated websites, and bank clerks by ATMs. Lawyers start to feel the heat now that smart algorithms can search case law, evaluate the issues at hand, and summarize the results. Software has already shown it can perform legal discovery far more cheaply and more thoroughly than lawyers and paralegals in many cases. Radiologists, who can earn over $300,000 a year in the United States after 13 years of college education and internship, are in a similar boat. Automated pattern-recognition software can do much of the work of scanning tumor slides and X-ray images at a fraction of the cost. Advances in driverless car technology make a future where truck and taxi drivers are no longer needed a distinct possibility (provided we have the energy to fuel the engines).

Society could be entering a new phase—one in which fewer and fewer workers are needed to produce and distribute all the goods and services consumed. Take retail: we already purchase many items from websites whose algorithms, with no human intervention, suggest what we might like. Soon the warehouses might be fully automated, and one day self-driving trucks could deliver the parcels. Some people lament the loss of jobs, but that perspective fails to see the possibly revolutionary implications. Up until now, the vast majority of human population has had to perform less-than-exciting work to make a living. For the first time in history, we can contemplate a future where all people, not just a happy few, are free to follow their calling, to live a life of creative self-expression.

Evolutionary democracy

Democracy as we know it emerged with the Orange/Green worldview. In all probability, Teal governance will deepen democracy with more citizen involvement (crowdsourcing technology applied to both the executive and legislative branches of government at all levels of power, for example). And we might find ways to ground human decision-making in the basic evolutionary unfolding of the world. Rather than projecting what people want onto the world (the basic premise of democracy), we might look for ways to listen in to what the world is calling for.

Spiritual re-enchantment

The fixed religious belief systems of traditional (Amber) societies have been challenged by the scientific and materialistic outlook of (Orange) modernity. In response, some people cling to their traditional worldviews with all the more passion and vehemence, leading to the many religious, sectarian, and ethnic flashes of violence we experience all over the world today. Some people read this as a sign of religious resurgence. From a developmental perspective, these are probably signs of Amber's waning power, as society moves to later stages.

In Teal, people are satisfied neither with religious dogma (Amber) nor with the exclusively materialistic outlook of modernity (Orange). They seek unity and transcendence through personal experience and practices. This offers the perspective of Teal societies that heal previous religious divisions and re-enchant the materialistic world of modernity through non-religious spirituality.

Collapse or gradual transition?

Only time will tell if and when these predictions will play out. To people seeing the world through Evolutionary-Teal lenses, the destination sounds attractive. How we will get there is a more worrying matter. Will we sail through the transition more or less unscathed? Or are we bound for a shipwreck, a collapse in civilization? Never before in history have we faced such a perfect storm of predicaments that each on its own could cause widespread decline of human life: climate disruption; the accelerating extinction of animals, plants, and ecosystems essential for human survival; land degradation; ocean acidification; depletion of scarce resources (fossil fuels, minerals, and groundwater); chemical pollution; nuclear wars; global epidemics. These are all time bombs, many with fuses only two or three decades long. All the while, human population is forecast to increase by at least another two billion, adding more strain to these predicaments.

> *There is a natural rate of growth, a rate of growth that is consistent with the expansion of the universe. And our current demand for growth is not only unsustainable but will invoke a natural balancing. Can we consciously facilitate this balancing or will we have to let the universe do it to us?*
>
> Norman Wolfe

That large-scale disasters can happen has been amply demonstrated. In his book *Collapse,* Jared Diamond reviews cases of societies that broke down from environmental degradation they brought upon themselves. The Maya, a once-vibrant civilization of at least 3 million people in 900 AD had lost 99 percent of its population and dwindled to 30,000 people by 1524 when Cortez arrived. Easter Island changed from a well-populated and prosperous island society to being barren and uninhabitable. How could the Easter Islanders push deforestation so far as to rob themselves of a future, we wonder? But then again, after just a bit more than a century of modern living, 95 percent of the large fish are gone, along with 75 percent of the forests and about 50 percent of the oil.

We don't have much time. Because our mind predisposes us to think of trends as linear, we often fail to grasp the urgency of the situation. The demand we place on the planet grows, like our economies, not linearly but exponentially, compounding like interest rates. To show how the time shortens when changes are not linear but exponential, imagine putting a drop of water in the palm of your hand, and then doubling the water every minute. In six minutes, there would be enough water to fill a thimble. How long would it take to fill a sports arena? Just 50 minutes. Only 5 minutes earlier, the stadium would still be 97 percent empty and it would feel like there was still plenty of time left to find a solution. Of course we don't double GDP in a second, but at the current rate of growth, China doubles its GDP and its resource needs every 10 years. The planet cannot afford the current demands we place on it, much less so if we keep doubling them.

An increasing number of people believe that technology alone will not save us and that a change in consciousness is needed. Will humanity, in sufficient numbers, make the leap in time? We can draw some hope from the fact that consciousness seems to grow at an exponential rate too, moving to later stages ever more quickly: the half-life of each new paradigm seems to get shorter and shorter (see graph on page 35). Hope can come also from the millennial generation: it used to be that people shifted to a Teal perspective mostly in their 40s or 50s; more and more millennials make the shift in their 20s and 30s. We seem increasingly ready and hungry for change. On a small scale, Buurtzorg gives a hopeful example of an entire industry—neighborhood nursing in the Netherlands—that in less than 10 years transitioned smoothly from Orange to Teal, breathing truth into the affirmation of Harvard economist Kenneth Rogoff: "Systems often hold longer than we think, but they end up by collapsing much faster than we imagine."

Teal Organizations in a Teal society

The Teal Organizational model described in Part 2 of this book is derived from early pioneers that operate in a predominantly Amber/ Orange world. Let's assume for a minute that some of the commonly made predictions about future Teal societies summarized earlier in this chapter do play out. Would a Teal society evoke further innovations, beyond what we can observe in pioneer organizations today? In two areas, at least, I believe that the organizational model could evolve beyond what is possible today.

Shareholdership

Teal Organizations, as described in chapter 2, blur the line to some extent between for-profits and nonprofits. Both are in service to an evolutionary purpose, and at the end of the day both are likely to attract surplus funds (profits). The difference: nonprofits will plow back the entire surplus to achieve more of the evolutionary purpose, whereas for-profits might return some part of that surplus back to investors.

Now let's imagine a society and a monetary system where people don't try to accumulate wealth, and where ownership gives way to stewardship. In such a context, the lines between nonprofit and for-profit blur completely. I can only speculate what this would mean in terms of ownership structure (or stewardship structure, to be more precise). Perhaps it might look something like this: Organizations might all have stewardshipholders, instead of today's shareholders (in for-profits) and donors (in nonprofits). Stewardshipholders might contribute excess money that they currently don't need to a purpose dear to their heart. There would be no automatic dividends, but rather an understanding that when that person hits a rough patch, the organization would do what it can, in proportion to what the person contributed and the surplus funds her investment has generated, to support that individual. The same would hold true for organizations, which could channel excess funds to other organizations with like-minded purposes. In the end, there would be a rich fabric of stewardshipholding between people and organizations that could prove highly resilient and make them capable of supporting each other in times of need. The old dichotomy of for-profit and nonprofit will have disappeared, along with the notions of investors and donors.

Purpose and the porous organization

Today, organizations are fairly well delimited units. It's easy to draw walls around them. Take the assets, offices, and factories, all the employees on the payroll, and you have the organization. This is true for traditional organizations and for the pioneer organizations researched for this book. I wonder whether that will still be true when we transition to a Teal society.

There is a strong case to be made that the more central purpose becomes in people's lives, the more porous organizations will become. Today, fulltime employment is the standard contractual relationship that binds people and organizations. The arrangement is pretty inflexible, but it gives both employer and employee a sense of safety and control over the future. Even if a job doesn't offer much satisfaction, it provides a paycheck, which is not a bad thing in uncertain times.

When people transition to Evolutionary-Teal, they often tame their need to control the future and learn to trust in abundance. The security of fulltime employment becomes less important than pursuing what is really meaningful. They are ready, sometimes positively happy, to be self-employed or work on a freelance or part-time basis. They value the flexibility to shift how they allocate time to the different commitments they have in their life. Teal Organizations can accommodate this flexibility much more easily. No approval is needed from human resources or the hierarchy if you want to reduce hours, as long as you find a way to transfer the commitments you made to colleagues. If you want to come back and work more hours, you can explore with colleagues what new roles and commitments you could take on that would add value to the organization.

People might not just reduce or increase the number of hours they work as employees. They might switch between employment (fulltime and/or part-time) and freelance work; they might at other times choose to volunteer, donate money, or temporarily have no involvement at all with an organization, only to come back later. There can be combinations; there are examples of people paying to volunteer.[2] The boundaries of the organization blur when people get involved over time in so many different capacities.

The boundaries between organizations might become porous, too. Today, companies in the same sector hold each other at arms' length, viewing one another as competitors. Even nonprofits tend to think competitively and find it hard to partner when their purpose requires them to join forces. Often, such attempts exhaust themselves in endless discussions about governance and power. What structure will coordinate the efforts? How will the voting rights be divided? Whose philosophy will prevail? Who gets to chair which committee?

With Teal, serving the purpose becomes more important than serving the organization, opening up new possibilities for collaboration across organizational boundaries. Like a flock of birds, people could join forces temporarily and disband again. One organization might join another for a project; a team of colleagues could decide to move over to another organization, on a temporary basis or permanently; a company might share its intellectual capital or some assets with another organization or give it away.

In its budding international expansion, Buurtzorg gives an example of this kind of flexibility. A year ago, a Swedish nurse who worked for Buurtzorg in the Netherlands decided it was time to move back home. She asked Buurtzorg to help her establish a team there. The Dutch organization set up a nonprofit subsidiary in Sweden to host the team within a legal entity. Buurtzorg has also been approached by people from a dozen countries in Europe, Asia, and the Americas, asking it for help to set up local versions of the successful Dutch model. Jos de Blok, who is often the first contact point in these discussions, is eager to help. Whether the local entities fly Buurtzorg's flag or another one doesn't much matter to him; purpose clearly comes before consideration of power and governance. De Blok envisions a network of nurses that federate around a purpose, whatever the legal entities involved:

> *The more [the partners] do, the more we can play a facilitating role. They can use the IT system we developed and adapt it to their circumstances. What is important to me is that we plant seeds that can grow into something beautiful. I would find it wonderful if a Global Nurses Network would emerge, in which nurses from countries everywhere could exchange with each other. Each country has its own expertise. Nurses all over the world think in the same terms. They want the best for their patients.*[3]

It's conceivable that in the future the evolutionary purpose, rather than the organization, will become the entity around which people gather. A specific purpose will attract people and organizations in fluid and changing constellations, according to the need of the moment. People will connect in different capacities—fulltime, part-time, freelance, volunteering—and organizations will join forces, or disband, in reaction to what best serves the purpose at the moment. The boundaries of an organization might be harder to trace, and the very notion of an organization less relevant.

Creating the future

Speculating about the future can be fun, but of course there is wisdom in Drucker's words: *The best way to predict the future is to create it.* Due to the work of researchers and psychologists, we have a good grasp of the emerging stage of consciousness that will help us create a different future. In Evolutionary-Teal, we seek wholeness beyond ego and see the inner lives—the emotional, intuitive, and spiritual—as valuable domains of learning. We define a life well-lived by inner, not outer, standards. We see life as an unfolding journey and seek to live from trust in abundance, not fear of scarcity. We are able to transcend the either-or thinking of modernity through the ability to reason in polarities and paradoxes.

Such a worldview is bound to produce new ways of working. Many of us sense that the current way we run organizations is deeply limiting. We will come up with better ways- because there is simply too much life, and too much human potential, waiting to express itself. Almost 20 years ago, Margaret J. Wheatley and Myron Kellner-Rogers began *A Simpler Way*, a prophetic book about what organizations could be, with these words:

> *There is a simpler way to organize human endeavor. It requires a new way of being in the world. It requires being in the world without fear. Being in the world with play and creativity. Seeking after what's possible. Being willing to learn and be surprised.*
>
> *The simpler way to organize human endeavor requires a belief that the world is inherently orderly. The world seeks organization. It does not need us humans to organize it.*
>
> *This simpler way summons forth what is best about us. It asks us to understand human nature differently, more optimistically. It identifies us as creative. It acknowledges that we seek after meaning. It asks us to be less serious, yet more purposeful, about our work and our lives. It does not separate play from the nature of being. ...*
>
> *The world we had been taught to see was alien to our humanness. We were taught to see the world as a great machine. But then we could find*

nothing human in it. Our thinking grew even stranger—we turned this world-image back on ourselves and believed that we too were machines.

Because we could not find ourselves in the machine world we had created in thought, we experienced the world as foreign and fearsome. … Fear led to control. We wanted to harness and control everything. We tried, but it did not stop the fear. Mistakes threatened us; failed plans ruined us; relentless mechanistic forces demanded absolute submission. There was little room for human concerns.

But the world is not a machine. It is alive, filled with life and the history of life. … Life cannot be eradicated from the world, even though our metaphors have tried. …

If we can be in the world in the fullness of our humanity, what are we capable of? If we are free to play, to experiment and discover, if we are free to fail, what might we create? What could we accomplish if we stopped trying to structure the world into existence? What could we accomplish if we worked with life's natural tendency to organize? Who could we be if we found a simpler way?[4]

The book muses on the possibilities that could open up if we built organizations not on the template of machines, but seeking inspiration from life and nature. Thanks to extraordinary pioneers—the founders of Buurtzorg, Resources for Human Development, Morning Star, Heiligenfeld, AES, FAVI, and HolacracyOne, to name but a few—we can now go a step further: we have insights into how to put these musings into practice, how to bring to life truly soulful organizations. We have, perhaps for the first time, a good grasp of the structures, practices, and cultures that are needed to create purposeful and energizing ways to come together in organizations.

All of this is still very much emerging, of course; by no means does this book answer all possible questions about this new way of organizing. As more people and more organizations follow in the pioneers' footsteps, they will enrich and refine our understanding of this emerging model by pushing the boundaries a bit further, by inventing new practices, and experimenting in new directions.

> *We are the people we have been waiting for.*
> Navajo Medicine Man

This book hopes to be an inspirational guide for people wanting to help Evolutionary-Teal Organizations come to life. And yet it isn't meant to be read in a prescriptive way, as a list of structures and practices that must be rigidly implemented. I no longer believe that we need to design and shape organizations in the way we design machines and buildings—objectively, from the outside. What we *can* do is seek inspiration from these pioneers to evoke new ways of being, new ways of operating, from within an organization. These pioneers show that we can create radically more productive, soulful and purposeful businesses, nonprofits, schools or hospitals, and that in some cases we can transform even an entire industry. We are not dealing here with a theoretical model or a utopian idea, but with a reality waiting to be imitated and propagated. I hope their example will inspire and energize you, and many others, to join their ranks.

These are extraordinary times to be alive. Sometimes I can't wait to see what the future will bring. In the words of Wheatley and Kellner-Rogers, I can only wonder: *If we can be in the world in the fullness of our humanity, what are we capable of?*

Appendices

APPENDIX 1

RESEARCH QUESTIONS

The introductory chapter laid out the essence of the research methodology used to uncover what has been shared in this book. With varying degrees of depth, 12 organizations were analyzed so as to understand their pioneer practices in the fields of management and collaboration. Two sets of research questions were used. The first relates to 45 fundamental business practices and processes, to understand how these pioneer organizations operate on a daily basis. The second set comprised 25 questions related to the past and the future: the conditions that allowed a novel organizational model to emerge, and the critical factors for it to keep operating along these new lines.

Research questions part 1: Structure, processes and practices

For each of the following 40-plus practices and processes: In what ways do you sense **your organization approaches them differently** than other organizations in your field, be it in terms of **actions** or in terms of **intention**?

Major organizational processes

1. Purpose and strategy
   For example: What process is used to define purpose and strategy? Who is involved? Who senses when it is time to review purpose or strategy? ...
2. Innovation (product development, process development, R&D)
   For example: What practices and processes are used to foster innovation? Who is involved? Who filters and decides what gets attention and funding? ...

3. Sales
   For example: What is the sales strategy? Who is responsible? What are the targets and incentives? ...
4. Marketing and pricing
   For example: What marketing philosophy and practices are used? How are customer needs understood? How are offerings defined? How are prices set? ...
5. Purchasing and supplier management
   For example: Who is responsible for purchasing? What is the criteria for supplier selection? What is the relationship with suppliers? ...
6. Operations (production, manufacturing, back office...)
   For example: What operational practices and methodologies are used? What is the emphasis on costs, quality, continuous improvement, outsourcing? ...
7. Environmental footprint
   For example: How is environmental impact analyzed and tracked? How are decisions made to reduce the environmental impact of the organization? ...
8. IT
   For example: How does IT support the purpose? What are the choices of platforms and architectures? ...
9. After sales
   For example: How does after sales support organizational purpose? Who is responsible? ...
10. Organizational learning and change
    For example: What are the practices to capture organizational learning? To support the organization's embrace of change? ...
11. Budgeting and controlling
    For example: How are budgets established and followed? What control and audit practices are in place? How is risk managed? ...
12. Investments
    For example: How are yearly investments prioritized and approved? What level of management can spend what amount? ...
13. Financing and funding
    For example: How is the organization funded? What practices involve funders in the organizational purpose? What practices resolve trade-offs between funding and purpose? ...
14. Reporting and profit attribution
    For example: What indicators, what bottom lines, do you use most prominently to track if the organization is performing well? What gets reported to whom? What process is used to divide profit between stakeholders? ...
15. Executive committee and board governance
    For example: What governance, meeting, and decision-making practices are used at the level of the ExCo and/or the board? ...

Human resources

16. Organizational structure
    For example: What is the overall structure (units, hierarchy, reporting lines, etc.)? What is the size/role for central support functions? ...
17. Project teams and task forces
    For example: What project or team management practices are used? Who decides on project staffing? How are resources prioritized across projects? ...

18. Recruitment
    For example: What are the recruitment practices? Who recruits? What are the criteria? ...
19. Onboarding
    For example: How are new coworkers supported in joining the organization, the purpose, their role? ...
20. Training
    For example: What training is offered? What is mandatory or open enrollment? Who is faculty? ...
21. Coaching and mentoring
    For example: Who gives and receives coaching? What are the expectations? What training, what models, are used? ...
22. Team and trust building
    For example: How is trust built in teams? How are teams supported in performing at their best? ...
23. Feedback, evaluations, and performance management
    For example: What are the feedback culture and practices? Who gives feedback to whom? What formal and informal appraisal mechanisms are in place? Who does the appraising? What are consequences for good/poor performance? ...
24. Succession planning, promotions, and job rotation
    For example: What are the processes for changes in responsibility? Who makes decisions? How are coworkers supported in preparing for change in responsibility? ...
25. Flexibility
    For example: What career flexibility is there to care for family? To study? ...
26. Titles and job descriptions
    For example: What practices are there around titles and job descriptions? Who defines them? ...
27. Target setting
    For example: What practices are used to set targets? Are they individual or group targets? Who defines them? Who follows up? ...
28. Compensation, incentives, and benefits
    For example: What are the compensation practices? Who decides on compensation levels? What incentive practices, individual or team, are used? What criteria are used in defining incentives? ...
29. Non-financial recognition
    For example: What practices are in place to recognize individual and team contributions? ...
30. Dismissals and layoffs
    For example: What processes are used to dismiss coworkers for low performance? For not living up to values or purpose? Who decides? How do the person and the organization learn from the dismissal? What practices are used in the event of layoffs? ...
31. Leaving the organization/alumni
    For example: What practices and processes are used when people leave the organization? What relationship is maintained between ex-coworkers? ...

Daily life

32. Office space
    For example: What principles govern the design of office space? What is the relationship to nature and community? What are the amenities? What is the atmosphere? ...
33. Working hours and work-life integration
    For example: What practices are maintained around working hours? Can and do people work remotely, from home? ...
34. Community building
    For example: How is community built among coworkers inside the organization? How does the organization connect with the external communities it operates in? ...
35. Meetings
    For example: What are the key recurring meetings that take place? How are decisions reached? Are there specific roles allocated during the meeting? Are there specific meeting practices? ...
36. Decision-making
    For example: What are the decision-making mechanisms? Who can decide on what? What sources of data and insights are tapped? ...
37. Conflict resolution
    For example: What practices are used to resolve interpersonal conflicts? How do conflicts come to the surface? ...
38. Dealing with failure
    For example: What practices are used to deal with failure—individually and collectively? To learn from failure? ...
39. Leadership and management style
    For example: What are the expectations for leadership behavior? What is considered "not done"? ...
40. Employee alignment
    For example: What practices are there to create alignment among coworkers around purpose and objectives? ...
41. Internal communication
    For example: Who gets access to what information? How does information flow from the top to the frontline? From the frontline to the top? Horizontally across groups? ...
42. External communication
    For example: What information is shared with whom? What is the tone of communication? Who can speak on behalf of the organization? ...
43. Culture and values
    For example: What process is used to define/update values and culture? What are the practices to maintain and transmit them? How do you keep track of whether they are alive in the organization? ...
44. Rituals, retreats, and celebration
    For example: What gets celebrated? By whom? What are the objectives for rituals and retreats? At what frequency and with whom are they held? ...

Other

45. Other significant practices or processes not already mentioned

Research questions part 2:
Conditions for emergence and resilience

History and intentions

1. Can you tell me a bit about the history of the organization?
2. How would you define the purpose of the organization? What is its offer to the world?
3. What is or has been the intention that has brought your organization to operate the way it does?
4. What are the key assumptions and values of the organization?
5. How far along the way would you say you are today in defining a way of operating that meets your purpose, intent, and values?

Emergence and resilience

6. What were the critical conditions, in your opinion, that allowed a different way of operating to emerge in your organization?
7. What were some key moments and turning points in creating this way of operating?
8. Of all the processes and practices that set your organization apart, which are most critical to maintain?
9. How resilient or fragile do you assess your way of operating to be?
10. What could cause this way of operating to unravel? What could cause the organization to fall back on more traditional methods?

Culture

11. How would you describe the culture of the organization?
12. How homogeneous is it across the organization? And how homogeneous would you want it to be?
13. What would you say are the dominant emotions/moods in the organization?
14. Is there some specific language that has developed inside the organization?
15. What kinds of individuals tend to not fit in with your culture?

Holding tensions: how do you deal with tensions ...

16. Between pursuing your purpose vs. being profitable/sustainable?
17. Between leadership from the top vs. initiative from below?
18. Between reducing risks vs. upholding trust and freedom?
19. Between planning and controlling vs. sensing and adjusting?
20. Between individual freedom to decide vs. collective wisdom in collaboration?
21. Between the need for specialist skills and knowledge vs. empowerment of frontline decision makers?

Leadership questions specific to the founder/CEO

22. How do you deal with being the CEO?—The loneliness at the top, the weight of responsibility, the need for renewal, the shadows you cast?
23. How do you stay in the right presence? How do you work on your own ego?
24. How much do you feel the organizational model depends on your presence as a leader?
25. Do you have a network of like-minded peers outside of the organization? What references or role models do you have?

APPENDIX 2

BEYOND EVOLUTIONARY-TEAL

At all times, some people have operated from stages higher on the developmental ladder than the majority of the population. The number of people operating from stages beyond Evolutionary-Teal is, percentage wise, very small presently. For that reason, our knowledge about these stages is somewhat hazy. There are comparatively fewer "subjects" to research. And there are also fewer researchers: many of the scholars that have researched, thought, and written about stages of human consciousness have stopped their exploration at Teal, or even earlier. For instance, it seems fair to say that Conformist-Amber corresponds with the most advanced stage in Freud's writings; Piaget saw "Formal Operational," the cognitions corresponding to Achievement-Orange, as the final stage; and Maslow's pyramid ends at Teal "Self-Actualization," although he later hinted at the possibility of a further stage of self-transcendence. Only a small number of researchers have explored stages beyond Evolutionary-Teal, probably for a simple reason: one must to some degree have tasted these stages oneself to discern them with clarity and write about them competently.

What we know about these higher stages varies along the dimensions of development (the "lines" in the language of Integral Theory). There is much we know about spiritual development beyond Teal, because spiritual traditions, especially in the East but also in the West, have explored this area for hundreds, even thousands, of years. We know less about other dimensions, for instance the psychological, cognitive, and moral. Ken Wilber and Jenny Wade have both critically reviewed and summarized the work of scholars who have written about these later stages. I invite readers who are interested in deepening their understanding beyond the few paragraphs below to read their work, referenced in the bibliography.

Transcendent consciousness[1]

People who transition to Evolutionary-Teal become aware that ego is merely one part of themselves (some traditions refer to it therefore as the "small self"). If the ego is just an object in their awareness, *who* is being aware? A deeper part of themselves—the soul, or the "big self." This realization prompts people at this stage to seek wholeness, to integrate all parts of the self, big and small. Sometimes, through meditative practices, or sheer luck, they have a peak experience beyond even the big self; they merge and become one with the absolute, with nature, with God.

Such peak experiences can happen at any stage. People who transition to transcendent consciousness start to actively seek such experiences. They become keenly aware that not only is the ego a construct, but so is the soul, the big self. Ultimately it is nothing more than nothingness, the ultimate contraction of focus, the ultimate illusion of separateness. Personal development at this stage blends with a spiritual quest—often through a disciplined daily practice of meditation, yoga, altered breathing techniques, or other methods that help to access non-ordinary states of consciousness—to experience, beyond separateness, beyond time and space, the oneness with all of manifestation. Along the spiritual dimension, the path to self-transcendence has been described in great detail by various spiritual traditions. Some Buddhist traditions, for example, divide this stage into 27 sub-stages. Wilber, who contrasted many of these traditions, highlights three broad types of transcendent consciousness: the psychic, subtle, and causal, where consciousness experiences respectively oneness with nature, divinity, and the Absolute. With practice, these transcended states of consciousness can be accessed ever more easily and blend into everyday awareness.

The limits of Evolutionary-Teal

From the perspective of one particular stage, in hindsight all previous stages of consciousness appear limiting. Sometimes I am asked, "What are the limitations of the Evolutionary-Teal worldview?" The corollary question is, "In what aspects might Teal Organizations one day feel as limiting as the current organizational models do today?" I believe it is fair to assume that to people who have moved on to the stage of transcendent consciousness, the practices of Teal Organizations, as outlined in Part 2 of the book, will seem very much grounded only in one level of reality—the level of tangible experience in waking consciousness. They could seek to break through this limitation and create organizational practices that work directly with the world of energy and spirit to help manifest an organization's evolutionary purpose with less effort and more grace.

Unity consciousness[2]

Is there an end point in our human development? Most spiritual and mystical traditions seem to think there is such an end point (which might of course just be a beginning to something entirely new), when our consciousness fuses with the Absolute itself (referred to variously as God, Oneness, the Ground of all Being, and Emptiness, among other names). It is the *nirvana* of Buddhism, the *samadhi* of yoga, the *satori* of Zen, the *fana* of Sufism, and the *kingdom of heaven* of Christianity. Unity consciousness is enlightenment; it is to possess clear insight and pure compassion. Accounts of people in various traditions reaching this stage show that they fully transcend duality. Unlike people operating from transcendent consciousness, they are no longer in the unmanifest *or* in the manifest, in the material *or* in the spiritual, in ordinary waking consciousness *or* in altered states, but in both at the same time. They live in the time-bound *and* the timeless, they see the current reality through the eyes of no space *and* no time. Esoteric traditions maintain that this state of being is the potential and true state of every human being, when we stop clinging to attachments and accept to be still, simply with what already is and always has been.

APPENDIX 3

STRUCTURES OF TEAL ORGANIZATIONS

All organizations prior to the emerging stage of Evolutionary-Teal were structured in a pyramidal shape, for a simple reason: the hierarchical boss-subordinate relationship cannot stack into anything other than a pyramid. In self-managed organizations, peer commitments replace hierarchical relationships, and the pyramid can finally collapse and rest with history. But it would be a mistake to think that because there is no hierarchy, self-managing organizations are simply flat and structureless. How then are self-managing organizations structured? Unlike the single template of the pyramid, self-managing organizations can adopt different forms to fit the context they operate in. From the pioneer organizations researched for this book we can derive three broad types of structure (and perhaps others are yet to emerge). This appendix describes these three structures and discusses how certain contexts might call for a certain structure above another.

1. Parallel teams

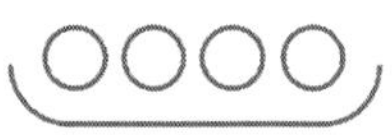

This is the structure I've encountered most often in my research. FAVI has structured its 500 factory workers in 13 self-managing "mini-factories;" RHD operates its programs with self-managing "units;" Buurtzorg's 7,000 nurses are clustered in hundreds of teams of 10 to 12 colleagues working in a specific neighborhood. This model is highly suitable when work can be broken down in ways that teams have a high degree of autonomy, without too much need for coordination across teams. They can then work in parallel, side by side. In this model, it is within the team setting that colleagues define their roles and the mutual commitments they make to each other. Teams also handle their own planning, establish their investment needs, devise a budget (if a budget is needed), track their financial and non-financial results, do their recruitment, determine their training needs, and so on.

In an ideal situation, every team is fully autonomous in bringing the purpose to life and performing all tasks from start to finish; when that is the case, every single person in the organization has the satisfaction of seeing the entire purpose come to life, and not just a small slice of it, which is often the case in large organizations or when work becomes very specialized. In practice, there will often be a need for some people or teams who take on coordinating or supporting roles with a more narrow focus:

- *Team coaches*: In Teal Organizations, there are no middle managers. But teams often feel a need to be supported by someone external that can help them work through problems. At Buurtzorg, they are called regional coaches; at RHD, hub leaders.
- *Supporting teams*: For some tasks, duplication in every team doesn't make sense. At FAVI, for example, the great majority of mini-factories are client facing—the Audi team, the Volkswagen team, the Volvo team, the water meter team—but a few teams are supporting other teams, such as the foundry team, which, at the beginning of the value chain, casts metal for all client-facing teams. It would not be practical for the teams to operate the foundry in turns, nor would it make sense to duplicate the equipment and have a foundry within each team. RHD has units responsible for topics such as training (its "miniversity"), real estate, and payroll, that support all the units in the field.
- *Supporting roles*: The self-management model pushes expertise down to the teams, rather than up into staff functions. But for certain specific expertise or for coordination purposes, creating a supporting role can make sense. At FAVI, for instance, there is an engineer who helps teams exchange innovations and best practices. One of the roles of founders and CEOs belongs in this category too: they offer support across teams by holding the space for Evolutionary-Teal practices.

2. Web of individual contracting

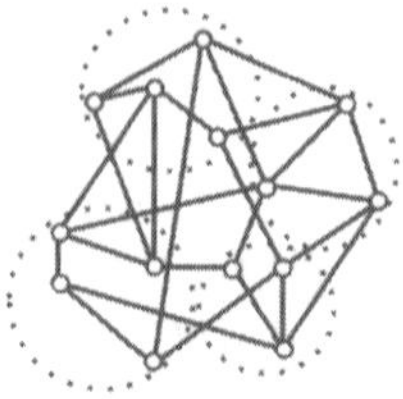

This is the model pioneered by Morning Star in California. In this model, as in the previous one ("parallel teams"), investment budgets and financial results are set up and discussed in teams. Morning Star calls them "Business Units," and each Business Unit is linked to a particular step in the food processing (say, tomato preparation, dicing, canning, or packaging) or to a support service (for instance, steam generation or IT).

Roles and commitments, though, are not discussed in teams, but in a series of one-on-one discussions between colleagues who work closely together. These commitments can then be formalized in a written document. For instance, at Morning Star, each colleague establishes a document called a "Colleague Letter of Understanding" (CLOU) that records the different roles and commitments that the person has agreed to.

3. Nested teams

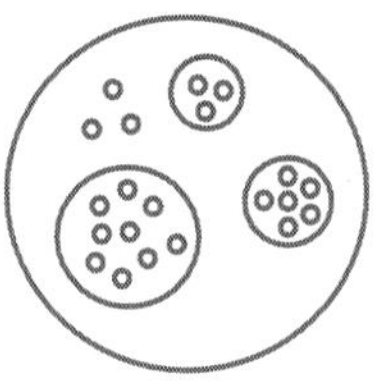

Holacracy is a self-management approach first pioneered at Ternary Software, a Philadelphia-based company, which has now turned into a fully documented operating model. It relies on a structure of nested teams. Like in the first model, teams (called *circles* in Holacracy[1]) are fully autonomous to discuss and decide on how roles will be allocated within the team, what commitment team members make to each other, and so on. But there is an important difference in the relationship between teams and the supporting structure. In the first model, all teams work side by side, with a minimum supporting structure. In Holacracy, circles are part of a nested structure.

Let's imagine a 7,000-person pharmaceutical company structured in a holacratic manner. The overall purpose of the organization might be "to help individuals and communities to live healthy lives." What works in the case of Buurtzorg does not work for a pharmaceutical company: you cannot simply break down the 7,000 people into 700 teams of 10 people working in parallel doing the same thing. A team of 10 people cannot go and develop a series of drugs, get them approved by the FDA, and sell them across the world. For a pharmaceutical company, you need specialization on a bigger scale. A holacratic, nested structure allows for such specialization. How would this work? The overall purpose of the company ("to help individuals and communities to live healthy lives") would be pursued by the circle at the top, while a number of sub-circles would pursue a specific part of the overall purpose. One of the sub-circles could be responsible for research and development, and its specific purpose might be "to discover new medication that helps individuals and communities to live healthy lives." This sub-circle could in turn break down its purpose into more manageable parts and create its own sub-circles. For instance, one sub-circle could delve into the specific purpose of "developing groundbreaking medication for epilepsy." If this purpose is still too complex to manage for a reasonably-sized team, it might be broken down again.

If this seems to you like a traditional pyramid, you would be both right and wrong. Indeed, there is a stacking up of levels that gradually reach into ever-bigger questions, so there is a hierarchy of *purpose, complexity,* and *scope.* The research circle at the "bottom" senses what is needed to develop a drug for epilepsy, a more narrow purpose than the one of the top circle that senses what is needed to make individuals and communities more healthy. Yet it is no hierarchy of *people* or *power*. In the holacratic system of practices, the epilepsy research team has full authority to make any decision within the scope of its specific purpose. Decisions are not sent upwards, and cannot be overturned by members of overarching circles. A given person may show up filling roles in more than one circle throughout the organization; there is not a one-to-one relationship between people and their "place in the structure."

Circle and sub-circle are bound together by a double link, not by a boss-subordinate relationship. The sub-circle elects a representative to the overarching circle that sits on all that circle's meetings, and the overarching circle sends a representative of its own to be part of the discussion in the sub-circle. There are elegant meeting processes that ensure that everybody's concerns are heard and acted upon, and that no voice trumps the others. The result is a structure that allows complex purposes to be broken down into smaller parts through a hierarchy of purpose, complexity, and scope, without a hierarchy of people or power.

What structure is most appropriate?

Of the three structures, or possible variations or hybrids, which would be most appropriate for your specific organization? In many cases the answer is straightforward: the size and type of activity the organization engages in will naturally call for one type of structure, just like surrounding terrain determines the shape of a lake.

Small organizations

The first matter is one of size. If your organization is relatively small, say less than a dozen employees, then the three types of structures essentially boil down to the same thing: an organization run as a single self-governing team (with the minor distinction that in the second model, roles and commitments are not discussed as a team, but in a series of one-on-one meetings; given the small size, it probably makes sense to have these discussions together with the whole group). This structure can work for any type of company in any type of industry—construction companies, coffee shops, design firms, local museums, daycare centers, private health clinics, boutique consulting firms, homeless shelters, startups, or any number of others. Depending on the nature of the work and how fluid or how stable it is, there might be more or less frequent reshuffling of roles and change of direction. This will determine how often or not team meetings will be needed to discuss roles, commitments, and purpose.

When organizations grow larger, say beyond 20 employees, running the show as a single team becomes unpractical. For large organizations, the length of what is called in business jargon the "value chain" is a defining factor for the most appropriate structure. Neighborhood nursing has a very short value chain. A single nurse can perform all tasks—getting to know the client, reading the prescription, performing the medical intervention, and so forth—and can do it all in an hour or less. A pharmaceutical company has a very long value chain that can involve thousands of people and take several years: there is a lengthy drug research process (computer simulations, lab tests, clinical trials); molecules must receive regulatory approval; pricing strategies must be established; product launches prepared in every country; and global sales forces trained to inform doctors about the product.

Short value chains

If the value chain is relatively short, then the first model—parallel self-managing teams supported by minimal central functions—is a natural candidate. Parallel teams can work side by side performing similar tasks: mini-factories producing gearbox forks for different car manufacturers at FAVI or units running separate shelter and care programs at RHD, for example. The beauty of the short value chain is that the overall purpose doesn't need to be broken down into sub-purposes (except for a few supporting teams). Almost everyone is part of a team that senses the whole purpose and helps it manifest. Everyone sees how their work makes clients happy.

Luck has it that most industries have a relatively short value chain. For some examples:

- *Retail:* Stores can easily be operated by self-governing teams. In the case of small store formats, the whole store works as a single self-governing team. Retailers with larger stores, like supermarkets, can break down each store into several teams, like Whole Foods does. The teams in the stores are assisted by a few central or regional supporting teams—logistics, purchasing, marketing, and so on.
- *Service sector:* Almost all companies operating in the service sector—maintenance services, catering, cleaning, and security services, for instance—can easily be operated as self-governing teams serving a particular geographical area. Professional services such as law firms, IT and management consultancies, and advertising agencies are often already broken down into geo-graphical sectors or topical units, which naturally lend themselves to becoming self-governing teams.
- *Manufacturing and assembly:* Many manufacturing operations such as automotive suppliers, toy manufacturers, and apparel makers have relatively short value chains and can use FAVI's model of parallel teams.

- *Farming:* Larger farms can work with parallel teams, split along geographical areas, type of crop, or type of livestock.
- *Schools:* Large schools can be broken down into smaller, self-governing units, ideally with dedicated classrooms and faculty rooms to create a sense of community within mini-schools, as is the case with ESBZ.
- *Hospitals:* Hospitals can structure themselves into self-governing teams. Most hospital units would make natural teams of nurses and doctors (such as the orthopedic team, the cardiology team, the emergency room team), with a few supporting services (labs, maintenance, and so on).
- *Foundations and nonprofits:* Large nonprofits, like RHD, also tend to have natural groupings, often by geography, activity, or type of client.
- *Public services:* Like nonprofits, almost all public services can be easily broken down into teams on the basis of geography, activity, or type of client.

Long value chains

When supply chains are longer, the model of parallel teams isn't practical. You can't break down a bank or a pharmaceutical company into mini-banks and mini-pharmas. (It is possible, though, for certain steps of the value chain: a pharmaceutical sales force and the branches of a bank can operate as parallel self-managing teams.) In this case, a structure based on individual contracting or on nested teams makes more sense.

Morning Star's model of individual contracting is a natural fit for continuous and relatively stable processes, such as can be found in the chemical industry, in food processing, or in long assembly chains. Each major step in the process often involves only a few people, and so a nested structure is not needed. Through individual contracting, colleagues can make clear agreements with their upstream and downstream counterparts.

Some industries have not only *long*, but also *deep* value chains, when certain steps in the value chain involve both a large number of people and complex tasks (for instance, research in a pharmaceutical company or marketing in a large retail bank). Consumer electronics firms, large media companies, banks, insurance companies, car manufacturers, aerospace companies, and airline companies are likely to have *long and deep value chains*. For these types of companies, Holacracy's structure of nested teams might be particularly appropriate, as it allows an overall purpose to be broken down into successively less complex and more manageable pieces.

Which type of context most naturally lends itself to each of the three structure archetypes is summarized in the table on page 325. When trying to discover the most suitable self-managing structure for your organization, the key is to try to understand how colleagues without managers would most naturally cluster to coordinate their efforts. The issues raised in this table—the size of the company, the length and the depth of the value chain—can help you in your thinking, but other factors specific to your organization might play an important role, too. Take some time with colleagues from different parts of the organization to reflect on the question about the most appropriate structure. Let it simmer. The answer will emerge in time. And you don't have to start with a perfect solution. You can get going with a structure that seems about right and trust the self-organizing power of the organization to evolve into the structure that best suits its needs, and to keep evolving as the environment changes.

Organization	Type	Structure	Examples
Small organization			✓ A small organization in any sector can be run as a single, self-managing team
Large org. with short value chain		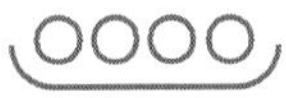	✓ Retail ✓ Service industries ✓ Some manufacturing ✓ Schools ✓ Hospitals ✓ Public services ✓ ...
Large org. with long value chain	*Continuous, stable processes*	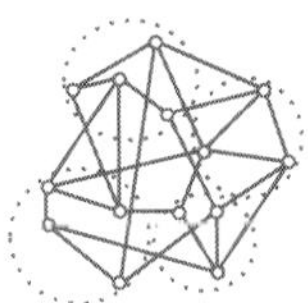	✓ Chemical industry ✓ Food processing ✓ Some manufacturing (e.g. long assembly chains) ✓ ...
	Deep value chains	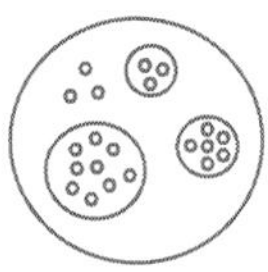	✓ Banking / Insurance ✓ Pharmaceuticals ✓ Automotive ✓ Aerospace ✓ Consumer electronics ✓ ...

APPENDIX 4

OVERVIEW OF TEAL ORGANIZATIONS' STRUCTURES, PRACTICES, AND PROCESSES

The tables below contrast the structures, practices, and processes of Teal Organizations with those of Orange Organizations (the predominant frame of reference in management thinking today).

	Orange practices	Teal practices
STRUCTURE		
1. Organization structure	• Hierarchical pyramid	• Self-organizing teams • When needed, coaches (no P&L responsibility, no management authority) cover several teams
2. Coordination	• Coordination through fixed meetings at every level (from executive team downwards), often leading to meeting overload	• No executive team meetings • Coordination and meetings mostly ad hoc when needs arise
3. Projects	• Heavy machinery (program & project managers, Gantt charts, plans, budgets, etc.) to try and control complexity and prioritize resources	• Radically simplified project management • No project managers, people self-staff projects • Minimum (or no) plans and budgets, organic prioritization
4. Staff functions	• Plethora of central staff functions for HR, IT, purchasing, finance, controlling, quality, safety, risk management, etc.	• Most such functions performed by teams themselves, or by voluntary task forces • Few staff remaining have only advisory role

HUMAN RESOURCES

1. Recruitment	• Interviews by trained HR personnel, focus is on fit with job description	• Interviews by future colleagues, focus is on fit with organization and with purpose
2. Onboarding	• (Mostly administrative onboarding process)	• Significant training in relational skills and in company culture • Rotation programs to immerse oneself in the organization
3. Training	• Training trajectories designed by HR • Mostly skill and management training	• Personal freedom and responsibility for training • Critical importance of common training that everybody attends
4. Job titles & job descriptions	• Every job has job title and job description	• No job titles • Fluid and granular roles instead of fixed job descriptions
5. Individual purpose	• (It's not the organization's role to help employees identify their personal calling)	• Recruitment, training, and appraisals used to explore juncture of individual calling and organizational purpose
6. Flexibility & time commitment	-	• Honest discussion about individual time commitment to work vs. other meaningful commitments in life • High degree of flexibility in working hours, as long as commitments are upheld
7. Performance management	• Focus on individual performance • Appraisals established by hierarchical superior • Appraisal discussion aims for objective snapshot of past performance	• Focus on team performance • Peer-based processes for individual appraisals • Appraisal discussion turned into personal inquiry into one's learning journey and calling
8. Compensation	• Decision made by hierarchical superior • Individual incentives • Meritocratic principles can lead to large salary differences	• Self-set salaries with peer calibration for base pay • No bonuses, but equal profit sharing • Narrower salary differences
9. Appointments & promotions	• Intense jockeying for scarce promotions leads to politics and dysfunctional behavior • Silos: every manager is king of his castle	• No promotions, but fluid rearrangement of roles based on peer agreement • Responsibility to speak up about issues outside of one's scope of authority

HUMAN RESOURCES (cont'd)

10. Dismissal	• Boss has authority (with HR approval) to dismiss a subordinate • Dismissal mostly a legal and financial process	➡	• Dismissal last step in mediated conflict resolution mechanism • In practice very rare • Caring support to turn dismissal into a learning opportunity

DAILY LIFE

1. Office spaces	• Standardized, soulless professional buildings • Abundant status markers	➡	• Self-decorated, warm spaces, open to children, animals, nature • No status markers
2. Meetings	• (Many meetings, but few meeting practices)	➡	• Specific meeting practices to keep ego in check and ensure everybody's voice is heard
3. Decision-making	• High up in the pyramid • Any decision can be invalidated by hierarchical superior	➡	• Fully decentralized based on advice process (or on holacratic decision-making mechanisms)
4. Conflicts	• (Conflict often glossed over, no conflict resolution practices)	➡	• Regular time devoted to bring to light and address conflicts • Multi-step conflict resolution process • Everyone trained in conflict mgmt. • Culture restricts conflict to the conflicting parties and mediators; outsiders are not dragged in
5. Information flow	• Information is power and is released on a need-to-know basis • Secrecy toward the outside world is the default position	➡	• All information available in real-time to all, including about company financials and compensation • Total transparency invites outsiders to make suggestions to better bring about purpose
6. Values	• (Values often only a plaque on the wall)	➡	• Clear values translated into explicit ground rules of (un)acceptable behaviors to foster safe environment • Practices to cultivate discussions about values and ground rules
7. Reflective spaces	-	➡	• Quiet room • Group meditation and silence practices • Large group reflection practices • Team supervision and peer coaching

DAILY LIFE (cont'd)

8. Mood management	-	• Conscious sensing of what mood would serve the organization's purpose
9. Community building	-	• Storytelling practices to support self-disclosure and build community

MAJOR ORGANIZATIONAL PROCESSES

1. Purpose	• (No practices to listen to the purpose; self-preservation against competition is the key driver of decision making)	• Organization seen as a living entity with its own evolutionary purpose • The concept of competition is irrelevant; "competitors" are embraced to pursue purpose • Practices to listen into the organization's purpose: – Everyone a sensor – Large group processes – Meditations, guided visualizations, etc. – Responding to outside prompting
2. Strategy	• Strategic course charted by top leadership	• Strategy emerges organically from the collective intelligence of self-managing employees
3. Innovation & product development	• Outside in: customer surveys and segmentation define the offer • Client needs are created if necessary	• Inside out: offer is defined by purpose • Guided by intuition and beauty
4. Supplier management	• Suppliers chosen based on price and quality	• Suppliers chosen also by fit with purpose
5. Purchasing & investments	• Authorization limits linked to level in hierarchy • Investment budgets steered by top mgmt.	• Anybody can spend any amount provided advice process is respected • Peer-based challenging of team's investment budget
6. Sales & Marketing	• Brands positioned to fit consumer segmentation (outside in) • Sales force driven by targets and incentives	• Marketing as a simple proposition: this is our offer to the world (inside out) • No sales targets

7. Planning, budgeting, & controlling	• Based on "predict and control" • Painful cycles of mid-term planning, yearly and monthly budgets • Stick to plan is the rule, deviations must be explained and gaps closed • Ambitious targets to motivate employees	➡	• Based on "sense and respond" • No or radically simplified budgets, no tracking of variance • Workable solutions and fast iterations instead of searching for "perfect" answers • Constant sensing of what's needed • No targets
8. Environmental and social initiatives	• Money as extrinsic yardstick: *Only if it doesn't cost too much initiate* • Only the very top can begin initiatives with financial consequences	➡	• Integrity as intrinsic yardstick: *What is the right thing to do?* • Distributed initiative taking, everyone senses the right thing to do
9. Change management	• Whole arsenal of change management tools to get organization to change from A to B	➡	• ("Change" no longer a relevant topic because organizations constantly adapt from within)
10. Crisis management	• Small group of advisors meet confidentially to support CEO in top-down decision making • Communication only when decision is made	➡	• Everyone involved to let the best response emerge from collective intelligence. • If advice process needs to be suspended, scope and time of suspension is defined

NOTES

Introduction • The emergence of a new organizational model

1 "Males have more teeth than females in the case of men, sheep, goats, and swine." Aristotle, *History of Animals*, 2.3.

2 The nervous systems in the heart and in the gut have 40 million and 100 million neurons, respectively, compared to an average of 85 billion for the brain in the head.

3 Smaller organizations often operate based on more informal processes and practices, and many of the most vexing issues raised by hierarchy are likely to show up beyond that number.

Chapter 1.1 • Changing paradigms: past and present organizational models

1 The term "Reactive" is borrowed from Wade. This stage corresponds to Gebser's "Archaic," Loevinger's and Cook-Greuter's "Pre-social" and "Symbiotic," Graves' "AN," Spiral Dynamics' "Beige," Piaget's "Sensorimotor," and others.

2 The term "Magic" is borrowed from Gebser. This stage corresponds to Loevinger's and Cook-Greuter's "Impulsive," Graves' "BO," Spiral Dynamics' "Purple," Piaget's "Pre-operational (Symbolic)," Wade's "Naïve," and others.

3 This stage corresponds to Loevinger's and Cook-Greuter's "Self-protective," Kegan's "Imperial," Torbert's "Opportunistic," Graves' "CP," Spiral Dynamics' "Red," Piaget's "Pre-operational (Conceptual)," Wade's "Egocentric," and others.

4 According to Wikipedia, the idea of an aggressively dominant "alpha wolf" in gray wolf packs has been discredited by wolf biologists and researchers, and so-called "alphas" in packs are merely the breeding animals. This news makes for an interesting discussion. If we projected a story of dominance onto the role of the alpha male in wolf packs, it is probably because we as human beings have long functioned this way. That researchers fairly recently began to see more subtle relationships in wolf packs might reveal that we ourselves are coming to operate from more complex worldviews. (Of course, it could be the other way around: that researchers operating from Pluralistic-

Green don't want to see alpha behavior in wolves and project their pluralistic stance onto them.)

5 The term "Conformist" is used by Loevinger, Cook-Greuter, and Wade, among others. This stage corresponds to Gebser's "Mythical," Loevinger's and Cook-Greuter's "Conformist," Graves' "DQ," Spiral Dynamics' "Blue," Kegan's "Interpersonal," Torbert's "Diplomat" and "Expert," Piaget's "Concrete Operational," and others.

6 Cognitively, in the Amber stage, there is a considerably higher capacity for abstract thought than in Red. Yet, neurologically, there is still a strong prepotency of the limbic system (the system primarily working with emotions) that the left hemisphere of the brain then proceeds to rationalize. For example, the Amber self's need to belong and fit in will rationalize away possible contradictions between rational thought and group norms.

7 Ken Wilber, *A Brief History of Everything* (Boston: Shambhala Publications, 1996), 273.

8 The term "Achievement" is borrowed from Wade. This stage corresponds to Gebser's "Mental," Loevinger's and Cook-Greuter's "Self-Aware" and "Conscientious," Kegan's "Institutional," Torbert's "Achiever," Piaget's "Formal Operational," Graves' "ER," Spiral Dynamics' "Orange," and others; it is often simply referred to as *modernity*.

9 Wilber, *A Brief History of Everything*, 185-186.

10 This stage corresponds to Loevinger's and Cook-Greuter's "Individualistic," Torbert's "Individualist," Wade's "Affiliative," Graves' "FS," Spiral Dynamics' "Green," and others; it is often simply referred to as *postmodernity*.

11 Often in history we find ideas, like democracy in ancient Greece, ahead of their times, meaning ahead of the developmental center of gravity of people at that moment in time. To flourish, these ideas have to wait for evolution to catch up with them, to provide the right "cultural womb" as the American philosopher Richard Tarnas calls it:

> *A big question here is why did the Copernican Revolution happen in the sixteenth century, with Copernicus himself, and in the early seventeenth century, with Kepler and Galileo? Why did it take until then, when a number of people prior to Copernicus had hypothesized the heliocentric universe and a planetary earth? There's evidence of this being proposed among the ancient Greeks and in India and Islamic cultures during the European Middle Ages. I think this question shows the extent to which a major paradigm shift depends on more than just some additional empirical data and more than just a brilliant new theory using a new concept. It really depends on a much larger context so that the seed of a potentially powerful idea falls on a whole different soil, out of which this organism, this new conceptual framework, can grow—literally a "conception" in a new cultural and historical womb or matrix.*

Richard Tarnas and Dean Radin, "The Timing of Paradigm Shifts," *Noetic Now*, January 2012.

12 In the corporate sector, worker cooperatives have failed to achieve any meaningful traction. The ones that prevail are often run on practices that are a combination of Orange and Green. One often-cited success story is Mondragon, a conglomerate of cooperatives based in a Basque town of the

same name in Spain (around 250 companies, employing roughly 100,000 people, with a turnover of around €15 billion). All the cooperatives are fully employee-owned. Bosses are elected; wage differentials are smaller than elsewhere (but still significant, at up to 9:1 or more); temporary workers have no voting rights, creating a two-tiered community where some are more equal than others.

In the educational sector, there have been several models of schools with no authority structures from adults over children, most notably the Summerhill School, a British boarding school founded in the 1920s. It practices a radical form of democracy, where students and adults have the same voting power, and lessons are not compulsory, among other differences.

In the institutional sphere, many supranational bodies—the United Nations, European Union, and World Trade Organization, and others—have decision-making mechanisms at the highest level that are, at least partially, molded along Green principles such as democratic or unanimous voting of the different member countries and rotating chairmanship. These Green decision-making principles are difficult to uphold, and richer or more powerful countries demand and often end up receiving more voting powers (often even implicit if not explicit veto powers). The staff departments of these institutions are most often run as Amber Organizations.

13 This practice was made famous by Semco, a Brazilian manufacturing firm, when the book that described the organization's practices became a bestseller (*Maverick* by Ricardo Semler). It has been practiced for decades by W. L. Gore (of Gore-Tex fame). The practice is starting to spread in tech startups in Silicon Valley and elsewhere. The English training company Happy has introduced the practice with a twist: people have two managers. One is responsible for matters of content (direction setting, decision-making) and appointed from above, the other for matters of management (coaching, challenging, supporting) and chosen by employees for themselves (see *The Happy Manifesto* by Henry Stewart for more details).

14 The first major study dates from 1992, when Harvard Business School professors John Kotter and James Heskett investigated this link in their book *Corporate Culture and Performance*. They established that companies with strong business cultures and empowered managers/employees outperformed other companies on revenue growth (by a factor of four), stock price increase (by a factor of eight) and increase in net income (by a factor of more than 700) during the 11 years considered in the research.

A more recent study by Raj Sisodia, Jagh Sheth, and David B. Wolfe, in what is arguably a defining book for the Green organizational model—*Firms of Endearment: How World-Class Companies Profit from Passion and Purpose*—came to similar conclusions in 2007. The "firms of endearment" studied by the authors obtained a cumulative return to shareholders of 1,025 percent over the 10 years leading up to the research, as compared to 122 percent for the S&P 500. From a methodological point of view, these results should be taken with a grain of salt. There is an obvious selection bias, as only exceptional companies that one would expect to outperform their peers were handpicked into the sample. The benchmark of the S&P 500 wasn't adjusted for industry, size, or other criteria. Furthermore, criteria other than the organization model, such as patents, innovative business models, and asset utilizations that could explain the superior result, were not filtered out.

Raj Sisodia's latest book, written with John Mackey, has a whole chapter with references of similar studies to which interested readers can refer.

Any research trying to make such general claims as the superior outcome of one organizational model over another is bound to hit methodological discussions (and on a principled level, one could question shareholder return or growth as the primary metric to gauge success, as most of these studies do). Perhaps direct experience ultimately matters more than academic claims. Anyone who spends time in organizations such as Southwest Airlines or The Container Store will return convinced that empowered workers in values-driven companies will on average outperform their peers in more traditional settings.

15 The 2006 Stanford Business Case on DaVita is highly readable and a good resource for readers wanting to immerse themselves in a more detailed description of Green organizational principles and practices.

Chapter 1.2 • About stages of development

1 It has been established that exposing people to developmental theory, to the notion that consciousness evolves in stages, also helps people make the leap. Studies show that introspective activities such as meditation also help.

2 It's a phenomenon we are familiar with from the realm of politics: autocratic rulers operating from a Red or Amber paradigm often feel obliged to pay lip service to the (Orange-Green) idea of democracy but at a fundamental level, haven't integrated its principles and practices. When democracy threatens to strip them of their power, they will respond in ways that are coherent with the paradigm they operate from (bullying to stay in power), and not in the ways that democracy calls for (stepping down and congratulating the victor).

Chapter 1.3 • Evolutionary-Teal

1 This stage corresponds to Gebser's "Integral," Loevinger's "Integrated," Cook-Greuter's "Construct-Aware," Kegan's "Inter-individual," Torbert's "Strategist" and "Alchemist," Graves' "AN," Spiral Dynamics' "Yellow," Maslow's "Self-actualization," Wade's "Authentic," and others; it is often referred to as *integral*.

2 To oversimplify: people who see the world differently are weaklings to be taken advantage of (Red), heretics to be brought back to the one true way (Amber), fools who don't know how to play the game of success (Orange), or intolerant people who won't give everyone a voice (Green).

3 Parker Palmer, *Let Your Life Speak: Listening for the Voice of Vocation* (San Francisco: Jossey-Bass, 2000), 5.

4 Ken Wilber makes the critical distinction between *stages of consciousness* and *states of consciousness*. States refer to the ephemeral, passing type of consciousness, while stages are longer-lasting structures that people grow into. States include waking consciousness, dreaming, sleeping, altered states (induced for instance by meditation, hypnosis, psychodrama, or drugs) and peak states of

mystical experience. (Wilber generally uses the categorizations of gross, subtle, causal, witnessing, and non-dual). States and stages sometimes get confused, because the language of peak experience is often similar to the language that describes the highest stages, but they are two distinct properties of consciousness (with quadrants, lines, and types being third, fourth, and fifth properties in Wilber's integral model).

Say someone has a *state* of peak mystical experience while generally operating from the Conformist-Amber *stage*: the peak state does not propel the person to bypass the Orange, Green, Teal, and subsequent stages of development to reach the top of the ladder. The person is still operating from Amber, as will be clear when he or she is again in a state of waking consciousness. Wilber and Combs have found evidence that any state can be experienced at every stage. For instance, people can take up meditative and other altered state practices at any stage. From Teal onward, there is a marked interest in taking up regular practices of non-ordinary consciousness to access the full spectrum of human experience.

5 David Rooke and William R. Torbert, "Organizational Transformation as a Function of the CEO's Developmental Stage," *Organization Development Journal*, April 2005.

6 Clare W. Graves, *The Never Ending Quest* (Santa Barbara: ECLET Publishing, 2005), 371.

Chapter 2.2 • Self-management (structures)

1 Jos de Blok and Aart Pool, *Buurtzorg: menselijkheid boven bureaucratie* (Den Haag: Boom Lemma Uitgevers, 2010), 20.

2 Ibid., 20.

3 Ibid., 21.

4 De Blok wrote a memo describing how the care organizations he worked for could adopt a structure where nurses worked in autonomous teams. He reckoned that the number of director functions would go down from 13 to three, his own function being among the casualties. Unsurprisingly perhaps, the memo wasn't well received by the executive team.

5 A method developed and taught by Ben Wenting and Astrid Vermeer of the Instituut voor Samenwerkingsvraagstukken in Groesbeek, the Netherlands.

6 Annemarie van Dalen, *Uit de schaduw van het zorgsysteem: Hoe Buurtzorg Nederland zorg organiseert* (Den Haag: Boom Lemma, 2010), 66.

7 Ibid., 73.

8 Productivity is defined as the billed hours (in other words, hours spent with patients based on a doctor's prescription) divided by the total contract hours of nurses on the team. Teams calculate their productivity themselves, typically once every month.

9 The story of Zobrist's appointment is worth telling. It seems straight from a movie. FAVI was owned by Max Rousseau, a colorful character who owned a number of industrial companies. In the late 1970s and early 1980s, Zobrist was working for Rousseau in a sister company. He occasionally interacted with FAVI's metallurgy department, so he knew the factory somewhat. One day, Rousseau called Zobrist to his office. He put a gold US dollar in Zobrist's

hand and added, "I'm not superstitious, but you could use some luck." With no further explanation, he stood up and asked Zobrist to follow him out of the office, where a helicopter was waiting. Zobrist knew better than to ask Rousseau what this was all about. An hour later, they arrived at FAVI, where Rousseau asked that the machines be stopped and called all workers to join him next to the helicopter. When everybody was assembled, he pointed to FAVI's CEO and said, "Dominique has asked to retire." He then pointed to Zobrist and said, "Here is his successor," and then stepped into his helicopter and left behind a promoted and baffled Zobrist pondering his unexpected appointment as CEO.

10 Some other organizations take another route: they do talk in dollar terms but train all operators to be fluent in accounting terms. In both cases, the intention is the same: make sure that everyone understands and can contribute to financial discussions and trade-offs.

11 Jean-François Zobrist, *La belle histoire de FAVI: L'entreprise qui croit que l'Homme est bon,* Tome 1, Nos belles histoires (Paris: Humanisme & Organisations, 2008), 93.

12 Linda Hill and Jennifer Suesse, Sun Hydraulics: Leading in Tough Times (A), case study (Cambridge: Harvard Business Publishing, 2003).

13 In normal times, Sun Hydraulics' gross margins range between 32 and 39 percent and net income margins between 13 and 18 percent.

14 Dennis Bakke, *Joy at Work: A Revolutionary Approach to Fun on the Job* (Seattle: PVG, 2005), 47-48.

15 Ibid., 19-20.

16 Alex Markels, "Blank Check," *The Wall Street Journal,* April 9, 1998.

Chapter 2.3 • Self-management (processes)

1 Bakke, *Joy at Work,* 82.

2 Ibid., 98-99.

3 Ibid., 44-45.

4 Ibid., 72.

5 Zobrist, *La belle histoire de FAVI, Tome* 2, 318.

6 Bakke, *Joy at Work,* 101-102.

7 Shari Caudron, "Meditation and Mindfulness at Sounds True," *Workforce,* June 2001.

8 Gary Hamel, "First, Let's Fire All the Managers," *Harvard Business Review,* December 2011, http://hbr.org/2011/12/first-lets-fire-all-the-managers, accessed April 11, 2012.

9 Ibid.

10 Brian Robertson, "Dialog: The History of Holacracy," Holacracy Community of Practice, October 2011, www.holacracy.org/resources, accessed Febuary 24, 2012.

11 Ibid.

12 Brian Robertson, interviewed by Jeff Klein, En*theos Radio, "It's Just Good Business," March 9, 2012, 2012, http://www.entheos.com/radio/shows/Its-Just-Good-Business, accessed April 12, 2012

13 This minimum set of practices is captured in a document called "Holacracy Constitution," which can be downloaded from Holacracy's web site at www.holacracy.org.

14 In Holacracy's language, I should use the term "circle" and not team. It comes back to the separation of people and roles: a team is a group of people; a circle is a group of roles.

15 Holacracy defines a tension more neutrally as a dissonance between what is and what could be.

16 Interested readers can dive deeper by reading Holacracy's constitution and other resources available on www.holacracy.org.

17 Daniel Pink's *Drive* provides a good overview of research on the matter.

18 A month later, in February, the whole company came together for two days off at a beach resort near Monterrey, California. Business Units made a 20-minute condensed presentation again, this time in front of the entire group of colleagues, with 10 minutes of Q&A. At the end, through a collective vote, teams were ranked in terms of the quality of their plans. People at Morning Star find this session of information sharing across Business Units essential to keep people knowledgeable about what happens in other units, to ensure everyone's plans benefit from everyone's insights, and to challenge teams to make the best plans.

19 O.J. Mason and F. Brady, "The Psychotomimetic Effects of Short-Term Sensory Deprivation," *Journal of Nervous and Mental Disease*, October 2009, http://www.ncbi.nlm.nih.gov/pubmed/19829208, accessed March 13, 2013.

20 Semco introduced self-set pay in the 1990s for white-collar workers. Fed up with managers haggling over their pay, Semco's owner and CEO, Ricardo Semler, decided to let everybody name his own salary (they didn't need to consult peers, as was the case in AES). What sounds like a recipe for disaster worked well in practice; very few people raised their salaries to levels others considered exaggerated. A number of reasons explain this, according to Semler: all compensation information is made public at Semco, so anybody with an inflated sense of self will have to face tough question from colleagues; the CEO and senior leaders make a point to set themselves low salaries by industry standards; and given the boom and bust nature of the Brazilian economy, people know that if a severe crisis were to call for removing redundancies, those who have granted themselves unjustified salaries might be first in line.

But something deeper seems to be at play: as long as someone holds power over us, as long as we are trapped in a child/parent relationship with our superiors, it's easy to feel treated unfairly and to ask for more. When our peers trust us to make the right decisions (and we in turn have to trust all our peers) we are likely to assess our contribution honestly. In the case of Semco, people have been willing on several occasions, when the country was hit by a deep recession, to scale back their salary temporarily to protect the organization's survival, something they might not have agreed to easily if the decision was handed down by their boss.

21 The "Gaining Agreement" (conflict resolution) process creates a space and time to explore in more depth where your and the committee's assessments diverge and to help you and the committee reach agreement.

22 Semco has devised an intriguing variation to protect the organization in times of crisis (to which Brazil has been prone over the last decades).

Employees are offered the option to opt into a risk salary program. They take a pay cut of 25 percent and then receive a supplement raising their compensation to 125 percent if the company has a good year. If the company does poorly, they are stuck with 75 percent of their salary. As the good years outweigh the bad, the deal is favorable to employees willing to take a risk. The program lets some of the labor costs fluctuate with the order books, protecting the company and reducing the risk for redundancies in case of recession.

23 "Fortune 50 CEO pay vs. our salaries," CNNMoney, http://money.cnn.com/magazines/fortune/fortune500/2012/ceo-pay-ratios/, accessed March 25, 2012.

24 Bakke, *Joy at Work,* 123.

25 CPP, a 40-person German self-managing company (no hierarchy, no job descriptions, decisions based on the advice process, and so on) active in the field of high-end event organization and film production, has taken the radical step of equal pay for all colleagues (we could call this "different work, same pay"). This means that some people—for instance, a highly skilled computer animation specialist—makes far less money than he would receive anywhere else. And some other people—say, the stagehand carrying boxes of equipment to and from the event—take home dramatically more money than they would otherwise. The company has been extremely successful for years, but it acknowledges that its pay structure brings interesting challenges. The organization must be particularly vigilant to keep an exceptional company culture, or the best talent will vote with their feet and collect a higher salary somewhere else. And the company finds it virtually impossible to hire experts with a specific, highly valued skill (say 3D rendering) from the outside. CPP believes it has turned this problem into a strength—out of necessity, the staff has turned autodidacticism into an art form, continuously picking up the latest technical skills to remain state-of-the-art.

26 Hamel, "First, Let's Fire All the Managers."

27 Ibid.

28 Brian Robertson, "The Irony of Empowerment," Holacracy Blogs, October 28, 2010, www.holacracy.org/blog, accessed November 2, 2011.

29 Gary Hamel, *What Matters Now* (San Francisco: Jossey-Bass, 2012), 176-177.

Chapter 2.4 • Striving for wholeness (general practices)

1 Brian Robertson, "Holacracy: Empowerment Built In," Holacracy Blogs, January 16, 2013, www.holacracy.org/blog, accessed January 20, 2013.

2 A similar effect is at play in schools where babies are brought into the classroom. Mary Gordon, a Canadian educator, pioneered a program where mothers (or fathers) and their babies come to spend time with a class of children at regular times. The results have been so spectacular that the program has by now been brought to thousands of classrooms in Canada, the United States, England, New Zealand, and elsewhere. A blogger at *The New York Times* writes:

"Tough kids smile, disruptive kids focus, shy kids open up. The baby seems to act like a heart-softening magnet. ... 'Empathy can't be taught, but it can be caught,' Gordon often says—and not just by children. 'Programmatically my biggest surprise was that not only did empathy increase in children, but it increased in their teachers,' she added. 'And that, to me, was glorious, because teachers hold such sway over children.' Scientific studies with randomized control trials have shown extraordinary reductions in 'proactive aggression'—the deliberate and cold-blooded aggression of bullies who prey on vulnerable kids—as well as 'relational aggression'—things like gossiping, excluding others, and backstabbing."

David Bornstein, "Fighting Bullying with Babies," Opinionator, *The New York Times,* November 8, 2010. For more information, see www.rootsofempathy.org.

3 Parker Palmer, *A Hidden Wholeness* (San Francisco: Jossey-Bass, 2009), 58-59. The second paragraph as published in the book is replaced here by a paragraph written by Parker Palmer for the essay "Teaching with Heart and Soul, Reflections on Spirituality in Teacher Education," www.couragerenewal.org/parker/writings/heart-and-soul, accessed October 21, 2012.

4 Robert Fishman and Barbara Fishman, *The Common Good Corporation: The Experiment Has Worked!* (Philadelphia: The Journey to Oz Press, 2006), 11.

5 Ibid., 24-26.

6 Ibid., 26-27.

7 Ibid., vii-viii.

8 Ibid., 165

9 Ibid., 165.

10 Conversation with the author in Bad Kissingen, Germany, February 2013.

11 Heiligenfeld runs four hospitals in Bad Kissingen and one in Waldmünchen, 200 miles away. Employees gather at the same time and join into a single meeting through an oversized two-way videoconference display.

12 I haven't come across any material on Intervisie in English. Parker Palmer's "Circle of Trust®," which has roots in ancient Quaker practices, works on almost identical principles and steps. Interested readers can learn more about it in Palmer's *A Hidden Wholeness.*

13 Parker Palmer, "On the Edge: Have the Courage to Lead with Soul," *Journal for Staff Development,* National Staff Development Council, Spring 2008.

14 Careful readers might have noticed the beautiful paradox around role and soul. Holacracy insists we should separate role from soul (stop confusing our identity with our job title). This separation is a necessary first step. Only then can we again reconnect role and soul, from a different place, as Parker Palmer invites us to do—bringing all of our selfhood to the roles we fill.

15 Conversation with the author, May 10, 2013.

16 Robertson interview.

17 Conversation with the author, March 14, 2013.

18 Fishman and Fishman, *The Common Good Corporation,* 15.

19 Yvon Chouinard, *Let My People Go Surfing: The Education of a Reluctant Businessman* (New York: Penguin Books, 2005), 161.

Chapter 2.5 • Striving for wholeness (HR processes)

1 Tami Simon, interviewed by Jeff Klein, En*theos radio, "It's Just Good Business," April 27, 2012, http://www.entheos.com/radio/shows/Its-Just-Good-Business, accessed October 3, 2012.
2 Charles A. O'Reilly, *Hidden Value: How Great Companies Achieve Extraordinary Results with Ordinary People* (Boston: Harvard Business Review Press, 2000), 162.
3 Bakke, *Joy at Work,* 101.
4 Colleen Kaftan and Louis Barnes, Sun Hydraulics Corporation, case study (Cambridge: Harvard Business Publishing, 1991), 5.
5 De Blok and Pol, *Buurtzorg,* 67.
6 Fishman and Fishman, *The Common Good Corporation,* 54-55.
7 Conversation with the author, April 9, 2012.
8 Rob LeBow and Randy Spitzer, *Accountability: Freedom and Responsibility Without Control* (San Francisco: Berrett-Koehler Publishers, 2002), 208.
9 Terry Chadsey, email message to author, May 22, 2012.
10 Hill and Suesse, Sun Hydraulics.
11 Bakke, *Joy at Work,* 185-186.

Chapter 2.6 • Listening to evolutionary purpose

1 I started to wonder if there were book titles that would epitomize other paradigms as well as Welch's *Winning* does epitomize Orange. *Lead with LUV,* the title of a book about Southwest Airlines' practices, might be an apt description of what Green business is all about. For Teal, *The Living Organization* by Norman Wolfe might take the crown.
2 Conversation with the author, April 9, 2013.
3 "Interview with Tami Simon, Sounds True Founder," YouTube video, interview by Lisa Spector on June 25, 2010, posted by "ThroughaDogsEar," June 19, 2011, http://www.youtube.com/watch?v=LbWEdmQw9PY.
4 Yvon Chouinard, *Let My People Go Surfing,* 3.
5 Ibid., 31.
6 Tami Simon, interviewed by Diederick Janse and Ewan Townhead, podcast series "Waking up the Workplace," episode "Even Sages need a Business Plan," April 14, 2011.
7 Robertson interview.
8 Brian Robertson "Outvoting the Low Voltage Light," blog post, July 9, 2012, http://holacracy.org/blog/outvoting-the-low-voltage-light, accessed November 4, 2012.
9 Judi Neal, "Spreading Spiritual Wisdom: Business Leader Tami Simon, CEO of Sounds True," electronic document (Louisville, Ken.: BrownHerron Publishing, 2003), 4-5.
10 Here is an intriguing thought: could we perhaps tap directly into an organization's purpose through techniques such as channeling or systemic constellations and ask it to provide guidance in making important decisions?

This idea is still largely uncharted territory within organizational settings and could perhaps yield unexpected breakthroughs.

11 This ritual involves beautiful stone pebbles. All 90 colleagues sit for a while in silence with a handful of pebbles and imbue them with blessings. Colleagues then walk around the premises and place a pebble in a place they feel might need a blessing.

12 Robertson interview.

13 A phrase often heard in organizations is that people should argue as long as it takes before a decision is made, but once it's made, a decision is a decision and people should stick to it. Allowing people to reopen any decision at any time sounds like a recipe for chaos. And indeed it is, when ego is in play: when decisions are viewed in terms of what department wins or loses, or how the decision will impact one's standing or career prospects, then people will be tempted to reopen decisions not to further an organization's purpose, but for their own benefit. The decision processes at Holacracy and Buurtzorg are explicitly designed to prevent ego-hijack from happening. A number of rules about what makes a "workable" solution and what "objections" are valid make it hard to justify a decision that would serve a person or a department but not the organization.

14 Margaret J. Wheatley and Myron Kellner-Rogers, *A Simpler Way* (San Francisco: Berrett-Koehler Publishers, 1996), 73.

15 Hill and Suesse, Sun Hydraulics.

16 Conversation with the author, January 29, 2013.

17 Casey Sheahan, interviewed by Jeff Klein, En*theos Radio, "It's Just Good Business," February 17, 2012, http://www.entheos.com/radio/shows/Its-Just-Good-Business, accessed October 3, 2012.

18 It is useful to make a distinction between *moods* and *emotions*, two notions that are often confused. Emotions are triggered by a specific event—someone says something and that makes me angry. Moods are emotions that we live in, often unconsciously, for a longer period of time. They are not triggered by a specific event. They live in the background and color how we view the events that happen in our life. If I live in a mood of anger, I will tend to read events as criticisms or threats. If, instead of anger, I lived in a mood of confidence or gratitude, I would give the same events very different interpretations, leading me to very different decisions and behavior. Learning to read and manage our moods is a powerful personal and organizational practice.

19 BerylHealth is a wonderful example of a company thriving on Green principles and practices. Paul Spiegelman, the co-founder and CEO, and Beryl employees have written two books (*Smile Guide* and *Why Is Everyone Smiling?*) that are great guides to creating culture-driven companies.

20 All of these books, to some extent, critique Orange leadership and management styles. They insist on the importance of empowerment, culture, and purpose. Notwithstanding these books' Orange titles, their content and recommendations stem at least partially from a Green perspective. In the introduction to the 2002 paperback edition, the authors of *Built to Last* share that they can't take credit for the title, which was devised, in a moment of genius, by the editor. I wonder if the "Orange" titles of other books in this list were also chosen by their editors, with the objective of appealing to the largely Orange readership of business books looking for ways to better play the game of success.

21 Wheatley and Kellner-Rogers, *A Simpler Way*, 35.

Chapter 2.7 • Common cultural traits

1 Video of Bob Koski, interviewed by one of Sun's operators, internal Sun Hydraulics material.
2 Brian Robertson, "Differentiating Organization & Tribe," blog post, August 28, 2013, http://holacracy.org/blog/differentiating-organization-tribe, accessed August 30, 2013.

Chapter 3.1 • Necessary conditions

1 Fishman and Fishman, *The Common Good Corporation*, 58-60.
2 Ibid., 31.
3 Bakke, *Joy at Work*, 55-56.
4 "Holacracy Distributes Heroes," YouTube video, posted by HolacracyOne, January 7, 2013, http://www.youtube.com/watch?v=QGphlvr4jdE, accessed June 16, 2013.
5 Conversation with the author, March 14, 2013.
6 Of course, the technological platform doesn't really matter. It can be a blog post or any other medium used with the same intention. A few years ago, Chris Rufer felt a need for a new strategic direction at Morning Star. He wrote a memo that he sent to all colleagues, with an invitation to a company-wide meeting (the different locations joined by videoconference) where he shared his ideas for the new strategic direction and the reason for it. He asked everyone to contact him personally after the meeting with any questions, concerns, comments, and advice on his plans.
7 Eckart Wintzen and Robert Jan Pabon, *Eckart's Notes* (Rotterdam: Wintzen, 2007), 184.
8 Bakke, *Joy at Work*, 207.
9 Ibid., 68-70.
10 Ibid., 208.
11 Deborah Boyar, "Living Holacracy: The Tip of the Iceberg," blog post, August 12, 2012, http://holacracy.org/blog/living-holacracy-the-tip-of-the-iceberg, accessed August 22, 2013.

Chapter 3.3 • Transforming an existing organization

1 Bakke, *Joy at Work*, 176-177.
2 Zobrist, *La belle histoire de FAVI, Tome 1*, 38.
3 Anthony S. Bryk and Barbara Schneider, *Trust in Schools: A Core Resource for School Reform* (New York : Russell Sage Foundation, 2002).

Chapter 3.4 • Results

1 Of course, we should be careful about the possibility of a selection bias. While I have researched all the organizations I have found that corresponded to the research criteria (more than 100 employees, operating for at least five years on principles and practices inspired to some significant degree by the Evolutionary-Teal paradigm), it could well be that only particularly successful organizations caught my attention.

2 For instance A. J. E. de Veer, H. E. Brandt, F. G. Schellevis, and A. L. Francke, "Buurtzorg: nieuw en toch vertrouwd—Een onderzoek naar de ervaringen van cliënten, mantelzorgers, medewerkers en huisartsen," Nederlands instituut voor onderzoek van de gezondheidszorg (NIVEL), 2008.

Chapter 3.5 • Teal Organizations and Teal Society

1 A. M. Diederen, "Metal Minerals Scarcity and the Elements of Hope," The Oil Drum: Europe, March 10, 2009, http://europe.theoildrum.com/, accessed March 20, 2012.

2 An example of people paying to volunteer comes from the Mankind Project (MKP), an educational nonprofit. MKP began in 1984, when Rich Tosi, a former Marine Corps officer; Bill Kauth, a social worker, therapist, and author; and Ron Hering, a university professor, created an experiential weekend for men called the "Wildman Adventure" (since then renamed the "New Warrior Training Adventure"). The weekend was designed as a two-day rite of passage, a process of initiation and self-examination, to catalyze the development of a healthy and mature masculine self, at a time when traditional models of masculinity were breaking down. The weekend proved so popular that it was held again and again, ultimately giving birth to a movement. The Mankind Project (MKP) is now an umbrella organization for 43 interdependent centers in eight countries over four continents. Close to 50,000 men have been initiated. The weekend costs around $650 for participants. For many, it is such a profound experience that they choose to come back as a volunteer to staff weekends where other men are initiated. A weekend usually involves 20 to 32 participants and some 30 to 45 staff (in other words a rather extravagant ratio of 1.5 staff for every participant). Except for a handful of more experienced staffers who travel the world for such training and get paid modestly for it, the majority of staffers are not compensated for their time and expenses … rather, they actually pay to be a staff member. Their contributions help to keep the fee for participants at reasonable levels and to offer grants. In 2010, more than 2,700 men staffed initiation weekends (more volunteered, but the volunteer slots quickly fill up). Pay to volunteer? For these men, it makes sense. They have been personally transformed by their own initiation weekend, and staffing provides not only the opportunity to give back, but also to deepen their learning and to deepen their relationships in the purpose-driven community they feel part of. MKP offers a good example of the fluidity in roles we might

see more of in the future. Men involved with MKP keep switching from and to: volunteering intensively, not at all, paid staffing roles, administrative roles on a volunteer or paid basis.

3 "Buurtzorg Nederland verovert Buitenland," *Zorgvisie Magazine,* June 29, 2012, http://www.zorgvisie.nl/Home/Nieuws/2012/6/Buurtzorg-Nederland-verovert-buitenland-ZVS014262W, accessed November 26, 2012.

4 Wheatley and Kellner-Rogers, *A Simpler Way*, 5-7.

Appendix 2 • Beyond Evolutionary-Teal

1 The term "Transcendent" is borrowed from Wade. It corresponds to Wilber's "Indigo," "Violet," and "Ultra-Violet;" Maslow's "Self-Transcendence;" Torbert's "Ironist;" Cook-Greuter's "Unitive;" and others.

2 The term "Unity Consciousness" is borrowed from Wade and corresponds to Wilber's "Clear light."

Appendix 3 • Structures of Teal Organizations

1 To be precise, in holacratic terms, circles and teams refer to two different realities. Holacracy is careful to always distinguish between people and the roles people happen to fill. In Holacracy a "team" refers to a group of people, while a "circle" refers to a group of roles.

SELECTED READINGS

The next pages list a selection of resources for readers who want to delve deeper into some of the themes discussed in this book.

Teal Organizations case examples

Some of the founders of the pioneer organizations who have inspired this book have written some highly readable firsthand accounts of their journey and of the organizational practices they have experimented with.

Bakke, Dennis. *Joy at Work: A Revolutionary Approach to Fun on the Job.* Seattle: PVG, 2005. (About AES)

Chouinard, Yvon. *Let My People Go Surfing: The Education of a Reluctant Businessman*. New York: Penguin Books, 2005. (About Patagonia)

De Blok, Jos, and Aart Pool. *Buurtzorg: menselijkheid boven bureaucratie*. Den Haag: Boom Lemma Uitgevers, 2010. (About Buurtzorg)

Fishman, Robert, and Barbara Fishman. *The Common Good Corporation: The Experiment Has Worked!* Philadelphia: The Journey to Oz Press, 2006. (About RHD)

Rasfeld, Margret and Peter Spiegel. *EduAction: Wir machen Schule.* Hamburg: Murmann Verlag, 2012. (About ESBZ)

Wintzen, Eckart, and Robert Jan Pabon. *Eckart's Notes*. Rotterdam: Wintzen, 2007. (About BSO / Origin)

Zobrist, Jean-François. *La belle histoire de FAVI: L'entreprise qui croit que l'Homme est bon*. Tome 1, Nos Belles Histoires. Paris: Humanisme et Organisations, 2008. (About FAVI)

Green Organizations case examples

Below is a selection of case studies about organizations operating predominantly along principles, structures, practices, and cultures inspired by Pluralistic-Green. Most organizations today are operating from Conformist-Amber or Achievement-Orange. Leaders who feel that in the current situation Teal would be a step too far, but Pluralistic-Green would be feasible, might find inspiration from these remarkable case examples of Green Organizations.

Blanchard, Ken, and Colleen Barrett. *Lead with LUV: A Different Way to Create Real Success*. Upper Saddle River: FT Press, 2011. (About Southwest Airlines)

Cohen, Ben, Jerry Greenfield, and Meredith Maran. *Ben & Jerry's Double-Dip: Lead with Your Values and Make Money, Too*. New York: Simon & Schuster, 1997. (About Ben & Jerry's)

Conley, Chip. *Peak: How Great Companies Get Their Mojo from Maslow*. San Francisco: Jossey-Bass, 2007. (About Joie-de-Vivre hotels)

Johnson, Judy, Les Dakens, Peter Edwards, and Ned Morse. *SwitchPoints: Culture Change on the Fast Track for Business Success*. Hoboken: Wiley, 2008. (About culture change at Canadian National Railway)

Nayar, Vineet. *Employees First, Customers Second: Turning Conventional Management Upside Down*. Boston: Harvard Business Press, 2010. (About HCLT)

Parker, James F.. *Do the Right Thing: How Dedicated Employees Create Loyal Customers and Large Profits*. Upper Saddle River: Wharton School Publishing, 2008. (About Southwest Airlines)

Pfeffer, Jeffrey. Kent Thiry and DaVita: Leadership Challenges in Building and Growing a Great Company. Case study. Stanford: Stanford University, 2006. (About DaVita)

Spiegelman, Paul. *Smile Guide: Employee Perspectives on Culture, Loyalty, and Profit*. Dallas: Brown Books Publishing Group, 2012. (About BerylHealth)

Stewart, Henry. *The Happy Manifesto: Make Your Organization a Great Workplace.* London: KoganPage, 2012. (About Happy—downloadable for free at happy.co.uk)

Organizational theory, management, leadership, inner life

Here is a selection of thought-provoking books about organizational theory, management, and leadership. This list is an unabashedly partial and personal selection from the massive amount of literature in the field. A particular favorite is Wheatley and Kellner-Roger's *A Simpler Way*, which muses poetically about what organizations could be like if we sought inspiration from life and nature, instead of thinking about them as machines. Parker Palmer's writings offer deep and personal explorations on life as seen from the Evolutionary-Teal perspective. These books fall neatly into the "Teal" category. Other books on this list speak mostly from a Pluralistic-Green or Achievement-Orange perspective, but are interesting to read because they have profoundly shaped the discourse on management.

Arbinger Institute. *Leadership and Self-Deception: Getting out of the Box*. 2nd ed. San Francisco: Berrett-Koehler Publishers, 2010.

Barrett, Richard. *Liberating the Corporate Soul: Building a Visionary Organization*. Boston: Butterworth-Heinemann, 1998.

Benefiel, Margaret. *Soul at Work: Spiritual Leadership in Organizations*. New York: Seabury, 2005.

Block, Peter. *Stewardship: Choosing Service Over Self-Interest*. San Francisco: Berrett-Koehler Publishers, 1993.

Carney, Brian M., and Isaac Getz. *Freedom, Inc.: Free Your Employees and Let Them Lead Your Business to Higher Productivity, Profits, and Growth*. New York: Crown Business, 2009.

Collins, James C. *Good to Great: Why Some Companies Make the Leap ... and Others Don't*. New York: HarperBusiness, 2001.

Drucker, Peter F. *The Essential Drucker: Selections from the Management Works of Peter F. Drucker*. New York: HarperBusiness, 2001.

Hamel, Gary. *The Future of Management*. Boston: Harvard Business School Press, 2007.

Hamel, Gary. *What Matters Now: How to Win in a World of Relentless Change, Ferocious Competition, and Unstoppable Innovation*. San Francisco: Jossey-Bass, 2012.

Hock, Dee. *One from Many: VISA and the Rise of Chaordic Organization*. San Francisco: Berrett-Koehler Publishers, 2005.

Lebow, Rob, and Randy Spitzer. *Accountability: Freedom and Responsibility without Control*. San Francisco: Berrett-Koehler Publishers, 2002.

Logan, David, John King, and Halee Fischer-Wright. *Tribal Leadership: Leveraging Natural Groups to Build a Thriving Organization*. New York: Collins, 2008.

Mackey, John, and Rajendra Sisodia. *Conscious Capitalism: Liberating the Heroic Spirit of Business*. Boston: Harvard Business Review Press, 2013.

Kofman, Fred. *Conscious Business: How to Build Value Through Values*. Boulder: Sounds True, 2006.

Morgan, Gareth. *Images of Organization*. 2nd ed. Thousand Oaks: Sage Publications, 1997.

O'Reilly, Charles A., and Jeffrey Pfeffer. *Hidden Value: How Great Companies Achieve Extraordinary Results with Ordinary People*. Boston: Harvard Business School Press, 2000.

Palmer, Parker J. *A Hidden Wholeness: The Journey Toward an Undivided Life*. San Francisco: Jossey-Bass, 2004.

Palmer, Parker J. *Let Your Life Speak: Listening for the Voice of Vocation*. San Francisco: Jossey-Bass, 2000.

Pflüger, Gernot. *Erfolg ohne Chef: Wie Arbeit aussieht, die sich Mitarbeiter wünschen*. Berlin: Econ, 2009.

Semler, Ricardo. *Maverick: The Success Story Behind the World's Most Unusual Workplace*. New York: Warner Books, 1993.

Senge, Peter M.. *The Fifth Discipline: The Art and Practice of the Learning Organization*. New York: Doubleday/Currency, 1990.

Sisodia, Rajendra, David B. Wolfe, and Jagdish N. Sheth. *Firms of Endearment: How World-Class Companies Profit from Passion and Purpose.* Upper Saddle River: Wharton School Pub., 2007.

Taylor, William C., and Polly G. LaBarre. *Mavericks at Work: Why the Most Original Minds in Business Win*. New York: William Morrow, 2006.

Torbert, William R. *Action Inquiry: The Secret of Timely and Transforming Leadership*. San Francisco: Berrett-Koehler Publishers, 2004.

Wheatley, Margaret J., and Myron Kellner-Rogers. *A Simpler Way*. San Francisco: Berrett-Koehler Publishers, 1996.

Wolfe, Norman. *The Living Organization: Transforming Business to Create Extraordinary Results.* Quantum Leaders Publishing, 2011.

About stages of human development

This is just a small selection of the large amount of material written about stages in human development. For readers new to the concept, I recommend in particular Wilber's *A Brief History of Everything* and Wade's *Changes of Mind*, both of which provide a good introduction to and a solid overview of the field.

Beck, Don Edward, and Christopher C. Cowan. *Spiral Dynamics*. Oxford: Blackwell Publishing, 2006.

Cook-Greuter, Susanne R. "Ego Development: Nine Levels of Increasing Embrace." S. Cook-Greuter: 1985.

Feuerstein, Georg. *Structures of Consciousness: The Genius of Jean Gebser: An Introduction and Critique*. Integral Publishing, 1987.

Fowler, James W. *Stages of Faith: The Psychology of Human Development and the Quest for Meaning*. San Francisco: Harper & Row, 1981.

Gilligan, Carol. *In a Different Voice: Psychological Theory and Women's Development.* Cambridge: Harvard University Press, 1993.

Graves, Clare W. *The Never Ending Quest.* Santa Barbara: ECLET, 2005.

Kegan, Robert. *In Over Our Heads: The Mental Demands of Modern Life.* Cambridge: Harvard University Press, 1994

Kohlberg, Lawrence. *The Philosophy of Moral Development: Moral Stages and the Idea of Justice*. San Francisco: Harper & Row, 1981.

Loevinger, Jane. *Ego Development: Conceptions and Theories*. San Francisco: Jossey-Bass, 1976.

Piaget, Jean, and Bärbel Inhelder. *The Psychology of the Child*. New York: Basic Books, 1969.

Wade, Jenny. *Changes of Mind: A Holonomic Theory of the Evolution of Consciousness*. Albany: State University of New York Press, 1996.

Wilber, Ken. *A Brief History of Everything*. Boston: Shambhala Publications, 1996.

Wilber, Ken. *Integral Psychology: Consciousness, Spirit, Psychology, Therapy*. Boston: Shambhala Publications, 2000.

INDEX

C

D

E

F

M

N

O

T

U

V

W

Z

GRATITUDES

Many people contributed to the creation of this book. Obviously, I owe particular gratitude to the founders and the employees of the trailblazing companies that are featured in the book. What they have achieved continues to fill me with awe. For many of them, what pushed them to explore new methods of managing (at least initially) wasn't to prove a point, but to act on a very personal urge to do things in ways that would agree with their values and beliefs. And yet their innovations have universal importance. They point to a better future at work; if these innovations were to spread on a large scale, they could help us usher in the next stage of consciousness more quickly and painlessly.

Many of the founders and employees of the organizations featured in Parts 2 and 3 (and of a few others that I researched but ultimately didn't include in this book) have taken time away from their work or their family to help me understand in detail the principles, structures, practices, processes, and cultures of their workplace. Without the time they generously offered, I couldn't have written this book.

I'm grateful, as well, to the friends and professionals interested in this topic who volunteered to read drafts of the manuscript along the way. Eric Meade helped me improve the chapters on developmental theory in Part 1 with important clarifications and challenging questions. Diederick Janse helped me crack the breakthroughs of Green Organizations and provided insightful comments on many other parts of the book. Bernadette Babault, Claudia Braun, David Puttick, Diego Cuadra, Joëlle Méric, Koen De Witte, Mollie Treverton, Nadine Thevenet, Natalyia Higbie, Norman Wolfe, and Terry Chadsey provided me with wonderful feedback by sharing with me (sometimes almost paragraph by paragraph) their reactions to what they were reading. Going through their comments, delights, questions, and doubts was like being given the secret key into the head of my readers (the dream of any writer!). It helped me understand what was working, avoid numerous misunderstandings, clarify many points large and small, and turn this into a better book. Other friends have read early versions of the manuscript and provided me with their general impressions. Researching and writing a book is a long process; their generally enthusiastic feedback gave me much encouragement and helped me keep spirits high all along the way.

Two persons spent more time with the manuscript than any other. Jessica Epstein and Elizabeth Goolsby patiently and painstakingly copy-edited and proofread every page of this book. I'm grateful for the countless, subtle improvements that their hard work and careful attention brought to this book. I felt in very safe hands with them, knowing that they were critically reviewing every detail of the text.

I also want to thank Lars Van Tuin, who pointed me to Buurtzorg; Mark Hollern, who suggested I research RHD; Christophe Mikolajczak, who first brought Gary Hamel's article on Morning Star to my attention; as well as Brian Carney and Isaac Getz whose book "Freedom Inc." brought FAVI and Sun Hydraulics to my attention. Margaret Benefiel, Michael Bischoff, Judi Neal, and Chuck Palus also took time to help me in trying to identify candidate organizations to research for this book.

Above all, my thanks go to Hélène, Raphaël, and Noémie. I was lucky that Raphaël and Noémie paid no regard to my eagerness to move forward with this project. Their recurring invitation to join them in their world of play and wonder kept me grounded in life beyond this book. Hélène unfailingly supported me with her love, encouragement, and interest. Being with and around her makes everything more fun, even writing a book. During the research, I witnessed workplace communities that make people feel safe to express their full potential and grow into their unique selfhood. That I can experience such community within my home, every day, is a gift that fills me with gratitude beyond words.